AMC

Let's Meet up!

1re/Tle

Anglais Monde Contemporain

DIRECTION D'OUVRAGE ET AUTEUR :

Erwan GOURAUD
- Formateur
- Enseignant au lycée Jean-Jacques Rousseau, Sarcelles (95)

AUTEUR.E.S :

Catherine ARCHAMBEAUD
- Formatrice
- Enseignante au lycée Fustel de Coulanges, Massy (91)

Aline CHARLES
- Lycée Descartes, Rabat (Maroc)

Léo CLERC
- Université Jean Monnet, Saint-Étienne (42)

Anne-Cécile COUTURIER
- Université Paris-Saclay, Université d'Évry (91)

Véronique DORGET
- Lycée Louis Lapicque, Épinal (88)

Sylvie DOUGLADE-VAL
- Lycée Claude Gellée, Épinal (88)

Sue GALAND-JONES
- École Navale, Lanvéoc (29)

Rachael HARRIS
- Lycée Töpffer, Genève (Suisse)

Mathilde HENRIOT
- Lycée Montgrand, Marseille (13)

Robert LIM
- Lycée Louis-le-Grand, Paris (75)

Jean-Marck MOLIGNIER
- Formateur
- Enseignant au lycée Saint-Michel de Picpus, Paris (75)

Amal NAVAILH
- Lycée Jacques Prévert, Boulogne-Billancourt (92)

Solène NICOLAS
- Lycée Henri IV, Paris (75)

Grammaire et phonologie :

Sylvain GATELAIS
- Université de Tours (37)

Hatier

Les experts de nos vidéos d'ouverture d'unité :

The expert's view
hatier-clic.fr/21amc

Monia O'BRIEN CASTRO est maître de conférences en civilisation britannique à l'Université de Tours, responsable des Agrégations d'anglais. Membre du laboratoire de recherche ICD, elle est l'auteure de nombreux travaux consacrés aux centres urbains socio-économiquement défavorisés au Royaume-Uni. Elle a en outre co-dirigé des ouvrages d'histoire et publié des manuels d'apprentissage de la langue.

Sébastien MORT est maître de conférences en sociétés et cultures des États-Unis à l'Université de Lorraine et membre du Centre de Recherche sur les Médiations (CREM). Auteur d'une thèse sur l'influence des talk-shows radiophoniques conservateurs sur le conservatisme de l'après-Reagan, il travaille sur l'intersection entre politique, médias d'information et journalisme aux États-Unis, sur les médias conservateurs et sur le phénomène d'intimidation politique des journalistes dans l'ère Trump. Il a récemment publié *Les médias conservateurs dans la campagne de 2020 : un soutien unanime au président ?* pour l'Institut Français de Relations Internationales.

Les auteur.e.s tiennent à remercier tous les élèves qui ont accepté de tester les contenus de ce manuel en classe.

Conception graphique : David Bart
Mise en page : Valérie Causse
Édition : Karin Albert, Catherine de Bernis
Iconographie : Katia Davidoff
Infographie : Olivier Aubert
Studio d'enregistrement : QualiSons
Vidéos "The expert's view": David Bart
Droits : Sophie Labrousse

ISBN : 978-2-401-07728-7

AMC

Let's Meet up!

1re/Tle

Avant-propos

Bienvenue !

La spécialité de LLCER Anglais Monde Contemporain est l'occasion d'approfondir vos connaissances du monde anglo-saxon. Pour vous accompagner, nous avons réfléchi à la meilleure façon de vous donner les outils pour comprendre, analyser et interpréter le monde qui vous entoure grâce à une double proposition : **un site et un manuel pour les classes de 1re et Tle**.

Tout au long des **22 unités**, nous avons sélectionné de nombreux supports dont la variété et les questionnements vous donneront envie d'en savoir davantage. Vous aurez ainsi l'occasion de travailler sur le journalisme d'investigation et son évolution avec les lanceurs d'alertes, vous pourrez aussi découvrir que le mouvement Black Lives Matter a des racines britanniques ou encore que de nombreuses nations cherchent aujourd'hui à s'émanciper dans le monde anglo-saxon – un monde riche, varié et passionnant !

Le manuel vous apportera les clés de compréhension nécessaires. Les pages *Focus on...* et les interviews de nos experts (deux maîtres de conférences à l'université) sont là pour vous donner un regard plus complet, plus profond sur les sujets que nous abordons. Nous avons aussi réfléchi à la meilleure façon de vous accompagner pour **les épreuves du BAC** qui sont exigeantes mais qui vous permettront de montrer tout votre potentiel lors des écrits comme des oraux ou du grand oral. Vous trouverez donc des **conseils méthodologiques**, des **activités d'entraînement** mais aussi des **pages Bac** pour vous mettre dans les conditions optimales pour les épreuves de fin de terminale.

Comme l'actualité est toujours en mouvement, **notre site vous donne accès à des ressources supplémentaires**, sélectionnées par l'équipe des auteurs, didactisées et mises à jour régulièrement afin que vous et vos professeurs soyez toujours à la pointe de l'actualité la plus brûlante !

L'équipe de Let's Meet Up AMC

1 UK education: a chance for everyone?

The expert's view
hatier-clic.fr/21amc/012a

In the news
hatier-clic.fr/21amc/012b

Projects
- You are a member of the Students' Union. Make a video to promote an event encouraging equality at university.
- You are an activist. Write an opinion article about inequalities in the UK education system.

2 Reinventing education in the USA

The expert's view
hatier-clic.fr/21amc/024a

In the news
hatier-clic.fr/21amc/024b

Projects
- You are a journalist. Write an article presenting a technologist with big ideas about education.
- You are a vlogger. Make a two-minute video presenting your genius idea for education.

3 Robots for better... or for worse

The expert's view
hatier-clic.fr/21amc /036a

In the news
hatier-clic.fr/21amc/036b

Projects
- You run a business. Debate the introduction of robots in your company.
- You are a journalist. Write an article on the impact of the introduction of robots.

7 Investigative journalism

The expert's view hatier-clic.fr/21amc/084a

In the news hatier-clic.fr/21amc/084b

Projects
You are a writer. Create a storyboard about an investigation that acted as a counter-power.
You are journalist. Create a podcast on the role of investigative journalism.

8 Talk shows: information or entertainment?

The expert's view hatier-clic.fr/21amc/096a

In the news hatier-clic.fr/21amc/096b

Projects
Write an article about the informative and entertaining power of talk shows.
Create your own talk show and present your project to a board of producers.

9 The Commonwealth: tradition and modernity

The expert's view hatier-clic.fr/21amc/108a

In the news hatier-clic.fr/21amc/108b

Projects
You are a Commonwealth citizen. Write an opinion article giving your views on the Commonwealth.
You are a young poet. Perform a poem you have written on the Commonwealth.

20 Secret agents, symbols of power?

p. 234

The expert's view hatier-clic.fr/21amc/234a

In the news hatier-clic.fr/21amc/234b

Projects
- You are a film critic. Write a review of a spy movie explaining the evolution of espionage.
- You are a recruiting agent at the CIA or MI6. Record a recruiting video for a cyber threat analyst.

21 Battle for the Arctic, a new cold war?

p. 248

The expert's view hatier-clic.fr/21amc/248a

In the news hatier-clic.fr/21amc/248b

Projects
- You are an intern at the UN. Take part in a panel discussion on geopolitical affairs.
- As a junior researcher you have been asked to write an article about what is at stake for the USA in the Arctic.

22 The royals: ambassadors for Britain?

p. 262

The expert's view hatier-clic.fr/21amc/262a

In the news hatier-clic.fr/21amc/262b

Projects
- You have a youtube channel about the royal family. Convince your subscribers that today's royals represent a modern image of Britain.
- Imagine an interview with a member of the royal family to question whether the members have evolved on the question of diversity.

ANNEXE

Les fiches de méthodologie

Des outils d'analyse

Des pistes pour préparer le BAC

Le + de Let's Meet up! AMC

UN ACCÈS DIRECT À L'ACTUALITÉ ET AUX RESSOURCES

Quels sont les contenus du site inthenews.hatier.fr ?

In the news

Pour chaque unité de ton manuel :

> **Des documents sélectionnés** et **didactisés** par les auteur.e.s

> **Une recherche facile** (tri par unité et par type de ressources)

> Des **mises à jour trimestrielles** en fonction de l'actualité

Comment fonctionnent les "hatier-clic" du manuel ?

Les mini-URLs « hatier-clic » permettent un accès direct aux documents audio, vidéo et texte en lien avec le manuel.

Repérage dans votre manuel

e-worksheet
hatier-clic.fr/21amc/097a

Sur **www.hatier-clic.fr** j'indique le code ressource du pictogramme

Pensez à mettre l'adresse dans vos favoris !

1 UK education: a chance for everyone?

The expert's view
hatier-clic.fr/21amc/012a

In the news
hatier-clic.fr/21amc/012b

Projects

- You are a member of a Students' Union. Make a video to encourage equality at university.
- You are an activist. Write an opinion article about inequalities in the UK education system.

Grammar p. 20 Phonology p. 21

Promoting a fair society?

A A past tradition?

1. Analyse the image focusing on the specific elements that make this school uniform old-fashioned.
2. Read the text and list the arguments for and against school uniforms.
3. Pick out the arguments of the article that are represented in the image.
4. PAIR WORK Research other examples of school uniforms and compare them to the image before designing your own.

e-worksheet
hatier-clic.fr/21amc/012c

1 *A bygone era?*

2 *Do we need uniforms?* **Britain's obsession with school uniform reinforces social divisions**

Other countries don't feel the need to strip children of their individuality.

It's September, and with it comes that back-to-school feeling […] cool, crisper mornings that hit you as you rush from the house trailing toast crumbs, and of course, new uniform – if your parents can afford it. […]

Uniforms prevent bullying, we are told – though for every study claiming this, there is another that concludes that school uniforms have no direct [positive] effect on behaviour, and some have argued they can even provoke bullying.

I went to a school that was fanatical about compliance with school uniform rules. […] The poorest children had school sweatshirts that had been washed so many times that they were badly discoloured. […]

These children were disciplined. I remember feeling the injustice of this, a child held up in front of other pupils, humiliated for the shabby[1] state of their uniform. As for uniforms somehow being a facilitator of better teaching: so much time was devoted to non-compliance checks that it ate into time that could have been spent learning. […]

Ultimately, uniforms are a form of social control and conformity in an education system that already doesn't focus enough on the individual. […]

Uniform policies reinforce gender and racial divisions as well as class ones. […] Ultimately, uniforms are a form of social control and conformity in an education system that already doesn't focus enough on the individual.

Rhiannon Lucy Cosslett, *The Guardian*, Sep. 5th, 2020

1. neglected

B Prefects, a controversial custom?

1 The qualities of a school prefect

A good school prefect possesses sound morals, good interpersonal skills and organizational skills. A good prefect should also be mature, empathetic and patient. School prefects are required to supervise students, promote a healthy work ethic, and fulfill any other duty delegated by the school's headmaster. "Prefect" is a term used primarily in British schools to describe a selected pupil who has authorization to discipline fellow students. Students applying for the position of prefect must exhibit leadership qualities and a willingness to help others. They must be able to organize and delegate tasks, as well as possess excellent time management and administration skills. A portfolio of personal achievements is also helpful in garnering the prefect role.

School prefects should have high integrity, be capable of communicating honestly and effectively, and be prepared to discipline peers. Prefects must also be firm and fair in their role of authority. Good prefects must be responsible, reliable and have high personal standards as well as strong self-discipline, as they are required to oppose and stop bullying. They should also be able to handle conflict and should have an open, genuine relationship with members of staff. Overall, prefects are exemplary students who are good role models and assist in keeping order in the school.

www.reference.com, Apr. 1st, 2020

2 Are school-imposed hierarchies good for students?

Hierarchies guide students

For the most part, I believe that school-imposed hierarchies are good for students. If there was no established sense of a power structure or hierarchy, students could just do whatever they wanted, learn essentially nothing, and not be held accountable for their actions.

Kids need structure

[…] Kids need structure; even if they're free to learn and be creative on their own, they need to do so in a framework, and having peers advising and patrolling them could be more constructive than an adult authority.

I believe that the prefect system is archaic and should be abolished.

I went to a girls private school in the 1970s/ early eighties, where there were no prefects in the sixth form. […] Every girl in both lower and upper sixth had a duty to perform, so that every girl felt worthwhile and the school had an egalitarian feel. A system, which is hierarchical and where some students are made to feel superior to others is not a system which has a place in today's society.

www.debate.org

1 Read text 1 and give a definition of a good prefect using the qualities mentioned.

2 PAIR WORK Summarise the disadvantages of the prefect system for schools, mentioned in document 2.

3 Grammar Find all the words or grammatical structures expressing obligation.

4 CONNECT. Pick out the advantages for someone becoming a prefect from both documents.

Culture Tip

A private school is a school where parents pay fees. State school is run and financed by the government. Despite the name, public schools are in fact fee-paying schools, the name comes from the Clarendon report 1864 which led to the formalisation of seven boys boarding schools, including Eton, Harrow and Rugby (where the sport was created). Today there are around 30 public schools.

C The end of private schools?

Should we abolish private schools?

Video hatier-clic.fr/21amc/013

1 Pick out the dates and figures in the video and use them to explain the origin and current status of private schools (see Culture Tip).

2 Read *Let's focus on...* n° 1, p. 18 and comment on the inequalities in private education and their consequences.

3 Phonology Listen and repeat the following words: education, abolition, proportion. Which syllable carries the main stress? What do these words have in common? What do you notice?

4 PAIR WORK Your friend is undecided about going to a private school. Discuss the pros and cons with him/her.

Education for all?

A A non-inclusive system

Akala is a British rapper, intellectual, activist and poet, brother of the musician Ms Dynamite. Born to a Jamaican father and a white Scottish mother, Akala grew up questioning his place in British society as a biracial boy from a poor family.

"I went into the British school system a nerdy boy who wanted to be an astronaut. I was from a materially poor but culturally very rich family. My stepdad was a stage manager of a theatre which was probably the most important black-led cultural institution in 1980s Britain. I think I met Angela Davis there, I met this South African jazz musician Hugh Masekela – you couldn't ask for culturally a better upbringing. I saw probably four pieces of theatre a week for the first ten years of my life.

"But I went into school too well prepared for school for a child from my ethnic and class backgrounds. And I found out very early that this offended some teachers' very sense of identity. My teacher at seven put me in a special needs group for kids who didn't speak English. She obviously knew I didn't have problems with English – I was reading *The Lord of the Rings* at home. This is a woman who was brought up in the 1930s, at a time when the idea that white people were innately genetically superior and that Britain's right to colonise the world were self-evident. This doesn't excuse her, but she was conditioned in a very particular way. I can now understand why she maybe felt like a traitor to her race, to her culture and to history if she allowed me to believe that I could access the best of British society. Even poor white kids are not taught 'of course you can be an astronaut, of course you can be an architect, of course you should aspire to run the country.' That's preserved for kids who go to Eton or who are privately educated and so a lot of this is about the pre-existing class hierarchies that were in Britain prior to even black and brown folks arriving in large numbers. Then we arrive with all of these aspirations to move up in the world because it's what our grandparents were fed in the colonies.

"Remember our grandparents leave Jamaica, in my case, believing everybody in Britain's rich, like the white people in Jamaica. One of the things that the British government was terrified about us coming in was precisely that we discover that most of people will be poor and non-educated and not treated that well. That we'd see actually this is what the British elite have done to their own people and we lose admiration for them, which is exactly what happened.

"Had I – remember I've got one white parent – had two white parents and had I been middle class, the chances I would've got put in a special needs group for kids who don't speak English, while reading *The Lord of the Rings*, is somewhere close to zero. My identity, whether I like it or not, had real world implications on my experiences. I wasn't interested in football at all, I wasn't even that much into music. I was a proper nerd. But I was socialised into being into football, socialised into being into music [...]

"My argument has always been and continues to be: even though Britain pretends to be a meritocracy, it is not. And the better young people from poor backgrounds, and particularly young black boys, understand the hurdles that are inevitably going to form in front of them, the easier they can jump over them. My argument has never been and never will be: oh, some people are racist, therefore you shouldn't try hard at school. It's the exact opposite. Some people come back at me with, 'oh, you're trying to make excuses,' and it really impresses me that people can look at everything I've achieved in my life and think I'm interested in making excuses. Quite the opposite. I'm trying to give people the arsenal to succeed because that's what I was given."

www.anothermag.com, 2019

1. Read the introduction and the first paragraph (l. 1-10). Pick out information about Akala's childhood.
2. Concentrate on lines 11 to 37. Focus on oppositions and comment on Akala's analysis of his experience of racism and classism at school.
3. Read the last paragraph l. 59-73 and show how his experience at school empowered him.
4. Write a short article in your school newspaper presenting Akala and his views about the British education system.

B Gender stereotypes at school

1 Difference between boys' and girls' subject choices at A-Level (UK, 2017)

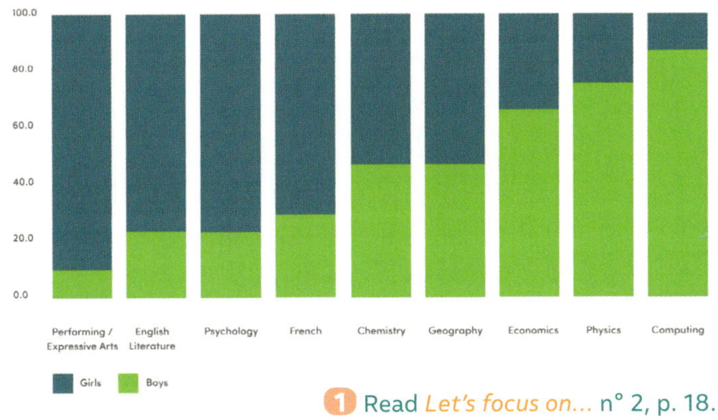

1 Read *Let's focus on…* n° 2, p. 18. Concentrate on the graph and explain the data it provides.

2

Why are gender stereotypes a problem?

Audio hatier-clic.fr/21amc/015

2 Listen to the recording, focus on key words and list both present and future consequences of gender inequalities.

3 **CONNECT.** Use both documents to show the urgency to tackle gender inequalities at school.

C Success for everyone?

1 *Grades of secondary schools*

Most recent overall effectiveness grades of secondary schools, by level of deprivation[1] and ethnicity, 30 April 2018. White british only.

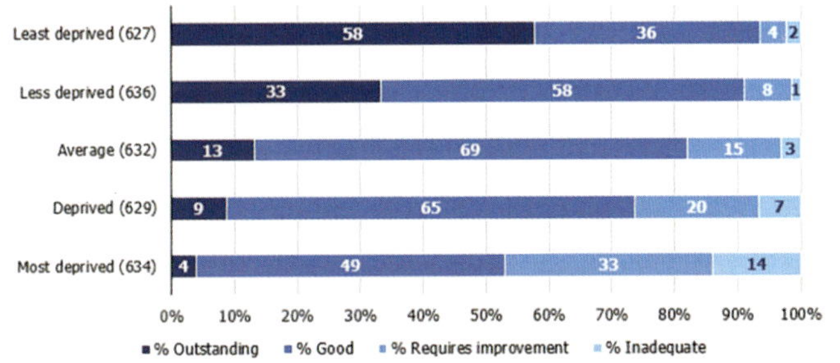

Source: Ofsted inspection data as at 30 April 2018
Source: Schools, pupils and their characteristics: January 2017

1. The indicator of deprivation used in this analysis is 'Eligible for free school meals on any census day in the last six years'.
2. Percentages are rounded and may not add to 100.

2 *Diversity at Oxbridge*

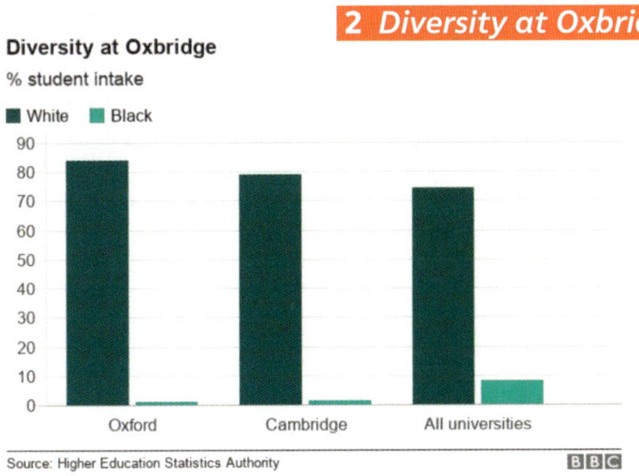

1 Analyse the two graphs (types, subjects of comparison) and comment on the link between education and social and/or racial origin.

2 Read *Let's focus on…* n° 3 p. 19 and explain the university UCAS points system in relation to the first graph.

3 Pick out dates and percentages from the article and account for the number of black students in British universities compared to Oxbridge.

4 **CONNECT.** Link the three documents and draw some conclusions about the chances of academic success for UK students.

3 *Diversity at the UK's top universities*

Attention has turned to the lack of diversity at the UK's top universities once again, as the University of Oxford publishes its admissions figures.

While Oxford says that the proportion of its undergraduate students from the UK who identify as black and minority ethnic rose from 14% to 18% between 2013 and 2017, Tottenham MP David Lammy says students are twice as likely to get in if they are white compared with their black counterparts.

On average in 2016, 8% of first-year undergraduates across the UK were black. In the same year, 1.5% of the University of Cambridge's intake was black, falling to 1.2% at Oxford University, according to the Higher Education Statistics Agency.

Oxford says in 2017, 1.9% of students admitted were black.

Oxford and Cambridge both admitted higher proportions of students from Asian and mixed-background minority ethnic groups. This is in line with the national trend.

According to the latest census, in 2011 about 3% of people of all ages in England, Wales and Scotland identified themselves as black. In Northern Ireland, black ethnic groups accounted for less than 0.1% of the population.

BBC News, 2018

Educ'action: towards a fairer future

A The Success Team

1

1. Use the words in document 1 and the information of document 2 to explain what the Success Team does.
2. Describe the link between the images and the titles in document 2.
3. Prepare arguments to explain what creating your own Success Team could bring to students.

1

B Universities evolving

1 The Edinburgh Seven

Video hatier-clic.fr/21amc/016a

2 University of the Year 2020

Audio hatier-clic.fr/21amc/016b

GROUP WORK

Group A on document 1 – Group B on document 2

1. Pick out dates, names and places and explain what happened in the university's past.
2. Explain how the university's actions to acknowledge and confront its past are important for today's students.
3. Show how this ceremony represents an evolution.
4. **PAIR WORK** Present your ceremony to the other groups in a one-minute presentation. Take notes on your classmates' presentations.

Culture Tip

Glasgow University came to terms with its past, its history and its links to slavery, with honesty. It decided to research this past in collaboration with universities from places where slavery actually took place, such as the West Indies. Furthermore, it decided to act on its findings and start a programme aimed at ethnic minorities, to make amends for its past.

C The teachers' role

Racism isn't just a US problem; to fight it in the UK we need to change how it's taught in schools

It's time to move away from a 'whitewashed' curriculum[1], where black history is omitted or taught only in terms of colonialism and slavery

The first time she was taught African history as anything other than a sidebar[2] to European adventures, Lavinya Stennett was at university. Reflecting on how little she and her fellow students had been taught about black history at school – usually short references to the American civil rights leader Martin Luther King or the South African anti-apartheid leader Nelson Mandela – inspired her last year to set up The Black Curriculum, a campaign for black British history to be embedded[3] into the UK curriculum rather than limited to Black History Month (if that). The proposal includes four modules: art history; migration; politics and the legal system; and land and the environment.

"[University] was the first time I had studied African history that incorporated a non-Eurocentric perspective," she told me, speaking at the end of a long day in a week that has seen her campaign propelled into the spotlight as Britain reacted to the killing of George Floyd in the US by a police officer. (…)

Social media is currently awash[4] with demands (including a petition to the Secretary of State for Education, Gavin Williamson) for children to be taught about the reality of Britain's racist, colonial past (exported, of course, to the US), and while Stennett agrees this is absolutely necessary, she stresses the importance of achieving "an equal balance between confronting the hard parts of black British history and [...] celebrating role models and the contributions black people have made to our society".

Learning beyond slavery and colonialism

Stennett's mother used to buy books on black inventors as part of ensuring a more comprehensive education, but not all black children – and very few white children, though of course this is the best place for families to start – may receive this independent investment.

And this is not the only major omission on the curriculum. The Black Lives Matter movement has woken many (white) people up to the sentiment of a much-cited Angela Davis observation: that "In a racist society it is not enough to be non-racist, we must be anti-racist."

The multicultural junior school I attended in the Nineties took a proactive approach to teaching pupils about racism – but my formal education did not make me aware of my own white privilege. It did not hold me accountable. […]

> **Culture Tip**
>
> First celebrated across the USA in 1976, **Black History Month** was introduced to the UK in October 1987 as part of the African Jubilee Year. The objective of BHM is to bring awareness but it has been criticised for reducing history to symbolic figures such as Nelson Mandela. In 2019 Lavinya Stennett, who was studying African Studies in London, created the Black Curriculum organisation. It aims to challenge the present white, eurocentric curriculum with a more balanced overreaching history of Black people.

Stennett, now age 23, started school eight years after me, and agreed: "The teaching of racism individualises it and removes the structure. It's very polarised, with no understanding of the complexity; of things like microaggressions and tokenism[5]."

I spoke to Ged Grebby, Chief Executive of Show Racism the Red Card, which works with schools to teach anti-racism, utilising the status of footballers and other high-profile individuals. The charity was established in 1996, and I remember it from my own youth. He confirms that "things haven't moved on" since then – anti-racism and black British history are still not part of the curriculum (though the charity does help train every teacher in Wales). […]

Grebby told me the teaching of "Citizenship", which includes lessons on politics, parliament and voting as well as human rights, justice, the law and the economy, offered some hope when it was made mandatory in 2001, but has ultimately failed to deliver as it is too vague. Asked what he thinks is the most important change we need in schools right now, Grebby said: "Anti-racism on the curriculum, and more time for teachers to teach it."

Rachel Cranshaw, *The Telegraph*, June 5th, 2020

1. school programme 2. (here) detail 3. inserted 4. full of 5. minor, symbolic effort of no real value

1. Read the Culture Tip and the text. Pick out the elements of Black History that are presently taught in British schools during Black History Month.
2. Describe the events and issues that encouraged Stennet to create the Black Curriculum.
3. Explain what Stennet wants to see in the Black Curriculum.
4. Write a blogpost arguing for a black curriculum in your school.

e-worksheet
hatier-clic.fr/21amc/017

Let's focus on...

Tuition fees 1

Students have had to pay to study at university ever since 1998 when Tony Blair's Labour government introduced the Teaching and Higher Education Act. Tuition fees were originally capped at £1,000 a year until 2004 under the new Higher Education Act. However, Blair deemed this amount insufficient and granted universities the right to top up their fees, according to the funding they needed. This sparked large student protests all over the UK, and consequently, to finance their education, many students have had to take on loans or part-time jobs, with adverse effects on their results. Today, fees can go as high as £9,250 a year in England and Wales, £4,000 in Northern Ireland and £1,800 in Scotland. Students can be offered scholarships to help finance their studies. Foreign students (including Europeans since Brexit) have to pay higher fees (up to double), depending on the course and university they choose.

What are A levels? 2

After GCSEs examinations, which are compulsory and take place at the end of Year Eleven, pupils aged 16 can continue their studies in Sixth Form at secondary school or at College (if they want to leave school) for 2 more years of academic education to prepare for their A-level examinations. A-levels (advance levels) are highly valued school-leaving qualifications which open the door to further studies and careers. Pupils usually study 3 to 5 subjects, which are then assessed by a series of exams and are graded from A* (A star) to E. There are more than 40 A-levels on offer in British schools (from photography or psychology to economics), although some universities limit the choice of subjects on offer to "facilitating subjects" such as English literature, history, modern and classic languages, maths etc.

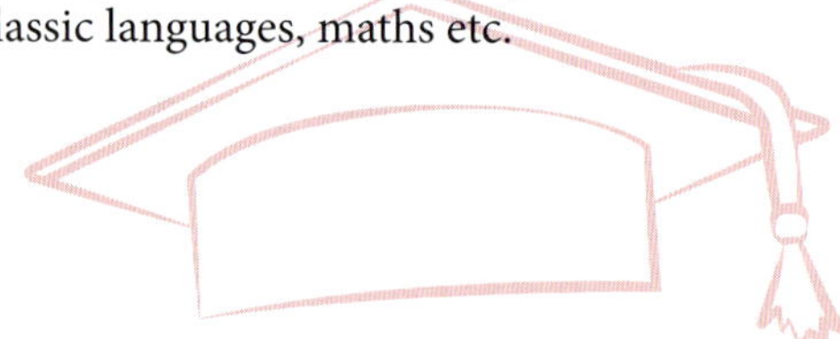

Timeline 4

First universities: Oxford and Cambridge.
13th century

"The Edinburgh Seven", University of Edinburgh.
1869

1868
"The London Nine": First women admitted at London university.

How to get into university? ③

Students apply to university through UCAS (Universities and Colleges Admissions Service). They must give details of how they will fund their course (see tuition fees) as well as a personal statement. This motivation letter is often the deciding factor for universities, as students describe what qualities and experiences will make them ideal candidates for a place on a course.
Universities also take students' predicted A-level scores into consideration to decide whether they will offer them a place. The results obtained at A-level are converted into UCAS points, with higher grades scoring higher points. The university courses require a certain amount of UCAS points which are usually dependent on the popularity of the course and the standard of grades that the university wants. For instance, a student will need 212 points to enter Cambridge University, and 167 to go to Manchester University.

@ e-worksheet
hatier-clic.fr/21amc/019

A-Levels and Highers: UCAS Points

	A-Levels	AS-Levels	Scottish Highers	Advanced Highers
A*	56			
A	48	20	33	56
B	40	16	27	48
C	32	12	21	40
D	24	10	15	32
E	16	6		

Christian Cole first black student at Cambridge.
1873

1908
Edith Morley first woman professor, University of Reading.

Education Act: local UK authorities pay for students' fees, and no repayment is required.
1962

1987
Black History Month celebrated for the first time in UK.

Higher Education Act: top-up tuition fees introduced in UK.
2004

2020
Glasgow University receives Times Higher Education Award for exploring its historic link with the slave trade.

Practice your grammar

Le génitif

▶ Le génitif permet de mettre en relation deux noms. Souvent, il s'agit d'une relation de possession (*Ted's uniform*), mais pas exclusivement (*yesterday's class*).

▶ Attention à la façon d'orthographier le génitif :

N's	un nom propre ou un nom commun singulier	***the teacher's*** *desk*
	un nom propre qui se termine par un *s*.	***James's*** *teachers* /ɪz/
N'	un nom commun pluriel qui se termine par un *s*	***the students'*** *school*

▶ Le premier nom (celui qui porte la marque du génitif 's) peut renvoyer à :

une personne	***the student's*** *uniform*
un pays, une ville	***Britain's*** *colonial past*
une institution	***the school's*** *headmaster*
une date repérée par rapport au moment *now*	***today's*** *society*, ***next week's*** *exam*, ***yesterday's*** *meeting*

▶ Les noms qui désignent **des objets**, **des sentiments** ou **des abstractions** se construisent en général avec la préposition *of* : *the evolution **of the education system***, *the end **of a long day***, *a portfolio **of personal achievements**...*

⚠ Lorsque le nom qui porte la marque du génitif est un nom propre, il n'est pas précédé de l'article défini : on ne dit pas ~~*the*~~ *William's uniform*.

▶ Le second nom peut parfois être sous-entendu, surtout quand on traduit *chez* ou *celui / celle de*. On parle alors **de génitif elliptique** :

*I forgot my uniform at **my mother's**, so I borrowed **Tom's**.*

1 Reliez les deux mots par un génitif ou par *of*. Si les deux structures sont possibles, précisez-le.

a. *Tom / friends*

b. *his brothers / school results*

c. *Monday / class*

d. *school year / beginning*

e. *education system / the UK*

f. *last week / match*

g. *gender inequality / consequences*

h. *company / debts*

2 Traduisez.

a. Le nombre d'étudiants étrangers a beaucoup augmenté à l'université de Leicester l'an passé.

b. Cette étudiante vit toujours chez ses parents.

c. Les notes de Ben sont meilleures que celles de Tom.

L'expression de l'obligation

▶ Pour exprimer **une obligation présente**, on peut utiliser **l'auxiliaire modal *must*** ou **le substitut de modal *have (got) to*** :

*You **must be** home by midnight.*

⚠ Avec *have (got) to*, l'obligation ne dépend pas de l'énonciateur : il peut s'agir d'une obligation morale, dictée par le bon sens, les circonstances ou par la loi.

*We **have (got) to** take exams at the end of each year.*

▶ Pour exprimer **une obligation passée ou future**, seul *have to* peut être employé :

*We **had to revise / will have to revise** the whole syllabus for the exam.*

▶ Pour exprimer **une absence d'obligation**, on utilise *have (got) to* à la forme négative :

*French students **don't have to** wear uniforms.*

⚠ La négation du modal *must* n'exprime pas une absence d'obligation mais **une interdiction** :

*You **mustn't interrupt** the teacher and the other students.*

▶ Notez aussi les expressions suivantes : *be **obliged** / **compelled** / **forced** / **required** / **supposed** to do sth.*

*School prefects **are required to** supervise students.*

3 Reformulez les phrases en utilisant l'une des formes suivantes : *don't have to, must, mustn't, had to*.

a. *You're not obliged to go to university if you don't want to.*

b. *She was forced to drop out of university.*

c. *You are required to submit your homework during the class on the due date.*

d. *You're not allowed to chew gum in class.*

4 Dites ce que les élèves avaient l'obligation de faire dans le passé et qu'ils ne font plus aujourd'hui. Produisez quatre phrases en utilisant chaque fois une structure différente.

Improve your pronunciation

La consonne *h*

▶ En anglais, **la consonne /h/** est prononcée avec **une aspiration**. Il s'agit d'une consonne comme une autre : ne pas la prononcer peut engendrer des difficultés de compréhension.

▶ Un mot commençant par /h/ est précédé de l'article *a* ou *the* (prononcé /ðə/) (***a hat***). On ne fait pas la liaison avec le premier son de ces mots.

▶ On ne prononce pas le /h/ initial dans les mots suivants : ***heir***, ***honest***, ***honour*** et ***hour*** (ainsi que dans leurs dérivés : ***honesty***, ***honourable***...). Ces mots sont donc précédés de l'article *an* ou de l'article *the* prononcé /ði/.

▶ La plupart du temps, on ne prononce pas le *h* à l'intérieur d'un mot quand il suit une consonne (***ghost***, ***exhibition***, ***which***). Notez les exceptions suivantes après un *w* : ***who*** /huː/, ***whose*** /huːz/, ***whole*** /həʊl/.

▶ Le son /h/ est également souvent omis dans **certains mots grammaticaux** (sauf quand ils apparaissent en début de phrase) : **les pronoms *he*, *him*, *her*, l'auxiliaire *have*...**

1 **Écoutez les paires de mots suivantes et répétez.**

Audio hatier-clic.fr/21amc/021a

a. *ill / hill*
b. *hate / eight*
c. *hear / ear*
d. *arm / harm*
e. *air / hair / heir*

2 **Recopiez les phrases suivantes. Rayez les *h* muets et soulignez les *h* qui se prononcent.** Écoutez l'enregistrement pour vérifier vos réponses et répétez.

Audio hatier-clic.fr/21amc/021b

a. *School prefects should have high integrity, be capable of communicating honestly and effectively.*
b. *The class started an hour ago.*
c. *Harry has just finished his freshman year in college.*

L'accent de mot

▶ **Une syllabe accentuée** est prononcée avec plus de force et est légèrement plus longue qu'une syllabe inaccentuée. En anglais, **tous les mots de deux syllabes ou plus ont au moins une syllabe accentuée.**

degree oO ***authority*** oOoo

▶ Les mots d'une seule syllabe peuvent ou non être accentués. Tout dépend de leur catégorie :
- **Les mots lexicaux** (noms, verbes, adjectifs) d'une syllabe sont accentués : ***home***, ***eat***, ***white***.
- **Les mots grammaticaux** d'une syllabe sont en principe inaccentués. Il s'agit **des déterminants** (***the***, ***an***, ***some***, ***this***), **des pronoms personnels** (***I***, ***me***, ***you***), **des prépositions** (***for***, ***in***, ***with***), **des conjonctions** (***and***, ***but***) et **des auxiliaires** (***have***, ***do***, ***be***, les modaux tels que ***can*** ou ***must***).

▶ Les mots de plus de trois syllabes ont souvent une seconde syllabe accentuée, de moindre intensité : on parle alors **d'accent secondaire**.

education /ˌedjuˈkeɪʃən/ OoOo

⚠ Un accent mal placé engendrera souvent des difficultés de compréhension. Pour connaître la place de l'accent dans un mot, il faut consulter un dictionnaire papier ou en ligne : le symbole ' précède la syllabe accentuée dans la transcription. La terminaison d'un mot nous permet également de localiser l'accent.

3 **Soulignez la syllabe qui porte l'accent principal.** Écoutez l'enregistrement pour vérifier vos réponses et répétez.

Audio hatier-clic.fr/21amc/021c

achievement • experience • commitment • uniform • graduate • degree • perfect • hierarchy • inclusive

4 **Recopiez ces mots et soulignez la syllabe qui porte l'accent principal après avoir écouté l'enregistrement.** Qu'ont tous ces mots en commun ? Ne peut-on pas en déduire une règle ?

Audio hatier-clic.fr/21amc/021d

academic • archaic • symbolic • empathetic • dyslexic • athletic

5 **Recopiez la phrase et entourez les mots grammaticaux inaccentués.** Écoutez l'enregistrement pour vérifier vos réponses et répétez.

Audio hatier-clic.fr/21amc/021e

I am the first child in my family to attend college.

Build up your vocabulary

Examinations

- sit an **exam** = take an **exam**
- pass an **exam** = succeed
- **succeed** in + V-*ing*
- fail
- **gra**duate
- re**vise**
- re**sults**
- marks = grades
- mid-term **exam**

Diplomas and university courses

- GCSE (**Gen**eral Cer**tif**icate of **Sec**ondary Edu**ca**tion)
- A **Lev**el (Ad**vanced Lev**el)
- under**gra**duate de**gree** = **bach**elor's de**gree**
- **mas**ters de**gree** = post**gra**duate de**gree**
- PhD (re**search**) de**gree**
- MA (**Mas**ter of Art)
- MBA (**Mas**ter of **Bus**iness and Admini**stra**tion)
- MSc (**Mas**ter of **Sci**ence)

Cambridge University

Academic excellence

- ex**per**ience
- a**lum**nus
- inno**va**tion
- **chall**enges
- pur**sue**
- **lea**dership
- top-**ran**king uni**ver**sity
- com**mit**ment
- **work**force
- ca**reer read**iness
- inter**na**tional re**pute**

Equality

- oppor**tu**nity
- **e**quity
- i**niq**uitous
- fair
- in**clu**sive
- high **stan**dards
- **ci**vic **a**gency
- afforda**bi**lity
- **so**cial responsi**bil**ity
- **po**sitive discrimi**na**tion
- **chall**enge **ste**reotypes
- undera**chie**ver

Higher education

- tu**i**tion /tʃuːˈɪʃ.ən/
- aca**dem**ic **know**ledge
- certifi**ca**tion
- **schol**arship
- en**roll** in
- at**tend**
- **spe**cialise in
- **lec**ture
- tu**tor**ial
- de**part**ment
- **sem**inar
- field of **stu**dy
- as**sign**ment
- term

1 **Complete the texts with words from the mind map.**

a. At the age of 16 in the UK students … … … called … if they … they can continue studying and pass … … around the age of 18. After, if they get the … they need, they can go on and study for a … … in three years at university, followed by a … … which usually takes about two years.

b. At university, there are different kinds of … a … involves a large number of students in a hall listening to a professor, a … is a class for around 15 students, where they have the opportunity to discuss and ask questions on a particular subject. A … is even smaller and involves more personalised learning for the students present.

2 **Use words from the boxes entitled "Equality" and "Academic excellence" to recap what today's universities are trying to offer.**

Projects

1 You are an activist and a member of the organisation The Brilliant Club. Write an opinion article about inequalities in the UK education system and the initiatives to improve it.

1. Gather information from this unit and the web (data, percentages, dates, people's account and stories).
2. Organise your ideas and arguments to show the evolution of the education system.
3. Give different suggestions to provoke positive change.
4. Use a convincing tone to voice your opinion. Make it personal to prompt action from your readers.
5. Provide a strong ending to your op-ed by summing up your arguments and proposing solutions.

2 You are a member of the Students' Union at Edinburgh University. Promote an event you are organising to encourage equality in higher education in a video posted on social media and on the university website.

1. Concentrate on the introduction of your video to attract viewers (with numbers, a quote, a striking picture or graph for instance).
2. Plan out the outline of your video using information and data from this unit and/or from the web.
3. Explain the situation and why evolution is necessary.
4. Focus on possible actions and suggestions for proactive change.
5. Use key words only to avoid reading.

2 Reinventing education in the USA

The expert's view
hatier-clic.fr/21amc/024a

In the news
hatier-clic.fr/21amc/024b

Projects

- You are a journalist. Write an article presenting a technologist with big ideas about education.
- You are a vlogger. Make a two-minute video presenting your genius idea for education.

Grammar p. 32 Phonology p. 33

Standardised or personalised learning?

A Testing for proficiency

Culture Tip

College is part of higher education. It is another commonly used word for university in the US. The SAT (Scholastic Aptitude Test) is a test aimed at students who want to go to college. The SAT score determines what college you are likely to get in. So there is a lot of pressure to be among the top-scoring SAT takers.

1. Analyse the cartoon focusing on how the tests are shaped and what the educators expect.
2. Study the facial expression of college students and imagine their feelings.

PAIR WORK

3. **Brainstorm:** What type of skills may the University lady have in mind? Imagine the conversation between her and a student.

B Empowering with technology

1

Patrick Newell led one of the first schools to adopt gamified learning programmes – and is a strong advocate of personalised learning. Here's what he had to say.

As an expert on the role of technology in education, what major changes do you think we should expect to see in the way students learn in the future?

I think our current education system is ridiculous. There's no other instance in our lives when we expect young people to have the same level of intellectual intelligence and emotional intelligence as required by current education systems. Technology has the ability to assess learners using AI and it's definitely going to shift things. We're already seeing it with people being forced to go online [due to COVID-19].

One of my core focuses right now is to see how we can use AI to assess learning and learners. It can also tell us what we need to learn next or give us ideas around options we have. This will have a huge impact on how we learn and work together to reach the highest level of creative, collective intelligence. […]

What impact has the current pandemic had on parents, educators and students, and how will the current use of online platforms like Zoom impact the way educators and students interact in the years to come?

It's been a huge wakeup call for everyone. It's definitely strengthened the triangle of parents, educators, and students aligning towards the goal of helping students reach their highest potential. Parents now understand what it's like for teachers, and teachers understand what it's like for parents. It's also really showing the weaknesses in our existing education system. Finding the right balance of online learning combined with human face-to-face interaction is definitely one of the most important things we can do moving forward. It's really shown the level technology can allow us to reach to develop their IQ[1] and EQ[2].

Cheyelene Singh, hivelife.com, May 26th, 2020

1. intellectual quotient 2. emotional quotient

2

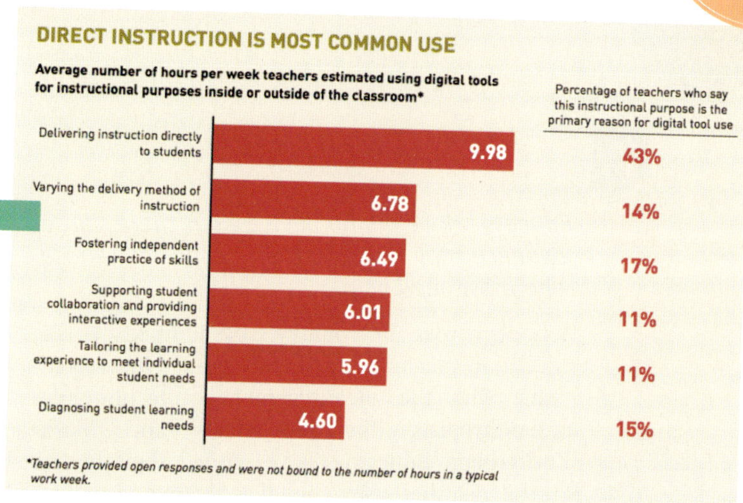

1. Look at the graph. Focus on percentages and explain what they reveal about teachers' views on digital tools.
2. Read the text and focus on lines 5-10. Explain what Patrick Newell thinks is wrong with current education systems.
3. Pick out the modern elements that can move education forward and list them in your own words.
4. **Grammar** Identify an infinitive clause of purpose. Rephrase it by means of an equivalent structure.
5. **CONNECT.** Use both documents to write your conclusions about the gap between American teachers' current use of digital tools and their real potential.

@ e-worksheet
hatier-clic.fr/21amc/025a

C Flip the classroom

Flipped classroom

Audio hatier-clic.fr/21amc/025b

1. Read *Let's focus on...* n° 2, p. 30 and watch the clip. Pick out the keywords Salman Khan stresses the most and use them to explain what Khan Academy is and how it works.
2. Describe what Khan Academy students do at home and what they do in class. Compare the benefits with the "one-size-fits-all" lecture format.
3. Explain what you like and dislike about watching teachers' videos online in a post in the comment section of the video.

Equal access to education 3.0?

A The richer takes it all

1

Educators love digital devices, but there's little evidence they help children – especially those who most need help.

Schools across the country have jumped on the education technology bandwagon[1] in recent years, with the encouragement of technophile philanthropists like Bill Gates and Mark Zuckerberg. Educators have pinned their hopes on the idea that instructional software and online tutorials and games can help narrow the massive test-score gap between students at the top and bottom of the socioeconomic scale. A recent Gallup report found that 89% of students in the United States (from third to 12th grade)[2] say they use digital learning tools in school at least a few days a week.

In fact, the evidence is equivocal[3] at best. Some studies have found positive effects, at least from moderate amounts of computer use, especially in math. But much of the data shows a negative impact at a range of grade levels. A study of millions of high school students in the 36 member countries of the Organisation for Economic Co-operation and Development (OECD) found that those who used computers heavily at school "do a lot worse in most learning outcomes, even after accounting for social background and student demographics." According to other studies, college students in the US who used laptops or digital devices in their classes did worse on exams. Eighth graders who took Algebra I online did much worse than those who took the course in person. In some states, the gap was significantly larger.

Judging from the evidence, the most vulnerable students can be harmed the most by a heavy dose of technology – or, at best, not helped. The OECD study found that "technology is of little help in bridging the skills divide between advantaged and disadvantaged students." In the United States, the test score gap between students who use technology frequently and those who don't is largest among students from low-income families. A similar effect has been found for "flipped" courses, which have students watch lectures at home via technology and use class time for discussion and problem-solving. A flipped college math class resulted in short-term gains for white students, male students, and those who were already strong in math. Others saw no benefit, with the result that performance gaps became wider.

Even more troubling, there's evidence that vulnerable students are spending more time on digital devices.

Natalie Wexler, *The MIT Technology Review*, Dec. 19th, 2019

1. adopted the trend 2. from 8 to 18 years old 3. uncertain

2

Plugging the digital divide

Video hatier-clic.fr/21amc/026

PAIR WORK

Student A on document 1
Student B on document 2

1. Study your document and give the consequences of moving education online.
2. Share your findings about the obstacles standing in the way of moving education online.
3. You both work for Students for Equal Educational Opportunities. Write a tract on the bright and dark sides of education moving online.

B Meet the learning pods

Education pods

Video hatier-clic.fr/21amc/027

1. Define Mrs Dehaas's situation and how a learning pod works.
2. Show why lifeboats and speedboats perfectly illustrate the education divide.

PAIR WORK

3. Imagine a conversation between the sociologist and Mrs DeHaas.

C Staying apart but connected

1. Look at the cartoon. Compare and contrast the two students' school situations and comment on the irony of their conversation.
2. Study the graph. Compare the situation of students from lower- and upper-income families
3. **CONNECT.** Use both documents to comment on how the digital gap affects educational outcomes.

1

2

Roughly six-in-ten parents with lower incomes said it's likely their homebound children would face at least one digital obstacle to doing their schoolwork

*Among parents with children whose schools were closed, % who said it was **very** or **somewhat** likely that as their children did schoolwork at home during the coronavirus outbreak, they would ...*

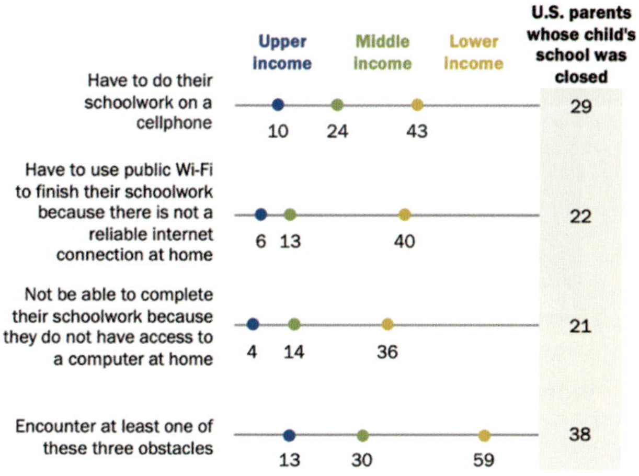

Note: Only parents of elementary, middle, high school students whose school was closed at the time were asked these questions. Family income tiers are based on adjusted 2018 earnings. Those who did not give an answer or who gave other responses are not shown.
Source: Survey of U.S. adults conducted April 7-12, 2020.

PEW RESEARCH CENTER

GAFAM in the US classroom

A Moving online

1 Read *Let's focus on...* n° 4, p. 31 and the caption below. Explain what equipment and learning apps the whole class is using.

2 Find what or who is missing from the photograph. Explain the potential consequences on the pupils.

1

American elementary school students using Google-powered laptops and Google education apps for classwork. More than half the nation's primary and secondary-school students – more than 30 million children – use Google education apps, the company says.

B Supporting immediate, individualised feedback

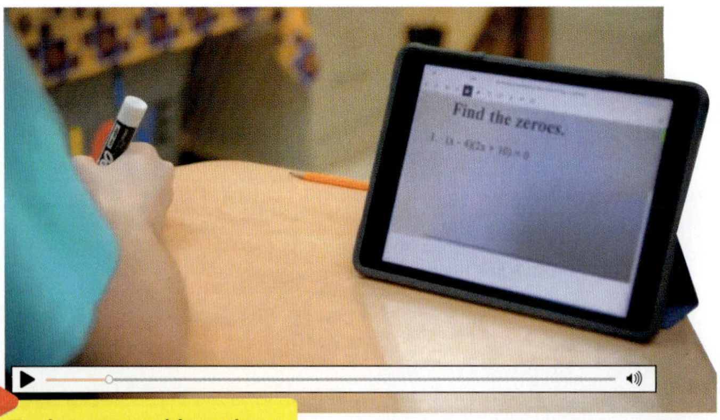

Tech-powered learning

Video hatier-clic.fr/21amc/028

1 Watch the video and pick out the stressed words said by Ms. Miller and her students at Greene Central High. Use them to present the main benefits of tech-powered learning.

2 Focus on how Ms. Miller and her students use their tablets and interact with each other. Explain why it is "immediate, individualised feedback."

3 You are an exchange student at Greene Central High. Write an email to your family about your immersion in math class.

Culture Tip

STEM is an umbrella word for science-related school subjects, namely science, technology, engineering and math.

2 Google's education tech has a privacy problem

New Mexico's attorney general sued the company, claiming its school tools continue to track kids after the final bell.

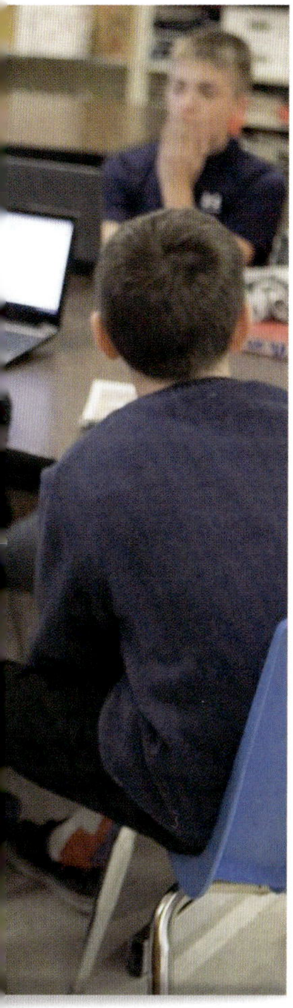

New Mexico is suing Google for allegedly invading children's privacy through educational products it provides to the state's schools, claiming it tracks students' activities on their personal devices outside the classroom. The suit calls into question what a major for-profit player in the nonprofit educational space – which counts millions of children among its users – is doing with whatever data it collects from them.

Google offers its educational products to schools for little to no obvious cost. New Mexico's attorney general, Hector Balderas, claims the hidden price is children's data, which it collects without their knowledge or the required parental consent, even when the technology isn't being used for educational purposes. While Google denies the charges, the very existence of the lawsuit could prompt other states and school systems to reevaluate their agreements with the company.

"While purporting to offer only educational services, Google instead has stripped children and parents of autonomy and control of their most sensitive personal information, forcing children to acquiesce to constant monitoring, in perpetuity, in exchange for their education," the suit says.

Any companies that collect online data about children under the age of 13 must have their parents' consent first. (This is why Facebook, for example, does not allow children under 13 to have accounts.)

"Google tracks children across the internet, across devices, in their homes, and well outside the educational sphere, all without obtaining verifiable parental consent," Balderas wrote. "Google has used this access to collect massive quantities of data from young children not to benefit the schools you have contracted with, but to benefit Google's own commercial interests."

Google says its educational products comply with COPPA and industry standards, that it does not own or sell G Suite data, and that it does not use any personal information to target ads in G Suite school products. It also says schools must obtain parental consent before allowing users under the age of 18 to use Google's services, according to its contract with schools.

Sara Morrison, www.vox.com, Feb. 21st, 2020

1. Read *Let's focus on...* n° 1, p. 30 and the text. List all the legal charges against Google and report on Google's response to the lawsuit.

PAIR WORK

2. "If you're not paying for it, you're the product." Discuss why the sentence applies to Google's education tech and other Google products.

3. **Phonology** Pick out all the words containing the diphthong /eɪ/ (as in *great* or *say*). Classify them into several groups based on their spelling.

4. **CONNECT.** Link documents 1 and 2 and comment on the impact of Google education apps on schoolchildren.

C Free computers, really?

1. Pick up the names of iconic Apple products and of its founder. Describe his vision for personalised computers.
2. Explain why Apple was a gamechanger in the education marketplace.
3. Present this initiative in a one-minute video for a Ted Talk.

Classroom computers

Audio hatier-clic.fr/21amc/029

Let's focus on...

Data protection 1

Europe has embraced a legal revolution recently with the adoption of the General Data Protection Regulation (GDPR), and you are now regularly asked to give your "consent" when surfing the web. There is no such framework in the US, and there are regular calls in the press for a better protection of pupils' and students' privacy. Pupils should not be handing over free information to Tech Giants when going to school, yet parents are routinely asked to consent to their children's data being used: their names, their internet activity and their grades are no secret to these firms. A majority of students are now using Gmail and Doc Apps: what if this data fell into the wrong hands? This is, of course, the worst-case scenario. But more generally, more structurally: Should we sit on our hands when the young are being targeted by adverts because of the devices and technology they use in class? Commerce should not rule the American classroom, and public awareness is being raised by parent groups or privacy advocates. Efforts such as that of the Do Not Track Kids Act need to be strengthened, clarified and generalised for American students to have the best of both worlds: information AND privacy. Technology should be the product, not students!

Khan Academy 2

Khan Academy is named after its founder, Salman Khan, who first started creating online videos to help his cousins who were struggling with their math class. It proved to be such a success that in 2008 he started a non-profit organisation creating online tools to help educate students, and it is now offering content in a whole range of subjects. It is very optimistic about the possibility for each individual to learn and rise, and speakers typically conclude their presentations with the words "You can learn everything". In 2020, Sal Khan used the COVID crisis as a stepping stone to push for a full revolution in the US educational system: in his opinion, teachers should stop creating their own Khan-Academy-style videos, use the real thing, and spend their time and energy on direct interactions with their students.

TEDtalks 3

TED is the acronym for Technology, Entertainment, Design. TEDtalks are short lectures of approximately 15 minutes that can tackle a vast variety of subjects. They are organised by a non-profit and non-partisan organisation. A scientist, an artist, a philosopher, an activist or whoever, shares his/her findings in a way that can be understood – and appealing – to the vast majority of people. The lectures have two things in common. First, in terms of content, they aim at sharing world-changing ideas and making knowledge pleasant – its motto being "Ideas worth spreading". Second, in terms of form, speakers offer a combination of inspiration and personal testimony: they have a story to tell, they stage their intellectual or personal journey, go into the details of their tribulations and, usually, triumphs. This has been a recipe for success since the dawn of the internet, and the videos are all available for free on YouTube – and hugely popular.

Google in the classroom

4

Google education is used by some 80 million users, and that number keeps growing. The firm sums up its ambition like this: "to help expand learning for everyone". Accessibility is guaranteed: these tools are free-of-charge and they are easy-to-use. They are the perfect place to develop group work, as all the members in a group can edit the documents they share, without the hassle of endless emails that do not always integrate the latest remarks and thoughts. Since G-Suite-for-Education also provides teachers and educators with emails, chats and videos, it comes as no surprise that these devices, offered by a private company, came in very handy in state-schools nationwide when the Covid 19 pandemic forced education to move online for several months. The recent boom in distance learning was first correlated with school closures. The educators, who were left scrambling to find creative ways to engage their students remotely, massively turned to Google. Interestingly, in May 2020, New York governor Andrew Cuomo publicly questioned the existence of physical classrooms. He champions edtech so much that he announced that former Google CEO Eric Schmidt and Bill Gates would help rethink education in his state. This pragmatic approach considers that if the private sector provides the most adequate tools, they should be adopted in the public sector with no hesitation.

5

HISTORY OF E-LEARNING

1960s
First computer based training program.

1970s
Mouse and graphical user interface (GUI) created.

1980s
Mac enables individuals to have computers in the home.

1990s
First digital natives born.

1999
The term "e-learning" is first used during the TechLearn conference at Disney World.

2008
The term MOOC (Massive Open Online Course) is used for the first time.

2012
3 major e-learning platforms – Coursera, Udacity, and edX – emerge.

2014
98% of US public colleges and universities are already offering fully online learning programs.

2020
About 90% of US corporations use online learning.

2020 and beyond
Towards adaptive personalised e-learning.

EFFICIENCY GAINS

40% to 60%
E-learning typically requires from 40% to 60% less employee time than the same material delivered in a traditional classroom setting.

X 5
E-learning participants learned nearly five times more material without increasing time spent learning.

25-60%
The E-learning experience increases the retention rate by 25-60% by providing participants control over their learning and the ability to easily revisit material later.

Practice your grammar

Les comparatifs

▶ On forme les comparatifs des adjectifs ou des adverbes de la manière suivante :

supériorité	adj. court ***-er than...*** *She's brighter than me.*	***more*** adj. long + ***than***... *She's more intelligent than me.*
égalité	***as*** + adjectif + ***as...*** *He's as hard-working as his brother.*	
infériorité	***less*** adjectif + ***than...*** *He's less brilliant than his brother.* ***not so / as*** + adjectif + ***as...*** *He isn't as / so brilliant as his brother.*	

▶ Les adjectifs courts sont les adjectifs d'**une syllabe**. Ceux de deux syllabes qui se terminent par ***-y*** (*happy* → *happier*), ***-le*** (*simple* → *simpler*) ou ***-ow*** (*narrow* → *narrower*) forment souvent leur comparatif au moyen de la terminaison *-er*.

▶ Notez ces formes irrégulières :
good / well → ***better*** *bad / badly* → ***worse***
far → ***farther / further***

▶ Le complément du comparatif introduit par ***than* ou *as*** peut être à **la forme complément ou sujet**. Dans ce cas, on a parfois recours à **une reprise d'auxiliaire** : *You are more intelligent **than I (am) / me**.*

▶ On peut renforcer les comparatifs au moyen **d'adverbes** tels que ***much, way, even, significantly***, etc.

*In some states, the gap was **significantly larger**.*

▶ Notez la construction **du double comparatif** pour traduire « de plus en plus » (***more and more* + adj**. ou **adj.+ *-er* and adj.+*-er***) ou « de moins en moins » (***less and less* + adj**.).

*It's getting **more and more difficult** for schoolteachers to do their jobs well.*

L'expression du but

▶ On peut exprimer le but au moyen d'**une proposition infinitive** en ***to* + V**, en ***in order (not) to* + V** ou en ***so as (not) to* + V**. On traduit toutes ces structures par ***pour* + infinitif**.

*These teachers have used technology **(in order) to** humanise the classroom.*

▶ Il est également possible d'utiliser une proposition introduite par ***so that*** ou par ***in order that* (afin que, pour que)**. Dans ce cas, la proposition contient souvent un modal tel que *can*, *could* ou *may*.

*The students used webcams **so that** their teacher **could** see them.*

▶ Notez aussi les structures suivantes :
- *aim to do sth*
- *be designed / meant / intended to do sth (for sb)*

*This blog **is intended / aims to** provide useful information about e-learning tools.*

*The course **is designed for beginners**.*

1 Mettez le verbe à la forme du comparatif de supériorité qui convient.

a. *75% of teachers report that home schooling made them ... (aware) of their students' needs.*

b. *Students participating in this exchange programme have ... (low) absentee rates and ... (high) SAT scores.*

c. *His schoolmates work ... (fast) than he does.*

d. *Are educational games ... (effective) than traditional learning methods?*

e. *Over the course of the term her son's grades have got ... and ... (bad).*

2 Comparez l'éducation à distance avec les méthodes traditionnelles. Utilisez des comparatifs d'égalité, de supériorité et d'infériorité. Produisez six phrases utilisant les adjectifs suivants.
stressful • flexible • easy • funny • widespread • interactive • attractive

3 Dans quel but un professeur peut-il utiliser les nouvelles technologies dans sa classe ? Produisez quatre phrases utilisant ces structures :
aim to do sth • in order (not) to do sth • so that • be designed / meant to do something.

Exemple : *My English teacher has created a class blog **in order to encourage** his students to improve their writing skills.*

Improve your pronunciation

La diphtongue /eɪ/

▶ La diphtongue que l'on retrouve dans *say* ou *may* est représentée par **le symbole /eɪ/**. Ce son est orthographié par les graphies suivantes :

ai **(à l'intérieur d'un mot) ou** ***ay*** **(en fin de mot)**	*day, pay, essay, fail, pain* Exceptions : *said, again* /e/
ei **(à l'intérieur d'un mot) ou** ***ey*** **(en fin de mot)**	*prey, they, eight, weight* Exceptions : *height* /aɪ/, *foreign* /ə/
a **dans** ***ation, ange***	*education, nation, strange, change, angel*
et **et** ***é*** **dans des mots français**	*fiancé, café, cliché, ballet, buffet*
ea **dans quelques mots**	*steak, great, break* (mais *breakfast* /e/)

⚠ En position inaccentuée, la graphie *ai* se prononce souvent /ə/ ou /ɪ/ : *Britain*, *certain*, *mountain*.

▶ Lorsque **la graphie *a*** est suivie d'**une consonne unique suivie d'un e (*a* + C + e) en position accentuée**, on la prononce /eɪ/ : *game*, *make*, *paper* (exception : *have* /æ/).

⚠ La terminaison *-age* se prononce /ɪdʒ/ en position inaccentuée : *image*, *advantage*, *manage*.

1 **Écoutez et répétez les mots suivants.**

Audio hatier-clic.fr/21amc/033a

a. *paper / pepper* **b.** *fail / fell* **c.** *pen / pain* **d.** *taste / test* **e.** *let / late*

2 **Chassez l'intrus (le mot qui ne rime pas avec les autres) dans ces listes.**

Audio hatier-clic.fr/21amc/033b

a. *explain – mountain – remain – entertain*
b. *plain – gain – obtain – certain*
c. *foreign – reign – neighbour - vein*
d. *page – stage – cage – manage*

3 **Pour chacun de ces mots, trouvez un homophone (un mot qui ne s'écrit pas de la même manière mais qui se prononce de façon identique).**

pray • male • weight • plane • tail • stake

L'alphabet phonétique international

▶ L'alphabet phonétique international (API ou IPA) permet de retranscrire fidèlement la prononciation d'un mot. Il est particulièrement utile quand on n'a pas la possibilité d'écouter un mot dont on ignore la prononciation.

▶ Les transcriptions en API suivent quelques conventions :
- les mots apparaissent **entre barres obliques /…/**.
- **les symboles ˈ (accent primaire) ou ˌ (accent secondaire)** placés **avant** une syllabe indiquent que celle-ci est accentuée.

education /ˌedjuˈkeɪʃən/

▶ **L'apprentissage des consonnes** ne pose pas beaucoup de problèmes car la plupart des symboles sont les mêmes que dans l'alphabet latin : /p/, /t/, /d/, /g/… Voici quelques symboles sources de difficultés :

/k/	*come, kill, school*	/ʃ/	*shoot, shame*
/ð/	*this, they, the*	/ʒ/	*measure*
/θ/	*think, math*	/tʃ/	*chair, catch*
/j/	*you, yet*	/ŋ/	*ring, king*

▶ **L'apprentissage des voyelles** est plus complexe (voir Unit 10, p. 129). **Le signe ː** indique que la voyelle est **longue**. Par exemple, le symbole /iː/ représente le *i* long de *meet*.

4 **Écrivez les mots correspondant aux transcriptions suivantes.**

a. /bed/ **b.** /bɪg/ **c.** /niːd/ **d.** /tiːtʃ/ **e.** /ˈtiːtʃə/ **f.** /geɪm/ **g.** /skuːl/ **h.** /tuːl/ **i.** /ðeɪ/

5 **Transcrivez les consonnes en gras dans ces mots.**

day • paper • she • book • can • fail • that • say • think • yes • hot • leasure • choose

6 **Recopiez les mots suivants et soulignez la syllabe accentuée après avoir consulté la transcription du dictionnaire en ligne.**

ignorant • beginning • analysis • eighteen • proficient • consider

Build up your vocabulary

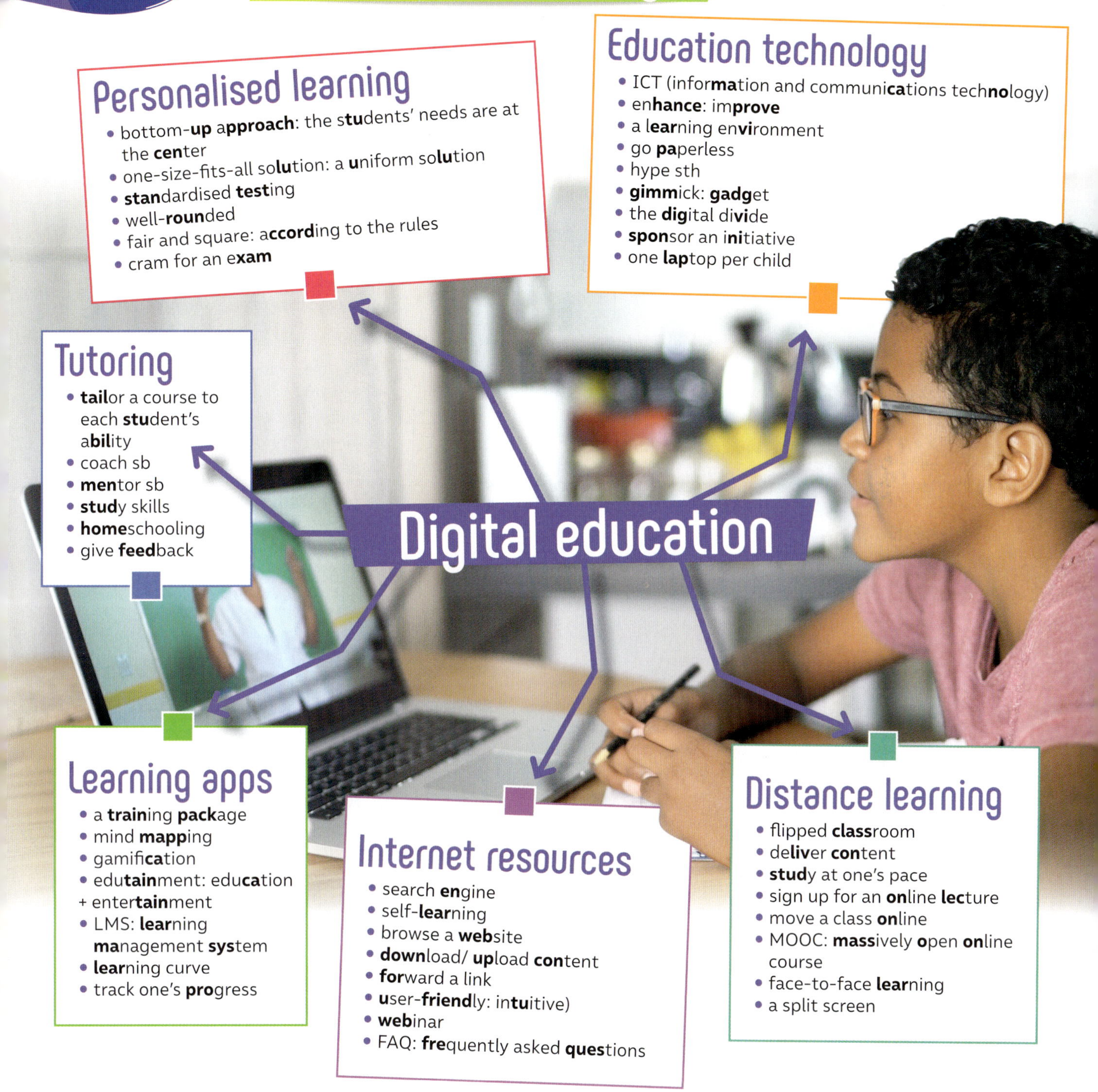

Personalised learning

- bottom-**up approach**: the **stu**dents' needs are at the **cen**ter
- one-size-fits-all so**lu**tion: a **u**niform so**lu**tion
- **stan**dardised **test**ing
- well-**roun**ded
- fair and square: ac**cord**ing to the rules
- cram for an e**xam**

Education technology

- ICT (infor**ma**tion and communi**ca**tions tech**no**logy)
- en**hance**: im**prove**
- a **lear**ning en**vi**ronment
- go **pa**perless
- hype sth
- **gimm**ick: **gadg**et
- the **dig**ital di**vi**de
- **spon**sor an i**ni**tiative
- one **lap**top per child

Tutoring

- **tail**or a course to each **stu**dent's a**bil**ity
- coach sb
- **men**tor sb
- **stud**y skills
- **home**schooling
- give **feed**back

Digital education

Learning apps

- a **train**ing **pack**age
- mind **mapp**ing
- gamifi**ca**tion
- edu**tain**ment: edu**ca**tion + enter**tain**ment
- LMS: **lear**ning **ma**nagement **sys**tem
- **lear**ning curve
- track one's **pro**gress

Internet resources

- search **en**gine
- self-**lear**ning
- browse a **web**site
- **down**load/ **up**load **con**tent
- **for**ward a link
- user-**friend**ly: in**tu**itive)
- **web**inar
- FAQ: **fre**quently asked **ques**tions

Distance learning

- flipped **class**room
- de**liv**er **con**tent
- **stud**y at one's pace
- sign up for an **on**line **lec**ture
- move a class **on**line
- MOOC: **mass**ively **o**pen **on**line course
- face-to-face **lear**ning
- a split screen

1 Complete the text with words from the mind map.

... learning may well be phased out by the myriad ways you can deliver educational ... straight to students through ... lectures. Further progress in artificial intelligence will enable educators to ... courses and assignments to individual students and let them study at their own ... . The ability to view and ... your ... will promote self-... and generally ... student performance. Critics may argue that digital learning platforms are nothing more than ... and get ... beyond their real value. The jury is still out on whether ... learning will propel schools into the twenty-first century.

2 Use five words or expressions from the mind map to describe one of your interactive classes in an email to your American pen pal.

Projects

1

You are a journalist. Write an article presenting an American technologist with big ideas about education.

1. Choose an original initiative from a philanthropist who is very active in the education field (Bill Gates, Jeff Bezos, Elon Musk or Mark Zuckerberg). Look for specific information online about their initiatives.
2. Find an attention-grabbing headline.
3. Use words from *Build up your vocabulary* to write the article.
4. Read-proof your article: pay special attention to your English and make sure that you can answer the Who / What / When / Where / Why questions.

2

Ted Talk: you are a vlogger. Make a two-minute video presenting your genius idea for education.

1. Find your genius idea: the needs that it addresses, the way it would affect teachers and learners.
2. Think about your narrative: the story of a life-changing moment when you realised that change was needed.
3. Practice and record yourself.
4. Pay attention to intonation and allow for pauses to make your story more dramatic.
5. Spice it up with a joke or find a way to involve the audience.
6. Start recording your talk!

3 Robots for better... or for worse

The expert's view
hatier-clic.fr/21amc/036a

In the news
hatier-clic.fr/21amc/036b

Projects

You run a business. Debate the introduction of robots in your company.

You are a journalist for a science magazine. Write an article on the impact of the introduction of robots.

Grammar p. 44 Phonology p. 45

Rise of the robots

A Elektro & Steam man

1

In 1868, American author Edward S. Ellis wrote about a prodigy that constructed an automaton called the Steam Man, the first American robot.

"It was about ten feet in height, measuring to the top of the 'stove-pipe hat,' which was fashioned after the common order of felt coverings, with a broad brim, all painted a shiny black. The face was made of iron, painted a black color, with a pair of fearful eyes, and a tremendous grinning mouth. A whistle-like contrivance[1] was made to answer for the nose. The steam chest proper and boiler were where the chest in a human being is generally supposed to be, extending also into a large knapsack[2] arrangement over the shoulders and back. A pair of arms, like projections, held the shafts[3] and the broad flat feet were covered with sharp spikes[4], as though he were the monarch of baseball players. The legs were quite long, and the step was natural, except when running, at which time, the bolt uprightness[5] in the figure showed differed from a human being.

"In the knapsack were the valves, by which the steam or water was examined. In front was a painted imitation of a vest, in which a door opened to receive the fuel, which, together with the water, was carried in the wagon, a pipe running along the shaft and connecting with the boiler.

https://www.syfy.com

1. device 2. backpack 3. metal or wooden pieces attaching a horse to a vehicle 4. pointed objects 5. rigid straightness

2

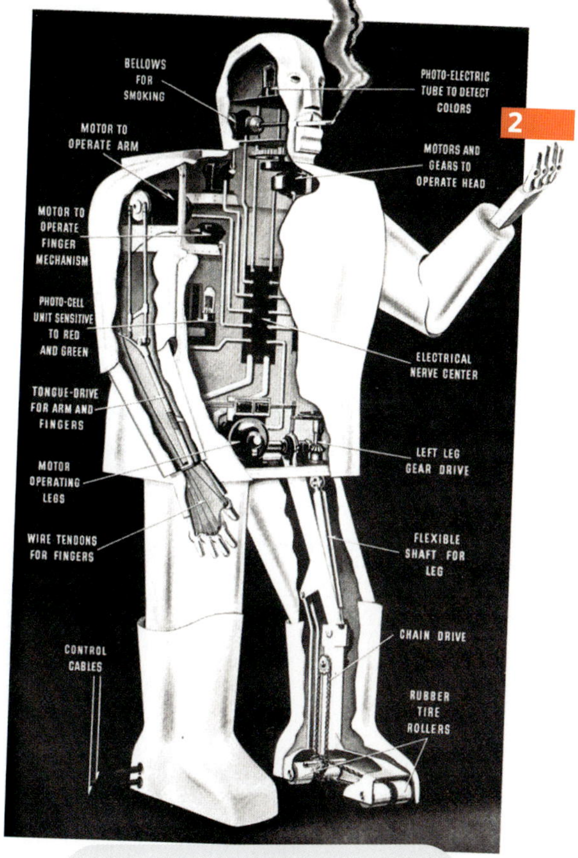

The first robot, presented at the 1939 New York World's Fair.

1. Look at the illustration. Describe Elektro and list what he can do.
2. Read the text. List what makes Steam Man look human and explain how he is powered. Draw your version of this robot.
3. **CONNECT.** Use both documents to comment on the way men imagined the first robots.

B On the origins of robots

History of robots

Video hatier-clic.fr/21amc/037a

e-worksheet hatier-clic.fr/21amc/037b

1 Watch the video and comment on the images of the montage and what they mean about the evolution of robots.

2 List the different stages of this evolution and give examples of robots. Explain how people view them.

3 Read *Let's focus on...* n° 1, p. 42 and present the Turing test.

4 **Phonology** Listen and repeat the following words: *elaborate, navigate*. Which syllable carries the main stress?

5 Imagine and ask each other four new questions for the Turing test.

C Teaching robots right from wrong

You're rushing across the school parking lot to get to your first class on time when you notice a friend is in trouble. She's texting and listening to music on her headphones. Unawares[1], she's also heading straight for a gaping hole in the sidewalk. What do you do? [...]

To figure out the best solution, such a decision balances the effects of your choice. It's an easy decision. You don't even have to think hard about it. You make such choices all the time. But what about robots? Can they make such choices? Should a robot stop your friend from falling into the hole? *Could it?*

Not today's robots. They simply aren't smart enough to even realize when someone is in danger. Soon, they might be. Yet without some rules to follow, a robot wouldn't know the best choice to make.

So robot developers are turning to *philosophy*. Called ethics, it's a field in which people study differences between right and wrong. And with it, they are starting to develop robots that can make basic ethical decisions. [...]

Such research should help robots of the future figure out the best action to take when there are competing choices. This ethical behavior may just become part of their programming. That will allow them to interact with people in safe, predictable ways. In time, robots may actually begin to understand the difference between right and wrong. [...]

The most famous set of rules for robots comes not from research but from a science fiction story by Isaac Asimov. "Runaround," published in 1942, features two men and Robot SPD-13, nicknamed "Speedy." They're sent to the planet Mercury in the year 2015. Speedy is programmed with three basic rules:

1) A robot can't hurt a person or, through inaction, allow a person to get hurt.

2) A robot must obey people, as long as this doesn't break the first law.

3) A robot must protect itself, as long as this doesn't break the first two laws.

In later robot stories, Asimov added a "zeroth" law: A robot can't harm[2] humanity or, through inaction, allow harm to humanity.

Asimov's rules sound good. But the story shows that such simple rules may not be enough. [...]

These rules would certainly compel[3] a robot to rescue your friend. But they wouldn't help a robot decide what to do if two people were about to fall and it could only save one. The robot also wouldn't try to rescue a kitten.

It's very difficult to write a set of rules that will apply in all possible situations. For this reason, some scientists instead build robots with the ability to learn ethical behavior.

Kathryn Hulick, *Science News For Students*, April 20th, 2017

1. not knowing 2. damage 3. force

1 Mime or draw what is happening in the first paragraph.

2 Rephrase Asimov's three laws of robotics and say if they are ethical or not.

3 Explain if today's robots are capable of making ethical choices.

4 **Grammar** Observe the following sentence: "Asimov's rules sound good. But the story shows that such simple rules may not be enough." Pick out the modal auxiliary. Rephrase the sentence by using one of the following adverbs: *probably – certainly – perhaps*.

5 You are part of the ethics committee of a large robotics industry. Write five rules for today's robots.

I'll be back

1

A Evolution or revolution?

PAIR WORK

1. Describe your document and comment on the layout, the colours, the characters. Highlight the evolution of the place of robots in our lives.
2. Share your findings with your partner and explain the message of your artist.

2

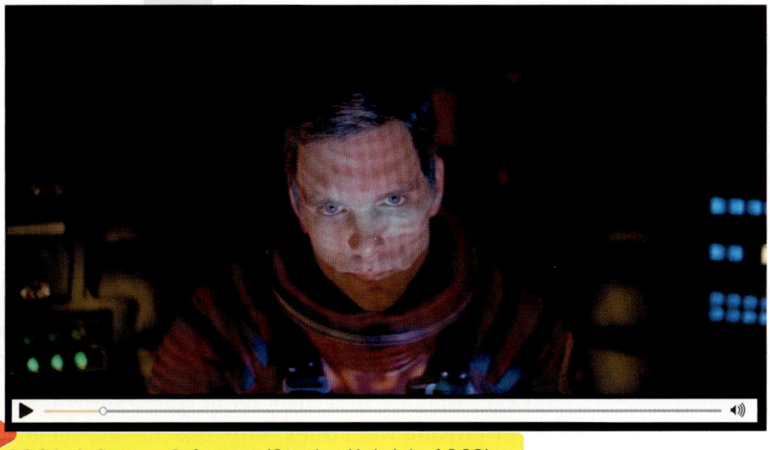

2001: A Space Odyssey (Stanley Kubrick, 1968)

Video hatier-clic.fr/21amc/038

B "I'm sorry, Dave..."

1. Present the two characters in this extract.
2. Comment on the setting (colours, shapes, places) and the intonation of both voices. Describe the atmosphere they create.
3. Account for the superiority of one of the characters and explain the end of the scene.
4. Record Dave's message to his base where he explains the situation and warns them about what robots plan to do on earth.

C The rise of robots

Since the oldest times people have sought[1] for ways to save them from hard physical work and menial[2] activities. To find solutions they have invented new tools, domesticated animals, and created new machines. As new technological innovations were created, people quickly adopted them and assimilated them into their lives. While many of them understood that technology brings them new opportunities to improve their living standards and to grow their wealth, many others have started to fear what would happen once the robots will reach a certain level of intelligence. [...]

People don't like interacting with robots

Do you know what the Turing test implies? In 1950, Alan Turing established the benchmark for AI, if people are interacting with robots in conversation, and they cannot distinguish them from persons, they have to admit that the machines are capable of true intelligence.

No one could doubt people were dealing with machines when they had the first interactions, but in the present times when people can talk to their mobile phones via programs like Siri, they are no longer sure if they can distinguish them from persons.

Now people are having difficulties to integrate robots and AI into their lives because they no longer feel comfortable to interact with robots. It remains to be seen if people will see robots as part of their life, and they will decide to accept their presence or if they will continue to be frightened of machines.

Only because a thing does not make us feel comfortable it doesn't mean it's not good for us. No one can deny the incomparable advantages technology integration brings to both individuals and companies. By using machines, businesses are able to improve their business effectiveness and to protect their employees from hazardous[3] activities. They count on robot software to create and control machines that help them grow their businesses without posing risks to the human workforce and the surrounding environment.

Fiction and movies were not kind to AI and robots

How did people create robots a bad image? The depictions of the media had an important role in influencing their impression. *Westworld*, *Alien*, *Matrix*, and *Ex Machina* are only some of the movies that showed how things can go wrong if robots gain intelligence. From the earliest depictions[4] of robots in science fiction the message was the same, robots have a single purpose to dominate the world. [...]

People are afraid that robots will take their jobs away

More and more people feel this immediate fear. For example, in the automotive industry, robots are used to assemble cars, but it doesn't mean that no human is working on the premises[5]. Humans have other tasks to accomplish, they no longer complete the jobs that would pose danger to their life, they are supervising the robots making sure they are 100% efficient. AI may threaten some jobs, but it leads to the growth and rise of others. [...]

People are afraid of the Uncanny[6] Valley

It looks like human-like robots are the ones that generate the greatest fear among people. The perception gained the name Uncanny Valley and it describes the situation when people feel uncomfortable with the human-like traits of robots. They are not experiencing fear of robots, but fear of the robots that look like humans, the ones that are able to mimic a person.

Bogdan Butoi, www.techzone360.com, May 24th, 2019

1. searched 2. unskilled 3. dangerous 4. portrayal 5. site 6. strange, supernatural

GROUP WORK

1. Group A: List the positive uses of robots. Group B: List the negative uses of robots.
2. Groups A + B: Share your findings and recap what you have found out about robots.
3. Read *Let's focus on...* n° 8, p. 43. Explain the role of robots in the four films mentioned.
4. Account for the negative vision people can have of robots.
5. React to this article. Write a post to give your opinion about the impact a robot could have on people's lives.

Good, better, the best

A Musk's quest for immortality

There will always be a myriad of ways our mortal forms can go wrong. And we've seen that physiological constraints seem set to always hold us back from drastically extending our lifespans and remedying the root cause of ageing – if there even is one.

But on the border between science fiction and pioneering science rest exciting technological ideas that could perhaps unlock a different kind of immortality. Technology can already help us catch age-related defects early, but it holds the potential to become even better: what if we were able to circumvent[1] biological trade offs[2] entirely?

Billionaire Elon Musk's company Neuralink is already on the march to set us down this transhumanist path. It envisages a future where humans are far more intimately connected with their electronic devices than we are today. It invites us to work towards a brain-machine interface that would fundamentally integrate us with our technology, achieving a truly symbiotic relationship.

The research is still in its early stages, but brain-machine interfaces are already in use in the form of ear and eye implants that can restore our senses, and brain implants that allow disabled people to remotely control computers and robots. Neuralink aims to take this a step further by seamlessly[3] connecting us to electronic devices, the internet and even other humans. Essentially, we'd all have encyclopaedic information on hand and be able to communicate with one another telepathically.

To make this remarkable enhancement possible, a brain-machine interface would be injected into our bloodstream and travel to the brain. There it would self-assemble into a mesh[4]-like structure on the outside of the cerebral cortex, entwining technology to the core[5] of our intelligence and sentience[6].

Despite the invasiveness of Neuralink's implants, there are already a host of healthy individuals who are eager for such artificial enhancement. Some have even gone so far as to perform surgery on themselves just to install a gadget of meagre real-world value. But this may be just the start.

Neuralink and the technology it inspires could become a gateway to a post-human future. Through research in this area, we may decipher the means to accurately translate our organic, chemical neuronal pathways into electronic data that could encapsulate them. And so we may, eventually, be able to capture our beings within a computer, living forever as digital memory accessed by a piece of software.

This might be an extreme solution to the question of how to live forever, but there are wealthy individuals, such as entrepreneur Dmitry Itskov, devoted to the idea of merging with a computer. Itskov's 2045 Initiative views brain-machine interfaces as just the first step in a four-part journey that culminates in an artificial brain housing a human personality that controls a hologram-like avatar.

Itskov and other futurists are promising immortality, but to attain it we'll have to make possibly the biggest trade off of them all, giving away one of our most precious and defining gifts: our human form. The organic brain has forever been the vessel of our soul. An artificial copy may go as far as capturing your entire network of 100 trillion connections, but would it truly be you?

James S. Horton & Nicholas K. Priest, "Silicon Valley's quest for immortality – and its worrying sacrifices", *The Conversation*, Dec. 12th, 2018

1. avoid 2. change 3. smoothly 4. web 5. centre 6. consciousness

1. Read lines 1 to 6. Give the main concern some human beings have about their bodies.
2. Read lines 10 to 25. List the different aims of Elon Musk's Neuralink project. Explain how they can answer the concern mentioned above.
3. Use the article to write a definition of transhumanism.
4. Read lines 35 to the end. Comment on our possible future selves, as seen by entrepreneur Itskov.
5. You work for Elon Musk. Present his new transhumanist project to a board of investors.

e-worksheet
hatier-clic.fr/21amc/040

B Half man, half machine

go rogue: cease to follow orders

Rigid exoskeleton

A rigid frame with motorized joints could greatly boost strength and load capacity.

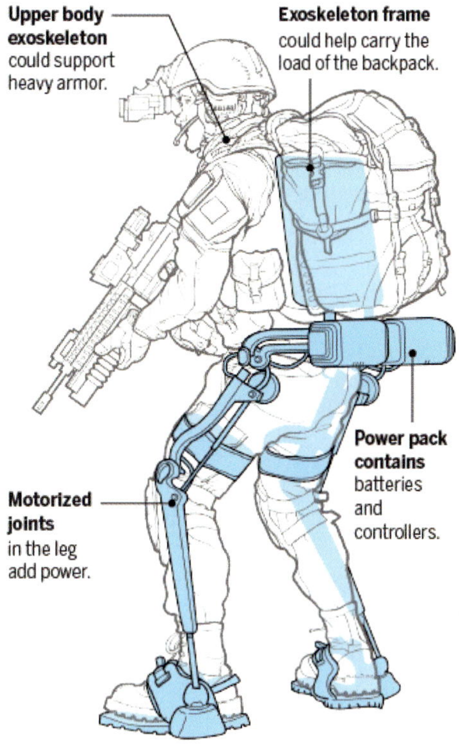

e-worksheet
hatier-clic.fr/21amc/041a

1. Describe the documents.
2. Give a definition of an exoskeleton.
3. List all the positive options it can give a soldier.
4. **CONNECT.** Use both documents to think of other fields where these exosuits can be used and list the advantages they offer.

C Real life Iron Man

1 Amputee gamer shows off 'Iron Man Arm'

Video hatier-clic.fr/21amc/041b

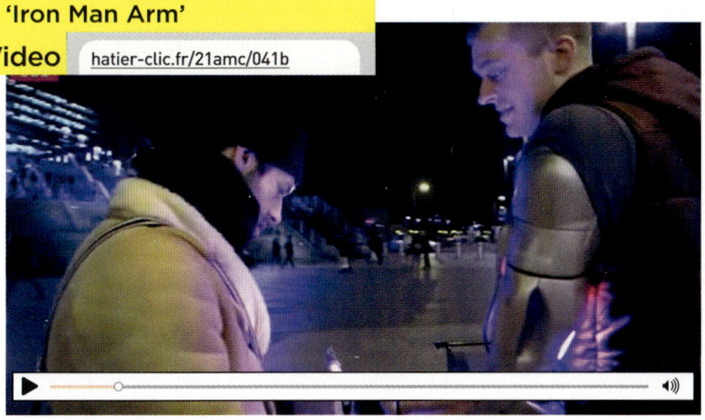

2 Body hack – metal gear man

Video hatier-clic.fr/21amc/041d

GROUP WORK

Student A on video 1.
Student B on video 2.

e-worksheet
hatier-clic.fr/21amc/041c

1. Watch your video and note down details about James Young.
2. Share your findings and recap what you know about the young man.
3. Student A: You work for the computer games company. You are interviewing several candidates interested in your bionic prosthetics.
Student B: You promote the company. Explain why your product is revolutionary.

Let's focus on...

Alan Turing (1912-1954) 1

Alan Turing was a brilliant British mathematician who is considered the father of computer science and artificial intelligence. He broke the Nazis' Enigma Code which helped the Allies win WW2. In 1950 he imagined a set of questions known as the "Turing test", meant to test machine intelligence and distinguish human beings from robots. Being a homosexual, he also broke the social codes of the time and was forced to undergo chemical castration which led him to take his life at the age of 42.

Elon Musk (1971-) 2

Elon Musk is a South African-born American entrepreneur and businessman who became a multimillionaire by founding many companies operating in very different sectors (X.com in 1999 which later became PayPal, SpaceX in 2002 and Tesla Motors in 2003). Elon Musk has always been ahead of his time: with a team of neurologists his firm Neuralink, founded in 2017, invented devices to be implanted in the brain, firstly to treat disease and then eventually for human enhancement.

Timeline 3

Elon Musk's Neuralink human test of brain-computer interface.
2020

First applications of exoskeletons designed in the field of industry.
2014

First biomedical applications designed to assist mobility.
2001

IBM supercomputer Deep Blue beats world chess champion Kasparov.
1997

James Cameron directs *Terminator*, presenting one of the most iconic robots.
1984

First exoskeleton used for military purposes.
1965

First industrial robot, called UNIMATE for "Universal Automation", designed by American engineers.
1954

Alan Turing proposes the "Turing Test" to determine if a machine has gained the power to think for itself.
1950

American author I. Asimov popularises the term "robotics" and sets out his "three laws of robotics" in his story *Runaround*.
1942

Elektro, the first voice-controlled robot, is presented at New York world's fair.
1939

American author E. Ellis writes one of the first science-fiction novels, *The Steam Man in the Prairies*, featuring the first mechanical man.
1868

Bionic man 4

Hugh Herr: How we'll become cyborgs...

Video hatier-clic.fr/21amc/043

Robots for rehabilitation 5

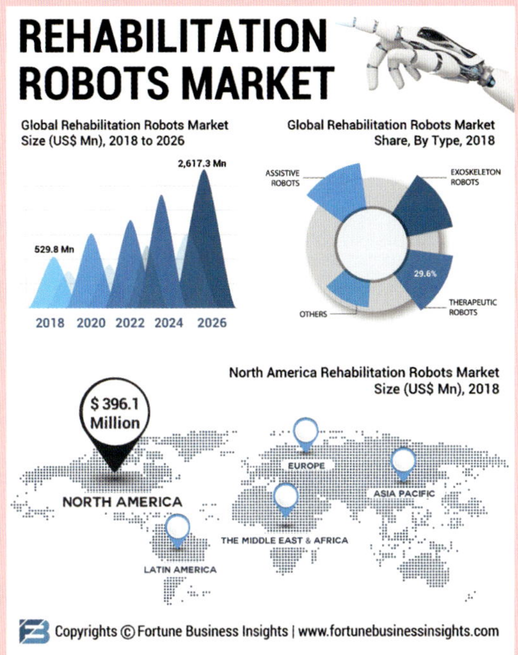

Exoskeletons 6

An exoskeleton (also called a power armor, an exoframe, a hardsuit or an exosuit) is a wearable device powered by different types of technologies. It goes around users' bodies or part of their body. Sensors monitor and respond to the users' motion. Exoskeletons can support the shoulder, waist and thigh, and assist movement for lifting and holding heavy loads, thus increasing strength and stamina and lowering back strain. Exoskeletons are more and more common in both the industry and the army. In the medical field, they help patients with limb movements and even enable some people in wheelchair to walk again.

AI – Artificial Intelligence 7

Based on algorithms, Artificial Intelligence is a science which imitates the cognitive abilities of a human brain, such as learning and problem solving. It has led computers to perform increasingly complex tasks, which could previously only be carried out by a human being and also make predictions. AI is synonymous both of fear and fascination. British physicist and author **Stephen Hawkings** warned that "the development of full artificial intelligence could spell the end of the human race." Entrepreneur and scientist **Elon Musk** calls AI humanity's "biggest existential threat."

Science fiction and robots 8

Robots have always been at the core of science fiction films and made viewers dream or… freak out. Lucas's ***Star Wars*** features some of the most iconic robots. Asimov's laws of robotics inspired ***I, robot***, released in 2004, starring Will Smith as a police officer investigating a murder. In Crichton's 1973 science-fiction thriller ***Westworld*** androids malfunction and kill visitors from an amusement park. Ridley Scott's 1979 ***Alien*** introduces one of the most terrifying killer beings who will wipe out the whole crew of a spaceship. ***The Matrix*** (1999) depicts a dystopian future in which computer hacker Neo discovers he is trapped in a simulated reality created by an evil cyber-intelligence. In the sci-fi psychological thriller ***Ex Machina*** (2014) a programmer is asked to have an intelligent humanoid robot take the Turing test.

Practice your grammar

Utiliser les modaux pour faire des prédictions

▶ Pour faire des prédictions, on utilise souvent **les modaux** pour exprimer des degrés de certitude divers :

C'est quasi certain.	***will*** *One day, robots* ***will*** *replace us.*
C'est possible ou vraisemblable.	***could / might*** *One day, robots* ***could / might*** *take over the world.*
C'est incertain (= je ne sais pas).	***may*** *In the future, robots* ***may*** *be able to cure cancer. I don't know.*

▶ L'expression ***be likely to*** **+ V** permet de dire qu'un événement futur est **très probable**.

Artificial intelligence ***is likely to*** *improve our lives.*

▶ On peut également associer l'un de **ces adverbes ou locutions à l'auxiliaire *will*** : *probably, certainly, maybe, perhaps, surely, in all likelihood...*

Exprimer la permission ou l'interdiction

▶ Pour exprimer **une permission au présent**, il est possible d'utiliser les modaux ***can* ou *may***. Le modal ***could*** peut être utilisé au passé :

May / Can *I use your phone?*

▶ Pour exprimer **une interdiction au présent**, il est possible d'utiliser **les modaux *can't, mustn't* ou *may not***. Au passé, on peut employer ***couldn't***.

A robot ***may not / can't*** *harm a human being.*

▶ Pour exprimer l'interdiction, il est également possible d'utiliser **l'impératif à la forme négative (*do not / don't* + V)** :

Don't *hurt a human being!*

▶ On utilise également la structure ***(not) be allowed*** **/ə'laʊd/ *to do sth*** à tous les temps :

Scientists ***aren't / won't be / weren't allowed to*** *clone other human beings.*

▶ Les verbes ***forbid (forbade – forbidden), ban*** **et *prohibit*** se construisent avec **la préposition *from*** suivie d'un verbe au gérondif (V-*ing*) :

The First Law ***forbids / prohibits*** *a robot* ***from injuring*** *a human being.*

1 Reformulez ces phrases en utilisant un modal, un adverbe modal (*certainly, maybe, probably...*) ou *be likely to*. Produisez deux phrases chaque fois.

a. *I don't know if one day scientists will discover the secret of eternal youth or not.*

b. *I'm absolutely certain that the development of artificial intelligence will be a hallmark of the 21st century.*

c. *In the near future it is possible that scientists will use robots to repair damage to cells, muscles and bones.*

d. *In the years to come, our company will probably become a pioneer in artificial intelligence technology.*

2 Que seront capables de faire les robots dans l'avenir ? Produisez cinq phrases avec des degrés de certitude variés. Vous pouvez utiliser les compléments de temps suivants :
in the future • in the near / distant future • one day • sooner or later • in the years to come • very soon

3 Reformulez chaque phrase en utilisant une structure qui exprime la permission ou l'interdiction. Produisez deux phrases chaque fois.

a. *You aren't allowed to tell anyone about the scientific project you are working on.*

b. *Politicians should write more laws restricting what scientists may or may not do.*

c. *Geneticists are forbidden from carrying out experiments on human embryos.*

4 Inventez vos propres lois de la robotique. Dites ce qu'un robot a le droit ou n'a pas le droit de faire. Produisez quatre phrases en utilisant chaque fois une structure différente.

Improve your pronunciation

La diphtongue /aɪ/

▶ La diphtongue que l'on retrouve dans *die* ou *my* est représentée par **le symbole /aɪ/**. Ce son est le plus souvent orthographié par **la graphie *i* ou *y*** dans les contextes suivants :

***ie* en fin de mot d'une syllabe**	*die, lie, tie*
dans *ild* ou *ind*	*wild, child, behind, find*
dans *igh*	*night, might, light*
dans *ign* (on ne prononce pas le *g*)	*sign, align, resign*
***y* en fin de mot d'une syllabe ou si la syllabe finale est accentuée**	*my, fly, rely, apply*
***y* dans des mots d'origine grecque**	*hypothesis, hybrid*

⚠ **Lorsqu'un *i* est suivi d'une consonne unique suivie d'un e (*i* + C + e) en position accentuée**, on le prononce /aɪ/ : *wine*, *line*, *device* (exceptions : *give* et *live* /ɪ/, *machine* /məˈʃiːn/).

1 Écoutez et répétez les mots suivants.

Audio hatier-clic.fr/21amc/045a

while • write • biological • pioneer • mankind • scientific • despite • height

2 Pour chacun des mots suivants, trouvez un homophone. (Un mot qui ne s'écrit pas de la même manière mais qui se prononce de façon identique.)

write • cite • eye • night • by

3 Dans les phrases suivantes, relevez les mots contenant la diphtongue /aɪ/. Écoutez l'enregistrement pour vérifier vos réponses.

Audio hatier-clic.fr/21amc/045b

a. *Isaac Asimov is famous for his science fiction novels.*

b. *A cyborg is a hybrid creature, composed of organic elements and cybernetic devices.*

Prononciation et accentuation des mots en *-ate*

▶ La terminaison *-ate* peut avoir deux prononciations en fonction du type de mot :

/eɪt/	dans les mots d'une syllabe : *late, date, plate*
	si le mot est un verbe : *create, communicate*
/ət/	si le mot est un adjectif ou un nom de deux syllabes ou plus : *climate, immediate, elaborate* Exceptions : *debate, candidate, estate*

▶ Leur accentuation peut aussi varier :
– **les verbes de deux syllabes** sont accentués sur **la 2e syllabe** en anglais britannique : *create* oO
– **les noms et adjectifs de deux syllabes** sont accentués sur **la 1ère syllabe** : *pirate* Oo
Exceptions : *debate* et *estate*.
– **les mot de trois syllabes ou plus** portent leur accent principal sur **l'avant-avant-dernière syllabe** : *calculate* Ooo

▶ L'accentuation de ces mots restera la même si on leur ajoute les suffixes *-ing*, *-ed*, *-or* ou *-ly* : *calculate* → *calculator*

4 Classez les mots dans un tableau en fonction de la prononciation de la terminaison *-ate* : /eɪt/ ou /ət/ ? Justifiez votre choix. Écoutez l'enregistrement pour vérifier vos réponses, puis répétez.

Audio hatier-clic.fr/21amc/045c

dominate • debate • accurate • rehabilitate • private • desperate • intimately • translate • encapsulate • certificate

5 Recopiez les mots suivants et soulignez la syllabe accentuée. Justifiez votre réponse. Écoutez l'enregistrement pour vérifier vos réponses, puis répétez.

Audio hatier-clic.fr/21amc/045d

dominate • communicate • culminate • rehabilitate • debate • inappropriate • approximately

Build up your vocabulary

Robotics

Pros
- fascination
- rehabilitate
- enhance = improve
- augmented strength
- increased endurance
- replace hazardous jobs
- undeniable /ˌʌn.dɪˈnaɪ.ə.bəl/ = cannot be disputed
- lifespan = lifetime
- mobility-impaired people wheelchair

Cons
- threat
- overcome
- ethical issues
- unemployment
- biohacking
- threaten = menace
- freak out = get angry
- exterminate
- harm = hurt / damage

AI
- implant = insert
- machine learning
- neural network
- chatbot
- computer brain
- mimic = imitate
- algorithm
- merge with = become one
- transhumanism

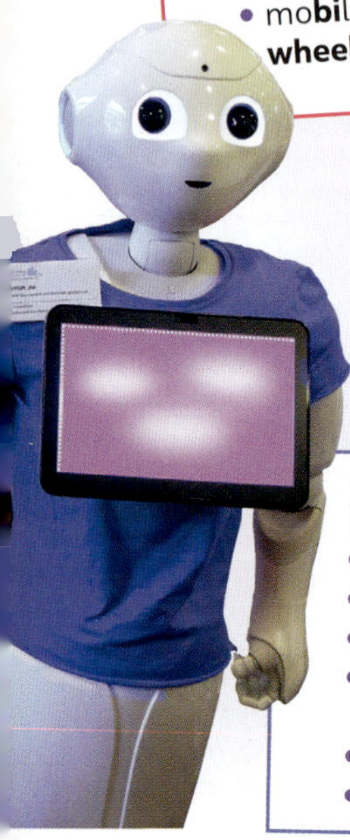

Robots
- bot = robot
- automation
- chip
- humanoid / android / cyborg /ˈsaɪ.bɔːɡ/
- industrial robot
- rehabilitation robot
- the Uncanny Valley
- replicate
- exoskeleton = exosuit = wearable device
- prosthetics /prɒsˈθet.ɪk/
- wheelchair

Ethics
- distinguish between right and wrong
- behaviour
- deontology
- ethical dilemma
- law
- moral
- theory of evolution

1 Draw this grid on your copy book and complete the missing words.

Nouns	Adjectives	Verbs
Behaviour		
		Enhance
Threat		
	Strong	

2 Complete these sentences with words from the mind map.

a. Ethics is a science based on … principles that govern a person's … and help them … between … and ….

b. A robot is a … machine able to … certain human movements and functions automatically. The … … refers to the development of … robots that look so real and human they freak people out.

c. A … combines living and non-living systems.

d. A powered … is a … mobile machine that is powered by a system of electric motors, pneumatics, levers, hydraulics, or a combination of technologies that allow for limb movement with … strength and endurance.

e. … is the part of philosophy that studies moral duty.

3 Use ten words / expressions of the mind map to comment on this picture.

Projects

1

You run a business. Debate the introduction of robots in your company.

1 Choose your role.

Student A : you are the boss of the company.

Student B: you are a young engineer in favour of robotics.

Student C: you are a 55-year-old engineer who fears for his job.

Student D: you are an employee working at the assembly line.

Student E: you are a trade union representative defending the workers' interests.

Student F: you are the sales manager from a robotics company, invited to explain why robotics is the future.

2 Get ready

- List the positive and negative impacts robots could have on your job.
- Prepare arguments and imagine how to react to counter arguments.
- Think about useful vocabulary to debate, give your opinion and convince.

3 Time to debate!

Help shy classmates enter the conversation if needed.

2

You are a journalist for a science magazine. Write an article on the impact / benefits / risks of using robots.

1 Prepare the content of your article.

- List the positive and negative impacts robots could have on companies, individuals and society in general.
- Choose the point of view you will adopt (for, against, mixed).

2 Write your article.

- First paragraph: key fact to appeal to the readers, question you will answer in the body of your article.
- Body of the article: one paragraph = one idea = one or two examples.
- Last paragraph: raise another question to widen the subject.
- Use link words to organise your ideas.
- Choose specific vocabulary to make your article sound more technical and scientific.
- Find a title and choose a picture to illustrate your article.

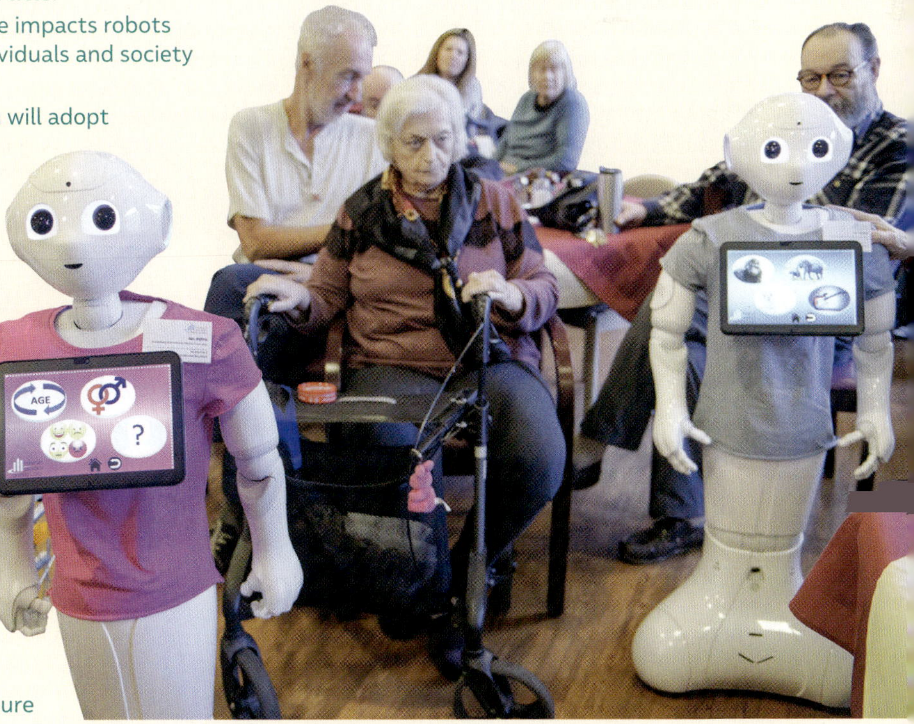

4 Art 3.0: the American experience

The expert's view
hatier-clic.fr/21amc/048a

In the news
hatier-clic.fr/21amc/048b

Projects

- You are a team of video game developers. Create the press kit for the game you present at the Tribeca Festival.
- You work in the art world. Take part in a talk show about the use of technology in 21st-century art.

Grammar p. 56 Phonology p. 57

When technology popularises art

A Movie screen vs mobile phone screen

1

2

"Filmmakers shouldn't complain about people watching movies on smartphones."
Headline of an article by James Vincent, *The Verge*, May 1st, 2015

3

4

"I would suggest, if you ever want to see one of my pictures – or most films – please, please don't look at it on a phone, please."
Martin Scorsese in a *Vanity Fair* interview, Dec. 3rd, 2019

1. Compare the two pictures and list the advantages and drawbacks of watching films on movie and mobile screens. Use them to discuss your personal habits and preferences.
2. Explain Martin Scorsese's and James Vincent's statements and imagine their reasons.
3. Record a short radio message to persuade people to go to the movies and enjoy big screens. Be convincing.

B Digital hijacking at the MoMA

Internet artists invaded the MoMA with a guerrilla augmented reality exhibit

"Hello, we're from the internet" is an art project that took over the MoMA's Jackson Pollock room without permission.

A collective of eight internet artists transformed the Jackson Pollock room in the New York City Museum of Modern Art into their own augmented reality gallery – without the museum's permission.

The collective, which calls itself "MoMAR," is making a statement[1] against elitism and exclusivity in the art world with its group art installation *Hello, we're from the internet*. The eight artists had their own works overlaid[2] on top of seven Jackson Pollock paintings using augmented reality technology. By downloading their MoMAR app, anyone with a phone can see their work.

"Our main idea is to democratize open spaces," Danjan Pita, one of the artists who goes by Damjanski told me. "The act of being open to the public is a little bit ironic because you still have an elite who is defining what is open to the public."

Friday, the artists made their way up to the MoMA's fifth floor two hours before closing. The museum, which was handing out[3] free tickets at the time, was packed full of visitors. While most visitors stuffed[4] in the Pollock room were there to see the American abstract impressionist's original art, a handful of people were seen holding up their phones using the MoMAR app. […]

Many visitors without the app were looking over the shoulders of people viewing the augmented reality versions of the paintings. One of AR installations, created by artist Gabriel Barcia-Colombo, turned Pollock's *White Light* painting into an interactive game. In the game, mini skeletons quickly climbed up all sides of the painting like spiders. Players controlled a spinning wheel in the center which they have to use to knock down the scaling skeletons. […] Damjanski said he and his partners are not worried about any retaliation[5] from the museum. The MoMA did not immediately respond to a request for comment.

Mack DeGeurin, www.vice.com, March 5th, 2018

1. make a statement: convey a message 2. covered 3. giving 4. crowded 5. revenge, punishment

1 Imagine what you usually get on a museum app, then contrast it with the artists' collective's actions described in the text. Use *Let's focus on...* n° 1, p. 54 to enrich your paragraph.

2 Clarify what the artist means when he says: "Our main idea is to democratize open spaces."

3 **CONNECT.** Leave a message to a friend describing what the hijacking consists in and the reactions of spectators around you.

C Museums and social media

PAIR WORK

Student A on video 1
Student B on video 2

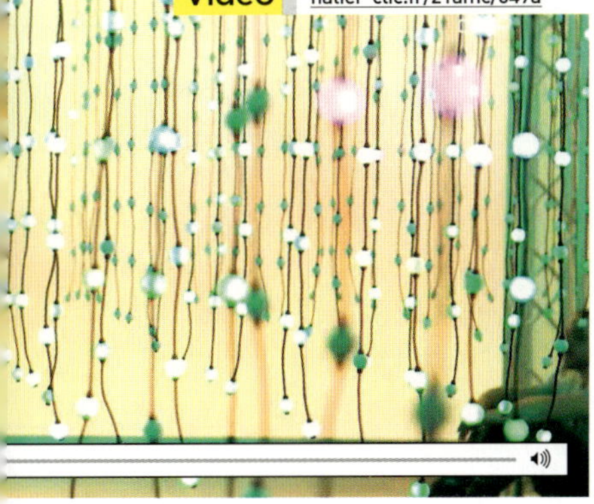

1 Interactive art museums

Video hatier-clic.fr/21amc/049a

2 "Instagram traps" are changing art museums

Video hatier-clic.fr/21amc/049b

1 Explain the use of technology in the exhibition(s) mentioned.

2 Pick out the different expressions used by the visitors to communicate their enthusiasm.

3 Present the video to your classmate. Compare the exhibitions and discuss your reactions.

4 You have been to one of these exhibitions. Write the post which would accompany your selfie in the art show.

Technologies in the creative process

A Computer-generated music

1 "It's the screams of the damned." The eerie[1] AI world of deepfake music

Artificial intelligence is being used to create new songs seemingly performed by Frank Sinatra and other dead stars. "Deepfakes" are cute tricks – but they could change pop for ever.

"It's Christmas time! It's hot tub time!" sings Frank Sinatra. At least, it sounds like him. With an easy swing, cheery bonhomie, and understated brass and string flourishes, this could just about pass as some long lost Sinatra demo. Even the voice – that rich tone once described as "all legato and regrets" – is eerily familiar, even if it does lurch[2] between keys and, at times, sounds as if it was recorded at the bottom of a swimming pool.

The song in question is not a genuine track, but a convincing fake created by "research and deployment company" OpenAI, whose Jukebox project uses artificial intelligence to generate music, complete with lyrics, in a variety of genres and artist styles. Along with Sinatra, they've done what are known as "deepfakes" of Katy Perry, Elvis, Simon and Garfunkel, 2Pac, Céline Dion and more. Having trained the model using 1.2m songs scraped from the web, complete with the corresponding lyrics and metadata, it can output raw audio several minutes long based on whatever you feed it. […]

Admirable as the technical achievement is, there's something horrifying about some of the samples, particularly those of artists who have long since died – sad ghosts lost in the machine, mumbling banal cliches.

Derek Robertson, *The Guardian*, Nov. 9th, 2020

1. strange, mysterious
2. make an abrupt sway

e-worksheet
hatier-clic.fr/21amc/050

2 How AI-generated music is changing the way hits are made

The idea that artificial intelligence can compose music is scary for a lot of people. But music-making AI software has advanced so far in the past few years that it's no longer a frightening novelty; it's a viable tool that can and is being used by producers to help in the creative process. This raises the question: could artificial intelligence one day replace musicians? […]

Using AI as a tool to make music or aid musicians has been in practice for quite some time. In the '90s, David Bowie helped develop an app called the Verbasizer, which took literary source material and randomly reordered the words to create new combinations that could be used as lyrics. In 2016, researchers at Sony used software called Flow Machines to create a melody in the style of The Beatles. […]

Now, there's an entire industry built around AI services for creating music. […]

Most of these systems work by using deep learning networks, a type of AI that's reliant on analyzing large amounts of data. Basically, you feed[1] the software tons of source material, from dance hits to disco classics, which it then analyzes to find patterns[2]. It picks up on things like chords, tempo, length, and how notes relate to one another, learning from all the input so it can write its own melodies. […]

Sure, an algorithm making music sounds scary because it mirrors human capabilities that we already find mysterious, but it's also a compelling[3] tool that can enhance[4] said human capabilities.

"You're collaborating and working with the AI to achieve your goal," Amper co-founder Hobe says. "It's not that the AI is just doing its own little thing. It's all about the process between it and you to achieve that final artistic vision."

Dani Deahl, *The Verge*, Aug. 31st, 2018

1. give 2. repetitive arrangement 3. convincing 4. improve

Text 1

1 Explain what a "deepfake" song is and list the adjectives used to define the process.

Text 2

2 Describe how computers can be used to create music.

Texts 1 & 2

3 Grammar **"Admirable as the technical achievement is,** there's something horrifying about some of the samples." Rephrase the clause in bold. What kind of logical relationship does it express?

4 CONNECT. Explain why people find these technologies "horrifying" or "scary" and what precautions should be taken. Give your opinion about this use of technology in music.

B Technology and visual art

1 Using AI to create art: Refik Anadol
Video hatier-clic.fr/21amc/051a

2 Ipad painting by David Hockney
Video hatier-clic.fr/21amc/051b

3 How artists are using technology: Miral Kotb
Video hatier-clic.fr/21amc/051c

GROUP WORK

Group A on video 1 – Group B on video 2 – Group C on video 3

1. Watch your video. Present the artist and his/her work. Use *Let's focus on...* n° 3, p. 54 to justify whether it is immersive or not.
2. Identify the reasons why they have chosen to use technology in their artworks and explain the adaptations necessary when exhibiting these artworks.
3. Present your video to the other groups.
4. Find the common points and differences between the three artists and their works. Explain which one you prefer and why.

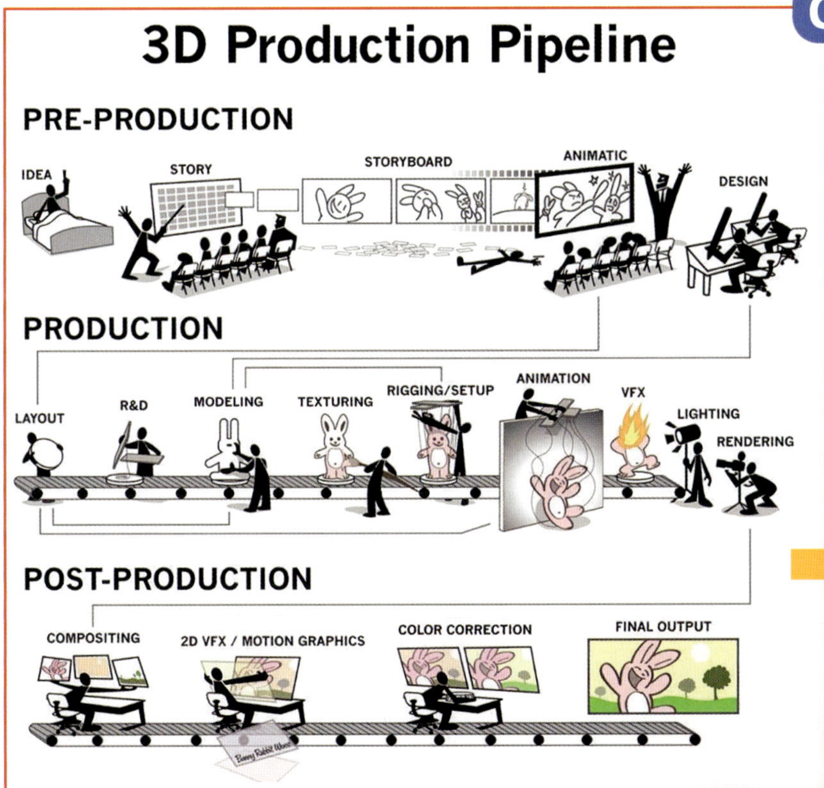

C Computers in animated movies: CGI

Working for Pixar and Dreamworks: from the idea to the CGI project

1

2

1. Look at document 1. Analyse the importance of new technology in the creative process today.
2. Show how the idea of a stimulating, cheerful spirit is conveyed.
3. Use document 2 to explain the advantages of the technique.
4. You work for Pixar Animation Studios. Explain to the new intern how you work.

The art of video games

A Digital art

1

2

Still from the indie video game *Whispering Willows*, developed by Night Light Interactive in 2014.

PAIR WORK

Student A on document 1
Student B on document 2

1. Analyse the visual elements and composition of your document and deduce the effect on the viewer. Find who the document targets.
2. Explain why the document reveals the artistic aspect of video games.
3. Present your document to your classmate and, together, write a short article for *Imagine FX* to explain that video games have become an art form.

B World video game Hall of Fame

World video game Hall of Fame
Video hatier-clic.fr/21amc/052

1. Explain what the The Strong is, give its main purpose and describe what visitors can do.
2. Four criteria are mentioned: icon status, influence, geographical reach and longevity. Explain each criterion in your own words and pick out the examples given.
3. **Phonology** Listen and repeat the following words: *art, VR, large*. Focus on the pronunciation of the vowel /ɑː/.
4. You are a game developer. Present your game to the curators of The Strong to convince them it should enter the Hall of Fame.

C The debate over video games as art

1 Tribeca Film Festival to add video games to official selections

The Tribeca Film festival which has announced its 20th anniversary edition for June 2021 is adding video games as an official selection for the first time. In an announcement, organisers say that for years, video games have been none of a kind medium for storytelling, innovation, art and education. This festival, however, has welcomed games for the past ten years, exposing titles like *League of Legends*, *God of War*, *Shadow of the Tomb Raider* and so on.

Tribeca was far ahead for the time when in 2011 included L.A. Noire as the first video game ever honoured and accepted as part of the film festival official selection. What might have seemed then like a marketing trick, soon revealed the start of a movement that will bridge the gap between two art forms.

In 2021, video games will become eligible for the first Tribeca Games Award. The festival says it will honour games that demonstrate artistic excellence in storytelling. It will include titles created for web, console, virtual reality, augmented reality and mobile devices. It's not a surprise that online games make an impact on different spheres of entertainment. (…)

Tribeca's film festival co-founder Jane Rosenthal says that Tribeca has a tradition to bring artists and diverse audiences together, to celebrate storytelling in all its forms. She adds that it's fantastic to see how game creators develop these worlds on their own, with unique stories, characters and language. As storytellers want to say, they always have the interest to push the boundaries of storytelling on different platforms. Games offer a new realm of narrative expression that is both film and gaming. Where there was once a clear line between media, now the line is blurred, with stories becoming games and vice versa. (…)

www.nerdly.co.uk, Sept. 9th, 2020

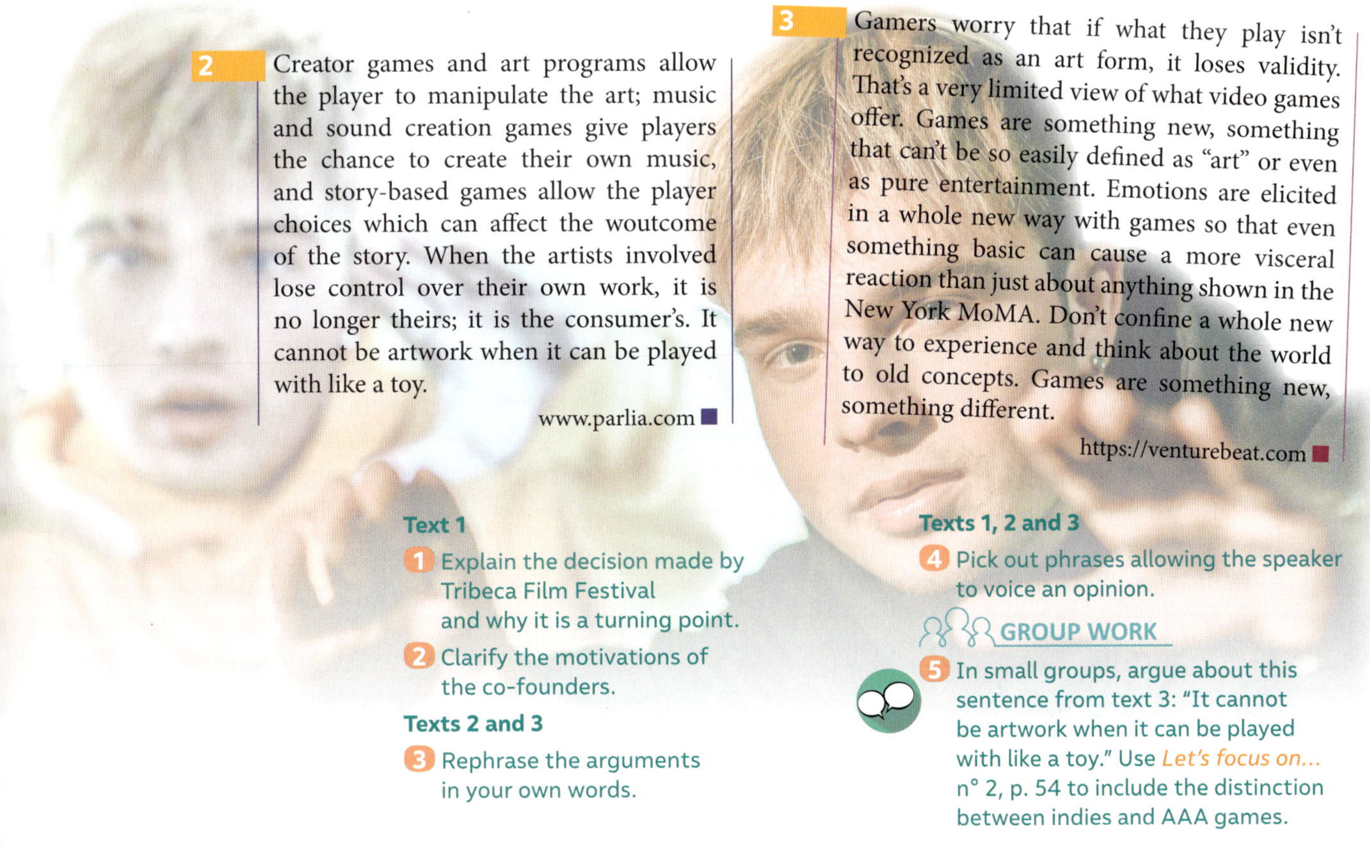

2 Creator games and art programs allow the player to manipulate the art; music and sound creation games give players the chance to create their own music, and story-based games allow the player choices which can affect the woutcome of the story. When the artists involved lose control over their own work, it is no longer theirs; it is the consumer's. It cannot be artwork when it can be played with like a toy.

www.parlia.com

3 Gamers worry that if what they play isn't recognized as an art form, it loses validity. That's a very limited view of what video games offer. Games are something new, something that can't be so easily defined as "art" or even as pure entertainment. Emotions are elicited in a whole new way with games so that even something basic can cause a more visceral reaction than just about anything shown in the New York MoMA. Don't confine a whole new way to experience and think about the world to old concepts. Games are something new, something different.

https://venturebeat.com

Text 1

1. Explain the decision made by Tribeca Film Festival and why it is a turning point.
2. Clarify the motivations of the co-founders.

Texts 2 and 3

3. Rephrase the arguments in your own words.

Texts 1, 2 and 3

4. Pick out phrases allowing the speaker to voice an opinion.

GROUP WORK

5. In small groups, argue about this sentence from text 3: "It cannot be artwork when it can be played with like a toy." Use *Let's focus on…* n° 2, p. 54 to include the distinction between indies and AAA games.

Let's focus on...

The MoMA ❶

The NYC Museum of Modern Art, situated in Middle Manhattan, opened in 1929 at the instigation of two ladies, Mrs Abby Aldrich Rockefeller and Mary Quinn Sullivan. It was the first museum dedicated to modern art in the USA back then. Little by little, the MoMA gained international prominence by organising successful exhibitions of artists like Picasso, Edward Hopper, Whistler, Rothko, Walker Evans or native American artists.
It has now a very rich permanent collection of more than 200,000 works of modern and contemporary art. The American painter Jackson Pollock, a major figure of the abstract expressionist movement, features highly in this collection thanks to the donation of major works made by Pollock's wife after his death.

Video games industry: indies vs AAA (triple A) games ❷

An "indie" is a video game created by a small, independent development team contrary to AAA video games which are developed by mid-sized or major game publishers such as Electronic Arts or Ubisoft. Company size obviously makes a huge difference to the development and marketing budgets.
The succession of generations of video game consoles (Play station, Wii, Xbox) led to an increase in costs and staffing.
The video game industry is now considered a very lucrative one: in 2019, the gaming market value amounted to $145 billion and it is expected to reach $200 billion by 2023. This is more than double the revenue of the international film industry.
In 2020, some studios started using the term AAAA (quadruple A) to describe their upcoming games adapted to a new level of technology.

Immersive art ❸

Immersive art consists in putting the spectator inside a world which is often illusory, a world that is artificially created thanks to augmented reality and computer-generated images. It may also, more simply, refer to an exhibition including interactive elements.
The artists use immersive virtual reality art to allow the spectator to visit the artwork and be part of it, making it an interactive experience.
Interactive installations appeared in the late 1980s. *Legible City* by the leading figure of the new media art, Jeffrey Shaw, is considered a pioneering immersive installation.

David Hockney ❹

David Hockney (born in 1937) is a British painter, but also printmaker, stage designer and photographer. He was part of the pop art movement of the 1960s and is now considered a hugely influential artist worldwide.
In 1963 he moved to California where he painted his famous sensual scenes of athletic men in swimming pools, thus tackling the subject of homosexual love. After coming back to England for a while, he has recently settled in Normandy.
He has experimented with several techniques, such as painting, prints, drawings, photography, photocollages with polaroid pictures and even cutting-edge technology with fax machines or iPads.
In 2018, one of his most famous paintings, *Portrait of the Artist (Pool with two Figures)*, sold for $90 million at Christie's auction house in NYC.

Timeline

5

Wonder Woman 1984 released both on HBO Max and in movie theaters.
2020

Immersive Art experience, San Francisco.
2019

First MoMA app.
2010

I-pad paintings by David Hockney.
2009

Creation of streaming service providers (Amazon Prime videos, Netflix, Hulu by Disney).
2006-7

Development of computer based interactivity.
1990s

IBM first commercial scientific computer.
1953

Snoop Dogg brings out a "hologram" of the rapper Tupac Shakur at Coachella Festival.
2012

Toy Story, first feature-length computer animated film.
1995

Early digital computer animation developed by Bell Telephone Laboratories.
1960s

First computer generated music by Alan Turing.
1951

Practice your grammar

Some, any et *no*

▶ *Some* exprime **une quantité vague ou inconnue**. On le traduit en général par **l'article partitif *du, de la, des*** ou par ***certain(e)s*** :

__Some people__ think that video games are not art.

Some indique que l'on ne remet pas en cause l'existence de ce dont on parle : c'est pourquoi on le retrouve le plus souvent dans **des phrases affirmatives**.

▶ *Any* et ses composés (*anyone, anything*...) indiquent que l'existence de ce dont on parle **est mise en doute ou pose problème** : c'est pour cette raison qu'on les retrouve surtout dans **des phrases négatives, interrogatives** ou encore **dans des propositions en *if*** :

He and his partners are __not__ worried about __any__ retaliation from the museum.
Are there __any__ tickets left for the exhibition?

▶ À la place de ***not... any...***, il est possible d'utiliser ***no***.

We __don't__ know __anything__ about this artist.
→ *We know __nothing__ about this artist*

⚠ *No* et ses composés (*nothing, no one*...) sont utilisés dans des phrases où **le verbe est à la forme affirmative**.

▶ *Any* peut aussi exprimer **une indétermination** et se traduire par **« n'importe quel / quelle »**.

By downloading their MoMAR app, __anyone__ with a phone can see their work.

▶ Quand on combine *some, any* ou *none* avec **un autre déterminant** (*the, these, my*...) ou **un pronom** (*them, you*), il faut utiliser *of* :

Some __of__ __these artists__ / Some __of__ __them__ are now very popular abroad.

1 Complétez avec *some, any* ou *no* ou l'un de leurs composés.

a. *... video games that were popular in the 1990s are worth hundreds of dollars today. Yet, I have ... intention of selling my collection.*

b. *I haven't downloaded ... of those new apps yet.*

c. *Are ... of those paintings for sale?*

d. *If I can be of ... assistance, please, let me know.*

e. *In 2013, the exhibition attracted ... 10,000 visitors.*

f. *The video game industry is evolving faster than ... other in the world.*

g. *I promised to say ... about his new project to ...*

2 Traduisez.

a. Certains artistes ne sont soutenus par personne.

b. N'importe qui peut utiliser un ordinateur pour créer une œuvre d'art.

Les propositions concessives en *(as)* + adjectif + *as*...

▶ Les propositions ***(as)* + adjectif (ou adverbe) + *as* + sujet + verbe** expriment la **concession**, c'est-à-dire une contradiction logique. On peut, par exemple, les reformuler par des propositions introduites par *although* (bien que) ou *even though* (même si). Notez que le premier *as* est facultatif :

__(As) boring as this movie is__, it was a big success.
__(= Even though this movie is boring...)__

__Admirable as the technical achievement is__, there's something horrifying about some of the samples.
__(= Although the technical achievement is admirable...)__

▶ Le verbe dans ces propositions est souvent employé avec **les modaux *may* et *might*** :

__Unlikely as it may / might seem__, my father liked the exhibition.

▶ On trouve parfois *though* à la place du second *as* :

__Strange though it may sound__, I'm not into video games.

3 Reformulez en utilisant la structure concessive *(as)* + adjectif + *as / though* + sujet + verbe.

Ex. : *Even though this story is shocking, it is true.* → *(As) shocking as this story is, it is true.*

a. *Although she's talented, she isn't a very popular artist.*

b. *Even though it sounds amazing, I've never visited the MoMA.*

c. *Even though this remake film looks impressive, it doesn't capture the full magic of the original.*

Improve your pronunciation

La voyelle longue /ɑː/

▶ La voyelle **/ɑː/** est une voyelle longue. Sa prononciation ressemble à la voyelle française de *pâte*. Pour la prononcer, la bouche doit rester bien ouverte et la langue doit se placer en position arrière.

▶ Cette voyelle peut correspondre à la graphie *a* dans les contextes suivants, **en position accentuée** :

***ar* en fin de mot ou avant une consonne**	*car, art, large*
alm	*palm, calm*
dans des mots d'origine étrangère	*banal, Sinatra, avant-garde*

⚠ En position inaccentuée, la graphie *a* se prononce souvent /ə/ comme dans : *liar*, *original*...

▶ En anglais britannique standard, la voyelle **/ɑː/** apparaît aussi dans les contextes suivants :

ass, ast, ask, ath	*rather, pass, ask, fast, brass* Exceptions : *mass*, *math* /æ/
alf, af(f), aph	*photograph, half, staff*
ance	*dance, chance*

⚠ Dans les contextes du tableau ci-dessus, la voyelle *a* se prononce /æ/ en anglais américain. Il s'agit d'un son plus bref. La bouche est plus fermée et la langue doit se placer en avant de la bouche.

1 Écoutez et répétez les paires de mots suivantes. Dites chaque fois quel mot se prononce avec la voyelle longue /ɑː/ de *car* et quel mot se prononce avec la voyelle brève /æ/ de *cat*.

Audio hatier-clic.fr/21amc/057a

a. *back / bark* **b.** *park / pack*
c. *part / pat* **d.** *heart / hat*

2 Classez les mots dans un tableau en fonction de la prononciation britannique de la graphie *a* : /ɑː/ ou /æ/. Écoutez l'enregistrement pour vérifier vos réponses et répétez.

Audio hatier-clic.fr/21amc/057b

sad • manner • far • market • partner • pass • app • artist • calm • lack • abstract • ask

3 Lisez la phrase à voix haute après avoir relevé les mots contenant la voyelle /ɑː/. Écoutez ensuite l'enregistrement et répétez.

Audio hatier-clic.fr/21amc/057c

This artist's paintings are rather too avant-garde for my tastes.

Prononciation et accentuation des auxiliaires modaux

▶ **Les auxiliaires modaux** sont susceptibles d'être prononcés de deux façons différentes en fonction du contexte : ils ont une **forme forte** et une **forme faible**.

▶ La forme faible est la prononciation **la plus fréquente et la plus naturelle** : on la trouve dans la plupart des contextes. La voyelle est prononcée le plus souvent **comme un *schwa* /ə/**. Parfois, certaines consonnes disparaissent.

Artificial intelligence ***can*** /kən/ *compose music.*

▶ La forme forte est rare : dans ce cas, la voyelle de l'auxiliaire est « pleine », c'est-à-dire qu'on la prononce telle qu'elle est écrite. Elle n'est utilisée que dans les réponses brèves, lorsque l'auxiliaire est utilisé seul ou quand on insiste fortement sur ce dernier : *Of course, I can!* /kæn/

⚠ À **la forme négative**, les auxiliaires sont accentués dans la phrase et n'ont pas de forme faible :

Games are something new, something that ***can't*** /ˈkɑːnt/ *be so easily defined as "art".*

4 Forme faible ou forme forte ? Recopiez ces phrases et entourez les auxiliaires modaux prononcés à la forme faible. Ensuite, écoutez les phrases et répétez-les.

Audio hatier-clic.fr/21amc/057d

a. *I can't help you with your homework now.*
b. *"I can do it immediately." "I don't think you can."*
c. *You MUST see this movie as soon as you can!!*
d. *"I would buy a more powerful computer if I had some money." "Would you?"*
e. *That'll be fine.*
f. *I shall see the film later.*

Build up your vocabulary

Art 3.0

Video games
- **graph**ics
- **av**atar
- **Batt**le **Roy**ale game
- **al**pha/ **be**ta re**lease**
- con**sole** (n.)
- co-**o**perative **game**play (co-op)
- **joy**stick
- **play**er
- **char**acter

Cinema
- shoot
- re**lease**
- **spe**cial ef**fects**
- stunts
- ani**ma**ted **pic**ture
- CGI : com**pu**ter-**gen**erated **im**age
- **mo**vie **thea**tre
- dis**tri**bute a **mo**vie

Museums and galleries
- exhi**bi**tion
- **mul**tiple **vid**eo pro**jec**tion
- dis**play** (v.)
- cu**ra**tor
- **tick**et **off**ice

Music
- **lyr**ics
- **mel**ody
- tune
- **cov**er song
- re**cord** (v.)
- track (n.)
- on tour
- band
- on stage

Visual art
- sketch (v.)
- **pen**cil
- **can**vas
- **ea**sel
- brush
- frame
- sculpt
- en**grave**
- cre**a**tive tools

Digital uses
- **immer**sive exhi**bi**tion
- aug**men**ted re**al**ity (AR)
- **strea**ming **plat**form
- **down**load an app
- **au**dio and **me**dia **ser**vice pro**vi**der
- **deep**fake
- **soft**ware
- **da**ta

1 Fill in the gaps with words from the mind map.

a. The MoMA organises many ... . Visitors can download an ... on their phones to have precise information about the artworks which are ... .

b. Computer generated music consists in using ... to compose the ... or even ... of a song. Then, the ... can be diffused on ... like Spotify or Deezer.

c. For centuries, painters have used a ... , an ... and ... to make an artwork while now, some artists like David Hockney use ... to create ... paintings and others use ... to invite the spectator in an ... experience.

d. The movie industry, and especially ... has evolved a lot: for decades, spectators had to go to ... to see movies which were ... on a big ... whereas now, thanks to ... they can watch movies on their ... .

2 Choose one video game and explain its rules using as many words as possible from the mind map.

Projects

1 You are a team of video game developers. Create a new game and get ready to promote it for the Tribeca Festival.

1. In groups of 4, imagine a new video game: characters, settings, visual style, avatars, possible actions by the gamer…
2. Each member of the team will write one part of the **press kit** (the dossier introducing the game to the journalists):
   - description (characters, place, plot, roles and choices offered to the player)
   - style (colours, atmosphere, soundtrack, 3D…)
   - statement of intent about the originality of your project (comparison with other games)
   - business aspects (target, platform, packaging, distribution, marketing)
3. Read the different parts and discuss how to organise your kit.
4. Edit an attractive kit with online tools like canvas, issuu or Madmagz.

2 You are invited to take part in a talk show to discuss the importance and influence of digital technologies in museums and the art world in the 21st century. Get ready to explain your point of view.

1. In groups of 4 or 5, choose one part: host, museum curator, digital engineer, musician, artist organising immersive exhibitions, art teacher for teenagers, art critic, student, simple visitor.
2. Choose a precise context which would justify the choice of the debate in a talk show: new museum app, release of a movie on streaming platforms only, new immersive exhibition, computer generated album…
3. Take ten minutes to prepare arguments, using examples studied in class or from your personal experience to support them. Meanwhile, the host prepares his/her presentation of the debate and possible questions.
4. Start the talk show, reacting to the other speakers' arguments.

5 US elections: people's choices and voices?

The expert's view
hatier-clic.fr/21amc/060a

In the news
hatier-clic.fr/21amc/060b

Projects

- You are part of a youth organisation. Write a poem and create a video to encourage young people to vote.
- You are an activist. Write an opinion article for *The New York Times*.

Grammar p. 68 Phonology p. 69

How does the US presidential election work?

A If maps could talk

2016 Election Results

	Candidate	Party	Electoral Votes	Popular Votes
✓	Donald J. Trump	Republican	304	62,984,828
	Hillary R. Clinton	Democratic	227	65,853,514
	Gary Johnson	Libertarian	0	4,489,341
	Jill Stein	Green	0	1,457,218
	Evan McMullin	Independent	0	731,991
	Other: See Election Facts Below		7	

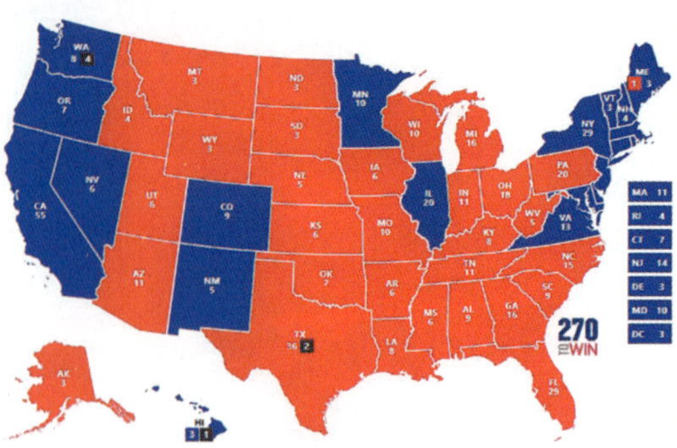

2020 Election Results

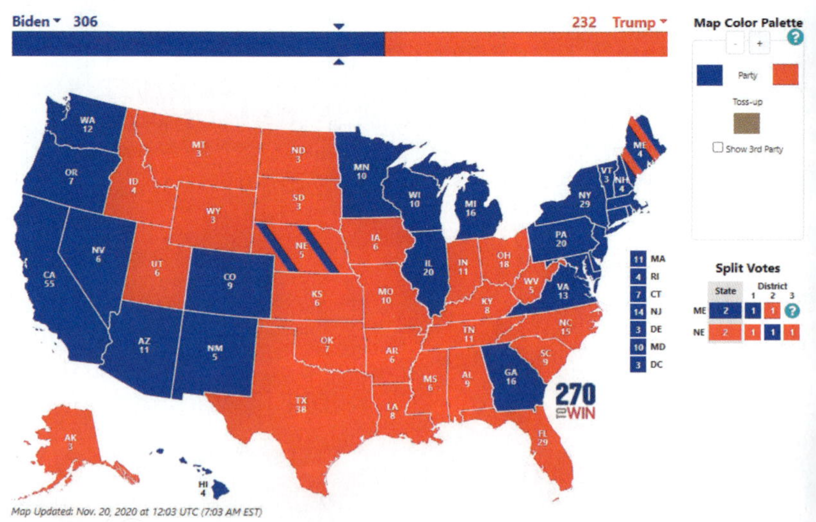

1. Identify the states that voted democrat or republican.
2. Oppose the number of electoral votes to the popular votes and conclude, focusing on election years, the candidates, the parties, the electoral votes won.
3. Look at *Let's focus on...* n° 1, p. 66 and say which electoral system you like best.
4. Explain to a friend the difference between electoral and popular elections. Take examples that you studied in class and visit this site: 270towin.com.

B Citizens denied to vote?

Voter suppression as a tactic – from strict ID laws to closing polling places to purging voter rolls – is deliberately making it hard for minority communities in America to exercise their democratic right.

In an interview last year Barack Obama said, "We're the only advanced democracy that deliberately discourages people from voting." […]

Struggle for the franchise

The struggle for the right to vote in the US has existed as long as the country itself. In 1789, after the ratification of the constitution, suffrage was extended only to white, property-owning men. Following the abolition of slavery in the 19th century, black people were permitted to vote, but after a brief period when black politicians began to win elections, the white majority began to institute restrictions like those that motivated King's march from Selma.

International comparisons show how voting restrictions are a stain on US democracy. In Australia, voting is compulsory. In Sweden, all voters are automatically registered. Both nations rank high on an "electoral integrity index" produced by academics at Harvard University and the University of Sydney.

Yet rather than being ranked with other major western democracies, the US falls lower down the list alongside countries like Kosovo and Romania.

Of particular concern in the US, said Sarah Repucci, senior director at Freedom House, a thinktank in Washington DC, "are the techniques that target minority (mostly black) voters, instituted by Republican-controlled state governments. Countries that have targeted minority voters include Cameroon, Kosovo – hardly regimes that Americans would consider to be our peers."

It's no surprise that the US trails behind other democracies in voter turnout – about 55% of eligible Americans voted in the 2016 elections, compared with around 87% in Belgium and 78% in South Korea.

Partisan officials

At every stage of the voting process, Americans face hurdles determined by where they live. Election law is set by partisan state lawmakers and administered, in most places, by secretaries of state, who are partisan officials.

In several Republican-leaning states, the difficulties voters face start with the documents they are required to produce in order to exercise their democratic right. Legislators across the country have tightened the requirements for acceptable forms of identification – this in a country where 7% of Americans do not have photo IDs, and the number is higher among black and Hispanic populations.

In 2016, Wisconsin reinstated strict voter ID laws, ostensibly to fight voter fraud, which experts have repeatedly found to be almost non-existent. […]

Voter purge

[…] "Voter purging" is when officials scrub names from the voter rolls ostensibly to ensure people don't vote twice and that people who have died or moved get removed from the rolls. These are perfectly legitimate justifications. Yet it tends to be on the rise, the Brennan Center reported, in areas and states that previously would have been prevented from making such changes by the Voting Rights Act. Places, that is, with a history of voting discrimination. And as the Brennan Center reports, "Problems arise when states remove voters who are still eligible to vote. States rely on faulty data that purport to show that a voter has moved to another state".

The Guardian, Nov. 8th, 2019

1. List the obstacles minorities may have to overcome to be able to vote and explain why the right to vote is at the heart of US history.
2. **Grammar** Lines 8 to 10, "Following … vote", say which nouns are used with no article at all and classify them as follows: singular count nouns, plural count nouns, uncountable nouns.
3. Show what the comparison between the USA and other countries reveals.
4. Comment on Barack Obama's quote (l. 1-3) in a tweet expressing your concern.

C Want to become president?

How to become president of the United States

Video hatier-clic.fr/21amc/061

1. Pick out the three requirements to become a presidential candidate and explain them.
2. Compare the systems of caucuses and primaries. Identify their role in the nomination of a candidate.
3. Indicate what these numbers and date correspond to: 270, 538, January 20th.

PAIR WORK

4. Create an infographic to recap what you have learnt about the presidential election process.

A fair representation?

A Trust in the system?

1. Describe the graph and show what it indicates regarding public trust in government. Use the timeline and explain the reasons the trust began eroding in the 1960s and why it rose after 2001.
2. Listen to the recording. Spot negative adjectives, nouns, expressions as well as numbers and figures and explain how they convey the lack of trust in government.

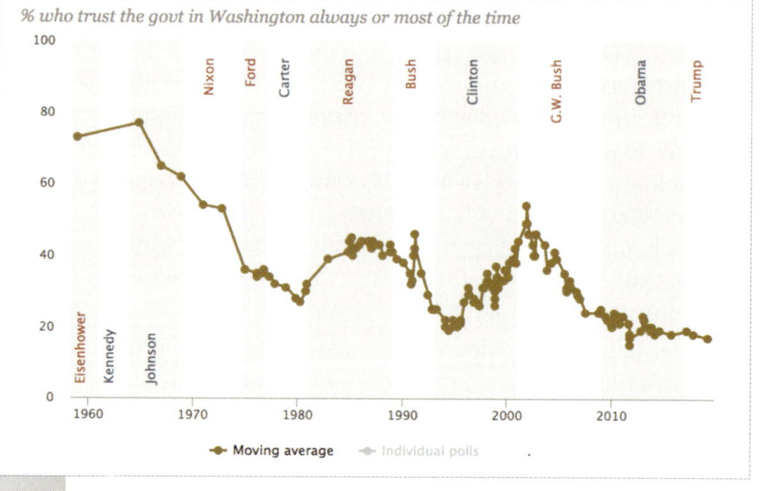

Trust in the institutions?
Audio hatier-clic.fr/21amc/062

3. Focus on the commission and comment on the solutions they suggested.
4. **Phonology** Listen and repeat the following words: pandemic, economic. Which syllable carries the main stress? What do these words have in common?
5. **CONNECT.** Use both documents to explain the lack of trust in democracy in the USA.

B Why is voting so complicated?

As the nation mourns civil rights icon **John Lewis**, a congressman and lifelong advocate of voting rights, the mayhem[1] in his home state's most recent election serves as another egregious[2] example of how a citizen's most sacred act in a democracy – voting – was undermined and even denied after a federal law protecting voters' rights was abandoned by a 2013 Supreme Court ruling.

Georgia's presidential primary election on June 9 was a nightmare mix of inefficiency and discrimination that shows how difficult it is for many Americans – particularly Black Americans – to participate in their democracy.

Hundreds of voters, many in majority Black areas, waited four, five and even seven hours to cast their ballots[3]. Some even faced down police seeking to send them home without having voted. [...]

The state's primary was an example of what should not happen in a democratic country. It is an experience that has implications beyond Georgia, and that carries warnings for problems with the November presidential election and the legitimacy of the results.

Not enough places, ballots or help

Georgia's primary election was postponed[4] twice from its original March 24 date, because of fears of spreading the coronavirus pandemic through in-person voting.

A million and a half Georgians applied to get absentee ballots that would have let them vote by mail. But an unknown number of them never received their ballots and were forced to vote in person to ensure that their votes would be counted. Ultimately only 943,000 ballots were cast by mail.

Georgians didn't always know where to go to vote: 10% of polling places – including 80 in the state's most populous county alone – were closed because of the COVID-19 pandemic. The state-run website that let voters look up where they should vote was down for several hours in the morning and worked only intermittently throughout the day. When the site was up and running, some voters still could not find their correct polling locations and visited precincts[5] where poll workers told them they couldn't vote.

Experienced poll workers were ill or feared getting sick, so the state had to recruit, train and dispatch new ones right before the election. Many poll workers were insufficiently trained and uninformed, especially about when voters were entitled to absentee, emergency and provisional ballots.

There weren't enough polling places, either. Several sites that normally serve 2,000 to 3,000 voters had to accommodate as many as 10,000 because of the consolidation.

Some polling places, especially in majority Black areas, had major delays because new voting machines weren't working correctly. Many polling places across the state opened two and three hours late. The new systems, including printers, scanners and tablets, had trouble throughout the day, causing additional delays.

Precincts ran out of provisional ballots and envelopes and printer paper. County governments, the NAACP and other civil-rights groups appealed to county courts to get orders extending polling hours beyond the usual 7 p.m. to make up for the delays. One precinct didn't close until 10:10 p.m.

As if that weren't enough, it rained on voters in long lines with no shelter.

Adrienne Jones, *The Conversation*, July 21st, 2020

1. disorder 2. shocking 3. cast ballots: vote 4. delayed 5. election district

1. List at least five obstacles Americans faced when voting or trying to vote.
2. Spot the impacts of COVID-19 during Georgia's election.
3. Write a post commenting on the difficulties that some Georgians faced and suggest solutions.

Culture Tip

John Lewis was an American politician and civil rights leader in the 1960s. As an activist, he fought to abolish segregation in the USA and organised the March on Washington in 1963 with Martin Luther King. He was member of the US House of Representatives for Georgia for the Democrats.

C Gerrymandering explained

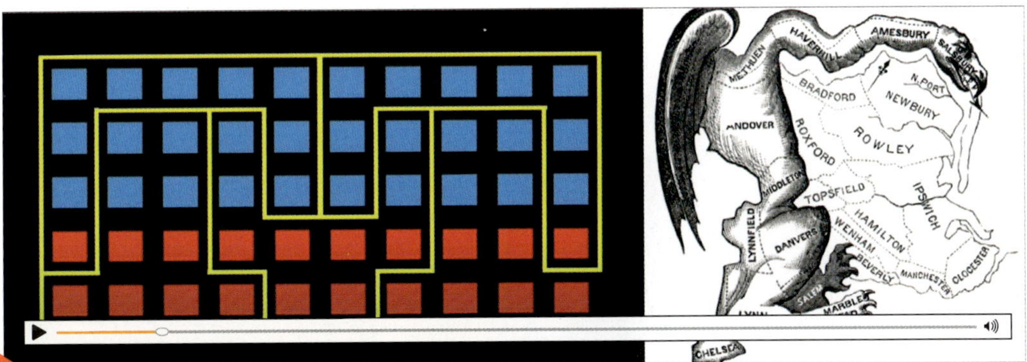

What is gerrymandering?

Video hatier-clic.fr/21amc/063a

1. Give the definition of gerrymandering with the help of the video and the picture using these words: redistricting • lines • state • monster • shape • benefit • political.
2. Look at the first still from the video and say which colour wins (blue or red) and why.
3. Explain the conclusion of the voice-over and why some politicians need gerrymandering.

PAIR WORK

4. With a classmate, explain how you can use gerrymandering to win an election.

e-worksheet hatier-clic.fr/21amc/063b

Standing up for a better political representation

A Representing the people

1. Read the captions and analyse the different portraits (colours and symbols).
2. Comment on the name of the foundation and explain the goal of the artists.
3. Act out an interview between a journalist and the artist.

B A common goal

Video hatier-clic.fr/21amc/064

1. Pay attention to the diversity of the participants and identify the common goal the different participants share.
2. Spot at least four reasons why citizens are no longer interested in their democracy and give at least four solutions.
3. Read *Let's focus on...* n° 1, p. 66 and choose what's the most democratic electoral system for the participants in the video.
4. As a future voter, react to what you saw and heard and give other recommendations in your blog.

C Poem for the Republic

In this poem Amanda Gorman refers to several fundamental texts and symbols in the history of the USA, such as the Declaration of Independence, Lincoln's Gettysburgh address or the American motto: E Pluribus Unum.

Believer's Hymn for the Republic

12 score and 3 years ago, to be exact,
Our founders dared to declare
The world's most revolutionary act:
A pact sworn for liberty and equality.
Out of many, was born one people;
A teeming nation made of nations,
At its very foundation a dream
For life, liberty, and the pursuit of happiness.

Today, we gather so that our Founders' words do not go diminished.
But also so that the work does not go unfinished.
For it's not just in a declaration of independence
But the everyday declaration of its descendants
That make a people equal.

It is our right and our role
To remember these words scratched on a scroll,
So we may live them and heal our nation whole.
We roll up our sleeves, we believe in the dream,
And these American stories, in the glory of the struggle,

For it is from our struggle that comes our nation's strength,
For the lengths that we fight for what is right
Is the fullest measure of our country's might.

And while we cannot shake or cast aside our past,
Every day we write the future. Together we sign it,
Together we declare it, we share it,
For this truth marches on inside each of us:

Americans know one another by our love of liberty.
When in fact, we are liberated by our love for one another.
We understand that a house divided cannot stand.
So let us make a pact to be the country that acts
As compassionate as we are courageous.

In the declaration's pages, we write a new order for the ages,
Where out of many, we are one,
Bright as a sun, and bold as an eagle,
A nation of all people, by all people,
For all people.

Let this fourth of July
Move forth our cry to redeem the dream.
As we remember those words forever ignited
That we the people have so long heard and recited.
That we are right to stand
But are revolutionary when we stand united.

Amanda Gorman © 2019 CBS Interactive Inc.

Believer's Hymn for the Republic
Video hatier-clic.fr/21amc/065

GROUP WORK

Group 1 will work on the first three stanzas, Group 2 on the last three.

1. Compare the reference of the founding of the USA to today's situation with nouns and adjectives referring to American values.
2. Focus on repetitions and find words and metaphors showing the poet's call for a collective response to the country's current crisis.
3. Listen to the poem and describe the effects of prosody (rhythm, rhymes, alliterations and assonances).

PAIR WORK

4. Write another stanza of this poem focusing on the power of people's voices. Use recent historic and political events and poetic devices (prosody, repetitions, metaphors etc.).

Let's focus on...

UNITED KINGDOM: Parliamentary monarchy

Voters

First-Pass-The-Post (FPTP): the candidate who gets the most votes wins, even if he or she doesn't poll an absolute majority of the ballots

Vote for or elect

Upper house **House of Lords**

Lower House **House of Commons**

Appoints

Appoints

Monarch **Head of State**

Prime Minister (PM) **Head of government** 5 years

REPUBLIC OF IRELAND: Parliamentary republic

Voters

Single Transferable Vote (SVT)

Universities + Councils Appoints

Single Transferable Vote (SVT): the voter ranks the most preferable candidate (1, 2, 3...)

Upper house **Seanad**

Lower House **Dáil**

Appoints

Ceremonial President **Head of State** 7 years

Taoiseach (PM) **Head of government** 5 years

NEW ZEALAND: Parliamentary monarchy

Voters

Mixed-Member Proportional (MMP): each voter has two ballots, one for a candidate and one for a party

Unicameral House **House of Representatives** (Beehive)

Monarch **Head of State**

Prime Minister (PM) **Head of government** 3 years

SOUTH AFRICA: Parliamentary republic

Voters

Provinces and other delegates

Party-List Proportional system: electors vote for a party, seats are distributed proportionally

Upper house **National Council**

Lower House **National Assembly**

Head of State and government 5 years

Anglo-Saxon electoral systems 1

Electoral systems vary in English-speaking democracies. Votes may be cast for candidates or for political parties. People may vote by checking marks, crossing out names, writing in names, or ranking candidates in order of choice. Winners may be required to win a majority of the votes or more votes than the other candidates (but not a majority).

The US Supreme Court 2

The Supreme Court is the highest Court of Justice in the USA. Its greatest power is judicial review: it can strike down laws passed by federal and state courts if the Supreme Court considers that they violate basic principles in the Constitution. It is composed of nine judges (called "justices"), appointed for life, who are nominated by the president, then confirmed by the Senate. Nearly all of the most controversial issues of American politics end up before the Court. With the death of Ruth Bader Ginsburg, the Court is politically unbalanced.

The Supreme Court in 2019.

Front row, left to right: Stephen Breyer, Clarence Thomas, John Roberts (Chief justice), Ruth Bader Ginsburg (deceased 9/18/2020, replaced by Amy Coney Barrett), Samuel Alito.
Back row, left to right: Neil Gorsuch, Sonia Sotomayor, Elena Kagan, Brett Kavanaugh.

Timeline 4

Landmark Supreme Court cases

1857
Dred Scott v. Sandford (7-2 decision)
Denied African American slaves citizenship.

1896 Plessy v. Ferguson (7-1 decision) Upheld "separate but equal" segregation laws in states.

1954
Brown v. Board of Education (9-0 decision)
Separating black and white students in public schools is unconstitutional.

1967
Loving v. Virginia (9-0 decision)
Invalidated state laws prohibiting interracial marriage.

Amy Coney Barrett, born in 1972 in Louisiana, is the fifth woman to serve as an associate Justice of the Supreme Court of the USA, where she replaced Ruth Bader Ginsburg who died on September 18, 2020. Barrett's nomination by President Donald Trump only a few days before the new presidential election sparked heated debates. Indeed, her conservative views on the death penalty, abortion or LGBTQ+ rights come in stark contrast with Ruth Bader Ginsburg's liberal stance.

Ruth Bader Ginsburg. After brilliantly completing law school, RBG became a professor and a lawyer, fighting for gender equality and women's rights. In 1993, she was appointed an associate justice of the Supreme Court, where she voted to protect minorities and the environment until her death in September 2020. Her courageous and liberal views made her a pioneer and an icon of the fight against discriminations.

Is the Supreme Court democratic? 3

There has always been a debate on whether the Court itself is a democratic body. Some argue that it is not democratically elected, and therefore should not be able to impose its judgements nationally. They accuse the justices of delivering their own interpretation of the Constitution and they argue that the Supreme Court is a super-legislature whose power is largely uncontrolled. On the other hand, its proponents believe the Court to serve democracy rather than work against it, to defend fundamental principles of freedom and equality in the face of popular opposition, in short to settle major civil right issues and protect individual liberty.

The ideology of the US Supreme Court

1973
Roe v. Wade (7-2 decision)
Women have a constitutional right to an abortion during the first two trimesters.

2000
Bush v. Gore (5-4 decision)
No recount of the 2000 presidential election was feasible in a reasonable time period.

2008
District of Columbia v. Heller (5-4 decision)
Citizens have a right to possess firearms at home for self-defense.

2015 Obergefell v. Hodges (5-4 decision)
Same-sex marriage is legalised across all 50 states.

2020
Bostock v. Clayton County (6-3 decision)
Prohibits an employer from discriminating against an individual on the basis of sexual orientation.

Practice your grammar

L'article Ø

- L'article Ø (c'est-à-dire l'absence d'article) est souvent utilisé pour désigner une généralité :
  – avec des **noms au singulier** qui désignent **des concepts et des idées** :
  The First Amendment to the U.S. Constitution guarantees Ø freedom of Ø speech and Ø religion.
  – avec des **noms pluriels** pour désigner toute une classe d'individus :
  Do you trust Ø politicians?
- L'article Ø est également utilisé avec des noms pluriels pour traduire l'article indéfini pluriel ***des***. On peut alors le remplacer par ***some*** :
  The president has been interviewed by Ø / some European journalists.
- Ø est également utilisé devant un **titre suivi d'un nom propre** :
  Ø President Obama, Ø Queen Elizabeth.
  ⚠ En revanche, on dit : ***the President of the United States, the Queen of the United Kingdom.***
- Les **noms de pays** ne sont pas précédés d'article : *Ø France, Ø Canada.* Il existe quelques exceptions : ***the United States, the United Kingdom, the Netherlands.***

1 Complétez avec l'article qui convient : *the* ou Ø.

a. *... President of ... United States of ... America is elected every four years, in November. ... new President takes ... office in January, two months after ... election.*

b. *In 1920 ... American women went to the polls for ... first time.*

c. *... President Roosevelt was elected four times but died during his fourth term in 1945. After Roosevelt's presidency, a law was passed allowing ... presidents to serve a maximum of two terms.*

d. *Nationwide, almost 60 % of ... Cuban voters say they affiliate with or lean toward ... Republican Party. ... Cubans are ... only people who can become ... U.S. residents after one year in ... country. After five years, they can get ... citizenship, making them eligible to vote.*

Les comparatifs des quantifieurs

- Pour traduire ***moins, autant*** ou ***plus* + nom**, il faut être attentif **au type de nom** (dénombrable ou indénombrable) :

	Dénombrable pluriel	**Indénombrable (ex : money)**
supériorité ***(plus de ...)***	*more* **+ nom** *more voters / money*	
égalité ***(autant de...)***	*as many* **+ nom** *as many voters*	*as much* **+ nom** *as much money*
infériorité ***(moins de ...)***	*fewer* **+ nom** *fewer voters*	*less* **+ nom** *less money*

- Les compléments du comparatif de supériorité et d'infériorité sont introduits par ***than*** /ðən/ :
  Fewer / More than 30% of people under the age of 40 consider it essential to live in a democracy.
- Les compléments du comparatif d'égalité sont introduits par ***as*** :
  Trump raised nearly as much money as Joe Biden.
- Pour exprimer une évolution dans le temps (de plus en plus de / de moins en moins de), on utilise ***more and more, fewer and fewer*** ou ***less and less*** :
  Fewer and fewer Americans trust the mainstream media.

2 À partir des données suivantes, produisez des phrases contenant les structures comparatives ci-contre. Produisez deux phrases chaque fois.

Exemple : *More people said they would vote in person than by mail.*

a. *According to a survey conducted in October, 54% of respondents said they would vote in person on Election Day, while 13% said they planned to vote early in person. Another 13% said they would vote by mail.*

b. *During the campaign, the Republican candidate spent $4 million on TV ads. The Democrat candidate and the independent candidate both spent $2 million.*

c. *A new poll finds that, nationally, the Democrat candidate leads the Republican incumbent by a 52% to 42% margin.*

3 Décrivez la courbe d'opinion p. 62 en utilisant les structures comparatives ci-contre. Produisez quatre phrases.

Improve your pronunciation

L'accentuation des mots en *-ic(s)*, *-ical* et *-ity*

▶ Les mots se terminant par le suffixe contraignant *-ic(s)*, *-ical* ou *-ity* portent leur accent principal sur la syllabe qui précède immédiatement le suffixe :

republic oOo *minority* oOoo

- Il existe quelques exceptions :
rhetoric (mais *rhetorical* est régulier),
Arabic, *politics* (mais *political* est régulier),
Catholic (mais *Catholicism* est régulier),
lunatic, *heretic*, *arsenic*…
- La terminaison d'un mot a donc parfois une incidence sur la place de son accent principal. Des mots de la même famille peuvent ainsi porter leur accent primaire sur des syllabes différentes :

democrat /ˈdeməkræt/ Ooo
↓
democratic /ˌdeməˈkrætɪk/ oooOo

1 Recopiez ces mots. Encadrez chaque fois le suffixe, puis soulignez la syllabe qui porte l'accent principal du mot.
Écoutez l'enregistrement pour vérifier vos réponses.

Audio hatier-clic.fr/21amc/069a

polemical • popularity • political • priority • politics • reality • community • Hispanic • academics • pandemic

2 Recopiez ces mots puis soulignez la syllabe qui porte l'accent principal du mot.
Écoutez l'enregistrement pour vérifier vos réponses.

Audio hatier-clic.fr/21amc/069b

a. *economy* → *economic*
b. *diplomat* → *diplomatic*
c. *history* → *historical*
d. *stupid* → *stupidity*
e. *major* → *majority*

La diphtongue /əʊ/

▶ La diphtongue /əʊ/ est le son qu'on trouve dans *g**o*** ou *sl**ow***.

▶ Elle est représentée par des graphies qui contiennent toutes la voyelle *o* dans les contextes suivants :

o en fin de mot	*tomato, go, no*
dans *oll, old, oul*	*old, poll, shoulder*
dans *ost*	*most, ghost, post* Exceptions : *lost, cost* /ɒ/
ow	*show, slow, know*
oa	*road, boat, goal* Exception : *abroad* /ɔː/
des auxiliaires	*won't, don't*

⚠ La graphie *ow* se prononce parfois /aʊ/ (comme dans ***out***) : ***down, now, how***…

▶ La voyelle *o* se prononce également /əʊ/ quand **elle est suivie d'une consonne unique suivie d'un e en position accentuée** : ***note, bone, hope***…
Il existe quelques exceptions :
- ***love, glove, done, some, come, none*** /ʌ/ (prononcés comme dans ***duck***)
- ***gone*** /ɒ/ (prononcé comme dans ***hot***)
- ***move, prove*** /uː/ (prononcés comme dans ***food***)

3 Les mots suivants contiennent tous la diphtongue /əʊ/.
Écoutez, puis répétez.

Audio hatier-clic.fr/21amc/069c

vote • only • roll • photo • toast • home • close • unknown • so • Joe Biden

4 Dans ces suites de mots, chassez l'intrus qui ne contient pas la diphtongue /əʊ/.
Écoutez l'enregistrement pour vérifier vos réponses.

Audio hatier-clic.fr/21amc/069d

a. *hotel – note – wrote – lot*
b. *how – low – own – show*
c. *bone – done – alone – phone*

5 Dans les phrases suivantes, relevez les mots qui contiennent la diphtongue /əʊ/.
Écoutez, puis répétez les phrases.

Audio hatier-clic.fr/21amc/069e

a. *All those aged 18 or over are eligible to vote.*
b. *The United States goes to the polls in November.*

Build up your vocabulary

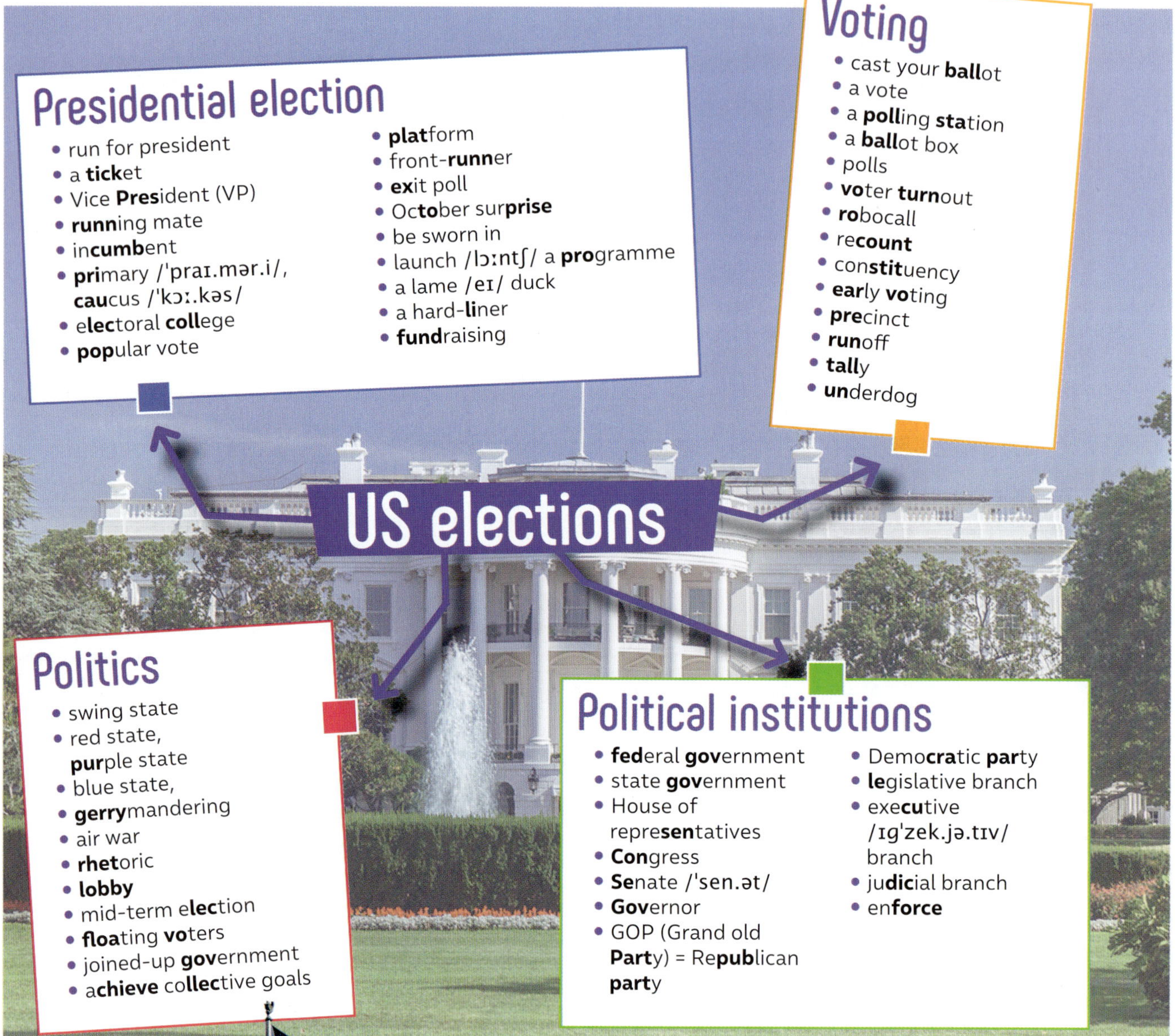

US elections

Presidential election

- run for president
- a **tick**et
- Vice **Pres**ident (VP)
- **runn**ing mate
- in**cumb**ent
- **pri**mary /'praɪ.mər.i/, **cau**cus /'kɔː.kəs/
- e**lec**toral **coll**ege
- **pop**ular vote
- **plat**form
- front-**runn**er
- **ex**it poll
- Oc**to**ber sur**prise**
- be sworn in
- launch /lɔːntʃ/ a **pro**gramme
- a lame /eɪ/ duck
- a hard-**li**ner
- **fund**raising

Voting

- cast your **ball**ot
- a vote
- a **poll**ing **sta**tion
- a **ball**ot box
- polls
- **vo**ter **turn**out
- **ro**bocall
- re**count**
- con**sti**tuency
- **ear**ly **vo**ting
- **pre**cinct
- **run**off
- **tall**y
- **un**derdog

Politics

- swing state
- red state, **pur**ple state
- blue state,
- **gerry**mandering
- air war
- **rhet**oric
- **lobby**
- mid-term e**lec**tion
- **floa**ting **vo**ters
- joined-up **gov**ernment
- a**chieve** col**lec**tive goals

Political institutions

- **fed**eral **gov**ernment
- state **gov**ernment
- House of repre**sen**tatives
- **Con**gress
- **Se**nate /'sen.ət/
- **Gov**ernor
- GOP (Grand old **Par**ty) = Re**pub**lican **par**ty
- Demo**cra**tic **par**ty
- **le**gislative branch
- exe**cu**tive /ɪg'zek.jə.tɪv/ branch
- ju**dic**ial branch
- en**force**

1 Complete the following paragraph with words from the mind map (one blank = one word).

a. The American ... consists of two chambers: the ... and the ... ...

b. In the USA, to become president, winning the ... ... is not enough: the candidate must win a majority of votes from the ... .

c. Florida and Arizona are ... ... : it is difficult to know in advance if they will vote for a Republican or a Democratic candidate and become ... or ... .

d. In 2020, the Democratic presidential ... was composed of Joe Biden, who ... ... and Kamala Harris, his ... ...

e. The voting process in the USA is rather simple: to ... ... , you can send your vote by post or go to the nearest ... ...

2 Write an email to a friend explaining how people vote and elect their president in the USA.

Projects

1 You are an activist and a member of ***Democracy Matters***. Write an opinion article for ***The New York Times*** entitled "Elections Not Auctions."

1. Find information about Democracy Matters to decide what will be your point of view.
2. Explain carefully why elections are not auctions.
3. Don't just try to teach your readers, touch them emotionally: make it personal.
4. Use interesting details and examples and show why the readers should care. You may use a quote from any document in the unit. That can be a good start for your article.
5. Give a solution to the problem.

2 You are part of a youth organisation. Write a poem to encourage young people to vote and create a video of your performance.

1. Think about the message you want to convey. Decide which youth organisation you'd like to be part of.
2. Choose the structure of your poem (acrostic, sonnet, free verse...) Try to use poetic devices such as metaphors, alliterations... to insist on key points.
3. Use concrete imagery to convey your message: you must be inspired, and inspiring!
4. Read your poem out loud. Use your voice to catch your viewer's attention.
5. Prepare a storyboard with meaningful camera shots (examples: close-ups, medium or full shots). Customise your video by adding filters or texts, and background music.

6 Brexit: past, present & future

The expert's view
hatier-clic.fr/21amc/072a

In the news
hatier-clic.fr/21amc/072b

Projects

- Write an email to the editor of a newspaper giving your opinion on Brexit and its impact.
- In groups of four, debate on Brexit and its consequences.

Grammar p. 80 Phonology p. 81

Origins of a crisis

A How Britain voted

1

Older people with fewer formal qualifications most likely to have voted Leave

		Remain	Leave
2015 vote	Conservatives	39	61
	Labour	65	35
	Liberal Democrat	68	32
	UKIP	5	95
	Green	80	20
Age	18-24	71	29
	25-49	54	46
	50-64	40	60
	65+	36	64
Education	GCSE or lower	30	70
	A level	50	50
	Higher below degree	48	52
	Degree	68	32

YouGov | yougov.com June 23-24 2016

2 **Britain Votes to Leave**

The U.K. voted to leave the European Union

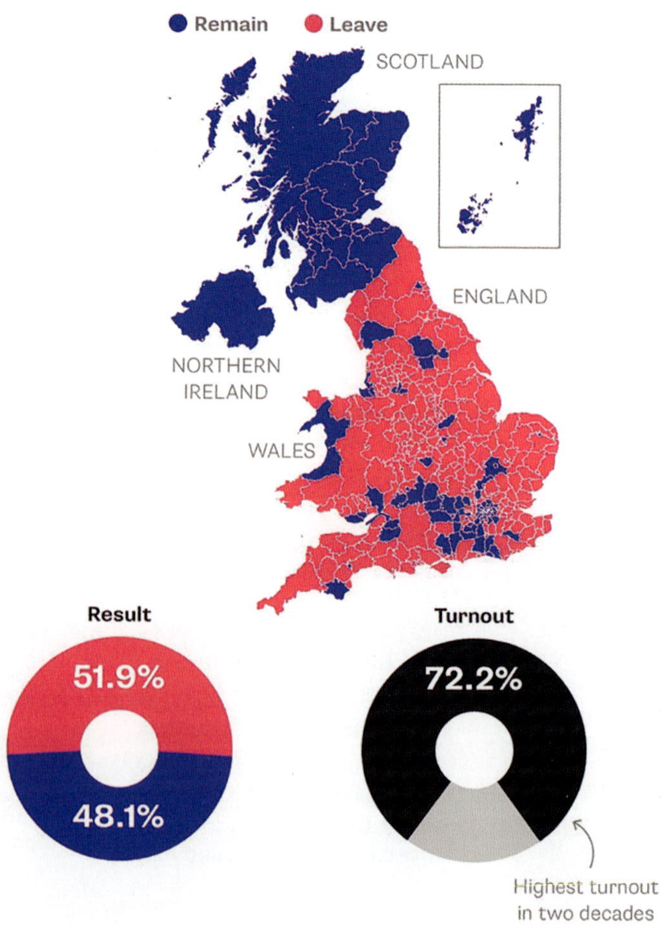

1. Analyse document 1 and explain how British people voted in terms of age and education.
2. Look at document 2 and describe how the different countries that make up the UK voted as well as how urban areas voted in comparison to rural areas.
3. **CONNECT.** Use both documents to sum up how the various segments of the British population voted.

B The roots of Brexit

What is Brexit all about?

Why did people vote to leave in favor of Brexit? […] Some of the key reasons Leavers wanted out of the EU included the following:

- Having to make financial contributions to the EU's annual budget
- Free movement of people and the perception that immigration from Europe was too high
- Wanting the UK to be able to negotiate its own trade deals, instead of negotiating as part of the EU bloc
- Perceived lack of UK "sovereignty" or control, with the UK being bound by EU rules and regulations

The key elements of the Brexit negotiations

[…] To ensure the UK's exit would be as smooth as possible, the two sides negotiated the following key points as part of the withdrawal agreement:

- The *divorce bill*, or how much the UK has to pay to cover its existing commitments to the EU.
- The *transition period* (also known as *implementation period*), which is designed to ensure a controlled transfer, and give governments and businesses time to prepare for life after Brexit.
- The rights of EU citizens already living in the UK (and the rights of UK citizens living in the EU) to retain their residency status after Brexit. Also, that the free movement of people would continue until the end of the transition period. Theresa May had made it clear during negotiations that free movement of people would have to end after the transition period – it was one of her "red lines" that she refused to budge on.
- The fact that the UK will have to abide by EU laws for the duration of the transition period – something that raised a lot of eyebrows among Brexiteers.
- How to avoid a hard border between Northern Ireland and the Republic of Ireland. The withdrawal agreement includes a provision for a temporary customs union between the UK and the EU until a trade deal is agreed upon, and this is known as the This backstop measure proved extremely unpopular among Brexiteers (and even many Remainers), even though it was designed to prevent a hard border and protect peace on the island of Ireland.

Nicholas Wallwork, www.dummies.com

1 Pick out the reasons that people voted remain or leave.

2 Explain the objectives of the Brexit negotiations.

PAIR WORK

3 Discuss whether you feel the YUK was really a part of the UE.

e-worksheet
hatier-clic.fr/21amc/073a

C Manipulated ?

1 Pick out the symbols of London present in the trailer.

2 Explain the reason why the characters meet and what they are trying to achieve.

3 Note the arguments for Brexit that are illustrated in this document.

4 Comment on the politician's position concerning Brexit in this trailer.

Brexit – how did it happen?
Video hatier-clic.fr/21amc/073b

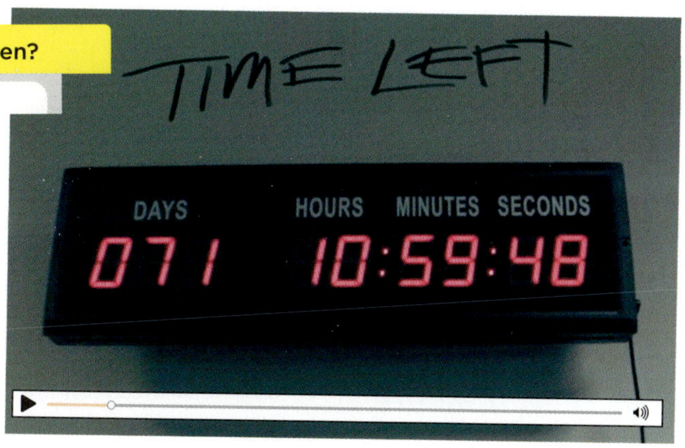

A nation divided

A Letters to the editor

1

SIR – You report that senior Tories dismissed by Theresa May have threatened to rebel over her Brexit plans if they are not reappointed.

They were dismissed because their new leader did not consider them competent or supportive enough to see through the wishes of the electorate. They should now knuckle down[1] and show the people who elected them that they are prepared to support the Prime Minister.

They are owed nothing, especially undeserved promotion, and will have to earn their re-election – or find another form of employment.

John H. Price, Holt, Wiltshire

2

SIR – Some people have forgotten that 48 per cent of those who voted in the EU referendum wanted to stay.

In our democracy, these people need representation as much as the 52 per cent with opposing views – so why should some MPs be castigated[2] for opting to represent them? Without effective opposition, government becomes dictatorship.

Sally Lawton, Kidlington, Oxfordshire

3

SIR – By arguing that the invocation of Article 50 could be reversed by Parliament, the Government risks undermining the process – even if its appeal[3] to the Supreme Court should succeed.

If the Prime Minister wishes to invoke Article 50, or any other device to initiate Brexit, she should table a Bill to that effect immediately, without detailing her strategy.

While the referendum was not decided by constituencies, it can be inferred that about two thirds of them voted Leave. In defeating the Bill, most disaffected MPs would provoke the wrath[4] of their constituents in the resulting general elections.

Chris Scott, Netherne-on-the-Hill, Surrey

4

SIR – As a pensioner who is one of an estimated 5.5 million British citizens resident overseas, I was denied the right to vote in the EU referendum. I only hold a British passport, and am already affected by the outcome of the vote. Yet I had no say in the matter.

When the Brexit debate comes before Parliament, as it should, I hope MPs will insist that this aberration of democracy will either be tested before a British or EU court.

A significant number of British citizens have been discriminated against, and this must be corrected before Article 50 is invoked – by way of a supplementary vote or by a referendum that includes all citizens.

Derek Rye, Durban, KwaZulu-Natal, South Africa

5

SIR – At a press conference during Barack Obama's farewell tour of Europe, he said that he "tries not to meddle[5] in other people's politics".

Is this the same Barack Obama who told Britain to remain in the EU or else we would "go to the back of the queue" for trade deals with America?

David Saunders, Sidmouth, Devon

www.telegraph.co.uk, Nov. 20th 2016

1. get to work 2. reprimanded 3. re-examination 4. anger 5. interfere

1 Read the Culture Tip and sum up the various points made in this selection of letters.

2 Read *Let's focus on...* n° 2, p. 78 and explain the objective behind invoking Article 50.

3 **Grammar** Turn the following passage into indirect speech, using the prompt "John H. Price wrote that...":
"They were dismissed because their new leader did not consider them competent or supportive enough to see through the wishes of the electorate."

PAIR WORK

4 Tell your partner which of these views you agree/disagree with and defend your opinion.

e-worksheet
hatier-clic.fr/21amc/074

Culture Tip

Letters to the editor are a common feature of British newspapers. Members of the general public write to the paper and give their opinions on a variety of topical issues – sometimes replying to previously published letters and often with humour. The editor then chooses a selection that represent a variety of different views. These letters always start and end in the same manner, SIR, and the name and town of the writer.

B An English town

How different classes voted

Video hatier-clic.fr/21amc/075

1. Describe the elements that illustrate Tewkesbury as a typical English town.
2. Explain how professionals can be the only majority group to vote Remain yet also contain the largest block of Leave voters.
3. Phonology Listen and repeat the two following verbs: *live*, *leave*. Are they pronounced in the same way?
4. Pick out and explain the numbers mentioned and then produce a series of pie charts to illustrate how Tewkesbury residents voted, how different social classes voted and where the majority of Leave voters lived.

C The Brexit Buses

1. Pick out and explain the figures mentioned on each bus.
2. Use this information to relate which bus is advertising for Remain and which for Leave.
3. Discuss how effective you consider the use of public transport as a means of advertising in this situation.

What does the future hold?

A The cost of Brexit

1 Describe the elements of the infographic and explain what they correspond to.

2 Use the figures to explain why Brexit will cost the British economy.

3 Read *Let's focus on...* n° 3, p. 79 and explain what is meant by the term "hard" Brexit, and its alternative – "soft" Brexit.

PAIR WORK

4 Convince your partner a soft Brexit is the better option. Take turns.

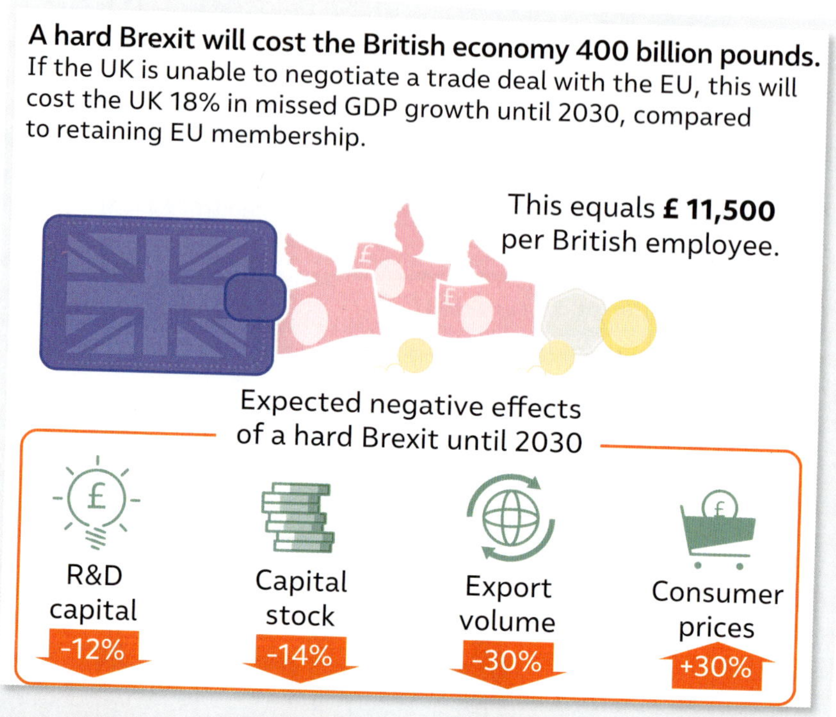

B Consequences for students

Erasmus: What could happen to the scheme after Brexit?

The Erasmus scheme is a European Union (EU) programme that helps students study in other countries.

Prime Minister Boris Johnson has announced that the UK will not continue to participate in it and will be replacing it with a new scheme named after the mathematician Alan Turing. He said leaving Erasmus had been a "tough decision" but that under the new scheme, students would "have the opportunity... not just to go to European universities, but to go to the best universities in the world." The EU's Brexit negotiator Michel Barnier said he regretted the decision. Students at universities in Northern Ireland will continue to participate in Erasmus, as part of an arrangement with the Irish government. [...]

The UK left the EU on 31 January, entering into a transition period until the end of 2020. During this time, the UK-EU relationship continued much as it was before – including the Erasmus scheme. Although coronavirus is now affecting student mobility, figures from before the pandemic showed that about half of UK university students who studied abroad did so through Erasmus. In 2017, 16,561 UK students participated in Erasmus, while 31,727 EU nationals came to the UK. Erasmus is also involved in vocational training and work overseas, as well as with teachers who want to work or train abroad.

A report from the House of Lords EU Committee warned the benefits of the Erasmus programme would be very difficult to replicate with a national programme as the government is planning. It added that vocational education and training would stop, and that leaving Erasmus would "disproportionately affect people from disadvantaged backgrounds and those with medical needs or disabilities."

Anthony Reuben, *BBC Reality Check*, Dec. 24th, 2020

1 Refer to *Let's focus on...* n° 1, p. 78 and explain what the Erasmus scheme does.

2 Use the numbers to explain the consequences of the U.K. pulling out of Erasmus.

PAIR WORK

3 Leave a message to a friend to persuade him/her to join you in a year at a European university on the Erasmus scheme.

C Consequences for the UK

What is the Northern Ireland backstop?

The Northern Ireland backstop was an arrangement for the Irish border that was part of Theresa May's Brexit deal. It would have come into effect if no other solutions to maintain the current open border were agreed once the UK had left the EU. It was intended to protect the Good Friday Agreement/Belfast Agreement and keep an open border between Northern Ireland and Ireland after Brexit.

Both the UK and EU agreed on the need for a backstop to ensure no hard border – physical checks and infrastructure – returns to Ireland. However, when Boris Johnson became prime minister in July 2019 he managed to obviate the need for a backstop by agreeing a permanent new relationship between Northern Ireland and the EU. This new relationship means Northern Ireland is treated differently to the rest of Great Britain and following EU rules in some areas.

Why might the border have hardened as a result of Brexit?

The UK's decision to leave the EU single market and customs union means that it will become a 'third country' to the EU. If the UK and EU had failed to find a new arrangement, the Irish land border would have become a customs and regulatory border involving the standard checks it has at its border with any third country. […]

Why were there concerns about the backstop?

The backstop proved one of the most contentious issues in parliamentary debates on the draft Withdrawal Agreement. The Democratic Unionist Party (DUP) opposed it because it would have introduced differences in regulation between Northern Ireland and the rest of the UK, which it saw as a threat to Northern Ireland's place in the Union.

A majority of people in Northern Ireland supported the backstop, however, as it gave them privileged access to both the UK and EU markets. In January 2019, the UK government published proposals on how the UK, including the Northern Ireland executive, could influence both the decision to use the backstop and its governance if it came into effect, as well as a commitment that the rest of the UK would unilaterally align with the single market regulations being applied in Northern Ireland.

Other Brexiteers are opposed to the backstop because it would mean the UK remaining in a customs territory with the EU, removing the UK's ability to vary its tariffs, a key component of trade deals.

There were also concerns that the UK would not be able to leave the backstop. It was intended to apply "unless and until" alternative arrangements, which both sides agree on, can replace it.

www.instituteforgovernment.org.uk, Feb. 24th, 2020

1. Read *Let's focus on…* n° 4, p. 79 and explain what differences between Northern Ireland and the rest of the UK the backstop would create.
2. Pick out the elements that show the backstop was not a popular solution with all parties.
3. Explain what the backstop agreement would mean practically for a person travelling between Northern Ireland and the Republic of Ireland.

e-worksheet
hatier-clic.fr/21amc/077a

D Brexit and the future of Britain

1

Scotland's future
Video hatier-clic.fr/21amc/077b

2 Scotland's first minister: Nicole Sturgeon

A future where our own parliament, our own government, accountable to the people of Scotland are responsible for the decisions and the international partnerships that shape our direction and our destiny, a future where we continue to be an open, welcoming place to live, study and work and a valued member of the European family of nations. Make no mistake, after tonight that future is only open to us with independence.

Extract of a speech given Jan. 31st, 2020

1. Watch the video. Describe the reasons mentioned for changing minds about Scottish independence.
2. Read the text. Explain what Nicole Sturgeon is calling for in her speech.
3. Read *Let's focus on…* n° 4, p. 79 and explain the relevance of the date of Nicole Sturgeon's speech.
4. **CONNECT.** Use both documents to give your opinion.

Let's focus on...

Erasmus 1

The European Community Action Scheme for the Mobility of University Students was established in 1987, with Erasmus Plus (including training, youth and sport) following in 2014. Thanks to these schemes over 3 million students have been able to study abroad for part of their university programme, learning languages and collecting experiences as they do so; the European Commission estimates that around one million babies have been born to Erasmus couples since the scheme was created!

Article 50 2

The Treaty of the European Union was signed in 2007, it replaced and modified the Treaty of Maastricht signed in 1992 which created the EU. Article 50 of this treaty declares that any member state may decide to leave the EU. The UK government "triggered" or invoked Article 50 on 29 March 2017 (almost a year after the referendum), and originally scheduled its departure for 29 March 2019, although this was extended until 31 January 2020.

A Brexit timeline 5

- UK votes to leave EU in referendum, David Cameron (PM) resigns. **June 23, 2016**
- **July 13, 2016** Theresa May becomes PM.
- **March 29, 2017** Theresa May triggers article 50 and informs EU the UK will leave March 29 2019.
- Brexit negotiation talks begin in Brussels. **July 17, 2017**
- Ministers including David Davis (Brexit minister) and Boris Johnson (foreign minister) resign over the Chequers plan (proposed Brexit plans). **July 6-8, 2018**
- **September 21, 2018** The Chequers plan is rejected by EU at summit in Brussels.
- Government loses parliamentary vote on Brexit deal by 432-202, worst government defeat in history. **January 15, 2019**
- **March 12, 2019** Government loses second vote.
- May asks for a delay. **March 20, 2019**
- **March 23, 2019** Thousands of demonstrators in London demand a second referendum.
- Government loses third parliamentary vote on Brexit. **March 29, 2019**
- **April 11, 2019** UK requests a further delay – until October 31.

"Hard" or "soft" Brexit? ❸

A "hard" Brexit meant the UK would leave the EU with no agreements on trade or the free movement of people, the UK would trade with the EU under WTO rules, just like any other country outside Europe. Whereas a "soft" Brexit would involve a closer relationship with the EU, perhaps similar to Norway, which is not a member state but has a free trade agreement and free circulation of workers agreement with the EU.

Irish backstop ❹

The Irish backstop was an appendix in the Brexit withdrawal agreement proposed by Theresa May's government in 2017. It would have involved keeping open the border between Northern Ireland and the Republic of Ireland – an important part of the peace treaty between the Republic and the UK in what was known as the Good Friday agreement, signed in 1998. It was called a backstop as it would have applied until a different trade agreement was made, which was the case in October 2019 when Boris Johnson renegotiated the withdrawal agreement.

May resigns, Conservative Party begins procedures to choose a new leader.
May 23, 2019

May 27, 2019
Nigel Farage and Brexit party win 29 seats (more than all other UK parties) in European elections.

Boris Johnson becomes PM.
July 23, 2019

August 19, 2019
Johnson's request to cancel the Irish backstop refused by EU.

Parliament is suspended for 5 weeks by Queen Elizabeth, at Johnson's request (later reopened by UK Supreme court).
August 28, 2019

October 17, 2019
Deal reached giving Northern Ireland unique position and EU advantages after UK concessions.

EU accepts Brexit delay until January 31.
October 28, 2019

EU approves Brexit deal.
January 29, 2020

Brexit day: UK officially leaves EU, and one year transition phase begins.
January 31, 2020

December 31, 2020
End of transition period, UK leaves EU.

Practice your grammar

Discours direct et discours indirect

▶ **Le discours direct** est placé entre guillemets. Il s'agit d'**une citation exacte** des paroles d'autrui.

"Britain will withdraw from the EU," he said.

⚠ Les guillemets « … » ne sont utilisés qu'en français. En anglais, il faut utiliser les guillemets qui ont la forme "…" ou bien '…' .

▶ **Le discours indirect** est introduit par un verbe de parole (*say, announce, add, explain*…) ou de pensée lui-même suivi d'**une proposition subordonnée introduite par la conjonction *that*** /ðət/ (qui peut être effacée).

*He **said (that)** Britain would withdraw from the EU.*

▶ Au discours indirect, quand le verbe introducteur est au passé, il faut respecter **la concordance de temps** :

Discours direct	Discours indirect
Présent simple ou en *be + ing* *"My father **supports** Brexit."*	Prétérit simple ou en *be + ing* *He said that his father **supported** Brexit.*
Prétérit / *present perfect* simples ou en *be + ing* *"Britain **left** the EU."*	*Pluperfect* simple ou en *be + ing* *He said that Britain **had left** the EU.*
Futur en *will* *"Britain **will** leave the EU."*	Futur dans le passé en *would* *He said that Britain **would** leave the EU.*

▶ Les compléments de temps subissent les transformations suivantes :
today → *that day, yesterday* → *the day before, last week* → *the previous week, tomorrow* → *the following day…*

▶ Il faut également modifier **les pronoms personnels et les possessifs**, surtout ceux de la 1ère et de la 2e personne.

1 Mettez les phrases suivantes au discours indirect. Commencez chaque phrase par l'amorce proposée.

a. *"My daughter is currently studying in an EU country."* → *She said that…*

b. *"Younger citizens voted overwhelmingly to remain in the EU."* → *The activist added that…*

c. *"A trade deal has been reached."* → *The Prime minister announced that…*

d. *"More than 50% of our exports go to EU countries."* → *The journalist explained that…*

e. *"Leaving the EU will result in an immediate cost saving, as the country will no longer contribute to the EU budget."* → *Brexiteers argued that…*

2 Mettez le passage suivant au discours direct.

Boris Johnson said leaving Erasmus had been a "tough decision" but that under the new scheme, students would "have the opportunity... not just to go to European universities, but to go to the best universities in the world".

La voix passive des verbes prépositionnels

▶ Certains verbes se construisent avec **des prépositions** (*with, about, for, on*…). C'est par exemple le cas du verbe *discriminate* dont le complément est introduit par la préposition *against*.

*The government **has discriminated against** a significant number of British citizens.*

▶ Ces verbes peuvent être mis **à la voix passive** (*be* + participe passé). Dans ce cas :
- le groupe nominal qui suit la préposition devient le sujet de la phrase passive.
- la préposition est utilisée seule après le verbe.
- le sujet de la phrase active devient le complément d'agent de la phrase passive introduit par *by*.

*A significant number of British citizens **have been discriminated against** (by the government).*

3 Mettez les phrases à la voix passive. Exprimez l'agent si nécessaire.

a. *The UK government asked for an extension to Brexit.*

b. *You can't rely on those corrupt politicians.*

c. *Several anti-Brexit activists shouted at Boris Johnson.*

d. *Someone broke into his office, but nothing is missing.*

e. *No one has ever heard of this small political party.*

f. *Nigel Farage and Brexiteers took advantage of the situation.*

Improve your pronunciation

Les voyelles /iː/ et /ɪ/

▶ La voyelle /iː/ est **une voyelle longue** qui ressemble au *i* français de *rive*. Elle est représentée par les graphies suivantes :

ea	*team, deal, leave*
ee	*keep, deep, free*
ie ou *ei*	*believe, piece, receive*
e dans *-ese, -ede, -eme, -ene*	*Chinese, intervene, extreme, scene*
i dans *-ique*	*technique, critique, unique*

▶ La voyelle /ɪ/ est **une voyelle très brève** qui n'a pas d'équivalent en français. Il s'agit d'un son intermédiaire entre le *i* de *nid* et le è de *père*. Elle est le plus souvent représentée par la graphie *i* surtout avant une consonne unique ou double : ***Brexit, tariff, is, did, admit.***

Notez aussi les graphies inhabituelles suivantes : *b**u**ild, b**u**sy, min**u**te, w**o**men* /ˈwɪmɪn/.

⚠ Quand la graphie *i* est suivie d'une consonne unique elle-même suivie d'un *e*, on la prononce /aɪ/ : *line, nine, hide, realise* (exceptions : *give* et *live* /ɪ/).

1 **Répétez les paires de mots suivantes.**

Audio hatier-clic.fr/21amc/081a

a. *sheep / ship* **b.** *rich / reach*
c. *leave / live* **d.** *feel / fill*
e. *fit / feet* **f.** *sit / seat*

2 **Pour chacun de ces mots, trouvez un homophone (un mot qui ne s'écrit pas de la même manière mais qui se prononce de façon identique).**

Audio hatier-clic.fr/21amc/081b

seen – peace – sea – meet

3 **Classez les mots en gras dans un tableau en fonction de leur prononciation : /iː/ ou /ɪ/.** Écoutez l'enregistrement pour vérifier vos réponses et répétez les phrases.

Audio hatier-clic.fr/21amc/081c

a. *The **UKIP** is a **Eurosceptic**, right-**wing populist political** party **in** the United **Kingdom**.*

b. *There **is** a **risk** that no **deal will** be **reached in** time.*

Les terminaisons accentuées

▶ Certaines terminaisons, souvent d'origine étrangère, sont accentuées : le mot porte donc son accent principal sur sa dernière syllabe.

▶ Ces terminaisons sont les suivantes :

-ette	*cigarette, laundrette* Exceptions : *etiquette, omelette*
-ee(r)	*agree, engineer, volunteer, Brexiteer* Exceptions : *coffee, toffee, committee, jubilee, Yankee, employee*
-ese	*Chinese, Japanese*
-ade	*parade, brigade* Exceptions : *marmalade, decade*
-oo(n)	*cartoon, kangaroo, tattoo* Exception : *igloo*
-aire	*billionaire*
-que	*grotesque, antique*

4 **Recopiez les mots suivants et soulignez la syllabe accentuée.** Écoutez l'enregistrement pour vérifier vos réponses.

Audio hatier-clic.fr/21amc/081d

degree • committee • decree • coffee • brunette • taboo • tycoon • Vietnamese • decade • blockade

5 **Relevez les mots se terminant par une terminaison accentuée.** Soulignez chaque fois la syllabe qui porte l'accent principal. Vérifiez vos réponses, puis répétez les mots.

Audio hatier-clic.fr/21amc/081e

a. *His crusade against corruption ruined his political career.*

b. *This is a unique opportunity to help Middle Eastern refugees.*

Build up your vocabulary

Vote
- call a refe**ren**dum
- cast a **ball**ot
- **turn**out
- cam**paign**
- e**lec**tor
- **lob**by (v.)
- poll
- sway the vote

People
- Brexi**teer**
- Re**main**er
- **Lea**ver
- the **gen**eral **pub**lic
- Joe **Pub**lic
- pro**tes**ters
- **Eu**rosceptics
- pro**po**nent
- sup**por**ter

Trade
- **cus**toms **u**nion
- trade deal
- opt in
- opt out
- get/make con**cess**ions
- con**trib**ute
- free trade
- **tar**iffs
- fluctu**a**tion
- goods

Brexit

Politics
- an MP (**Mem**ber of **Par**liament)
- the **Comm**ons
- the Lords
- **back**benchers
- the whip
- bu**reau**cracy
- be **bi**ased
- mani**fes**to

Media
- poll
- sway (v.)
- NHS: **Nat**ional Health **Ser**vice
- GDP: Gross Do**mes**tic **Prod**uct
- red tape
- ad / **ad**vert / ad**ver**tisement
- high-tech **pol**itics
- **tab**loids

1 Fill the gaps with words from the mind map.

a. There were many … in the streets of London, … of the … or the opposite side; the … .

b. Trade has been an important argument in the debate. The … allowed under EU rules has been replaced by … … between the UK and individual European states.

c. … and other media, ran … during the Brexit campaign, claiming money given to Europe could be spent on the … for example.

d. Politics became more complicated during Brexit, the … in the … did not vote to support Theresa May's Brexit deal, despite strong persuasion from the … .

e. Concerning the actual vote, … was relatively high for the referendum, and although … after the vote suggested that Remain would win, … were obviously … by the campaign and lobbying.

2 Choose five other words and make your own sentences with them.

Projects

1

Write an email to the editor of a newspaper giving your opinion on Brexit and its impact.

1. Choose a role from the following - a student about to go to university, a business owner, or your own perspective.
2. Focus on one main point and find arguments and examples from the documents in the unit or on the web.
3. Remain polite and calm, use humour if appropriate.
4. Check for mistakes before sending.
5. Use the proper format for your email.

2

In groups of four debate on Brexit and its consequences.

1. Choose one of the following people to represent:
   - a 50-year-old car factory worker who left school aged 16;
   - a 20-year-old university student doing a study exchange in Germany;
   - the CEO of a small company in Northern Ireland;
   - a British pensioner living in Spain.
2. Use the information in the unit to predict how they would have voted in the referendum and the implications of Brexit for them.
3. Research arguments you will use during the debate from the documents in this unit or on the web.
4. Imagine the arguments that will be made by the others and prepare your response.
5. Remember to stay polite and let everyone have their turn during the debate.

7 Investigative journalism

The expert's view
hatier-clic.fr/21amc/084a

In the news
hatier-clic.fr/21amc/084b

Projects

You are a writer. Create a storyboard about an investigation that acted as a counter-power.

You are a journalist. Create a podcast on the role of investigative journalism.

Grammar p. 92 Phonology p. 93

More than just journalism

A The impact of investigative journalism

1

Impact of Investigative Journalism in general

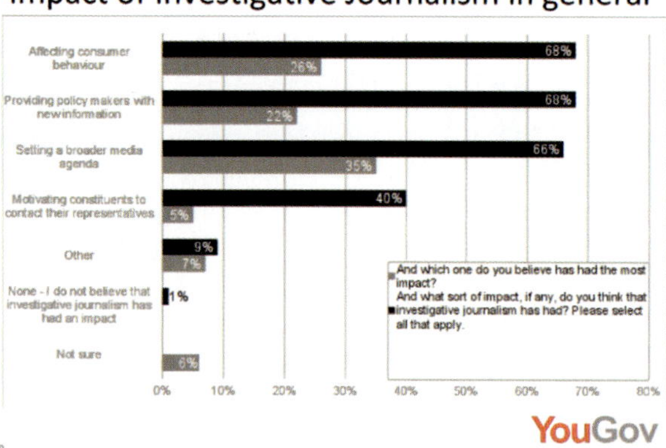

9 Base: 938 Opinion Formers

2

PAIR WORK

Student A on Document 1
Student B on Document 2

1. Watch your document carefully for 2 minutes. Take notes on the impact of investigative journalism.
2. Share information about your document with your partner.
3. Leave a short vocal message on an investigative media's website telling them why you admire their line of work and consider it essential.

B Defining investigative journalism

GROUP WORK

Student A on audio 1
Student B on audio 2
Student C on audio 3

e-worksheet
hatier-clic.fr/21amc/085a

1 Listen to your definition and sum it up.

2 Present it to your partners.

3 Phonology Listen and repeat the following words: *journalism, grouped, your, about, accountability*.

4 You attend the 10th Global Investigative Journalism Conference. Explain the characteristics of investigative journalism.

Global Investigative Journalism Network

Three definitions

Audio hatier-clic.fr/21amc/085b

C Goals & Means

1 Safeguarding the truth – ICIJ's manifesto

The International Consortium of Investigative Journalists represents a new journalism paradigm[1] for our troubled times. Its mission: to bring accountability[2] on a global scale. We are cross-border, networked, collaborative and thoroughly professional. We bring together journalists from around the world to safeguard the truth and each other. Along the way, we bring a new kind of scrutiny to world events and complex problems – using data and document-supported facts that cannot easily be dismissed.

We believe it is the job of journalists to arm the public with information, to empower citizens to strengthen democratic institutions and democracy itself. We believe that truth is society's best weapon against corruption, injustice and inequality.

By gathering massive teams of journalists from all over the world to work together on major investigative projects, ICIJ is able to expose the faults in national and international institutions that are supposed to protect us – but too often are failing. By working together, we can achieve results and impact that no single outlet could achieve on its own, and we can provide citizens around the world with the knowledge they need to hold the powerful to account.

We consider ourselves global leaders in data journalism and journalism technology. Our digital innovations, our secure international network and our access, through whistleblowers[3], to gigantic data sets that exist nowhere else, allow us to dig out information that would otherwise be hidden from view. […]

This is our contribution to democracy, to equality, to transparency. We believe this is the ultimate goal of great investigative reporting.

https://www.icij.org/about/icijs-manifesto

1. model 2. responsibility 3. informants who denounce illegal actions in an organisation

2

"Investigative journalism is absolutely essential," agrees Joseph Stiglitz, who won the Nobel Prize in Economics in 2001 for his analyses of markets with asymmetric information. "It's really part of the enforcement mechanism. It provides checks against the abuses. The very fact that there are investigative reporters out there… acts as a deterrent[1]. Its very presence is an important part of successful development… It's a key part of making our democracy work."

Investigative journalism enlightens. It shines a flashlight into the darkest corners of human, corporate and government behavior. It reveals the secrets that malefactors would like to keep hidden. And it prompts corrective action – from people, agencies, and institutions which can right the wrongs it exposes. […]

Indeed, the impact is often quite extraordinary: exposing abuses of power, curbing corruption, fostering[2] transparency, promoting accountability[3] and strengthening democracy, to name but a few of its more obvious contributions – particularly in emerging democracies and developing economies.

Global Investigative Journalism Network, *Investigative Impact: A Report on Best Practices in Measuring the Impact of Investigative Journalism*, 2017

1. way of discouraging 2. encouraging 3. responsibility

1 Identify the nature, source, topic and aim of each text. Then read *Let's focus on…* n° 2 and 4, p. 90-91 for more information.

2 Pick out the verbs that define the role of investigative journalism and classify them in three categories: supplying information, uncovering the truth, impacting reality.

3 Focus on key nouns and classify them along the following lines: what investigative reporting fights, what it promotes and who/ what organisations are concerned.

4 Grammar In text 1 (l. 12-16) pick out all the nouns and classify them into two categories: countable nouns and uncountable nouns.

5 CONNECT. Use both texts to explain why investigative journalism is a form of counter-power.

Uncovering the truth

A Julian Assange and Wikileaks

GROUP WORK

1. Identify the place and the characters. Read *Let's focus on...* n° 1, p. 90 and explain the situation.
2. Imagine what follows this scene and read the next page on the e-worksheet to see if you were right.
3. Act out your scene in groups of 4: Julian Assange and his collaborator meet the two characters to explain their goal.

@ e-worksheet
hatier-clic.fr/21amc/086

Pratap Chatterjee, Khalil, *Verax: The True History of Whistleblowers, Drone Warfare, and Mass Surveillance*, 2017

B Protecting whistleblowers

1 Guardian launches SecureDrop system for whistleblowers to share files

The Guardian has launched a secure platform for whistleblowers to securely submit confidential documents to the newspaper's reporters.

The launch comes a year to the day since the Guardian posted the first of a series of NSA documents leaked by former NSA contractor Edward Snowden, sparking a worldwide debate on surveillance, privacy, and civil liberties. [...]

The SecureDrop open-source whistleblowing platform provides a way for sources, who can choose to remain anonymous, to submit documents and data while avoiding virtually all of the most common forms of online tracking. [...]

"Protecting sources is at the core of journalism, and as the Guardian's revelations from the Edward Snowden documents over the last year have shown, it's getting ever more difficult," said Alan Rusbridger, the editor-in-chief of the Guardian.

"We're pleased to be able to use the best technology available to make sure we're doing everything we can to let sources talk to our journalists securely, and hope as many other outlets as possible do the same." [...]

Trevor Timm, the director of the Freedom of the Press Foundation, said the development of SecureDrop was part of a wider response to government crackdowns[1] on journalists and whistleblowers in the US and across the world.

"In an age where governments are increasingly using surveillance to uncover sources and chill[2] investigative journalism, technology can help whistleblowers and reporters safely get important stories to the public," he said.

"SecureDrop is designed specifically for news organizations so they can receive tips and documents in a much more anonymous and secure way than email or phone calls."

www.theguardian.com

1. repression 2. discourage

C Exposing the powerful

1 ***The Post*** (Steven Spielberg, 2017)

Video hatier-clic.fr/21amc/087a

Culture Tip 1

The **Pentagon Papers** were top-secret documents about US political and military involvement in Vietnam from 1945 to 1967. They were leaked to newspapers in March 1971 and revealed that the US government had not been honest and that decisions about the Vietnam War had been made without the consent of Congress.

2 ***All the President's Men*** (Alan J. Pakula, 1976)

Video hatier-clic.fr/21amc/087b

PAIR WORK

Student A on trailer 1
Student B on trailer 2

1. Find out the name of the newspaper, the revelations of the investigation and the possible consequences for the reporters.
2. Read the Culture Tip that corresponds to your trailer. See if it confirms your guesses.
3. Share your information with your partner.
4. Explain how investigative journalism served as a counter-power to the US administration in the early 1970's.

Culture Tip 2

The **Watergate Scandal** started when the Nixon administration tried to cover up a break-in at the Democratic National Committee's office in 1972. The robbery took place at the Watergate complex in Washington, D.C. The burglary and other illegal acts were exposed in investigations carried out by the media with the help of a mysterious informant, "Deep Throat." In the end, the scandal caused President Richard Nixon to resign.

2

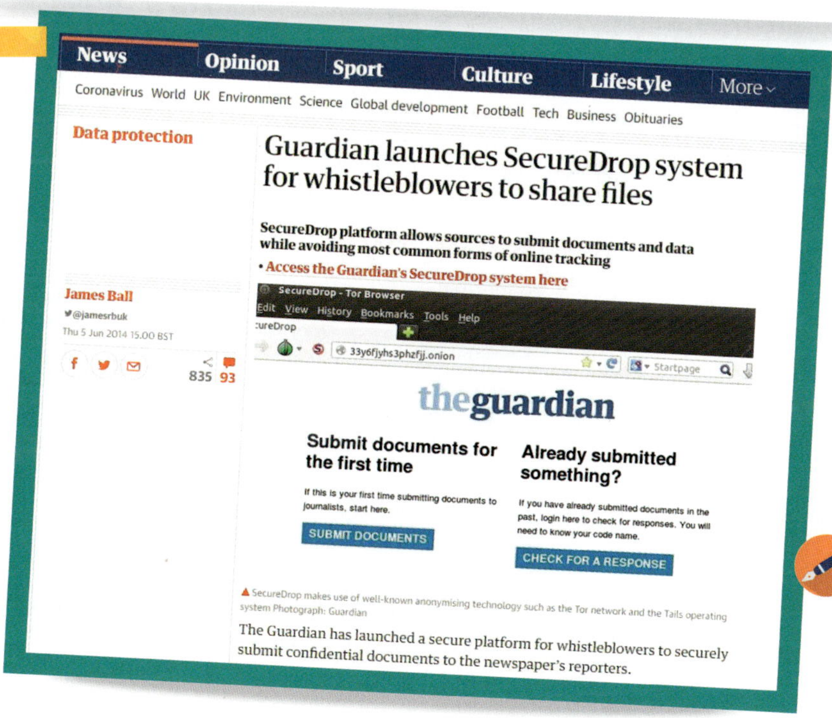
News Opinion Sport Culture Lifestyle More

Coronavirus World UK Environment Science Global development Football Tech Business Obituaries

Data protection

Guardian launches SecureDrop system for whistleblowers to share files

SecureDrop platform allows sources to submit documents and data while avoiding most common forms of online tracking

• Access the Guardian's SecureDrop system here

James Ball
@jamesrbuk
Thu 5 Jun 2014 15.00 BST

835 93

▲ SecureDrop makes use of well-known anonymising technology such as the Tor network and the Tails operating system Photograph: Guardian

The Guardian has launched a secure platform for whistleblowers to securely submit confidential documents to the newspaper's reporters.

1. Observe document 2. Identify its nature, source and aim. Then read the title of document 1 p. 86 to confirm or correct your answers.
2. Explain which events caused the creation of this platform.
3. Read *Let's focus on...* n° 3, p. 91 and explain why Snowden's revelations sparked "a worldwide debate on surveillance, privacy, and civil liberties."
4. Edward Snowden reacts to this article. Imagine his short reply to *The Guardian*.

Investigative journalism 3.0

A Open source journalism

These reporters rely on public data, rather than secret sources

LONDON — Leaked documents and interviews with whistle-blowing sources will always be a part of investigative journalism. But thanks to the rise of digital technology, and the easy availability of data that has gone with it, reporters have more ways to get stories than ever before.

"You can be on your couch in front of your computer and solve a mystery of a missile system downing a plane," said Aliaume Leroy, a journalist who is part of the BBC's Africa Eye team.

Internet sleuths[1] who piece together stories from available data, a practice known as open-source journalism, have helped identify the white nationalists who assaulted counterprotesters in Charlottesville, Va.; unmask the Russian intelligence officers who the British government said tried to kill a fellow Russian spy and his daughter in Salisbury, England. […]

With its emphasis on raw facts, open-source journalism has an immediacy that is effective at a time when readers all along the ideological spectrum have become skeptical of the news media.

"If the BBC tells you they've got a source that proves this, the BBC is the middleman and the source is behind it — you can't see it," Mr. Leroy said. "But if you've got the visual evidence, there is no middleman. You connect directly to the evidence."

The craft[2] of building a story on publicly available data was part of journalism in the analog[3] era, but it has come of age in recent years, with the ubiquity of smartphones and the expansion of social media.

The blogger Eliot Higgins made waves early in the decade by covering the war in Syria from a laptop in his apartment in Leicester, England, while caring for his infant daughter. In 2014, he founded Bellingcat, an open-source news outlet that has grown to include roughly a dozen staff members, with an office in The Hague. Mr. Higgins attributed his skill not to any special knowledge of international conflicts or digital data, but to the hours he had spent playing video games, which, he said, gave him the idea that any mystery can be cracked.

Marc Tracy, *The New York Times*, Dec. 1st, 2019

1. detectives 2. technique 3. not digital

GROUP WORK

Student 1 on document A
Student 2 on document B
Student 3 on document C

1. Look at your group's document(s).
2. Explain the differences between past and present techniques of investigation.
3. List the advantages of modern investigative techniques.
4. You participate in a course about investigative journalism. Share your findings with the other trainees in your group.

e-worksheet hatier-clic.fr/21amc/088a

B New journalism = new tools

Is the truth open-source?

Audio hatier-clic.fr/21amc/088b

C The golden age

1 Global Investigative Journalism Network

GIJN's reach extends worldwide through interlocking networks of training conferences and workshops, member organizations, a help desk, and online publishing.

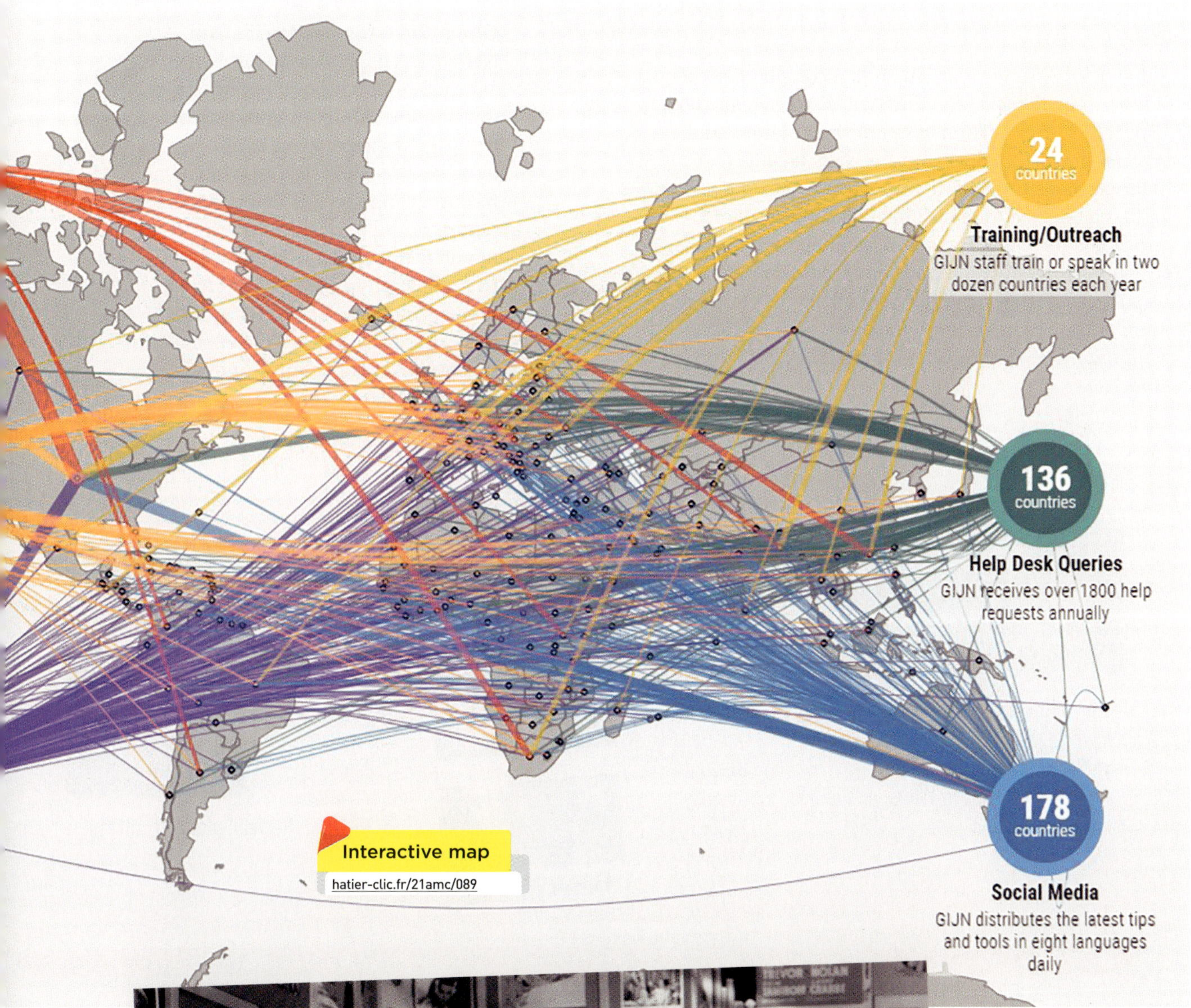

2

Let's focus on...

Julian Assange and Wikileaks ❶

Julian Paul Assange is an Australian computer hacker, editor and publisher who founded WikiLeaks in 2006. This media organisation has published a large number of classified documents on its website. It came to international attention in 2010 when it leaked a series of files about the Afghanistan and Iraq wars, which prompted the United States government to launch a criminal investigation into the organisation. The WikiLeaks 2010 revelations (and others that followed) were published by major newspapers such as *The Guardian*, *The Washington Post* and *The New York Times*.

GIJN ❷

Global Investigative Journalism Network is a US- based worldwide association of nonprofit organisations that support, promote, and provide investigative journalism, even in repressive regimes. It supplies resources and services to investigative reporters and encourages free access to public documents and data. Since its foundation in 2003, it has grown to over 200 member organisations in 80 countries. It holds the Global Investigative Journalism Conference every two years.

Timeline ❺

1892
Ida B Wells's pamphlets exposing the lynching of African Americans in the south of the US.
→ documentary *Ida B. Wells: A Passion for Justice* (William Greaves, 1989).

1902-1903
Ida M. Tarbell's articles about Standard Oil Company and its violation of the Anti-Trust Act.

1906
Upton Sinclair's novel *The Jungle*, about working conditions in Chicago's meatpacking factories.

1954
CBS News Edward Murrow's report on Senator Mc Carthy
→ movie *Good Night and Good Luck* (George Clooney, 2005).

1969
Seymour Hersh's story of the 1968 US Army massacre of civilians in My Lai, South Vietnam.

1971
The Pentagon Papers
→ movie *The Post* (Steven Spielberg, 2017).

1972
Woodward and Bernstein's revelations about the Watergate Scandal
→ movies *All the President's Men* (Alan J. Pakula, 1976) and *Frost/Nixon* (Ron Howard, 2008).

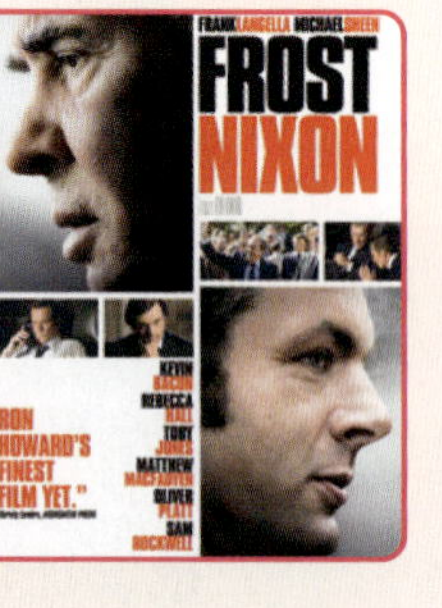

Edward Snowden and NSA documents

3

Edward Joseph Snowden is an American whistleblower who leaked classified documents from one of the world's most secretive organisations, the National Security Agency, in 2013, when he was a Central Intelligence Agency (CIA) employee. He handed out the material to several journalists, who had it published in news media such as *The Guardian*, *The New York Times*, *The Washington Post*. This material disclosed global surveillance programs, many run by the NSA, with the help of telecommunication companies and European governments. The revelations had a major impact as they triggered off debates over freedom of speech, privacy, national security and even democracy.

ICIJ

4

International Consortium of Investigative Journalists, founded in 1997, is an international news organisation based in Washington, D.C. It includes over 260 investigative reporters in 100 countries who collaborate on in-depth investigations. This non-profit organisation has disclosed a number of important stories in the world such as Panama Papers in 2016. Their media partners include some of the world's most famous news outlets like the BBC, *The Guardian* in the UK and *The New York Times*, *The Washington Post* in the U.S.

Dana Priest and William Arkin investigating US intelligence work.
2010

2010
Wikileaks documents on the Iraq and Afghanistan wars
→ movie *The Fifth Estate* (Bill Condon, 2013).

Disclosure of Edward Snowden's leaks on NSA surveillance
→ documentary *Citizenfour* (2014) and movie *Snowden* (Oliver Stone, 2016).
2013

Revelations about the Panama Papers: ICIJ's collaborative investigation into crime and corruption hidden by secretive offshore companies.
→ movie *The Laundromat* (Steven Soderbergh, 2019).
2016

2016
The New York Times investigation into D. Trump's connections with the Russians during his 2016 campaign
→ documentary series *The Fourth Estate* (Liz Garbus, 2018).

2017
Ronan Farrow's investigative reporting into Harvey Weinstein's sexual assaults for *The New Yorker*
→ documentary *Untouchable* (Ursula Macfarlan, 2019).

Facebook-Cambridge Analytica data scandal
→ documentary *The Great Hack* (K. Amer, J. Noujaim, 2019).
2018

Practice your grammar

Dénombrables et indénombrables

▶ **Un nom dénombrable** a deux formes : un singulier et un pluriel (*a house / two houses*). **Un nom indénombrable** (*money, information*) n'a qu'**une seule forme** : le singulier. Comme son nom l'indique, il ne peut pas être directement dénombré au moyen d'un numéral (on ne peut pas dire : ~~*two informations*~~). Le verbe s'accorde toujours au singulier.

▶ Par ailleurs, les deux types de noms ne s'emploient pas avec les mêmes déterminants :

	Dénombrables	Indénombrables
Grande quantité	*many*	*much*
Petite quantité *(peu de)*	*(a) few*	*(a) little*
Article indéfini *a(n)*	possible	impossible

*"Did you get **much information**?" "No, just **a little**."*

▶ Les noms indénombrables désignent en général des substances (*milk, gold, pasta*), des concepts (*justice, religion, honesty*) ou des activités (*swimming, whistle-blowing*).

▶ Certains noms sont indénombrables en anglais mais dénombrables en français. Ils ne peuvent donc pas être employés au pluriel. En revanche, on les traduit souvent par des pluriels français.

- *luggage*
- *damage* (des dégâts)
- *advice*
- *furniture*
- *information*
- *trouble*
- *toast*
- *evidence* (des preuves)
- *homework*

⚠ À cette liste, il faut ajouter ***news***, qui malgré la présence d'un *s* est un indénombrable toujours suivi d'un verbe au singulier : *The news **was** good.*

▶ Quand on veut compter un indénombrable avec précision, il est parfois possible d'utiliser l'expression ***X piece(s) of...*** (*a piece of news, two pieces of advice, three pieces of toast*).
*He told me **two** interesting **pieces of information**.*

1 Choisissez la forme appropriée.

a. *The news of his arrest **have / has** just leaked out.*

b. *This is **a / Ø** fake news!*

c. *The reporter leaked classified **information / informations** about a group of terrorists.*

d. *The police caused **a lot of damage / damages** in his apartment.*

e. *My publisher gave me some useful **advice / advices**.*

2 Complétez avec *much* ou *many*.

a. *How ... luggage can I take on the train?*

b. *I have too ... homework to do.*

c. *How ... phone calls did you make yesterday?*

d. *The President has lied so ... times that people no longer believe him.*

3 Traduisez.

a. *Les journalistes n'ont pas trouvé beaucoup de preuves de sa culpabilité.*

b. *Il a été arrêté à l'aéroport car la police avait trouvé de la drogue dans ses bagages.*

By et le gérondif

▶ La préposition *by* peut être employée pour dire comment accomplir une action ou une tâche. Dans ce cas, elle est suivie d'un verbe à la forme en *-ing* (appelée gérondif). Cette structure répond à la question *How?* :
*The blogger Eliot Higgins made waves early in the decade **by** covering the war in Syria from a laptop in his apartment in Leicester.*

▶ On traduit cette structure par **un gérondif français** (*en* + V-*ant*) :
*They covered up for the president **by** destroying evidence.*
→ *Ils ont couvert le président **en** détruisant des preuves.*

4 Vous enquêtez sur un homme politique malhonnête et corrompu.
Comment a-t-il violé la loi ? Produisez quatre phrases contenant la structure *by* + gérondif. Suivez ce modèle ainsi que les amorces proposées :
Ex. : The Senator broke the law by obstructing the investigation.

a. *The party leader broke the law...*

b. *The MP committed a crime...*

Improve your pronunciation

L'intonation

▶ Une phrase n'est pas une suite de mots prononcés de façon monotone. Comme dans la mélodie d'une chanson, la voix peut varier de hauteur : c'est ce qu'on appelle **l'intonation**.

▶ La voix peut suivre **une mélodie descendante** ↘. Cette intonation est utilisée dans **les phrases affirmatives ou exclamatives** :

It's fake news!

L'intonation est également descendante dans **une question ouverte** (*wh-* question), c'est-à-dire une question qui commence par un mot interrogatif (*who, what, why...*) :

What's the latest news ?

▶ La voix peut suivre **une mélodie montante** ↗. Cette intonation est utilisée **pour indiquer qu'une phrase ou une énumération n'est pas achevée** :

We are networked, collaborative and professional.

L'intonation **montante** est également utilisée dans **une question fermée** (*yes / no question*), c'est-à-dire une question qui appelle comme réponse *yes* ou *no* :

Have you heard the terrible news?

1 Prononcez les mots suivants avec une intonation montante ↗ ou descendante ↘. Écoutez l'enregistrement pour vérifier vos réponses, puis répétez.

Audio hatier-clic.fr/21amc/093a

a. *Maybe!* ↘ **b.** *Maybe?* ↗
c. *Right!* ↘ **d.** *Right?* ↗
e. *Yes, they did.* ↘ **f.** *They did?* ↗

2 L'intonation est-elle montante ↗ ou descendante ↘ dans les phrases suivantes ? Écoutez l'enregistrement pour vérifier vos réponses, puis répétez.

Audio hatier-clic.fr/21amc/093b

a. *The Prime Minister is involved in a financial scandal.*
b. *Who is Edward Snowden?*
c. *When did the Watergate scandal start?*
d. *Have they published your article?*
e. *What a nuisance!*
f. *Why did President Nixon resign?*

La prononciation de la graphie *ou(r)*

▶ La graphie *ou* se prononce le plus souvent **/aʊ/** comme dans *now* : ***about, ground, house***.
Il existe **quelques exceptions qu'il faut apprendre :**

/uː/ **comme dans *moon***	***souvenir, group, soup, wound, through***
/ʌ/ **comme dans *cut***	***country, couple, double, young, enough*** /əˈnʌf/
/ʊ/ **comme dans *book***	Dans les modaux ***should***, ***would*** et ***could*** (le *l* est muet).
/əʊ/ **comme dans *no***	Quand *ou* est suivi d'un *l* : ***soul***, ***shoulder***, ***boulder***
/ɔː/ **comme dans *short***	Dans ***ought*** : ***thought***, ***brought***, ***bought***

▶ En position accentuée, la graphie ***our* en fin de mot ou suivie d'une consonne** se prononce souvent /ɔː/ (comme dans *short*) : ***your***, ***four***, ***court***.
Exceptions : ***journalist*** et ***journey*** (prononcés /ɜː/ comme dans *girl*), ***hour*** et ***our*** (prononcés /aʊə/ comme dans *power*).

▶ Les terminaisons inaccentuées ***-ous*** et ***-our*** se prononcent avec la voyelle /ə/ comme dans *fath**er*** : ***colour***, ***mysterious***...

3 Classez les mots en fonction de leur prononciation : /aʊ/ (comme dans *now*), /uː/ (comme dans *moon*), ou /ʌ/ (comme dans *cut*). Vérifiez vos réponses avec l'enregistrement et répétez.

Audio hatier-clic.fr/21amc/093c

mountain • youth • young • sound • mouth • couple • account • country • group • cloud • courage

4 Chassez l'intrus. Vérifiez vos réponses avec l'enregistrement et répétez.

Audio hatier-clic.fr/21amc/093d

a. *about – loud – doubt – soul*
b. *course – neighbour – your – mourn*
c. *bought – thought – through – ought*

5 Lisez les mots en gras à voix haute. Écoutez l'enregistrement pour vérifier vos réponses, puis répétez les phrases.

Audio hatier-clic.fr/21amc/093e

a. *Protecting **sources** is at the core of **journalism**.*
b. *The **court adjourned** the trial until June **4th**.*

Build up your vocabulary

Investigative journalism

Tools
- in-depth reporting
- undisclosed documents/ classified information/ top-secret files
- informant
- leak information/ files
- investigate sth
- uncover/ disclose the truth
- expose sth

Counter-power
- watchdog
- keep in check
- shed light on sth
- hold sb accountable
- blow the whistle on sb
- stand up against sb
- trustworthy / reliable
- influential

Impact/ targets
- corruption / bribery
- corrupt official
- secrecy
- violation / abuse
- illegal/ unlawful/ law-breaking
- misconduct / illegal activity/ wrongdoing
- big business
- administration/ government
- people in power/ the powerful
- affair / scandal

Media
- Fourth Estate/ Fourth Power
- newspaper / print media
- offline ≠ online edition
- news outlet / media organisation
- a piece of news
- media coverage
- cover a topic
- hit the headlines/ be on the news

Investigative journalism 3.0
- fact-based/ data-based journalism
- collaborative journalism
- collect/ gather information/ data
- share material
- multi-media professional
- amateur journalist
- freelancer
- citizen journalist

1 Complete this summary about muckrakers with words from the mind map.

Muckrakers were the forerunners of modern investigative journalism during the Progressive Era in the United States (1890s–1920s). Their goal was to expose **...** officials and **...** practices in big business and government. They particularly shed **...** on such topics as urban poverty, unsafe working conditions and child labor, for which they held the powerful **...** .

Most early muckrakers wrote articles that were published in **...** media like *McClure's Magazine*, while others resorted to non-fiction, like Upton Sinclair who wrote a novel (*The Jungle*) based on information he **...** while working in Chicago 's meatpacking plants.

Thanks to these muckrakers' **...** reporting, social and economic issues got wide media **...** and as a result, laws were passed to reinforce protection for workers and consumers.

2 Rephrase the headlines using words from the mind map.

a. "250,000 leaked files that lay bare US view of world"
(*The Guardian*, Nov. 29th, 2010)

b. "UK watchdog fines Facebook over Cambridge Analytica data scandal"
(*Financial Times*, July 11th, 2018)

c. "Edward Snowden: the whistleblower behind the NSA surveillance revelations"
(*The Guardian*, June 9th, 2013)

Projects

1

You are a writer. Create a storyboard about an investigative reporter or an investigation that acted as a counter-power.

1. Choose a reporter or an investigation presented in the unit or do some research on the internet. It needs to be set in an Anglo-Saxon country.
2. Decide which protagonists and which aspect of the case you will focus on. Remember to highlight the counter-power action.
3. Write some captions giving the context and then the characters' dialogue / lines.
4. Use a digital tool to draw your storyboard or if you have art skills, draw it yourself. Then add the captions and balloons.

2

You are an investigative journalist. Create a podcast commenting on the role of investigative journalism as counter-power.

1. **Decide who you will be and which Anglo-Saxon news outlet you are working for.**
2. **Check the unit and your notes for information about some of the following topics:**
   - characteristics;
   - goals;
   - means and tools;
   - role and protection of whistleblowers;
   - one or two examples of investigative reporting and its impact on powerful people/ organisations.
3. **Prepare your arguments with a plan or a mindmap containing 15 words maximum.**
4. **Record the podcast:**
   - remain spontaneous;
   - don't read;
   - keep it as natural and lively as possible so as to involve listeners.

8 Talk shows: information or entertainment?

The expert's view
hatier-clic.fr/21amc/096a

In the news
hatier-clic.fr/21amc/096b

Projects

- Write an article about the informative and entertaining power of talk shows.
- Create your own talk show and present your project to a board of producers.

Grammar p. 104 Phonology p. 105

Symbols of American popular culture

A A white men's world?

1

Late Night with David Letterman

2

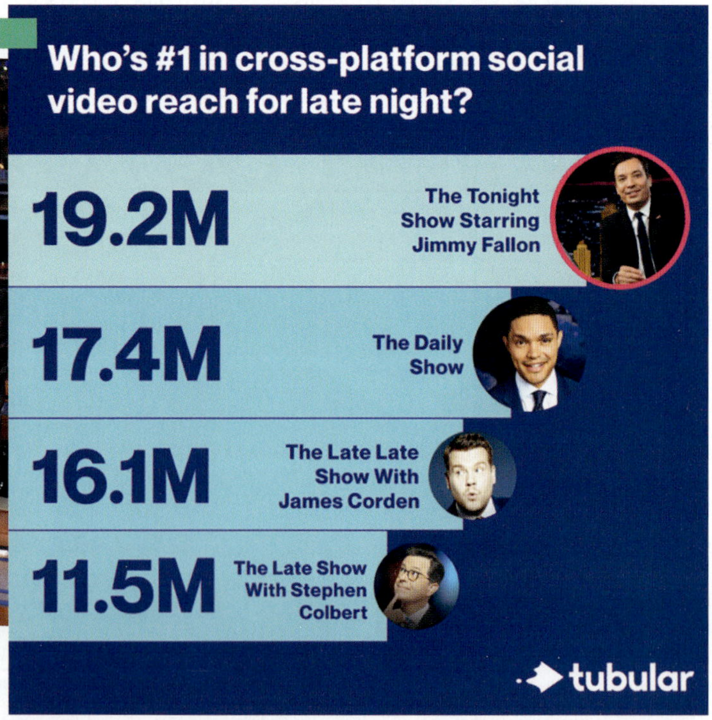

1. Look at the photo and the graph to present the hosts and the late-night shows: names, atmosphere, furniture.
2. Comment on the shows and their ratings. Imagine why they are so successful.
3. Use the graph and the image to show why some people may feel underrepresented.
4. You are a late-night show host. Thank your audience for the amazing ratings you had in 2019/2020.

B What's a talk show?

The talk show remains a fundamental feature within any economic, social, and cultural formation of television. This long reliance on the form results in part, as [Bernard] Timberg points out, from its status as an efficient and effective commodity. It is relatively cheap to produce. It is often extremely profitable when successful. And those successes need not, in most cases, rely on securing a "mass" audience. Almost always presented to a specific portion of the total viewing public […], the talk show, like the game or quiz show, can become a profitable staple of televisual entertainment and interaction within its specific niche. […]

First and foremost, this is a work framing television talk within a detailed historical perspective, an approach placing it within a strong development in the study of television. Perhaps as a result of the enormous technological, industrial, regulatory, and economic changes of recent decades, there is now a sense that it is possible to gain a much needed clearer perspective on this medium. Indeed, there is a sense that at least one, perhaps more than one, phase of television has passed. […]

One constant, however, clearly delineated by Timberg, is the formation of the talk show around the personality of the host.

Bernard M. Timberg, *Television Talk: A History of the TV Talk Show* (introduction by Horace Newcomb), 2010.

1. Read the text and explain why talk shows are described as fundamental.
2. List the reasons why talk shows are economically profitable.
3. Write down a post on social media about the benefits of having talk shows on television.

C Stars as talk show hosts

PAIR WORK

Student A on video 1
Student B on video 2

1. Find as much information as you can on the talk shows in your document (titles, hosts, ratings, broadcasting, network, etc.).
2. Read *Let's focus on…* n° 2 and 3, p. 102-103 and find information on the two hosts.
3. Share the information you found with your classmate.

e-worksheet hatier-clic.fr/21amc/097a

4. **CONNECT**. Compare and contrast the way talk shows are depicted in the videos.

1 Late-night talk show *Chelsea*
Video hatier-clic.fr/21amc/097b

2 Oprah Winfrey, the story of a success
Video hatier-clic.fr/21amc/097c

The show must go on!

A Celebrities showing off

1

2

Culture Tip

Michelle Obama (b. 1964) is not only an American attorney and author, but also the first African-American First Lady. Born and raised in Chicago, she graduated from both Princeton University and Harvard. She became a role model for women and raised awareness of poverty, education, etc. In 2020, she launched her podcast *The Michelle Obama Podcast*.

Culture Tip

Ellen de Generes (b. 1958) is an American TV host, writer and producer. She started her career as a stand-up comedian before moving on to acting. She became a symbol when she came out on TV in the *Oprah Winfrey Show*. Since 2003, she has been presenting *The Ellen DeGeneres Show*. In July 2020, she publicly apologised after former employees had revealed that the show was a toxic workplace.

1. Read the Culture Tips and look at the photos. Say who the hosts and the guests are, and comment on the atmosphere and what it reveals.
2. Choose one of the pictures and imagine the interview between the host and the guest.

B Show or entertainment?

The credibility of late night comedy

Late night comedy now has a much larger impact on audiences than it had just over a decade ago, thanks in large part to *The Daily Show* and all that it has spawned[1]. It has gradually become a more substantial[2] source for insight about what's happening in our world; it's become an outlet for news and valuable information.

For most of the history of televised media, comedy and news were not so tightly woven[3] that a perfect adherence to factuality was a real concern. And the increased intersection of news and comedy has led to mixed feelings, mostly related to the fact that, until recently, when late night comedy and the news did intersect, it was overtly trivial. For years, the closest thing America had to what it has now was *Saturday Night Live's* Weekend Update, which was simply comedians reading headlines and providing either puns[4] or comedically deliberate misinterpretations. The idea that anybody could gain any practical and informative news from late night comedy shows was laughable in itself.

But now, regardless of whether or not you draw your information *directly* from late night comedy shows, it is absolutely one of the channels of information that makes the most lasting impression. […]

With the rise of *The Daily Show*, it became apparent that Americans had grown wary of standard news media. Then and now, the news had a tendency to be exceedingly dramatic and theatrical. […] As Anthony Jeselnik [an American comedian, writer and actor] has said, "No matter how terrible something is, if you can find a way to laugh at it, then things are going to be all right."

Adding to the confusion, [Jon] Stewart [*The Daily Show* host from 1999 to 2015] and his team have always been eager to respond to criticism from other media outlets by underlining the unprofessional character of *The Daily Show*. After all, the show did begin by generally mocking the absurdity of political theater, especially as presented to us in the form of news. It wasn't supposed to be a channel for the news. What people learned in the course of enjoying *The Daily Show* was practically incidental. […]

Elkin, the show's fact checker, warned that "statistics and polls can very easily be misleading." Fortunately, Elkin's background has provided her with the experience to sort out what polls can and can't be trusted. "One nice thing about having a journalism background is that when you're looking at poll data, you have more tools at your disposal to know if this was a reliable poll, if the sample size was big enough, or if it was done over the phone or over the internet. There's a lot to take into consideration."

www.vulture.com

1. given birth to 2. considerable 3. connected 4. plays on words

1. List what people used to think about late-night shows before.
2. Compare people's opinion on standard news media and late-night shows today.
3. Explain why facts are so crucial for the show.
4. **Grammar** Pick out all the verbs in the present perfect. How are they formed? Pay particular attention to irregular verbs.
5. Student A prefers standard news media, student B prefers late-night shows. They end up agreeing. Act out the conversation.

C Voicing an opinion

1. Find out why Jill Biden is invited.
2. Analyse what it shows to invite the wife of a presidential candidate to a talk show.
3. Comment on the attitudes of the show hosts and what it means for viewers.
4. **Phonology** Listen to the video and repeat the following words: *election, generation, suppression*. What do they have in common? Identify the stressed syllables. What do you notice?
5. Imagine the tweet of a viewer who complains that the show is biased.

Jill Biden on Whoopi Goldberg's show

Video hatier-clic.fr/21amc/099

When talk shows get political

A Entertainment no more

A tribute to RBG

Video hatier-clic.fr/21amc/100

1. Watch the video and read the Culture Tip. Present Ruth Bader Ginsburg (job, personality, important facts about her...).
2. Find information about Ruth Bader Ginsburg's death and people's reactions.
3. Imagine a WhatsApp conversation about the tribute that Colbert paid to Ruth Bader Ginsburg in *The Late Show*.

Culture Tip

Ruth Bader Ginsberg (1933-2020) was the first woman to study and graduate at Columbia Law School. She dedicated her life to the fight for women's rights and she was a pro-choice supporter.

B Comedy news

Late night comedy not joking about news

The news can be tough to absorb after a while, even for a self-described "news junkie."

"News and current events are definitely something my life has always been centered around," says Hannah Zeller, 21, who says while in grade school, she knew the names of the news anchors[1] on her local evening news hour. But even for someone like Zeller, "there is such a thing as too much news," she says.

So, she turns to late-night programs to stay informed but also to find humor and solace[2].

Although watching television programs such as the "The Tonight Show Starring Jimmy Fallon," "The Late Show With Stephen Colbert" and "The Daily Show With Trevor Noah" may cover similar topics to traditional news outlets, they "certainly make the news of the day seem a little less intimidating," Zeller says.

A study by the Pew Research Center stated that "61 percent of young people reported regularly or sometimes learning campaign information from comedy television," according to the book *Laughing Matters: Humor and American Politics in the Media Age*, edited by Jody C. Baumgartner.

This is likely because hosts of late-night comedy shows make their news material more "digestible," Zeller says. Nevertheless, she recognizes that what she is viewing is not without bias.

"I think people often watch late-night shows and forget that what they're seeing isn't fact free from significant bias[3]," she says. "Not only are stories skewed[4] for entertainment's sake, but they're also targeted towards certain audiences with certain beliefs or opinions, and I think this can sometimes negatively impact a person's understanding of the facts of a news story."

Gainsboro, a Massachusetts native, says though he watches "usually around an hour a day" of late-night television, he also recognizes that "comedy news" has risks.

"Comedy news is a dangerous game," he says, "as people will seemingly believe anything nowadays. Same thing could be said for exaggerated news. I think we need to be better at sorting out the difference, as a society. They are too blurred." Yet simultaneously, hosts like Fallon, Colbert and Noah can help younger people feel like the world is a little less grim[5].

Ruby Rosenthal, www.voanews.com, June 16th, 2020

1. presenters 2. comfort 3. preconceived idea 4. distorted 5. dark

1. Explain Hannah Zeller's opinion on the news in general.
2. Use the figures in the text to show that the youth turned to late-night programs.
3. List the limits of late-night TV and conclude.
4. Debate with your partner: "Late-night TV is the best way to be informed." Make a list of arguments and voice your opinion.

C A political conversation

For more than three decades, Oprah has remained one of the most beloved TV personalities, with popularity spanning across[1] global audiences and demographics.

On July 27, Oprah took to social media to share her latest project, *The Oprah Conversation*, a new interview series which will feature conversations with newsmakers and thought leaders on current events and timely[2] topics. Tweeting to her over 40 million followers, Oprah said, “It’s time to bring humanity back to the conversation,” adding that the discussions will “unite us – not divide us.”

Deadline reports that the Apple TV+ series will begin by directly addressing racism in the United States. The debut episode, hitting the streaming service Thursday, July 30, is titled “How to Be an Antiracist,” and finds Oprah joined by bestselling author Professor Ibram X. Kendi to speak with white Americans about confronting their own racism. Professor Kendi’s book of the same name, which has received widespread praise[3], offers a deeper understanding of systemic and societal racism, and proposals for anti-racist individual actions and systemic changes.

Author Bryan Stevenson, whose story and memoir inspired *Just Mercy*, is also scheduled as a guest on the show.

Lauren Ramesbottom, www.theloop.ca, July 27th, 2020

1. including 2. current 3. positive criticism

1. With the help of the text and of *Let’s focus on...* n° 2 and 3, p. 102-103, introduce Oprah Winfrey.
2. Present her latest project.
3. Explain why this talk show is highly political.
4. In a tweet, insist on the fact that more shows like this are needed.

D Political bias

1. Observe the photos. Explain why this guest is on the show that you can see in the photo.
2. List the four most divisive hosts and use numbers to justify your answer.
3. **CONNECT**. Compare the hosts’ popularity (divisiveness/hostility) among Republicans’ and Democrats’ views and conclude.

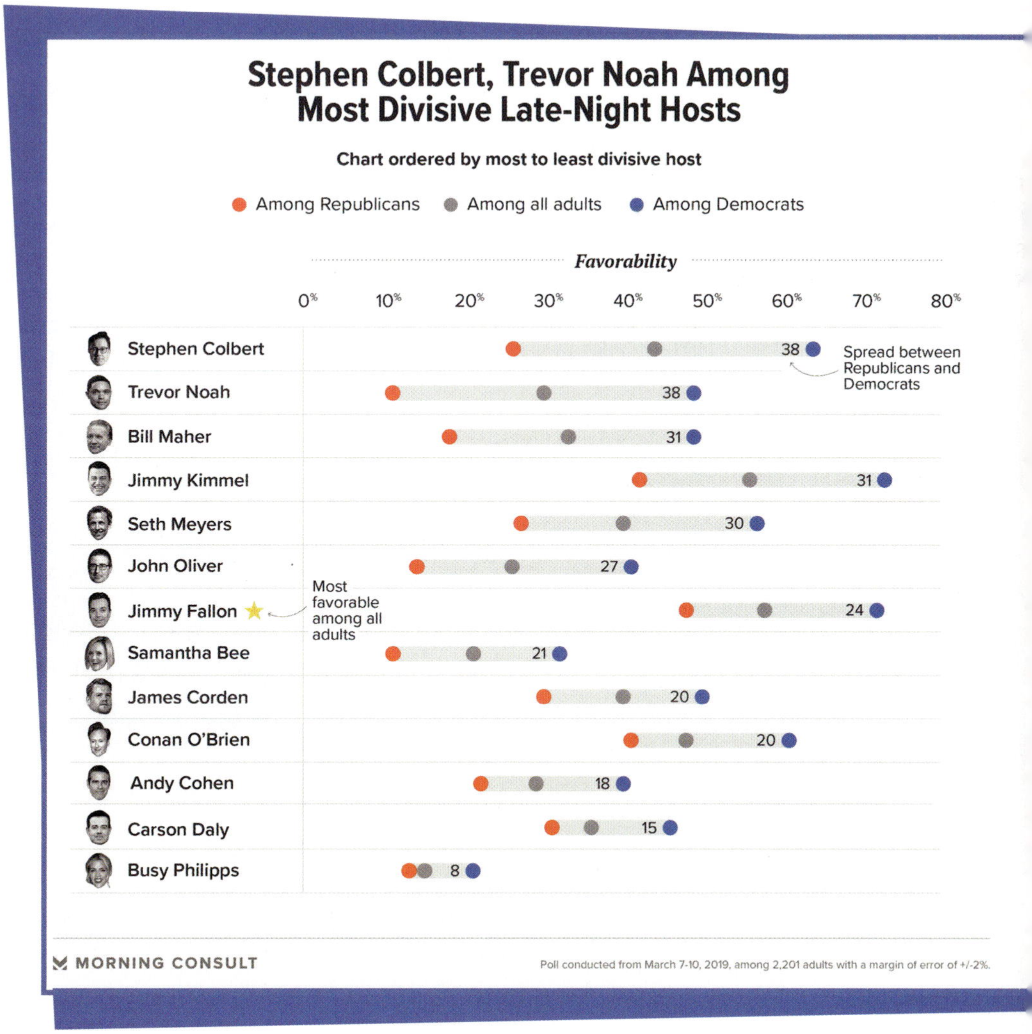

Let's focus on

Main American TV networks

NBC Short for National Broadcasting Company. NBC is an American radio and television network located in NYC and also in Los Angeles, Chicago and Philadelphia. It is part of the Big Three television networks along with ABC and CBS. Its logo looks like a peacock and is very colourful, to remind viewers that it was one of the first networks to broadcast in colour. On this channel, viewers can watch TV series such as *This is Us*, *The Good Place* … or talk-shows like *The Kelly Clarkson Show* or *The Tonight Show With Jimmy Fallon*. The current presidents of NBC Entertainment are George Cheeks & Paul Telegdy.

CBS The American television and radio network CBS has its headquarters in NYC and Los Angeles. It was founded in 1927. From 1928 to 1974, it used to be called Columbia Broadcasting System. It is also called the Eye Network due to its logo. CBS is part of the Big Three television networks along with ABC and NBC. The following programs are broadcast on CBS: NCIS (TV series), *The Late Night Show With Stephen Colbert*, *CBS Evening News*, *CBS This Morning* (news and information). Kelly Kahl has been its president since 2017.

abc Short for American Broadcasting Company, ABC is an American television network owned by Walt Disney Television. Its main headquarters are in Burbank, California. It is part of the Big Three television networks along with CBS and NBC. It was founded in 1948 by Edward J. Noble and Louis Blanche. The TV series broadcast on ABC are *Greys Anatomy*, *The Good Doctor* … Talk shows: *The View*, *Jimmy Kimmel Live!* … or *Good Morning America*, a popular morning news programme.

HBO HBO is a pay television network; its initials stand for Home Box Office. It was launched in 1972 as a pioneer for modern pay television. It is based in Manhattan's West Side district. The current slogan is "There's More to Discover."
There are several channels belonging to this network such as HBO, HBO 2, HBO Family, etc. It broadcasts TV series, comedies, sports, reality … There is a streaming partnership for its subscribers with Apple TV channels, Amazon TV channels etc.

FOX NEWS channel Fox News Channel, also known as FNC or Fox, is an American cable news television channel. It was first launched in 1996 and created by Rupert Murdoch (media mogul) to appeal to a conservative audience. *Hannity*, one of the most famous political talk shows, has been hosted by Sean Hannity since 2009.

Timeline

1948
Start of talk shows' golden age → talk programs as *Photographic Horizons, Omnibus; America's Town Meeting and We, -the People, Teenage Book Club and Author Meets the Critics, Meet the Press, Studio One.*

From 1949 to 1973
Majority of shows are talk-shows.

the 1950s
More and more American homes own a TV.

January 1984
Oprah Winfrey is the host of *A.M. Chicago*.

September 1986 to 2011
A.M. Chicago becomes *The Oprah Winfrey Show* and will be the most watched daytime talk show in the USA (25 seasons, 4,561 episodes, 47 Emmys).

1999-2015
Jon Stewart is the host of *The Daily Show*.

Leading talk show hosts

Oprah Winfrey
(*The Oprah Winfrey Show*, 1986-2011)

Wendy Williams
(*The Wendy Williams Show*, since 2008)

Jimmy Kimmel
(*Jimmy Kimmel Live!* since 2003)

Stephen Colbert
(*The Late Show*, since 2014)

Ellen Degeneres
(*The Ellen Degeneres Show*, since 2003)

Jimmy Fallon
(*The Tonight Show Starring Jimmy Fallon*, since 2014)

Joan Rivers
(*The Joan Rivers Show*, 1989-1993)

Kelly Clarkson
(*The Kelly Clarkson Show*, since 2019)

Trevor Noah
(*The Daily Show*, since 2015)

2003
Ellen DeGeneres launches *The Ellen DeGeneres Show*.

Oprah Winfrey creates the Oprah Winfrey Network (OWN).
2011

2014
The Tonight Show Starring Jimmy Fallon is launched on NBC.

Trevor Noah replaces Jon Stewart on *The Daily Show*.
Sept. 2015

2018
Stephen Colbert has the biggest ratings amongst all American late-night shows.

The first episode of *The Kelly Clarkson Show* is broadcast on NBC.
2019

Practice your grammar

Le *present perfect* simple

▶ **Le *present perfect* (*have* + participe passé)** permet de mettre en relation un événement passé et une situation présente.

▶ Il peut indiquer **un lien de cause à effet** entre un événement passé et une situation présente. L'emploi du *present perfect* implique donc **un résultat présent** :

I can't change the channel. ← explique — *I've **broken** the remote control.*

▶ On trouve souvent le *present perfect* avec des adverbes de temps ou dans des expressions qui permettent de faire **un bilan ou de parler de son expérience : *never / ever, always, already / yet*** (déjà), ***so far / until now*** (jusqu'à présent), ***it's the first time***…

*I've never **watched** this talk show.*

▶ **Avec *for* (+ durée) ou *since* (+ date) que l'on traduit par « depuis »**, le *present perfect* indique qu'une action ou un état a commencé dans le passé et s'est poursuivi jusqu'au moment présent. On le traduit par un présent en français.

*For more than three decades, Oprah **has remained** one of the most beloved TV personalities.*

⚠ C'est **le prétérit** qu'il convient d'utiliser dans une phrase qui contient **un complément de temps qui situe de façon ponctuelle un événement révolu** (*yesterday, last week, in 2015*…) ou dans une **question en *when?***. L'emploi du *present perfect* y est impossible.

*Michelle Obama **published** a memoir in November 2018.*

1 Formez une phrase en mettant le verbe entre parenthèses au prétérit ou au *present perfect*.

a. *I … (already / see) this film.*

b. *Oprah Winfrey … (be / always) my favourite TV host.*

c. *"When … (buy / you) your TV set?" "I … (buy) it last year."*

d. *The audience ratings of the show … (significantly / decline) since March.*

e. *His new talk show … (premiere) on NBC last week and … (receive) mixed reviews so far.*

f. *It's the first time Jimmy Fallon … (interview) the president.*

2 Produisez cinq phrases évoquant votre expérience et vos goûts en matière d'émissions télévisées. Utilisez les adverbes suivants (qui expriment un bilan) avec un verbe au *present perfect : never, so far, already, yet, always*. Produisez six phrases.

Ex. : *I've never liked reality TV shows.*

L'expression de la concession

▶ Pour exprimer la concession (une contradiction logique), il est possible d'employer **les prépositions *despite* et *in spite of*** (malgré) qui introduisent des groupes nominaux ou des pronoms :

***Despite / In spite of bad reviews**, HBO renewed the series for a second and third season.*

▶ On peut aussi avoir recours à **des propositions subordonnées introduites par *even though / if*** (même si), ***although*** /ɔːlˈðəʊ/ (bien que) ou ***while*** (tandis que) :

*The start of talk shows' golden age can be considered in 1948, **even though the television wasn't common in American homes until the 1950s.***

▶ Il est enfin possible d'utiliser **dans une phrase indépendante des adverbes de liaison** que l'on traduit par « cependant » et qui sont relativement mobiles dans la phrase : ***however, nevertheless, nonetheless, yet.***

*The TV show is very popular with young people. **However / Yet / Nevertheless**, it has been panned by critics.*

3 Reformulez les phrases en utilisant les mots ou expressions entre parenthèses. Produisez chaque fois deux phrases.

a. *The show caused a big scandal, but it received two Grammy Awards. (while, despite)*

b. *I rarely watch television, but I never miss my favorite sitcom. (however, although)*

c. *The program has been widely praised by critics. Unfortunately, it averages only one million viewers per week and might be canceled. (yet, even though)*

Improve your pronunciation

Les consonnes muettes

▶ On ne prononce pas le ***l*** dans les contextes suivants :

dans certains modaux	*could, would, should*
dans -*alk* /ɔːk/ (GB) ou /ɑːk/ (US)	*talk, walk, stalk*
dans -*alm*, -*alf*	*calm, palm, half*

▶ La **consonne *b*** est muette en fin de mot :
- après un m : *thumb, dumb, crumb*
- avant un t : *debt, doubt*

▶ En début de mot, **le *k* ne se prononce pas avant un *n* :** *know, knife, knock*

▶ **Le *t* est muet** dans les contextes suivants :

dans -*stle*	*castle,*
dans -*sten* ou -*ften*	*listen, hasten, soften, often*

⚠ Environ 25 % des anglophones prononcent le *t* dans *often*.

▶ **La consonne *w*** est muette avant un *r* : ***wrong, write***. Elle n'est pas non plus prononcée dans les mots suivants : ***sword, who, whose*** et ***whole*** /həʊl/.

▶ **La consonne *h*** est muette dans les quatre mots suivants ainsi que leurs dérivés : ***honest, honor, heir, hour***

▶ **La consonne *n*** est muette après un *m* : ***column, condemn, hymn***

1 Recopiez les mots suivants et repérez les consonnes muettes. Écoutez l'enregistrement pour vérifier vos réponses et répétez.

Audio hatier-clic.fr/21amc/105a

bomb • whistle-blower • Christmas • calm • honest • palm • climb • hasten • damn

2 Pour chacun des mots suivants, trouvez un homophone (un mot qui ne s'écrit pas de la même manière mais qui se prononce de façon identique).

new • knight • knot (nœud) *• wring* (tordre) *• whole • right • hymn • heir • hour*

La *ION rule*

▶ Les mots terminés par **un suffixe commençant par la voyelle *i*, *u* ou *e* et elle-même suivie d'une voyelle** portent leur accent principal sur **la syllabe qui précède ce suffixe**. On appelle cette règle **la *ION rule*** car les mots se terminant par *-ion* appliquent typiquement cette règle :

conversation - information

▶ Il s'agit, pour l'essentiel, des suffixes suivants :

-ion	*creation, opinion* (exception : *television*)
-ious, -uous, -eous	*courageous, luxurious*
-iar, -ian, -ia, -ial	*substantial, California*
-ient	*impatient*

▶ Il peut arriver que l'accent principal d'un mot soit déplacé si on lui ajoute l'un des suffixes ci-dessus. Les mots de la même famille ne sont donc pas toujours accentués sur la même syllabe.

president → *presidential*   *politics* → *politician*

3 Recopiez les mots suivants et soulignez la syllabe qui porte l'accent principal. Écoutez l'enregistrement pour vérifier vos réponses et répétez.

Audio hatier-clic.fr/21amc/105b

generation • administration • essentially • television • commercial • comedian • sufficient • individual • serious • Pennsylvania • controversial

4 Les mots suivants et leurs dérivés ne sont pas accentués sur la même syllabe. Recopiez les mots et soulignez la syllabe qui porte l'accent principal, puis écoutez l'enregistrement pour vérifier vos réponses. Répétez les mots.

Audio hatier-clic.fr/21amc/105c

a. *influence* → *influential*
b. *history* → *historian*
c. *industry* → *industrial*
d. *courage* → *courageous*

Build up your vocabulary

Talk shows

Talk shows and TV

- **net**work = **chann**el
- TV host = TV pre**sen**ter
- TV **pro**gram = TV **broad**cast
- TV set
- talk show = chat show (UK)
- **pro**gram = **sche**dule UK: /'ʃedʒ.uːl/ US: /'skedʒ.uːl/

On air

- **o**pening **cre**dits
- **wel**come = host
- guest
- being **broad**cast = on (the) air
- be on the screen
- daytime show / late-night show

Talk show set

- **fur**niture
- seats
- desk
- spec**ta**tors
- **cam**era
- in**ter**ior
- de**sign**
- **stu**dio
- **ligh**ting
- couch (UK)/**so**fa (US)
- props = **ob**jects used on a TV set

Popularity

- **ra**tings
- sta**tis**tics
- **au**dience share
- suc**cess**ful
- enter**tain**ing = recre**a**tional
- en**gross** = **cap**tivate
- spread news
- the **au**dience = **view**ers

Talk shows and politics

- de**bate**
- **in**terview
- com**mit**ment
- sa**tire**
- make fun of/mock
- **cri**ticise/**cri**ticism
- cam**paign**
- an**nounce**ment
- o**pin**ion

1 Complete the sentences with words from the unit.

a. Jon Stewart was … of the … called *The Daily Show* from 1999 to 2015.

b. The most popular talk shows are … on big … such as CBS or NBC.

c. Stephen Colbert has had very good … for his late-night show called … .

d. For many … late-night programs can be both … and … , which is different from standard … .

2 Write a definition of late-night shows including the following words : a host - a guest - to broadcast - daytime show - late-night show - entertaining - a channel - politics - news.

3 Change the words in bold letters using a synonym from the mind map.

a. TV presenters often **host** politicians in their shows.

b. In the U.S.A., some **TV programs** have been **broadcast** for more than ten years!

c. Some people find that talk-shows are really **recreational**.

d. Late-night shows are always **programmed** during the night.

e. Viewers are often invited to comment on **talk shows** on social media.

Projects

1 Write an article for your school magazine about the informative and entertaining power of talk shows.

1 Prepare the content of your article.
- Give a definition of a talk show and choose the talk-shows you are going to talk about: daytime talk-shows or late-time talk shows.
- Think about a catchy title for your article.
- Imagine a key question you will answer in the body of your article.
- Draw a two-column-grid or create a mind map about the power of talk shows: information / entertainment. List some arguments.

2 Write your article.
- Respect the rule: one idea = one paragraph.
- Give precise examples.
- Use the present to mention with their powers.

3 Time to conclude!
- Summarise your article in a few lines.
- Answer your key question.
- Use elements such as: to conclude, all in all, to sum it...

2 Create your own talk show and present your project to a board of producers.

1 Make your talk show yours.
- Choose a title, a TV host, a channel, the time it is broadcast...
- List the content(s): news, politics, entertainment, infotainment...
- Watch the videos of the unit or find some on the Web.

2 Prepare the content of your presentation.
- Choose who is going to appear on your video or in the pictures you will use in your presentation.
- List the words from the vocabulary mind map you will include in your video/presentation.

3 Prepare your notes.
- Make a list of 15 words from the mindmap.
- Use elements to promote your talk show: exclamations, adjectives...
- Check the pronunciation of difficult words on an online dictionary.

4 Film your trailer or present your new talk show.
- Look directly into the camera or in the eyes of the producers.
- Rehearse.
- Remember to speak loudly and clearly.

9 The Commonwealth: tradition and modernity

The expert's view
hatier-clic.fr/21amc/108a

In the news
hatier-clic.fr/21amc/108b

Projects

- You are a Commonwealth citizen. Write an opinion article giving your views on the Commonwealth.
- You are a young poet. Perform a poem you have written on the Commonwealth.

Grammar p. 116 Phonology p. 117

History and values

A The Commonwealth of Nations

1

COMMONWEALTH COUNTRIES BY GDP (NOMINAL)

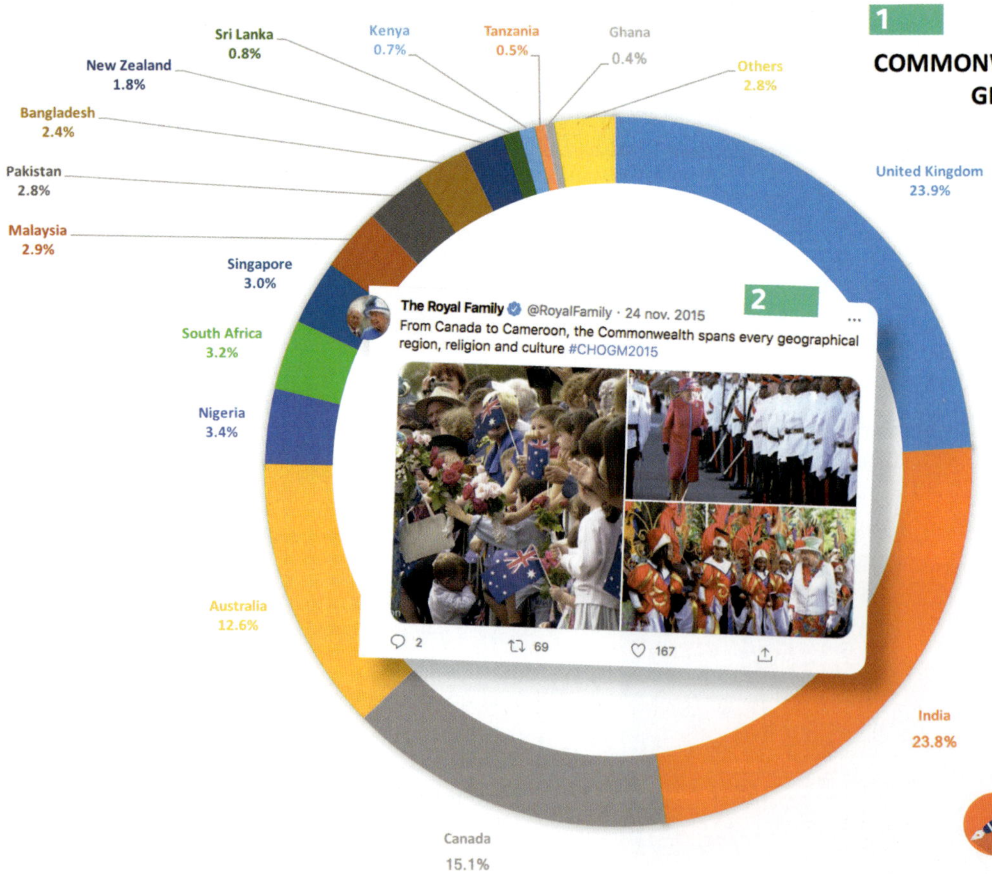

2

The Royal Family @RoyalFamily · 24 nov. 2015
From Canada to Cameroon, the Commonwealth spans every geographical region, religion and culture #CHOGM2015

2 69 167

1. Identify the Commonwealth countries with the highest GDP. Say whether they are the richest countries.
2. Compare how the different people are dressed in the image. Explain who stands out.
3. **CONNECT.** Explain how the two documents represent the Commonwealth.

B Unity

Unity, by Selina Tusitala Marsh

Audio hatier-clic.fr/21amc/109a

1. Identify the various places mentioned in the poem.
2. Read *Let's focus on...* n° 3, p. 114 and link the poem's message to the Commonwealth's work on the environment.
3. Show the reference to bees is related to the Commonwealth.
4. Write a short text explaining the message of the poem.

e-worksheet hatier-clic.fr/21amc/109b

C What exactly is the Commonwealth?

1 What the Commonwealth means to me

A veritable feast of different cultures make up the Commonwealth, but it is tied together by a shared language, values, interests, history, and purpose. In the latest edition of *Overseas*, we speak to ROSL members, music and arts scholars, and recipients of ROSL's humanitarian and education projects from araound the world to find out how they see the Commonwealth.

"In my youth I attended Roedean School in Sussex. One of my best friends, who also grew up in England, had spent her early childhood in India, whilst I had spent five years in South Africa. This week she sent me greetings from Australia where she's now living, having read my piece about my current hometown, Calgary, Canada in the *Overseas*.

That's the Commonwealth in my life – a necklace of countries spanning[1] the globe where you'll likely enjoy use of the English language, connections, common values and some shared education. And of course, the Anglican Church. The Commonwealth has allowed me to explore and make friends in Asia, Australia/New Zealand, Africa, North America and Britain. What a marvellous gift!"

Madeleine King, Calgary Branch President, Canada

"As a young girl, I was always fascinated by the huge diversity of the world with foreign names of cities, their leaders and their cultures all cohabitating on the same Earth. Working at ROSL in London gave me the opportunity to embrace the Commonwealth first hand. This common thread enables us to learn, understand and appreciate our differences."

Lyn Milne, NZ Branch Chair, New Zealand

www.rosl.org.uk

1. covering

2

Commonwealth, also called **Commonwealth of Nations**, formerly (1931-49) **British Commonwealth of Nations**: a free association of sovereign states comprising the United Kingdom and a number of its former dependencies who have chosen to maintain ties of friendship and practical cooperation and who acknowledge the British monarch as symbolic head of their association. In 1965 the Commonwealth Secretariat was established in London to organize and coordinate Commonwealth activities.

Historically, the Commonwealth was an evolutionary outgrowth of the British Empire. […]

Most of the dependent states granted[1] independence chose Commonwealth membership [...].

The Commonwealth differs from other international bodies. It has no formal constitution or bylaws[2]. The members have no legal or formal obligation to one another; they are held together by shared traditions, institutions, and experiences as well as by economic self-interest.

www.britannica.com

1. gave 2. regulation

1. Read texts 1 and 2. Explain what member states have in common, and what differentiates them.
2. Show how the Commonwealth joins these different countries together.
3. Create speech bubbles for the four women in the photo. They are talking about the Commonwealth.

Two sides of the coin

A Commonwealth or Empire?

What is the Commonwealth if not the British Empire 2.0?

While Britain is proud of the institution, its black and brown people are regarded with contempt. […]

This is not a question of conjecture, but of fact. Take Britain's relationship with the African continent, for example. At present, British companies control more than $1 trillion worth of Africa's key resources: gold, diamonds, gas and oil, and an area of land roughly equivalent to four times the size of the UK.

All countries use diplomacy to lobby in their own interests – there is nothing wrong with that. In Britain's case, the Commonwealth has served very nicely to advocate its particular shopping list: liberalised[1], extractor-friendly[2] regimes, low corporate tax rates, and a creative system of tax havens[3] predominantly located in – you guessed it – other Commonwealth countries. As a result, Africa loses £30bn more each year than it receives in aid, loans and remittances[4].

In the Caribbean 14 nations – including a good number of Commonwealth members – are attempting to sue[5] the British government for reparations for four centuries of slavery, and Britain is using jurisdiction issues arising from the Commonwealth to block the claim.

But why, to borrow the words of those who insist slavery left no trace of intergenerational injustice, talk ancient history? This very week, as the Commonwealth flags were proudly flying in Parliament Square, the government finally met Caribbean leaders after a public outcry over the cruel treatment of Windrush citizens forced a U-turn on immigration policy. The Caribbean heads of state wanted to know why Britain, having invited their strong, talented and motivated citizens to this country in the 1960s, has been seeking to deport their children in the 2010s. When the dust of the last minute U-turn has settled[6], the residue will be a realisation that while Britain is proud of the institution of the Commonwealth, its black and brown people are regarded with contempt. […]

Philip Murphy, director of the Institute for Commonwealth Studies at the University of London, has called it "an irrelevant institution wallowing[7] in imperial amnesia". The members like it, some will say, and can vote with their feet. The Commonwealth is ultimately a voluntary organisation – unlike, obviously, the empire – and its members choose to stay. At the end of the empire, only Burma, Aden and the Republic of Ireland did not. Has it been a meaningful choice? For the majority of members, the 32 countries whose population is less than 1.5 million, that's questionable. Having been brought into the globalised economy through the empire, under circumstances advantageous to Britain and not to them, and now grappling with rising sea levels, drug trafficking, high rates of crime, and brain drains that characterise so many small islands, can they really go it alone?

The Guardian, April 17th, 2018

1. freed 2. country that produces raw materials 3. place where little/ no tax is taken 4. payments 5. take to court 6. things calm down 7. lying in

e-worksheet
hatier-clic.fr/21amc/110

1. List the complaints against Britain mentioned in the article.
2. Pick out the problems facing certain members of the Commonwealth.

PAIR WORK

3. Discuss whether Commonwealth members are really free to leave.

Culture Tip

The **Windrush scandal** occurred in 2018 after British subjects were accused of being illegal immigrants. They had arrived in the UK from the Caribbean on the ship Empire Windrush in 1948. 70 years later they were threatened with detention and deportation. At least 83 were deported, many lost their jobs and some were not allowed to return to the UK.

B Spanning the globe

1. Explain what the image represents.
2. Comment on the body language of the people on the globe and compare their colour to the colour of the hands.
3. Imagine what they are saying.

C Famous quotes

"The Commonwealth makes the world safe for diversity."
Nelson Mandela

"At the moment the British Commonwealth is a Commonwealth of White nation."
Mahatma Gandhi

1. Use your background knowledge to explain why these two people thought the way they did.
2. Rephrase the quotes in your own words.

D A Commonwealth kid

1. List the references to Britain and the Commonwealth.
2. Explain the origin of Lenny's conflict.

PAIR WORK

3. One of you is a journalist, the other Lenny Henry. Continue the interview with questions and replies.

Lenny Henry about the Commonwealth

Video hatier-clic.fr/21amc/111a

Culture Tip

Knight is an honorary title given to someone by the monarch in recognition of their contribution to various fields such as acting, sport, charity, etc. The ceremony involves the Queen touching the recepient's shoulders with a sword as (s)he kneels before her.

e-worksheet hatier-clic.fr/21amc/111b

Commonwealth 2.0

A Representing the Commonwealth

1

BIRMINGHAM 2022

XXII COMMONWEALTH GAMES CANDIDATE CITY

HEART OF THE UK, SOUL OF THE COMMONWEALTH

2

3

The Commonwealth

Delivering a Common Future

Connecting, Innovating, Transforming

1. Describe the images and explain how the colours, symbols and logos are reflected in the tweet.
2. Read *Let's focus on...* n° 1, p. 114 and comment on how these images represent the various aspects of the Commonwealth.

GROUP WORK

3. Imagine the conversation between the people in the tweet.

B An uncomfortable past

1. Watch the video and explain the relevance of the participants.
2. Read *Let's focus on...* n° 2, p. 114 and explain what the Commonwealth has done to fight racism and what it still needs to do.

GROUP WORK

3. You are the participants in this meeting. Prepare the questions you will ask Harry and Meghan, and then imagine their answers.

Meghan Markle & Prince Harry on the past of the Commonwealth

Video hatier-clic.fr/21amc/112

C A modern club

1 Maldives accepted back into Commonwealth

Maldives, days after a meeting between Foreign Minister Abdullah Shahid and Secretary General of the Commonwealth, Patricia Scotland in Delhi was readmitted into Commonwealth on Saturday.

Within hours of the decision India congratulated the Government of Maldives on its readmission to the Commonwealth of Nations as its 54th member. "India has always been a key supporter of Maldives' readmission and for it to play a larger role in international organisations and the comity of nations. We are committed[1] to working closely with Maldives on shared Commonwealth goals like development, democracy and peace," MEA[2] said in a statement.

"India also acknowledges the efforts of the government of President Ibrahim Mohamed Solih to participate actively in international organisations like the United Nations and IORA and increase the global profile of Maldives as a democratic, dynamic and responsible member of the comity of nations. India will continue working with Maldives in achieving its democratic and developmental aspirations," according to the MEA statement. […]

Maldives withdrew[3] from the Commonwealth in 2016, under the then President Abdulla Yameen. He had accused the group of interfering with the country's internal affairs after it raised concerns over democracy and human rights. But the Solih government believes being part of Commonwealth will provide young Maldivians with opportunities to get educational scholarships[4] and for the country's athletes to play internationally.

The current government in Male also believes in importance of Maldives being a member of the Commonwealth is in keeping in line with other members of the international community with regard to upholding and promoting human rights, freedom of expression, and democracy.

The Economic Times, Feb. 1st, 2020

1. devoted 2. Ministry of External Affairs (India) 3. leave 4. studies paid for

1. Read text 1. Pick out the reasons the Maldives withdrew from the Commonwealth and the reasons it has returned.
2. Use *Let's focus on…* n° 5, p. 115 to comment on the role of Commonwealth countries during World War II.
3. Read text 2 and pick out the various reasons for creating a peace fund.
4. **CONNECT.** Use both texts to show how the Commonwealth promotes peace and human rights within its member states.

2 India considering new innovation, peace funds for Commonwealth

LONDON: India is in discussions with the Commonwealth of Nations over the introduction of new targeted funds to promote innovation and peace within the 54 member-countries.

Commonwealth Secretary General Baroness Patricia Scotland, who was in India on an official visit recently, said that one of the funds could be named after Sardar Vallabhbhai Patel - India's first Home Minister. […]

"One of the things we are exploring is an opportunity for a Sardar Patel Good Governance Innovation Fund, where India could share some of her wisdom and creativity with the rest of the Commonwealth," she said.

Highlighting India's role during the World Wars as part of the estimated 1.5 million volunteers from the subcontinent, the Secretary General also referred to the possibility of a dedicated peace fund.

"A Peace Fund because we have never needed peace more. We are now living in a very dangerous and volatile world and we need to honour that peace because the world's peace is very fragile right now," she said.

The Economic Times, March 11th, 2020

Let's focus on...

Commonwealth Games 1

The Commonwealth Games, an international sporting event similar to the Olympics, have been held every four years since 1930 (except 1942 and 1946). Unlike the Olympics, disabled athletes are full members of their country's team, and there is equality in the number of women's and men's medal events. The Queen's baton, which contains a message from the Queen, is sent on a relay around the Commonwealth – leaving London on Commonwealth Day, before arriving back at the opening ceremony to be handed back to the Queen who then reads the message aloud to officially open the games.

The Commonwealth and BLM 2

The **Lusaka Declaration on Racism and Racial Prejudice** was signed by the leaders of Commonwealth states in 1979. It declared that the Commonwealth is based on "legal equity, without discrimination or exclusion based on race, colour, sex or national or ethnic origin." However the slow condemnation of Apartheid in South Africa and scandals such as the Windrush affair have led to criticism of racism within the Commonwealth. On 30 June 2020 the Commonwealth Human Rights Initiative (CHRI) published a press statement recognising the need for the Commonwealth to acknowledge and correct its own systematic discrimination, following the worldwide spread of the Black Lives Matter movement. Prince Harry and Meghan Markle spoke to volunteers from the Queen's Commonwealth Trust on this topic in an online meeting in July 2020.

The Commonwealth and the environment 3

Many Commonwealth countries are already affected by climate change, such as Tuvalu, a group of low-lying islands in the South Pacific Ocean that will soon disappear due to rising sea levels. Other Commonwealth countries have been hit by flooding, drought and wildfires. The Commonwealth has been working to protect the environment since its Langkawi Declaration in 1989. The Climate Change Programme enables members to access funding in order to meet the Paris Agreement commitments. The Commonwealth Environmental Water Office works to deliver water where it is needed and to keep rivers flowing correctly to support local nature and avoid flooding.

The Commonwealth and the war 4

The Commonwealth was still referred to as the British Empire at the start of world war II, and many of the countries concerned fought for the Allies as well as supplying raw material and goods for the war effort. The countries governed from London, such as India, African and Caribbean colonies had no choice but to fight for the motherland, whereas the self-governing dominions (Australia, New Zealand, Canada and South Africa) chose to join the war on the side of the Allies. The Irish Free state remained neutral. The British Isles provided the Allied forces with over 8.5 million soldiers, 5 million of these coming from the British mainland.

Timeline

5

The Commonwealth celebrates 70th anniversary of the London Declaration.
2019

Queen Elizabeth II signs Commonwealth Charter- development of free & democratic states.
2013

South Africa rejoins.
1994

Harare declaration on democracy, human rights and equality signed in Zimbabwe.
1991

Langkawi Declaration on Environment signed at Heads of Government Meeting Kuala Lumpur.
1989

Fiji leaves after a military coup.
1987

Commonwealth envoy meets Nelson Mandela in prison and starts negotiating end of Apartheid with South African government.
1986

Lusaka Declaration on Racism and Racial Prejudice.
1979

First Commonwealth Day – second Monday in March (chosen as all Commonwealth children would be in school).
1977

Pakistan leaves to protest Commonwealth recognition of Bangladesh.
1972

Singapore Declaration of Common Principles signed.
1971

South Africa withdraws after criticism of Apartheid regime.
1961

Queen Elizabeth II's coronation. She becomes head of the Commonwealth on her father's (George V) death.
1953

Creation of the modern Commonwealth, all members are "free and equal members of the Commonwealth of Nations, freely co-operating in the pursuit of peace, liberty and progress".
1949

15 million Commonwealth soldiers fight alongside UK in World War II, Canada provides $4 billion in aid, Australia and New Zealand provide material aid to Pacific forces.
1939-45

Australia, Canada, New Zealand and South Africa become the first countries to join the Commonwealth after becoming independent.
1931

First Commonwealth Games.
1930

Prime ministers meeting between British MPs and Dominion leaders to discuss constitutional issues, trade and foreign affairs
Imperial conference – UK and Dominions declare they are equal in status.
1926

First Colonial conference – consultation between Britain and colonies (called Dominions).
1887

The British Empire is described as the Commonwealth of Nations for the first time.
1884

Practice your grammar

Le *pluperfect*

▶ **Le *pluperfect* (aussi appelé *past perfect*)** est formé au moyen **de l'auxiliaire *had* et du participe passé**. Sa forme négative est ***hadn't* (ou *had not*) + participe passé**. Il correspond au plus-que-parfait français.

▶ Le *pluperfect* indique que l'événement auquel renvoie le verbe est **antérieur à un autre événement passé, lui au prétérit**.

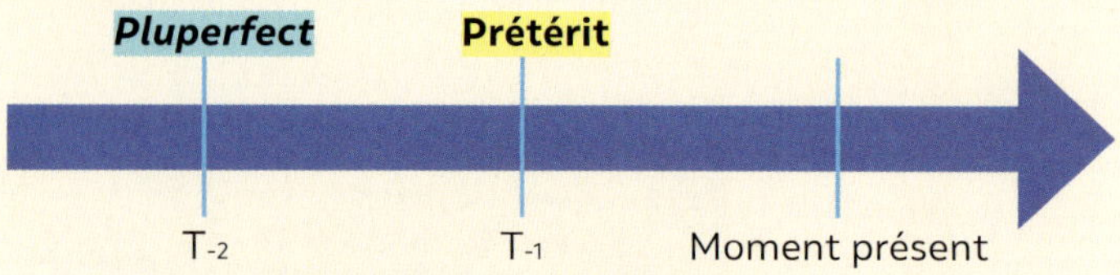

*In my youth I **attended** Roedean School in Sussex. One of my best friends, who also **grew up** in England, **had spent** her early childhood in India.*

Dans cet exemple, les années passées en Inde sont **antérieures** à celles passées en Angleterre.

▶ Il est fréquent de trouver le *pluperfect* avec **des adverbes ou des compléments de temps qui expriment une antériorité** (*just*, *already*, *a few years earlier*, *never before*, *by* + date...).

__By the mid-1960s__, Britain __had granted__ independence to all its colonies in West Africa.

▶ Le *pluperfect* est fréquent dans le **discours indirect**. Il s'agit d'une transposition d'un prétérit ou d'un *present perfect* du discours direct (voir Unit 6).

*"I **spent** my childhood in India," she said. → She said that she **had spent** her childhood in India.*

L'expression du contraste et de la différence

▶ Pour insister sur ce qui différencie deux éléments, il est possible d'employer **les prépositions *unlike* et *contrary to***, qui introduisent des groupes nominaux :

__Unlike South Africa__, Australia is a constitutional monarchy.

▶ **Les conjonctions *whereas* et *while* (alors que)** introduisent une proposition subordonnée :

__While Britain is proud of the institution of the Commonwealth__, its black and brown people are regarded with contempt.

▶ Les adverbes ou locutions adverbiales ***by/in contrast*, *on the contrary* et *conversely*** permettent de relier deux phrases indépendantes et sont **relativement mobiles** dans la phrase.

Australia is a constitutional monarchy headed by Queen Elizabeth II. __By contrast / Conversely__, South Africa is a republic.

1 Mettez le verbe au prétérit ou au *pluperfect*. Attention aux verbes irréguliers.

a. *Mahatma Gandhi ... (be assassinated) in 1948, a few months after India ... (gain) independence.*

b. *Cameroon ... (join) the Commonwealth in 1995, although only a fraction of its territory ... (formerly / be) under British administration.*

c. *Australian swimmer Emma McKeon ... (win) the bronze medal in the women's 200m freestyle at the Olympic Games on Tuesday night. She ... (already / take) part in the 2010 Commonwealth Games in Delhi.*

2 À partir de la chronologie suivante, produisez trois phrases contenant chacune un verbe au *pluperfect*. Utilisez des compléments de temps suivants : *X years after..., before..., X years earlier...*

1931: *Australia, Canada, New Zealand and South Africa become the first countries to join the Commonwealth after becoming independent.*

1961: *South Africa leaves the Commonwealth because of its policy of segregating white and black people.*

1994: *South Africa returns to the Commonwealth as a multi-racial and democratic country, under the leadership of Nelson Mandela.*

3 Complétez les phrases avec l'un des mots suivants : *while, unlike, by contrast, whereas, contrary to.* Indiquez toutes les possibilités.

a. *... many of my classmates were born and raised in the UK, I spent my childhood in Australia.*

b. *... many of my friends, I didn't spend my childhood in the UK.*

c. *In 2015, about 45% of UK goods and services went to the EU. ..., the entire rest of the Commonwealth received around 10% of UK exports.*

d. *... the Republic of Ireland is mainly Catholic, Northern Ireland is almost evenly split between Catholics and Protestants.*

Improve your pronunciation

La prononciation de *th*

▶ La graphie *th* peut être prononcée de deux façons différentes :
- le son de *the* et *this* est représenté par **le symbole /ð/**.
- le son de *think* et *math* est représenté par **le symbole /θ/**.
Pour prononcer ces sons, il faut placer **la pointe de la langue entre les dents**. Quand on prononce /θ/, les cordes vocales ne vibrent pas ; tandis qu'avec /ð/, elles vibrent.

▶ On ne trouve pas ces deux sons dans les mêmes contextes :

/θ/ (*think*)	/ð/ (*this*)
En début ou à la fin de **mots lexicaux** (verbes, noms, adjectifs) : ***Commonwealth***, ***math***, ***mouth***, ***theatre***, ***thin*** Exception : ***smooth***	En début ou à la fin de **mots grammaticaux très courants** (prépositions, pronoms, déterminants...) : ***this***, ***the***, ***them***, ***with***, ***though***, ***then***
	À l'intérieur d'un mot, entre deux voyelles (ou entre un *r* et une voyelle) : ***feather***, ***brother***, ***rather***, ***whether***, ***further*** Exceptions prononcées /θ/ : ***Catholic***, ***Catherine***, ***author***, ***Jonathan***, ***sympathy***, ***method***...

▶ Dans quelques noms propres ou mots étrangers, *th* se prononce /t/ : ***the Thames*** (la Tamise), ***Thomas***, ***Theresa***, ***Thailand***, ***apartheid***.

1 Écoutez et répétez les paires de mots suivantes.

Audio hatier-clic.fr/21amc/117a

a. *myth / miss*
b. *thought / sought*
c. *think / sink*
d. *sick / thick*
e. *seem / theme*

2 Classez les mots dans un tableau en fonction de la prononciation de la graphie *th* : /ð/ ou /θ/. Écoutez l'enregistrement pour vérifier vos réponses et répétez.

Audio hatier-clic.fr/21amc/117b

those • anthem • either • growth • north • northern • Elizabeth • anything • enthusiasm • Catholic • bath • bathe • bother • although • athlete

Les liaisons

▶ On fait une liaison quand un mot terminé par une consonne est suivi d'un autre mot commençant par une voyelle. Ils sont alors prononcés sans pause, comme un seul mot.

The Head‿of the Commonwealth‿is Queen‿Elizabeth II.

▶ On ne fait pas la liaison avant un mot qui commence par un *h* aspiré : ***The Queen* x *heard the bad news.***

⚠ Certains mots commencent par **un *h* muet**. C'est le cas de ***hour***, ***honest***, ***honour***, ***heir***. De plus, le *h* n'est pas toujours prononcé au début **de certains mots grammaticaux** (*he*, *him*, *her*, *his*, l'auxiliaire *have / had*). Il faut faire la liaison avant ces mots : ***with‿him, an‿hour‿ago***.

▶ Quand on fait des pauses dans la phrase (en général représentées à l'écrit par des virgules), on ne fait pas la liaison :

They are held together by shared traditions,* x *institutions,* x *and‿experiences.

▶ En anglais britannique standard, les *r* ne se prononcent normalement pas à la fin des mots (***father***, ***car***). Toutefois, ce *r* réapparaît pour assurer une liaison quand le mot qui suit commence par une voyelle : ***father‿and son***.

3 Recopiez le passage suivant et représentez les liaisons au moyen du symbole ‿. Écoutez l'enregistrement pour vérifier vos réponses et répétez.

Audio hatier-clic.fr/21amc/117c

Maldives, days after a meeting between Foreign Minister Abdullah Shahid and Secretary General of the Commonwealth, Patricia Scotland in Delhi was readmitted into Commonwealth on Saturday. Within hours of the decision India congratulated the Government of Maldives on its readmission to the Commonwealth of Nations as its 54th member.

Build up your vocabulary

The Commonwealth

Politics
- head of state
- rule (v.)
- com**mand**
- power
- adminis**tra**tion
- **lea**dership
- af**fairs**
- repre**sent**

Places
- do**min**ion
- **mi**crostate
- realm
- pro**tec**torate
- re**pub**lic
- **mon**archy
- ori**ent**al
- **aus**tral
- the **An**tipods
- the Far East
- the **Midd**le East
- span (v.)

Organisation
- **by**-law
- insti**tu**tion
- consul**ta**tion
- **em**issary
- com**miss**ioner
- decla**ra**tion
- negoti**a**tion
- as**so**ciate

Nature
- lush
- **vi**brant
- **viv**id
- scarce
- dense
- bare
- **moun**tainous
- **des**olate
- **ar**id

Aims
- grant (v.)
- with**draw**
- pro**mote**
- op**pose**
- re**suce**
- domi**na**tion
- in**eq**uity
- repa**ra**tions

Opinions
- roots
- out**da**ted
- inno**va**tion
- connec**tiv**ity
- sup**port**
- pros**per**ity
- **gov**ernance
- ir**rel**evant
- multi**lat**eralism
- **net**work

1 Complete the phrases with words from the mind map.

a. The aim of the Commonwealth is to … cooperation and trade between the various types of states; … , … or … .

b. The … … … continue to … their country, although the … of the Commonwealth hold a power of … .

2 Find a natural place to complete these phrases. Example: a lush jungle

a. a dense …

b. a desolate …

c. an arid …

d. a bare …

3 Complete the following sentences with word from the mind map.

a. The aims of the Commonwealth are…

b. However some find the Commonwealth…

Projects

1 Write an opinion article giving your views on the Commonwealth.

1. Find in the unit positive and negative points about the Commonwealth, its history and its current role.
2. Research further ideas on the web.
3. Organise your ideas into a balanced selection of views (for and against).
   Don't forget your introduction.
4. Include a conclusion where you will give and justify your own opinion.
5. Write your article and check for spelling and errors.

2 Perform a poem you have written on the Commonwealth.

1. Note your ideas about the Commonwealth and its members.
2. Brainstorm vocabulary from *Build up your vocabulary* p. 118.
3. Remember – poems don't have to rhyme!
4. Write your poem and practise reading it aloud.
5. Check on online dictionary for the pronunciation of any unfamiliar words.

10 Art in the city

The expert's view
hatier-clic.fr/21amc/120a

In the news
hatier-clic.fr/21amc/120b

Projects

- Your high school organises an exhibition entitled "London and NYC: two inspiring world cities?". Choose one artwork and present it.
- Create a video to pay a tribute to NYC or London.

Grammar p. 128 Phonology p. 129

Cities of the world or world cities?

A Particular architectures

1 World Trade Center Transportation Hub, New York

2 Lloyd's Building, London

3 Flatiron Building, New York

4 The Shard, London

GROUP WORK

Group A: picture 1 – Group B: picture 2 – Group C: picture 3 – Group D: picture 4

e-worksheet
hatier-clic.fr/21amc/120c

1. Describe your group's picture.
2. With the help of *Let's focus on...* n° 1 and 2, p. 126-127, take notes about your building.
3. Be ready to ask questions to the other groups and write down their answers.
4. Record a one-minute podcast for the website visitlondon.com or nycgo.com about the building you prefer. Explain why it's your favourite.

B New York's unusual skyline

How New York got its skyline

Video hatier-clic.fr/21amc/121

1. Pick up the rules set up for New York buildings.
2. Explain how architects adapted to these rules with a paragraph and a drawing.
3. Show how these rules defined the New York skyline.
4. **Phonology** Listen to the video and repeat these words: *city, limited, prohibiting, creatively, later*. Describe the pronunciation of the *t* consonant. Are all *t* sounds pronounced this way in the video?
5. Write an email to your best friend describing the particularity of the New York skyline.

C Are cities the new countries?

Do big cities have more in common with each other than with the rest of their own countries?

Are there meaningful comparisons between cities such as New York, London and Shanghai, rather than between nation states?

That is the suggestion of the Organisation for Economic Co-operation and Development (OECD).

Such mega-conurbations have bigger populations and economies than many individual countries – and the think tank argues that they face many similar challenges, whether it is in transport, housing, security, jobs, migration or education.

In a report on global trends shaping education, the OECD says cities could learn from each other's experiences, in a way that would be impossible at the level of national politics. [...]

They are the upsides and downsides of immense concentrations of people living in a small space, often two sides of the same coin.

There are more jobs, but also more unemployed. There are extremes of wealth and poverty. There are highly developed transport systems and then overcrowding as they struggle to cope with the demand.

The bright lights, the economy and innovation attract people which leads to extra pressures on housing and services and arguments over the levels of migration.

Modern mega-cities are highly connected places, but with corresponding levels of people who feel dangerously disconnected. [...]

The modern mega-city is also intensely international. Whether it's food, languages being spoken, local media, the multicultural mix of people, the rapid flux of money, ideas and fashions – these world cities are increasingly unlike anywhere else within their own countries.

They've developed their own cultural and economic micro-climates. Take a London bearded hipster and he might be more at home in Manhattan than a post-industrial part of his own country. [...]

In such diverse cities, what are the values and identities that need to be promoted or rejected? How do we respond to widening extremes of income inequality? How do we prepare young people for such a shifting jobs market?

What does it mean to be an individual in a huge city shaped by the unpredictable trade winds of a global economy?

Living in a mega-city doesn't necessarily make us feel like mega-citizens.

As the OECD guru asks, how do we make people "feel safe and at home in a city that changes rapidly around them?"

Sean Coughlan, www.bbc.com, Jan. 21st, 2016

1. List the issues that big cities have in common according to the OECD.
2. Comment on the evolution of modern mega-cities.
3. Discuss the importance of culture in big cities.
4. **Grammar** Observe this sentence: "*Living (...)* ***make us feel*** *like mega-citizens.*" Complete this statement: "The verb *make* is used when someone forces somebody else to do something. *Make* is followed by an infinitive without ..."
5. You have just moved to New York or London. Post your opinion on food, transportation, identity and evolution on Facebook. Use *Let's focus on...* n° 3, p. 127 to gather information.

The artists' muses?

A London and New York in literature

1 Strolling in the streets of New York City

And so when I began to go on evening walks last fall, I found Morningside Heights an easy place from which to set out into the city. The path that drops down from the Cathedral of St John the Divine and crosses Morningside Park is only fifteen minutes from Central Park. In the other direction, going west, it is some ten minutes to Sakura Park, and walking northward from there brings you toward Harlem, along the Hudson, though traffic makes the river on the other side of the trees inaudible. These walks, a counterpoint to my busy days at the hospital, steadily lengthened, taking me farther and farther afield each time, so that I often found myself at quite a distance from home late at night, and was compelled to return home by subway. In this way, at the beginning of the final year of my psychiatry fellowship, New York City worked itself into my life at walking pace. [...]

At first, I encountered the streets as an incessant loudness, a shock after the day's focus and relative tranquillity; as though someone had shattered the calm of a silent private chapel with the blare of a TV set. I wove my way through crowds of shoppers and workers, through road constructions and the horns of taxicabs. Walking through the busy parts of town meant I laid eyes on more people, hundreds more, thousands even, than I was accustomed to seeing in the course of a day, but the impress of these countless faces did nothing to assuage my feelings of isolation; if anything, it intensified them. I became more tired, too, after the walks began, an exhaustion unlike any I had known since the first months of internship, three years earlier. One night, I simply went on and on, walking all the way down to Houston Street, a distance of some seven miles, and found myself in a state of disorienting fatigue, labouring to remain on my feet. That night I took the subway home, and instead of falling asleep immediately, I lay in bed, too tired to release myself from wakefulness, and I rehearsed in the dark the numerous incidents and sights I had encountered while roaming, sorting each encounter like a child playing with wooden blocks, trying to figure out which belonged where, which responded to which. Each neighborhood of the city appeared to be made of a different substance, each seemed to have a different air pressure, a different psychic weight: the bright lights and shuttered hops, the housing projects and luxury hotels, the fire escapes and city parks. [...] Every decision – where to turn left, how long to remain lost in thought in front of an abandoned building, whether to watch the sun set over New Jersey, or to lope in the shadows on the East Side looking across to Queens – was inconsequential, and was for that reason a reminder of freedom. I covered the city blocks as though measuring them with my stride, and the subway stations served as recurring motives in my aimless progress. [...]

Teju Cole, *Open City*, 2011

1. Compare the way New York City and London are described in each text. Give information about the streets, the period, etc.
2. Pick out information on noise in text 1 and light in text 2. Sum up the atmosphere that prevails.
3. Focus on narration and discuss the differences in terms of point of view. Explain what it reveals about New York City and London.
4. **CONNECT.** Use both texts to compare and contrast how cities are represented in fiction and in today's reality.

e-worksheet
hatier-clic.fr/21amc/122

2 19th century London

It was by this time about nine in the morning, and the first fog of the season. A great chocolate-coloured pall lowered over heaven, but the wind was continually charging and routing these embattled vapours; so that as the cab crawled from street to street, Mr. Utterson beheld a marvelous number of degrees and hues[1] of twilight; for here it would be dark like the back-end of evening; and there would be a glow of a rich, lurid brown, like the light of some strange conflagration; and here, for a moment, the fog would be quite broken up, and a haggard shaft of daylight would glance in between the swirling wreaths[2]. The dismal quarter of Soho

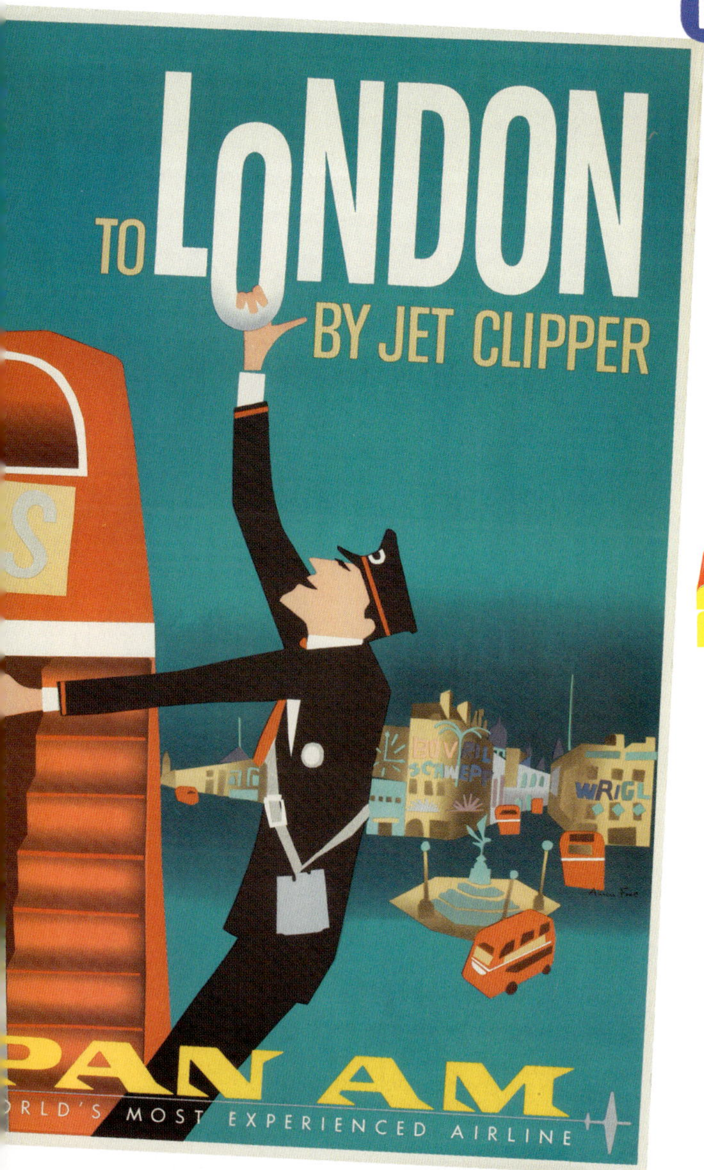

B Art pays tribute to London and New York

New York I Love You

Video hatier-clic.fr/21amc/123

PAIR WORK

1. Pick out the elements related to New York City and London in the documents.
2. Explain how each document pays tribute to New York City or London.
3. Discuss the effects of paying tribute to a city in a song or in an ad.

seen under these changing glimpses, with its muddy ways, and slatternly passengers, and its lamps, which had never been extinguished or had been kindled afresh to combat this mournful reinvasion of darkness, seemed, in the lawyer's eyes, like a district of some city in a nightmare. The thoughts of his mind, besides, were of the gloomiest[3] dye; and when he glanced at the companion of his drive, he was conscious of some touch of that terror of the law and the law's officers, which may at times assail the most honest.

As the cab drew up before the address indicated, the fog lifted a little and showed him a dingy street, a gin palace, a low French eating house, a shop for the retail of penny numbers and twopenny salads, many ragged[4] children huddled in the doorways, and many women of many different nationalities passing out, key in hand, to have a morning glass; and the next moment the fog settled down again upon that part, as brown as umber, and cut him off from his blackguardly surroundings. This was the home of Henry Jekyll's favourite; of a man who was heir to a quarter of a million sterling.

Robert Louis Stevenson, *The Strange Case of Dr Jekyll and Mr Hyde*, 1886

1. shades of colour 2. garland of flowers 3. darkest 4. wearing old clothes

The outsiders' perspective

A Through the eye of foreigners

1

PAIR WORK

Student 1 on document 1 – Student B on document 2

1. With the help of the Culture Tip and the article, give information about your artist or author.
2. Explain the elements that make New York City inspiring and why it is interesting to have a foreign artist depicting the city.
3. Exchange information with your partner and explain how New York City can be seen as an attractive place for foreigners.

Culture Tip

Zbar, also known as Nathan Walsh, is a contemporary realist painter living and working in Wales, United Kingdom. He was born in England in 1972. He is quite interested in big cities such as New York because of its visual complexity. His technique is to paint his model on a piece of paper and to take photos of specific urban areas. Then in his studio in Wales he paints large-scale paintings.

2

Why the world loves New York

I remember so well the first time I visited New York. I was 13, and though I had been to America once before, New York had deliberately been kept from me. The name alone conjured an adult world of glamour and excitement, the mythic New York of the 1980s: Andy Warhol and Studio 54. "It's not a place for children," my mother said firmly.

And my God, was she right! Within moments of our arrival in Manhattan, the gay pride parade started. [...] It was 1994. The AIDS epidemic raged and gay rights were a distant dream; the parade was full of the spirit of revolution.

I did not know at the time that I would later return to the city for the very same freedoms that were being fought for in the street that day. What I do know is that the Delhi prude in me died that June afternoon. I watched my mother's friend, a tall statuesque woman, stride casually into a restroom. When a big, burly man tried to point out that it was the men's toilet, she said, "So? This is New York!" [...]

I now live for part of the year in New York. My husband is here, and the city is my adoptive home. We who are fortunate enough to complain of delayed trains, traffic and astronomical rent often forget the power of the city as a symbol in the world beyond. I lived for years, on the outside, hankering after New York. I had spent one magical year here after college, living as a lodger in the Bowery loft of the feminist writer Kate Millet. [...]

But, all the time that I was away, the city came more and more to seem like a sanctuary. The freedoms that had seemed superficial turned out to have a more profound meaning: New York was where I would return when a populist demagogue took power in

Culture Tip

Aatish Taseer is a British-American writer and journalist. He was born in 1980 in England to Indo-Pakistani parents. He was raised in New Delhi then studied in India and Massachusetts, graduating with a BA in French and political science. He wrote in several British and American newspapers mainly about events related to Pakistan such as the assassination of his father in 2011 or the relation between India and Pakistan.

India. New York was where I would marry, and live freely, with a tall white man from Tennessee. New York was where I would feel insulated when a populist demagogue took power in America.

The Austrian writer Stefan Zweig was in New York a hundred years ago, as his own world of the Austro-Hungarian Empire was on the eve of ruin. He saw "foaming cascades of light in Times Square" and marveled at the city's "captivating nocturnal beauty." One thing that struck Zweig, a Jew who would die by his own hand in 1942 as Nazi night fell over Europe, was this: "No one asked about my nationality, my religion, my origin," he wrote in his memoir. "But there was work waiting for people to do it, and that was all that counted."

This is the New York that endures, and this is the New York that was attacked on a bright blue Halloween afternoon.

Aatish Taseer, www.nytimes.com, Nov. 2nd, 2017

B Through the camera's eye

1 *West Side Story* (1961)

Video hatier-clic.fr/21amc/125a

2 *Mary Poppins* (1964)

Video hatier-clic.fr/21amc/125b

1. List the common points between the two videos (setting, plot, period, etc.).
2. Focus on the characters and comment on the representation of social classes in both videos.
3. **CONNECT.** Give your opinion on the way New York City and London are represented in fiction and art.

Let's focus on...

Architecture in New York City

1

The Santiago Calatrava-designed **World Trade Center Transportation Hub** opened in the spring of 2016. From its initial design through to its final completion, the project proved to be tricky due to its symbolism, its physical complexity, as well as for the number of commuters it would need to accommodate. In 2016, the massive Westfield World Trade Center mall opened up, inside the Oculus (as it is commonly known), hosting some 113 retailers in roughly 365,000 square feet.

The 22-story, steel-framed **Flatiron Building** was completed in 1902. Its wedge shape, designed by architect Daniel Burnham, fitted perfectly into the triangular plot that intersects Broadway and Fifth Avenue in Manhattan. While many buildings at the time were designed with bulky, fortified bases, the Flatiron is consistent from the bottom to the top, making the architecture that much more charming.

Timeline

4

LONDON

- **1666** The Great Fire.
- **1710** St Paul's Cathedral is built and is the tallest building in London (111 meters).
- **1863** The world's first underground railway opens in London.
- **1886** *Dr Jekyll and Mr Hyde* written by Robert Louis Stevenson.
- **Feb. 2, 1901** Funeral procession of Queen Victoria.

NEW YORK CITY

- **1902** Completion of the Flatiron Building.
- **1904** First IRT (The Interborough Rapid Transit Subway) subway line opens with the City Hall station.
- **1916** The 1916 Zoning Resolution is the first citywide zoning code in the US.
- **1930** Construction of the Empire State Building, the world's tallest skyscraper until 1970 with the World Trade Center.
- **1933** Release of the first *King Kong* movie directed by Merian C. Cooper and Ernest B. Schoedsack.
- **1959** Opening of the Guggenheim Museum.

Architecture in London

2

Lloyd's Building, Richard Rogers' famous inside-out building is home to insurance company Lloyd's of London. Taking cues from the Centre Pompidou, this three-tower Bowellist construction features external elevators and service functions, allowing for easy maintenance and flexible, open-plan interiors.

Completed in 2012, Renzo Piano's instantly recognisable **Shard** building is home to a number of restaurants, offices, a hotel, and a viewing gallery. Inspired by the concept of a vertical city, the over 1,000-foot-tall structure is one of the tallest buildings in Europe.

New York and London boroughs

3

1961
Release of the American musical *West Side Story* directed by Robert Wise and Jerome Robbins.

1964
Release of the Walt Disney musical *Mary Poppins.*

1990's
The England-based street artist Banksy (pseudonym) comes to fame.

2000
For the new millenium, several monuments are built in London such as The London Eye on the South Bank of the River Thames or Millenium Bridge, a bridge for pedestrians linking Bankside with the City of London.

May 4, 2000
The election of the new Mayor of London is held for the first time.

May 12, 2000
Opening of the Tate Modern museum.

2001
9/11: attack on the World Trade Center; following its collapse, the Empire State Building becomes the world's tallest skyscraper again until 2012.

April 28, 2004
Opening of the Gherkin at 30 St Mary Axe in the City.

2012
Completion of The Shard, today's tallest building in London.

Spring 2016
Opening of World Trade Center Transportation Hub.

Practice your grammar

Les structures causatives

▶ Une structure causative est l'équivalent de la tournure ***faire faire qc à qn*** en français. Le sujet de la phrase provoque indirectement une action ou un état.

*Mary Poppins **makes me cry**.* → *Mary Poppins* **me fait pleurer**.

▶ Certaines de ces structures sont suivies d'**une base verbale** (l'infinitif sans *to*) : c'est le cas de ***make / have sb do sth***.

*Living in a mega-city doesn't necessarily **make us feel** like mega-citizens.*

⚠ À la voix passive, *to* réapparaît :

*We **were made <u>to</u> wait** in the cold.*

▶ D'autres structures sont suivies de l'infinitif en *to* : ***get / cause sb to do sth***. On utilise aussi l'infinitif en *to* avec des verbes qui ont un sens voisin : ***force / urge / oblige / prompt sb to do sth***.

*Rising rents **caused a lot of people to look** for more affordable housing outside Manhattan.*

▶ *Have* et *get* peuvent parfois être suivis **d'un participe passé (*have / get sth done*)**. Cette construction a **un sens passif**. On l'utilise pour ne pas dire qui a fait directement l'action :

*She **had her car repaired**.* **(= she didn't repair it herself)**

*The multi-millionaire tycoon **had a skyscraper built** near Central Park.*

1 Mettez le verbe à la forme qui convient : infinitif en *to*, base verbale ou participe passé.

a. *This Broadway musical made me ... (laugh).*

b. *Sinatra's song makes me ... (want) to live in NYC.*

c. *We were made ... (queue up) for over an hour in front of the British Museum.*

d. *In the 1970s, an economic recession caused NYC ... (suffer) from economic problems and rising crime rates.*

e. *The mayor had the old theatre ... (demolish) to make way for a new parking lot.*

f. *They're having their pub ... (paint) next week.*

Les adjectifs substantivés

▶ Un adjectif substantivé est **un adjectif utilisé comme un nom**. L'anglais n'utilise pas ce procédé aussi souvent que le français, surtout s'il s'agit de designer des individus particuliers. Ainsi, pour dire **un** *pauvre*, **un** *sans-abri*, etc., l'anglais utilise un adjectif suivi d'un nom : ***a** poor / homeless **person***.

▶ Les adjectifs substantivés en anglais sont uniquement utilisés **avec un sens pluriel et générique** (il s'agit de désigner **un groupe entier** et non des individus particuliers). Ils sont précédés de l'article défini ***the*** et restent **invariables** (ils ne prennent jamais de -*s* au pluriel). Ils sont également suivis d'**un verbe au pluriel**.

__The homeless need__ more than shelter and three meals a day.

⚠ Il est donc possible de remplacer un adjectif substantivé par **adjectif + *people*** précédé de **l'article Ø** :

__Ø Homeless people__ need more than shelter and three meals a day.

▶ Les **adjectifs de nationalité qui se terminent par *-ese*, *-ch* ou *-ish*** sont souvent employés de cette manière (***the** French*, ***the** English*, ***the** Dutch*, ***the** Chinese*). On désigne alors le peuple tout entier :

__The French don't celebrate__ Thanksgiving.

*Manhattan Island was purchased by **the Dutch** from the native peoples who originally lived there.*

⚠ Pour traduire ***un** Français* et ***un** Anglais*, il faudra dire ***a** Frenchman* et ***an** Englishman*.

▶ Les adjectifs de nationalité qui se terminent par ***-(i)an*** peuvent être employés comme des noms ordinaires et prennent donc un **-*s*** au pluriel : *Canadians*, *Americans*, *Italians*, etc.

2 Traduisez.

a. Il faut construire plus de refuges pour les sans-abris.

b. Quelques sans-abris vivent dans ce quartier du Bronx.

c. Au 19e siècle à Londres, les vieux et les malades vivaient souvent dans la pauvreté.

d. New York a été fondée par les Hollandais et fut baptisée New Amsterdam en 1624. Elle fut occupée puis annexée par les Anglais en 1664.

e. De nos jours, les riches deviennent plus riches et les pauvres deviennent plus pauvres.

Improve your pronunciation

Voyelles longues et voyelles brèves

▶ On classe souvent les 12 voyelles simples de l'anglais en deux groupes : **les voyelles brèves et les voyelles longues**. Le symbole **ː** est utilisé pour indiquer que la voyelle est longue.

Voyelles longues		Voyelles brèves	
/iː/	*seat, sheep, keen*	/ɪ/	*sit, ship, kin*
/ɑː/	*cart, park, dark*	/æ/	*cat, pack, back*
/uː/	*food, group, Luke*	/ʊ/	*cook, good, look*
/ɜː/	*girl, burn, world*	/ʌ/	*cut, duck, sun*
/ɔː/	*short, bought, law*	/ɒ/	*hot, God, not*
		/e/	*bed, net, head*
		/ə/	*alive, an, the*

▶ En position accentuée, une voyelle suivie d'un *r* (en fin de mot ou avant une consonne) est toujours **longue** (*car*, *short*, *park*, *girl*).

▶ **Les voyelles brèves** (à l'exception du *schwa* /ə/) n'apparaissent jamais en fin de mot et sont toujours précédées d'une consonne.

▶ **La voyelle /ə/** appelée *schwa* est la voyelle la plus fréquente de l'anglais : elle ressemble à un *e* muet français et a la particularité de ne jamais apparaître dans une syllabe accentuée.

1 Écoutez les paires suivantes. Dites chaque fois si la voyelle est longue ou brève. Indiquez si la graphie nous donne une indication. Répétez les mots.

Audio hatier-clic.fr/21amc/128a

a. *shot / short*
b. *sport / spot*
c. *seat / sit*
d. *kin / keen*
e. *fool / full*

2 Les graphies soulignées représentent-elles des voyelles longues ou des voyelles brèves ? Écoutez l'enregistrement pour vérifier vos réponses et répétez.

Audio hatier-clic.fr/21amc/128b

C<u>e</u>ntral Park is New Y<u>or</u>k's l<u>ar</u>gest <u>ur</u>ban p<u>ar</u>k. <u>I</u>t contains lakes, <u>a</u> castle, the Metropolitan Museum of <u>Ar</u>t, and a z<u>oo</u>.

Anglais britannique et anglais américain

▶ **Quand un *r* suit une voyelle** (en fin de mot ou avant une consonne), il ne se prononce pas en anglais britannique standard. En revanche, **la plupart des Américains prononcent ces *r*** :

park /pɑːk/ **(GB)** /pɑːrk/ **(US)**

▶ **Quand un *t* se situe entre deux voyelles** (ou entre un *r* et une voyelle) en anglais américain, on le prononce comme un *d* rapide et très doux appelé ***flap t*** : *better*, *later*, *party*...

▶ **Certains *t* disparaissent pratiquement** quand ils sont situés entre un *n* et une voyelle : *interview*, *twenty*, *center*. Cette prononciation n'est pas systématique, toutefois.

▶ Le son /juː/ de *new* en anglais britannique est prononcé /uː/ (comme dans *food*) après certaines consonnes en anglais américain. C'est le cas après un *n* (*new*), un *d* (*due*), un *s* (*pursuit*), un *t* (*Youtube*)...

▶ Le son de /ɒ/ que l'on trouve en anglais britannique dans *not* ou *hot* n'existe pas en anglais américain. Il est remplacé par la voyelle /ɑː/, un son plus long et plus ouvert. La voyelle longue /ɔː/, que l'on trouve dans *law* ou *thought*, est aussi remplacée par /ɑː/.

! Vous pouvez choisir la variété d'anglais qui vous plaît (britannique standard, américaine, voire australienne, écossaise...). **Veillez simplement à être cohérent.e.s** et à ne pas mélanger plusieurs variétés.

3 Vous allez entendre des mots prononcés par un Britannique, puis par un Américain. Dites ce qui les différencie. Répétez la forme que vous aurez choisie.

Audio hatier-clic.fr/21amc/128c

a. *short* **b.** *park*
c. *girl* **d.** *party*
e. *here* **f.** *substitute*
g. *better* **h.** *matter*
i. *not* **j.** *law*

4 Vous allez entendre une phrase prononcée par un Américain. Identifiez les traits typiquement américains de sa prononciation.

Audio hatier-clic.fr/21amc/128d

Manhattan is the most densely populated borough of New York City, its economic and administrative center, and the city's historical birthplace.

Build up your vocabulary

London & New York City

Visual aspects
- **breath**taking view
- ins**pi**ring
- **attrac**tive/**appea**ling
- de**pict**/de**scribe**
- paint
- **pain**ting/**art**work
- **paint**brush
- (large) scale
- **cap**ture
- street art
- street **ar**tist
- **sten**cil
- gra**ffi**ti

Architecture
- **ar**chitect
- **sky**line
- **buil**ding
- **sky**scraper
- bridge
- streets
- shape

Urban planning
- **land**scape
- **ur**banscape/ **ci**tyscape
- height
- width
- de**sign** (v.+n.)
- a set of rules
- **buil**ding regu**la**tions
- in**ge**nious
- environ**men**tal
- **struc**tured
- re**fur**bish
- **re**novate
- re**build**
- trans**form**

Filming NYC and London
- film/**mo**vie/**mo**tion **pic**ture
- scene
- **set**ting
- **cam**era
- pay a **tri**bute/ praise/ **cel**ebrate
- point of view/ **view**point
- shot
- shoot
- **cam**era **an**gle
- high-**an**gle shot/ low-**an**gle shot

1 Complete the sentences using words from the mind map.

a. I have visited New York City dozens of times but I am still impressed by its ... .

b. I think the Chrysler Building and the Empire State Building are the most beautiful ... .

c. In New York City, a set of rules was set for the ... of high buildings.

d. Even if I have been living in London for years, I have never been to the ... of Chelsea.

e. The ... of London are called Londoners.

2 Imagine an Instagram post using five words from the mind map to create your hashtags.

3 Complete the dialogues with words from the mind map:

a. "Did you know that in London, there is a borough where many ... draw graffiti on street walls? "
"No, I didn't!"

b. "Some ... had a lot of imagination to create such beautiful buildings in New York City and London!
"I completely agree! To me, London and New York City are the two most ... cities in the world."

c. "Have you ever seen the ... *West Side Story*?"
"No, why?"
"It's impressive how they managed to ... the city of New York perfectly."

d. "In London, there are many ... that go over the River Thames and link different parts of the city."
"That's true, but what I prefer is the way buildings are ... .

Projects

1

Your highschool organises an exhibition entitled "London or NYC: two arty world cities?" Choose one artwork studied in the unit or taken from the web and write down its presentation.

1 Gather information about the artwork.
- Go through the unit or the web and list as much information as possible.
- Link it to New York City or London's architecture, history, etc.
- Go to https://fr.nycgo.com/ or https://www.visitlondon.com/ for more inspiration.

2 Organise your ideas.
- List the elements you want to mention in your presentation.
- Go from the most obvious to the most implicit.

3 Present and describe your document.
- Make a small presentation of the context (the city, the artist, the period, etc.).
- Use *be + -ing* to describe it.

4 Make your presentation attractive!
- You can create a slideshow or use an app like *Genially*.
- Add symbols of New York City or London.

2

Create a video to promote the importance of art in New York City or London.

1 Choose the city you want to pay tribute to.
- Decide if you want to make a vlog, a promotional video or a video clip.
- Choose a title, a catchy slogan and some music.

2 List the elements you can use to be convincing.
- Look through the unit or on the web to find information.
- Use the adjectives studied in this unit and expressions such *as what a* + adj + noun! or *such a* + adj + noun!

3 Prepare the script of your video.
- The elements of your video : buildings, songs, extracts from novels, ads, etc.
- Choose ten words from the mind-map that you will include.

4 Practice and record your video.
- Go to the website www.wordreference.com to check the pronunciation of new words.
- Practise to be able to speak for around two minutes.
- Only use notes: do not read!

11 Religion in the USA: (dis)uniting?

The expert's view
hatier-clic.fr/21amc/132a

In the news
hatier-clic.fr/21amc/132b

Projects
- Prepare a presentation entitled "10 facts about religion in America."
- Comment on the Pledge of Allegiance in a TV show.

Grammar p. 140 Phonology p. 141

Roots of religion

A The religious landscape of the USA

The U.S. as 100 people: South home to 37, most of whom are Protestants

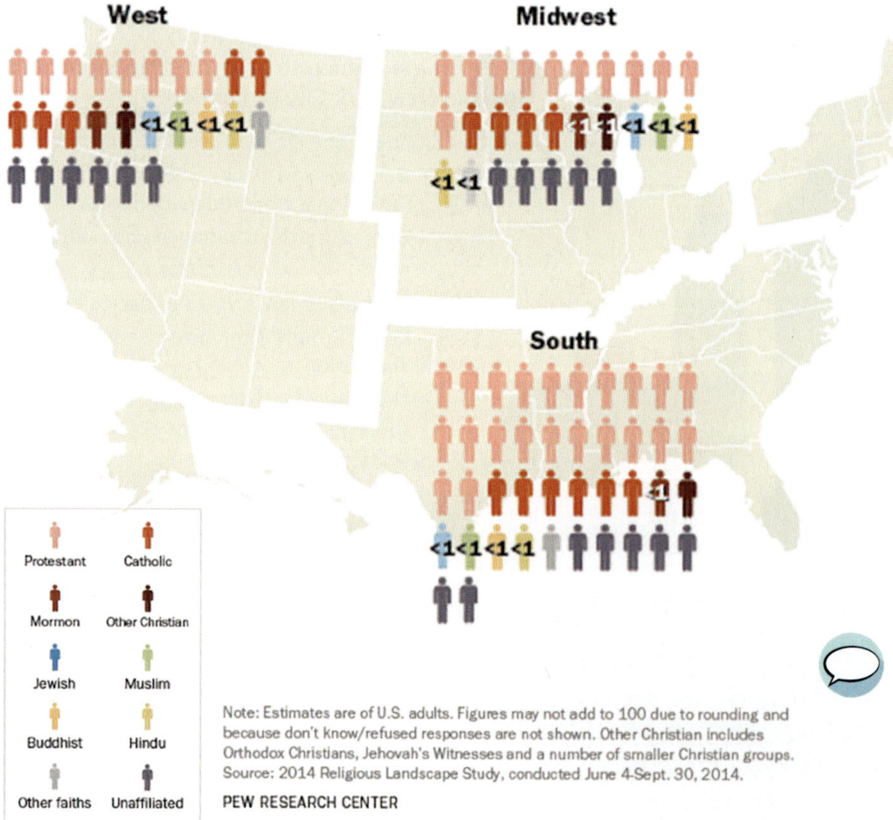

Note: Estimates are of U.S. adults. Figures may not add to 100 due to rounding and because don't know/refused responses are not shown. Other Christian includes Orthodox Christians, Jehovah's Witnesses and a number of smaller Christian groups.
Source: 2014 Religious Landscape Study, conducted June 4-Sept. 30, 2014.
PEW RESEARCH CENTER

1. Read *Let's focus on...* n° 2, p. 138 and comment on the high percentage of Protestants.
2. Describe the breakdown of the different religions in the USA.
3. Identify the geographical zone called "The Bible Belt" and explain this term.
4. You work for Pew Research Center. Present this graph.

B Religion: an American way of Life

Document 1

1. Define secularism and explain how America and Europe deal with it.
2. Read *Let's focus on...* n° 4, p. 139 and explain what is said about the Mormons.
3. Define the part science plays in the evolution of religion in the USA.

1 Why Americans are more religious than Europeans

Audio hatier-clic.fr/21amc/133a

@ **e-worksheet** hatier-clic.fr/21amc/133d

2 Obama's 2013 inauguration

Audio hatier-clic.fr/21amc/133b **Video** hatier-clic.fr/21amc/133c

Document 2

4. Listen to the audio first, then watch the video. Illustrate how religion is deeply rooted in American political life.
5. **Phonology** Listen and repeat the following words: *second, officially, Lincoln, Washington, commemorate*. Focus on the pronunciation of the letter *o*. Identify the stressed syllables. Is the vowel *o* stressed in these words?
6. **CONNECT.** Using both documents, write a short paragraph on the place of religion in the USA.

C Religion comes to America

The legacy of the pilgrims and the puritans is foundational. The work ethic. The fact Americans don't take much annual holiday. Notions of self-reliance and attitudes towards government welfare. Laws that prohibit young adults from drinking in bars until the age of 21. A certain prudishness. The religiosity. […]

All these national traits have traceable roots to the Puritans. The Frenchman Alexis de Tocqueville even wrote in his seminal work, *Democracy in America*: "I think we can see the whole destiny of America contained in the first Puritan who landed on these shores."

The Pilgrim Fathers – or more accurately, the Pilgrim Mothers – also created a gene pool from which tens of millions of Americans continue to draw. So many US citizens claim to have ancestors who arrived on the Mayflower that you'd be forgiven for thinking this three-sailed vessel was the size of an aircraft carrier.

For all that, just about the only time the Pilgrim Fathers loom large[1] in the national imagination is on Thanksgiving, that pre-Christmas feast of turkey and pumpkin pie when the whole of America comes to a calorific halt. This national holiday derives from the celebration marking the first harvest in 1621, when the colonists sat down with the Wampanoag Native Americans. It's been packaged up as an act of peaceful co-existence, a convivial banquet which suggests that the Pilgrim Fathers were welcomed by indigenous Americans with open arms. […]

That dominance persists to this day. A country colonised by Anglo-Saxon Protestants continues to favour Anglo-Saxon Protestants. Not until 1960 did America elect a Catholic president, John Fitzgerald Kennedy, a politician of Irish stock. Joe Biden is seeking to become only the second.

There's also a class dimension to WASP culture that means the Pilgrim Fathers are hardly regarded as populist heroes, the poster boys of the present incumbent[2] of the White House and his Make America Great Again supporters. WASP culture has traditionally been an upper class preserve, reinforced through marriage, inheritance, patronage, and elite schools and universities.

www.bbc.com

1. have great importance
2. Donald Trump

1. List the characteristics passed down from America's religious past.
2. Read *Let's focus on...* n° 5, p. 139. Show the impact of religion on American life today.

Religion debated

A Welcome to the club

1. Describe the cartoon and explain which religions are presented.
2. Analyse the visual and explain the artist's intentions.
3. Interview the cartoonist about his message.

B The pledge of allegiance under scrutiny

1. Sum up what happened to X.F.
2. Read the Pledge of Allegiance and explain XF's reaction.
3. Use some of the words from Court Justice Robert Jackson's quote (introduction) to comment on this event.
4. **Grammar** Pick out all the verbs in the passive voice. How are they formed? Turn the passive sentences into active sentences.
5. The headteacher of the school reacts to the decision. Write his/her tweet.

Forcing children to pledge allegiance is undesirable and unconstitutional. So why is it still happening?

Supreme Court Justice Robert Jackson explained that "no official, high or petty[1], can prescribe what shall be orthodox in politics, nationalism, religion, or other matters of opinion."

A 16-year-old junior at Lebanon High School in Eastern Pennsylvania is suing[2] his school district in federal court claiming his civil rights have been violated. As is the case across much of the country, everything at Lebanon High comes to a standstill for a minute or so every day as students recite the Pledge of Allegiance. Across the country, most people stand for the ritual, but every now and then someone chooses not to participate. This is usually less a problem than a curiosity. Right until it isn't.

Unconstitutional coercion

According to X.F.'s account (minor litigants are not mentioned by name), a teacher required him to stand for the pledge. When he refused, he was disciplined[3]. Repeatedly. After a number of in-school suspensions, X.F. was given a copy of the district's policy on the matter, which seems quite clear. "Each student shall," the policy reads, "be required to salute the flag and recite the Pledge of Allegiance during each day's opening exercises."

The policy goes on to say that conscientious objectors will be permitted to opt out[4] if they "maintain a respectful attitude throughout the ceremony," and if their parents "furnish the school with a written statement of their child's conscientious objection."

All of this is patently unconstitutional, and any educator – let alone[5] one who works for a government school – should know as much.

https://fee.org, Feb. 19th, 2020

1. low, inferior 2. taking to court 3. punished 4. not participate 5. let alone: not to mention

C Religion gets politicised

US election 2020: Trump says opponent Biden will 'hurt God'

7 August

US election 2020

BBC

Opinion

God help us: Religion's influence on the 2020 presidential election

Oct. 13, 2020 at 2:48 pm | Updated Oct. 13, 2020 at 2:48 pm

The Seattle Times

GROUP WORK

Group A on document C
Group B on document D

1. Sum up the issue mentioned in your article (topic, problems, consequences).
2. Read the headlines and identify the issues at stake.
3. Explain how religion interferes with politics and why it can be controversial.
4. Share your findings with the other group.
5. Debate with a partner: Does religion help Americans stand together?

Christianity for votes: How Republicans are using a religious facade to gain political power

Talk of God has been brought into and out of national politics throughout American history, with various partisan and non-partisan causes, but rarely in our history has any political group weaponized[1] faith for political goals as comprehensively as today's Republican Party. […]

The contradictory nature of devotional statements made by GOP[2] members was put on full display in a recent scandal in Congress, when Rep. Ted Yoho, R-Florida, was forced to resign from a Christian organization's board after publicly exhibiting a behavior profoundly opposite to the values he claimed to stand for.

The sinister nature of an ideology that weaponizes faith to justify divisive and dehumanizing rhetoric left little to the imagination as Yoho laid out his non-apology speech on the House floor for calling a fellow member of Congress, Rep. Alexandria Ocasio-Cortez (D-New York), a "f—-g b—h" while standing in front of the Capitol building. Not only did he not acknowledge how his actions were antithetical to Christian values, he also doubled-down on denying that he ever said the words that both Rep. Alexandria Ocasio-Cortez and a reporter from The Hill, who was a witness at the scene, had clearly heard. In the end of his non-apology speech, Yoho remarkably argued: "I cannot apologize for my passion or for loving my God, my family, and my country."

Jordan Rynning, www.minnpost.com, Aug. 2020

1. adapt sth as a weapon 2. (Grand Old Party) = nickname for the Republican Party

D Scientific progress versus religion

Many Americans die each day from diseases affecting the heart, liver, kidneys, brain and a whole host[1] of other bodily organs. Scientific researchers are constantly trying to develop new treatments for such medical conditions. Presently, the research community is working hard to develop medical treatments using stem cells[2] from human embryos. […] The expectation is that the stem cells will repair the patient's heart or other organs by curing diseases and otherwise improving the patient's medical condition and life expectancy. The only problem is that embryonic stem cell research is controversial because the embryos from which the researchers extract stem cells are destroyed during the extraction process. Some religious groups believe that the destruction of the embryos is immoral because embryos, even at the five-day developmental stage, have the same value as post-birth humans.

www.researchgate.net

1. whole host of: many 2. cells from which all other cells are generated

E Religion suffocates

Unorthodox (Anne Winger, 2020)

Video hatier-clic.fr/21amc/135

1. Watch the trailer and focus on the countries, the languages and the religion depicted.
2. Explain the heroine's reaction and illustrate her sentence: "God expected too much of me" with examples from the video.
3. Comment on the title *Unorthodox*.
4. You work for the film company. Write a short synopsis of the series to be published in a Netflix ad.

E pluribus unum

A The Amish way of life

Pennsylvania's Amish Country

Video hatier-clic.fr/21amc/136a

1. Sum up where the ancestors of the Amish came from and why they settled in Pennsylvania.
2. Account for their specific way of life and give examples.
3. Explain what the tradition of *Rumspringa* (= "running around") is and what it consists in.
4. Imagine the conversation an Amish teenager could have with his / her parents after his / her *Rumspringa*.

e-worksheet hatier-clic.fr/21amc/136b

B Freedom of worship then and now

1. Describe the visuals and the artist's depiction.
2. Read *Let's focus on…* n° 3, p. 139 and explain the context of *Freedom of Worship* by Norman Rockwell.
3. **CONNECT.** Use the two documents to comment on the diversification of religions in the USA.

Norman Rockwell,
Freedom of Worship, 1943

C Protecting religious freedom

Religious liberty should do no harm

The United States was founded on the principle of religious liberty – a principle that is now under threat. At the nation's outset[1], lawmakers established a unique society without a government-established religion, which is cemented in the First Amendment to the Constitution, and sanctioned rights for religious people. They also protected the rights of religious institutions and ensured that all Americans could express a diverse range of beliefs without interference from the government. In recent years, however, the right to religious liberty has increasingly been exploited and misused in order to favor the interests of select, privileged conservative Protestant Christians over the basic rights of the most vulnerable Americans.

The principle of religious liberty should extend to all people, not only ones who come from a specific set of religious beliefs. A 2014 study from the Pew Research Center reveals that the religious landscape in the United States is changing. As the Christian population is declining – particularly among mainline[2] Protestants and Catholics – the number of adults who do not identify with a specific religion is growing. With the changing demographics of Americans and their religious connections, it is even more important that people of all faiths[3] and people of no faith are granted the fundamental right to religious liberty.

Protecting religious liberty continues to be a priority for a majority of Americans: Almost two-thirds believe that there should be a "strict separation" between church and state, and nine out of 10 agree that the United States was founded with universal religious freedom that extends to people of all religions. Policymakers have an opportunity and a responsibility to enact policies that will ensure the right of religious liberty for all Americans without infringing[4] on the rights and religious freedoms of others. This report provides a menu of administrative and legislative options at the federal, state, and local levels to ensure that the right to religious liberty extends to all Americans – not solely those with the loudest voices, most power, or strongest political connections. In America – a country that has codified the necessity of freedom of religion for all – religious liberty policies should reflect the moral values of equality, inclusion, and freedom for all to live without fear of discrimination.

www.americanprogress.org, April 2019

1. beginning 2. traditional 3. religions 4. not respect

Hank Willis Thomas, Emily Shur, *Freedom of Worship*, 2018

1. Compare and contrast religious freedom when the First Amendment was written with now.
2. Analyse the statistics and say how the religious landscape in the US is changing.
3. Explain how religious liberty could be protected.
4. Record the teaser for the upcoming radio show entitled "Religious liberty should do no harm."

Let's focus on

The Pledge of Allegiance

1

Americans have been pledging allegiance to their flag for more than one hundred years. However, the first idea for a verbal pledge started in 1885 during the American Civil War, when Colonel George Balch created the vow "We give our heads and our hearts to God and our country; one country, one language, one flag."

This was quickly replaced by a salute composed by Francis Bellamy, a former Baptist, minister in 1892. He had been asked to come up with a new pledge that could be used for the 400th commemoration of Christopher Columbus' arrival in the new world.

He decided on the vow "I pledge allegiance to **my flag** and the republic for which it stands, one nation, indivisible, with liberty and justice for all."

This vow was popular in public schools for a number of years, with slight alterations. For instance, in 1923 it was changed to "I pledge allegiance to **the flag of the United States of America**..."

Congress officially agreed, in 1942, that citizens should recite the pledge while putting the right hand over the heart.

Then in "West Virginia State Board of Education v. Barnette" (1943), the Supreme Court confirmed that such ideological dogma was directly opposed to the principles of the country and ruled that public school students were not required to say the Pledge if they didn't feel concerned.

The final version of the pledge arrived in 1954 in the context of the Cold War. President Eisenhower passed a bill adding the words 'Under God' and since then the Pledge of Allegiance has not changed.

Fun facts

Did you know that Bellamy first thought about using the French revolution slogan *Liberté, Égalité, Fraternité*?

The Mayflower

2

In September 1620, the ship The Mayflower left Plymouth, England with a hundred men and women. Most of them were fleeing religious persecution, others were on board just to be sure of a safe passage and didn't have any religion. Thirty-five of them were radical Puritans who had been living in the Netherlands for 10 years after breaking with the Church of England. Others were Separatists, named 'the Pilgrim Fathers' only in 1820, who had a much more tolerant approach to religion. The repressive policies adopted by King James I and his successor, Charles I, toward religious nonconformists caused many people to follow the Pilgrims to the New World over the next decades.

Norman Rockwell's *Four Freedoms* 3

On January 6th, 1941, President Franklin D. Roosevelt used his State of the Union address to explain to Americans how their country was being affected by World War II events occurring across the Atlantic in Europe. At this time, America had not yet entered into the war and some citizens were calling for an act of neutrality to prevent precisely this. Roosevelt gave his speech focusing on the peace and harmony that Americans should fight to preserve, founded on four essential freedoms:

- Freedom of speech and expression
- Freedom of worship
- Freedom from want
- Freedom from fear

Norman Rockwell (1894-1978), an American illustrator, who drew the cover page for the *Saturday Evening Post* for around 40 years, was profoundly affected by Roosevelt's speech. He wanted to depict the four freedoms in visual terms to help Americans to understand both the significance of the President's words and the importance of the war effort. Rockwell's four paintings were published in the *Saturday Evening Post* from February to March 1943.

The Mormons 4

Mormonism is a Christian religious movement, founded by Joseph Smith. In 1819, he said he had had a vision from God asking him not to join a Christian denominal church. Furthermore, the angel Moroni told Smith to translate the sacred *Book of Mormon*, which had been written in the fourth century and named after Moroni's father, Mormon. Following the publication of the *Book of Mormon* in 1830, a divine revelation, the religion became official. Mormons belong to The Church of Latter-Day-Saints, whose headquarters are in Salt Lake City, Utah. They follow Christian principles but also have their own set of values and ethics. Their lifestyle is strict: they consume no coffee, tea, tobacco or alcohol. Missionary work is encouraged as are acts of kindness and respect for authority.

Jean Leon Gerome Ferris, *The First Thanksgiving, 1621*, 1912

The WASPs 5

The acronym WASP stands for White Anglo-Saxon Protestant. Although WASPs had been around for a while, probably since the American revolution, the social science term was first used in 1948. It describes a stereotypical group of white people who were traditionally of British upper class descent and practiced the Anglican religion. These elite families often lived in states on the eastern seaboard such as New England, enjoying a particularly privileged lifestyle. Their wealthy background, coming from "old money," led to positions of power within economic and political fields, in addition to domination in social and cultural spheres.

Practice your grammar

Le passif des verbes à deux compléments

▶ **Les verbes à deux compléments** tels que *give* ou *send* peuvent être mis **à la voix passive (*be* + participe passé)**. Dans ce cas, les deux compléments sont susceptibles de devenir le sujet de la phrase passive :

*The Indians **gave** the colonists furs and food.*

→ *The colonists **were given** furs and food (by the Indians).*

→ *Furs and food **were given** to the colonists (by the Indians).*

▶ Voici d'autres verbes à deux compléments susceptibles d'être mis à la voix passive : ***offer, show, teach, send, tell, ask, promise, grant…***

*The Pilgrims **were taught** how to grow corn and squash by the indigenous Wampanoag people.*

▶ Notez également les structures passives suivantes suivies d'un infinitif en *to* : ***be told / asked / required / expected / forbidden to do sth***

*Students **are required** to recite the Pledge of Allegiance.*

⚠ Ces structures n'ont pas d'équivalent en français. Il faudra donc les traduire par des phrases à la voix active.

1 **Mettez les verbes en gras à la voix passive en exprimant l'agent si nécessaire.** Commencez la phrase par l'amorce proposée.

a. *Someone **sent** me a postcard from Salt Lake City. → I…*

b. *Someone **told** me that Americans were more religious than Europeans. → I…*

c. *In 1520, King James **granted** the Pilgrims permission to settle in North America. → The Pilgrims…*

d. *I remember the first time somebody **asked** me about my religious beliefs. → I remember the first time I…*

e. *The teacher **required** the boy to stand for the Pledge of Allegiance. → The boy…*

2 **Quelles sont les règles que les Amish doivent suivre dans leur communauté ?** Aidez-vous de la vidéo p. 136 ou d'Internet. Utilisez les structures passives suivantes suivies d'un infinitif en *to* : *be required / expected / forbidden / asked / told (not) to do sth*. Produisez cinq phrases.

Ex. : *The Amish are forbidden to own cars.*

Les inversions sujet – auxiliaire

▶ Quand une phrase commence par certains adverbes ou expressions, il n'est pas rare que l'**on inverse le sujet et son auxiliaire**. C'est le cas avec *never* :

They had never celebrated Thanksgiving before.

→ *Never (before) had they **celebrated** Thanksgiving.*

⚠ Ces inversions sont surtout utilisées dans la langue écrite, voire soutenue et académique.

▶ Les expressions qui déclenchent cette inversion ont très souvent **un sens négatif ou sont précédées de *no* ou *not*** : *rarely / seldom* (rarement), *not until…*, *not only (but…)*, *under no circumstances*, *in no way*, etc.

*Not only did the first colonists **suffer** from the cold, **but** many of them **also** died of hunger and disease.*

▶ Notez également **les expressions temporelles** suivantes qui utilisent ces inversions : *hardly / barely… when…* (à peine… que…) et *no sooner… than…* (aussitôt… que…).

*No sooner had the Pilgrim Fathers **landed** in America than they met the Wampanoag Indians.*

⚠ Lorsque le verbe est au présent ou au prétérit simple, **l'auxiliaire *do / did*** apparaît dans ces inversions. Le verbe qui le suit est toujours une base verbale :

*Not until 1960 did America **elect** a Catholic president, J. F. Kennedy.*

3 **Reformulez les phrases en utilisant une inversion sujet – auxiliaire.** Utilisez les amorces proposées.

a. *His parents rarely went to church. → Rarely…*

b. *I'm in no way a religious person. → In no way…*

c. *The Amish can't own cars. → Under no circumstances…*

d. *In the US, the Christian population is not only declining, but the number of people who do not identify with a specific religion is also growing. → Not only… but…*

e. *White evangelical voters not only support President Trump but also make up the core of his electoral base. → Not only… but…*

f. *The first colonists had never seen a turkey before. → Never before…*

Improve your pronunciation

La voyelle /ə/ et la réduction vocalique

▶ **La voyelle /ə/ (aussi appelée *schwa*)** est l'un des sons les plus fréquents de l'anglais. Il s'agit d'une voyelle très brève qui ressemble à un *e* muet français (comme dans ***pe**tit*). La bouche est légèrement plus ouverte.

▶ Le *schwa* n'est pas une voyelle comme les autres : **elle n'apparaît que dans des syllabes inaccentuées.**

▶ Lorsqu'une syllabe d'un mot est inaccentuée en anglais, **sa voyelle est souvent réduite**. Cela signifie qu'elle est très brève, peu audible et prononcée **/ə/** (ou parfois **/ɪ/** comme dans *big*) : **l'accentuation influence donc la prononciation des voyelles en anglais.**

*A**mend**ment* /ə'mendmənt/ oOo

***Pro**testant* /'prɒtɪstənt/ Ooo

▶ **Les mots grammaticaux d'une syllabe** sont en général inaccentués dans la phrase. Leur voyelle est aussi souvent réduite en schwa. Il s'agit en particulier des articles *a(n)* et *the*, de certains auxiliaires (*can, be, have*), de pronoms personnels (*them, us*), de conjonctions (*and, but*) ou de prépositions (*of, for, from*), etc.

I can /kən/ *help them* /ðəm/.

1 **Recopiez les mots et soulignez la syllabe accentuée.** Vérifiez vos réponses en écoutant l'enregistrement. Les voyelles des syllabes inaccentuées sont-elles toujours réduites et prononcées /ə/ ? Répétez les mots.

Audio hatier-clic.fr/21amc/141a

tolerance • allegiance • freedom • foundation • Mormon • gospel • tradition • Boston • government • amendment

2 **Écoutez l'enregistrement et soulignez les mots grammaticaux inaccentués.** Dites lesquels sont réduits et prononcés avec la voyelle schwa **/ə/.** Répétez.

Audio hatier-clic.fr/21amc/141b

The Pilgrim Fathers came from England. They were a group of colonists who had fled to North America to escape religious persecution. Their desire to travel to America was considered risky, as previous attempts to settle in North America had failed. In 1620, they established a colony at Plymouth, Massachusetts

La prononciation de *have*

▶ Quand *have* est **un verbe lexical** qui signifie *avoir* ou *posséder* ou quand il exprime l'obligation (dans la structure ***have to*** **+ V**), il est **accentué** dans la phrase et sa voyelle se prononce toujours /æ/ (comme dans *cat*) :

*About 20% of Americans say they **have*** /'hæv/ *no religion.*

⚠ Dans ce cas, on ne peut normalement pas contacter *have*. Il est donc, en principe, incorrect de dire ou d'écrire *they'**ve** no religion*.

▶ Quand *have* est **un auxiliaire** (en particulier quand le verbe est au *present perfect* ou au *pluperfect*), il est en général **inaccentué** : sa voyelle est souvent réduite en *schwa* /ə/ et le *h* n'est pas toujours prononcé. Dans ce cas, il peut se contracter.

*The Pilgrim Fathers were a group of colonists who **had*** /(h)əd/ *escaped religious persecution in Europe.*

⚠ À la forme négative, ou quand l'auxiliaire est utilisé seul (par exemple, dans les réponses courtes ou les *tags*), la voyelle reste toujours pleine et le *h* est toujours prononcé :

*"Have you finished?" "No, I **haven't**!"* /'hævənt/

3 **Dites si *have* est un auxiliaire inaccentué ou un verbe lexical accentué dans les phrases suivantes.** Contractez-le quand cela est possible. Écoutez l'enregistrement et répétez les phrases en faisant attention à la prononciation du *h* et de la voyelle.

Audio hatier-clic.fr/21amc/141c

a. *Americans have been pledging allegiance to their flag for more than one hundred years.*

b. *The United States has the world's largest Christian population.*

c. *Do you have ancestors who came to the New World on the Mayflower?*

d. *I have never had Thanksgiving Day dinner at my cousin's house before.*

Let's translate

The principle of religious liberty should extend to all people, not only ones who come from a specific set of religious beliefs. A 2014 study from the Pew Research Center reveals that the religious landscape in the United States is changing. As the Christian population is declining – particularly among mainline[1] Protestants and Catholics – the number of adults who do not identify with a specific religion is growing. With the changing demographics of Americans and their religious connections, it is even more important that people of all faiths[2] and people of no faith are granted the fundamental right to religious liberty.

www.americanprogress.org, April 2019

1. traditional 2. religions

Traduire la voix passive

▶ L'emploi de la voix passive est plus courant en anglais qu'en français. Il n'est donc pas toujours possible de la traduire par un passif français.
Pour éviter cet écueil, on peut employer le **pronom indéfini *on*** :

*He **was offered** a good job.* → **On** lui a proposé un bon emploi.

▶ Le passif des verbes d'opinion et de parole (*be said / thought / believed to* + V) est utilisé pour indiquer qu'une nouvelle n'est pas vérifiée ou que sa source est inconnue. On peut le traduire par un conditionnel français.

*She **is said** to be abroad now.* → Elle **serait** à l'étranger en ce moment.

Translation Tip

▶ La conjonction *as* peut exprimer plusieurs types de relations : un lien temporel de simultanéité, un lien causal ou une comparaison.

▶ Sauf exception, il n'est en général pas nécessaire de traduire les noms d'organismes peu connus des francophones. Ce sera le cas pour le *Pew Research Center*.

À vous !

a. Comment traduira-t-on la voix passive *are granted* ?

b. Il n'est pas possible de traduire littéralement *With the changing demographics of Americans and their religious connections*. Ne faudra-t-il pas avoir recours à une transposition (voir p. 266) ?

Build up your vocabulary

1 Fill in your own mind map here: hatier-clic.fr/21amc/142

2 Draw the grid on your copy book and complete it.

Religion	Adjective	Person
Buddhism		a buddhist
Mormonism	mormon	
Catholicism		a catholic
Islam	muslim	
Judaism		a jew

3 Find a word / an expression from your mind map to match these definitions.

a. part of the US Constitution, ratified in 1791 as part of the Bill of Rights, prohibiting Congress from interfering with freedom of religion, speech, assembly, or petition

b. a solemn oath of fidelity to the US, part of many flag-saluting ceremonies in the US.

c. disbelief or lack of belief in the existence of God or gods.

d. English colonists who left the Church of England, sailed to America in 1620 aboard the Mayflower and founded the first permanent settlement in New England

e. a cell of a multicellular organism which can give rise to indefinitely more cells of the same type

Projects

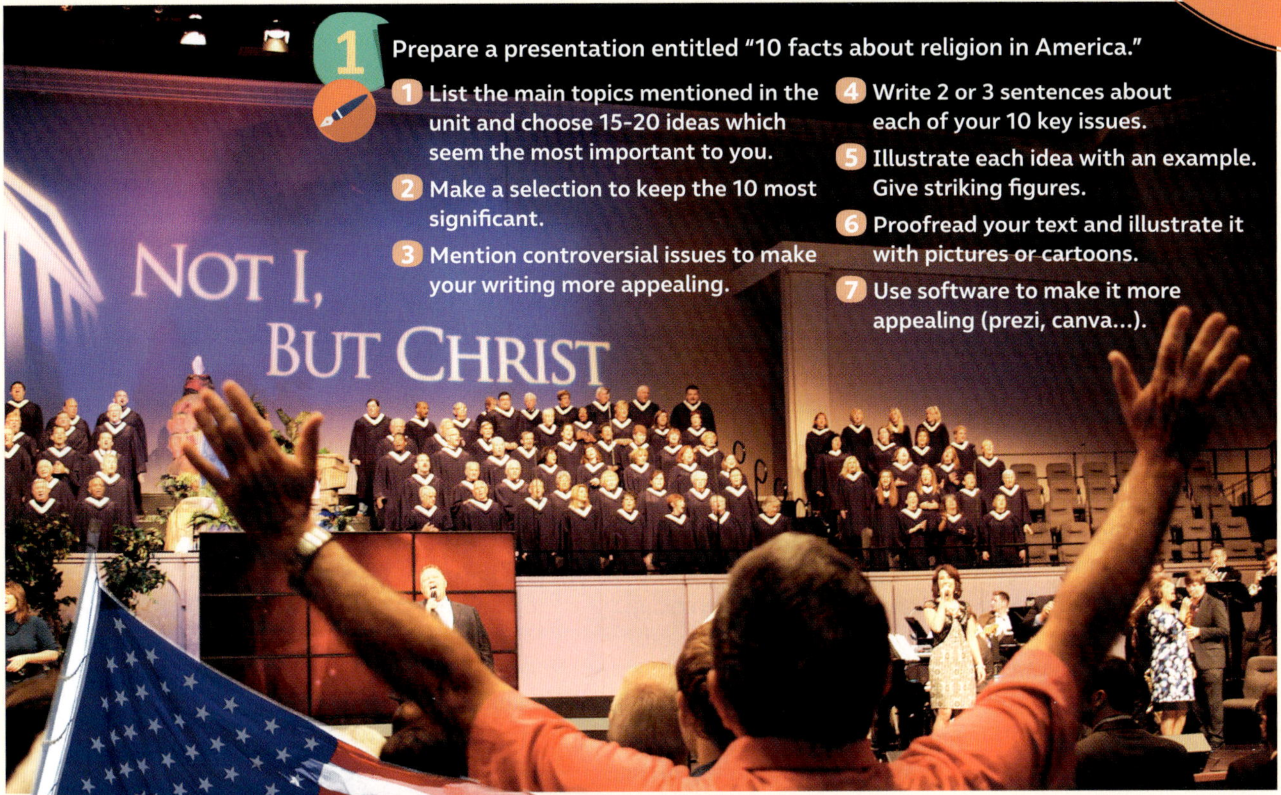

1

Prepare a presentation entitled "10 facts about religion in America."

1. List the main topics mentioned in the unit and choose 15-20 ideas which seem the most important to you.
2. Make a selection to keep the 10 most significant.
3. Mention controversial issues to make your writing more appealing.
4. Write 2 or 3 sentences about each of your 10 key issues.
5. Illustrate each idea with an example. Give striking figures.
6. Proofread your text and illustrate it with pictures or cartoons.
7. Use software to make it more appealing (prezi, canva...).

2

You take part in the David Pakman Show. Prepare an intervention about the issue of the 'Pledge of Allegiance in the USA.'

1. Read *Let's focus on...* n° 1, p. 138 and check you know the origin and evolution of this pledge.
2. List some elements from the unit or the web which have made it controversial.
3. Prepare a list of pros and cons and get ready to give your opinion.
4. Don't write a text but list key words to make sure you won't read.
5. Check the pronunciation of the words you're not sure about.
6. Record yourself and check the audio.

Pour l'écrit du Bac

A How the fight for religious freedom has fallen victim to culture wars

In theory, the commitment to religious freedom is straightforward. The First Amendment to the U.S. Constitution bars Congress from making any law "respecting an establishment of religion or prohibiting the free exercise thereof."

Most of the attention, especially in recent decades, has focused on the "free exercise" clause. An important case involved Adele Sherbet, a Seventh-day Adventist, who was fired for refusing to work on Saturdays and then denied unemployment benefits. In a 1963 decision, the U.S. Supreme Court ruled that Sherbet's free exercise right had been violated.

In a 1990 decision, however, the Court significantly narrowed the Sherbet precedent, ruling against a Native American man, Alfred Smith, who was dismissed from his job because he had illegally ingested peyote[1] as part of a religious ritual.

The Court's Smith ruling met with bipartisan outrage in the U.S. Congress and led to passage of the RFRA[2] legislation. Among the sponsors was a first-term liberal Democrat from New York, Jerrold Nadler.

"Unless the Smith decision is overturned," Nadler argued on the House floor, "the fundamental right of all Americans to keep the Sabbath, observe religious dietary laws, to worship as their consciences dictate, will remain threatened." The bill passed the House unanimously and was approved in the Senate by a vote of 97-3.

[…] the religious freedom cause has been politicized, with conservatives claiming it for their purposes and liberals shying away from it for reasons of their own.

When liberals started pushing for expanded protections for the LGBT population, conservatives grew alarmed, arguing that practices such as same-sex weddings go against biblical teaching. They've argued that religious freedom should mean they can't be forced to accommodate something they don't believe in. Liberals portrayed that stance simply as discriminatory and argued it should be illegal. […]

As conservatives focused the religious freedom debate narrowly around issues of sexuality and marriage, progressives doubled down on the promotion of LGBT rights. […]

"Religion is no excuse for discrimination in the public sphere, as we have long recognized when it comes to race, color, sex, and national origin," Nadler argued in a committee markup hearing, "and it should not be an excuse when it comes to sexual orientation or gender identity." […]

"RFRA was originally enacted to serve as a safeguard for religious freedom," he said, "but recently it's been used as a sword, to cut down the civil rights of too many individuals."

Some traditional advocates of religious freedom issues are dismayed by how the debate has evolved among both conservatives and liberals. […]

"It is unfortunate that some on the right will use religious freedom in order to advance a particular partisan issue," she says. "I think it is problematic on the left to cede arguments about religious freedom, to just say, 'Oh, people will use that now to advance an anti-LGBT perspective.' These are tough issues to work on, and religious freedom should not take the fall."*

www.npr.org

*Holyn Hollman, associate executive director Baptist Joint Committee for Religious Liberty

1. a type of cactus 2. Religious Freedom Restauration Act

PARTIE 1

Prenez connaissance des documents A, B et C et traitez le sujet suivant en anglais :

Write a short commentary on the three documents (minimum 300 words): taking into account their specificities, analyse how the documents deal with the themes of unity and plurality.

PARTIE 2

Traduisez le passage suivant du document B en français.

No. Religious freedom prevents the cultural majority from using the power of the state to impose their beliefs on others. This protects everyone – religious and nonreligious alike – from the government becoming so powerful that it can tell people what to think and how to act. Conscience has been considered the individual's most sacred right. A government that intrudes on conscience will not hesitate to intrude on our other freedoms.

B Religious freedom: what's at stake if we lose it?

First of all, what is religious freedom?

Religious freedom is more than the "freedom to worship" at a synagogue, church, or mosque. It means people shouldn't have to go against their core values and beliefs in order to conform to culture or government.

Religious freedom protects people's right to live, speak, and act according to their beliefs peacefully and publicly. It protects their ability to be themselves at work, in class, and at social activities.

Ok, that sounds good, but does such "freedom" allow people to do whatever they want under the cover of religion?

Well, that answer is no. The Supreme Court has said the federal government may limit religious freedom – but only when it has a "compelling[1] interest" to do so in order to protect the common good and limit people's ability to harm others.

Here's how that applies to the most common allegation in religious freedom cases today – charges of discrimination.

Should florists, photographers and bakers be forced to provide their services for same-sex weddings and celebrations that violate their religious beliefs?

Well, let's flip the question. Should a lesbian graphic designer or printer be forced to create a flyer for a religious group's rally opposing same-marriage?

In both cases, the answer should be no. [...]

And that's why the answer to this next question is very important… does religious freedom mean religious people get special rights?

No. Religious freedom prevents the cultural majority from using the power of the state to impose their beliefs on others. This protects everyone – religious and nonreligious alike – from the government becoming so powerful that it can tell people what to think and how to act. Conscience has been considered the individual's most sacred right. A government that intrudes on conscience will not hesitate to intrude on our other freedoms.

Additionally, forcing individuals and faith-based organizations to choose between living out their religious beliefs or serving their neighbors actually harms our communities.

Did you know that an estimated 350,000 religious congregations operate schools, pregnancy resource centers, soup kitchens, drug addiction programs, homeless shelters, and adoption agencies?

These efforts serve 70 million Americans each year and the value of their services are estimated at over a trillion dollars annually.

Ultimately, everyone benefits from religious freedom.

It covers all people equally – Christians, Jews, Muslims, agnostics, and atheists. Religious freedom preserves America's diversity, where people of different faiths, worldviews, and beliefs can peacefully live together without fear of punishment from the government.

Efforts to repress religious freedom is not just an attack on individual liberty and human dignity, but on the very foundation that has made America strong.

www.heritage.org

1. strong

C

Norman Rockwell, *Golden Rule*, 1961

12 Independence and identity

The expert's view
hatier-clic.fr/21amc/146a

In the news
hatier-clic.fr/21amc/146b

Projects
- Interact on a social media about your wish for your country to become independent or to maintain the status quo.
- Take part in a TV show about how countries have asserted their identity and claimed their independence.

Grammar p. 154 Phonology p. 155

I want out

A Brexit consequences

1

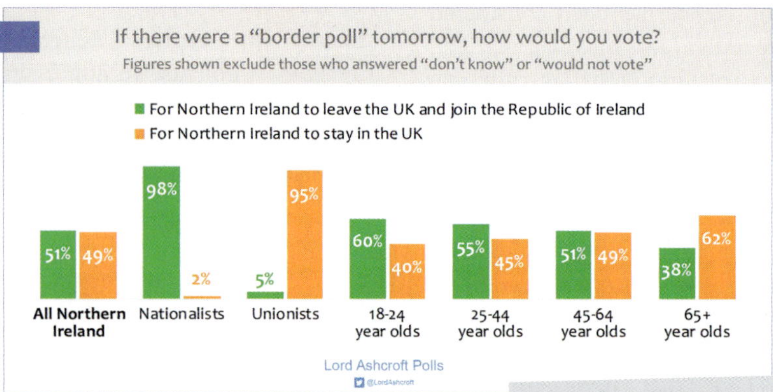

2

4

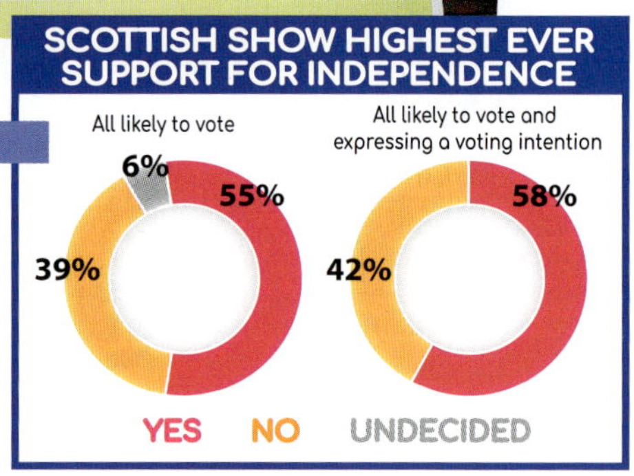

3

Oct. 14, 2020

"The Scots have Johnson presiding over a nationalist English government hell-bent on denying Scotland European heritage and identity"

Denis MacShane, former UK Europe Minister

GROUP WORK

Group A on documents 1 and 2.
Group B on documents 3, 4 and 5.

1. With your group, analyse the graph and comment on the results of the survey.
2. Using all the documents for your group, explain the consequences of Brexit for your nation.
   Group A, read *Let's focus on...* n° 5, p. 153, to answer the question.
   Group B, read *Let's focus on...* n° 3, p. 153, to answer the question.
3. Make a one-minute podcast to explain why these nations left the UK. Listen to the other group's podcast and discuss the two situations.

5

B Cameroon, a hidden conflict

DSCHANG, Cameroon — The battle lines of the conflict in this Central African country are drawn by language.

Around 80 percent of the country speaks French; the rest speaks English. For decades, Francophones and Anglophones lived in relative harmony.

But over the past two years, violence spurred by this linguistic split has brought Cameroon to the brink of civil war. Hundreds have died, close to 500,000 have been displaced, and activists have been rounded up[1] and jailed.

The government claims armed English-speaking separatists who want to create a new nation called Ambazonia have terrorized civilians and attacked government forces, prompting the military to retaliate[2] against them.

But in more than a dozen interviews, English speakers displaced by military raids on their villages recounted how Cameroonian troops opened fire on unarmed civilians and burned down their homes. Soldiers often arrived to Anglophone villages early in the morning, they said. But instead of looking for armed independence fighters, they fired indiscriminately, at times leaving the bodies of young men piled in the streets.

Witnesses and victims say the government's use of force has driven a growing number of moderate Cameroonians to throw their support behind the armed separatists, a shift that threatens to intensify the government crackdown[3] and deepen divisions between French and English speakers in the once-peaceful nation. If this conflict spreads beyond the Anglophone regions, it could destabilize the whole country, which is a key U.S. partner in fighting terrorism.

"I don't want Cameroon anymore," said Daniel, a civilian who fled to Dschang, a French-speaking city close to the border of one English-speaking region after government forces attacked his village and shot

an old woman dead. He spoke on the condition that his last name not be used out of fear of retribution for his comments, as did the other English-speaking Cameroonians in this story. "I want to fight for a new country." […]

Human rights groups have also accused separatists of attacking security forces and burning down schools, among other abuses.

The African Union has called for dialogue but affirmed its "unwavering[4] commitment to the unity and territorial integrity of Cameroon."

Siobhán O'Grady, www.washingtonpost.com, February 5th, 2019

1. gathered 2. counterattack 3. police enforcement 4. inflexible, firm

1. Read from line 1 to 13, look at the map and identify the reason of the conflict in Cameroon and its consequences.
2. Explain what happened when Cameroonian soldiers arrived in English-speaking villages. List the consequences and the governmental reaction.
3. Read from line 23 to the end of the article. Say why this conflict has an international dimension and why it is linked to identity.
4. One of your classmates couldn't attend the class, write him/her a short summary of what you understood about the conflict in Cameroon. Include the notions of identity and independence.

Nicola Sturgeon

Audio hatier-clic.fr/21amc/147

C Scotland: should I stay or should I go?

1. Read *Let's focus on…* n° 3, p. 153. Say who Nicola Sturgeon is and identify what she and the SNP want.
2. Pay attention to what the hostess says and sum up the British Prime Minister's answer to Nicola Sturgeon's wish. Qualify her reply.
3. Your history teacher asks you to explain Nicola Sturgeon's arguments on a second referendum on Scottish independence to one of his/her classes.

I'm torn

A An Australian republic?

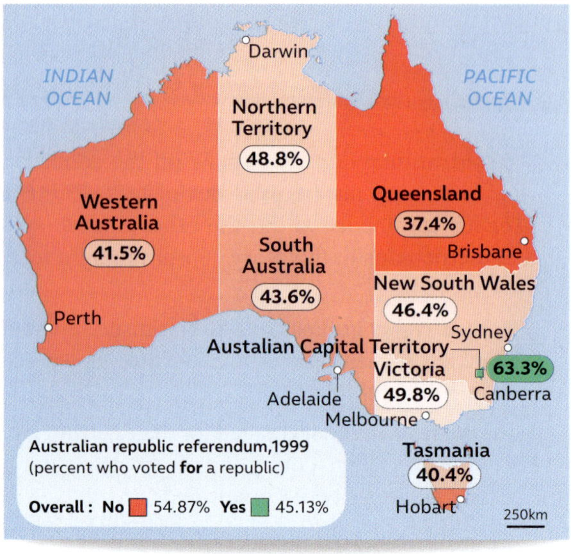

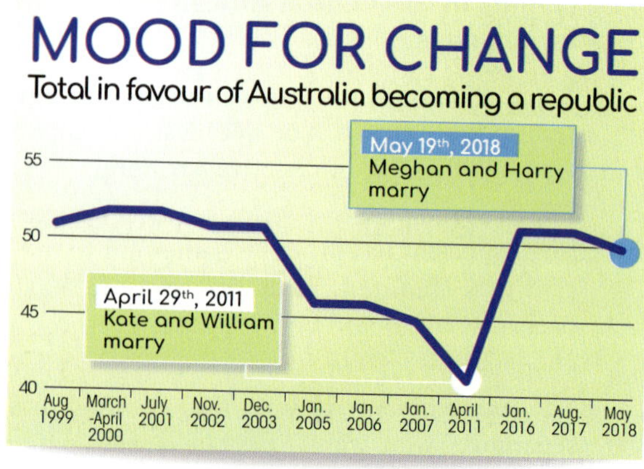

1 Analyse the map and the chart: explain Australians' view on becoming a Republic.

2 Read the first part of the text (l. 1-15) and *Let's focus on...* n° 4, p. 153. Make an organisational chart of the current Australian system of government.

3 Read the end of the article and pick out the different models of government possible for Australia. Compile the positive and negative aspects of each one in a chart.

4 **CONNECT.** Use the documents to explain why Australia is still a federal parliamentary constitutional monarchy (and not a republic).

e-worksheet
hatier-clic.fr/21amc/148

Is Australia ready for another republic referendum?

A recent poll […] suggests increasing popular support for a republic. According to the YouGov poll, 62% of Australians said they wanted the head of state to be an Australian.

The palace letters make clear the problem with our current set-up: we have a legal (what lawyers call *de jure*) head of state who is a resident and national of the UK (the queen), as well as an effective or *de facto* Australian head of state (the governor-general) who can operate as if that legal status was his/hers.

Aside from the symbolism of having a foreign head of state – a blow to nativist Australian pride – there is also the practical question of whether the legal status and system of appointment (and removal) of the Australian governor-general is the best we can do. […]

What happened in the 1999 referendum

The republican model put to voters in a referendum in 1999 didn't really fix that problem, as it still gave the prime minister the direct power to remove the head of state.

The other problem with the 1999 "minimalist" republic model was that it was attacked by some republicans who wanted a popular vote to select the head of state. […]

How republic models could work

[...] Some "hybrid" republic models have been proposed. […]

In 2001, the late constitutional law professor George Winterton proposed an alternative bipartisan choice idea. In this model, parliament would endorse[1] one candidate for head of state who would then be voted on in a popular national election (in which limited other nominees were free to stand). [...]

Another proposal is the "50-50" model, which aggregates the results of a parliamentary and popular vote, giving equal weight to both. This concept seeks to unite minimalists and direct electionists by requiring some sensible compromise from each side.

To avoid a repeat of Kerr's dismissal of Gough in 1975, Australia could choose a republic model that includes "concurrent expiration".

In this model, if a head of state acted to dismiss[2] a sitting prime minister, he or she would also face an early expiration of their own term. Voters would then decide the fates of both in the ensuing election.

Certainly, if there is to be change to a republic in Australia that maintains the Westminster system of responsible government, this will take time, considered thought and debate.

In the very long term, an Australian head of state may be inevitable, so it is important to get it right.

Michael Duffy, www.theconversation.com, July 15th, 2020

1. support, approve of 2. reject, fire

B Making Puerto Rico a state

With a historic vote, its people staked[1] their claim to statehood.

Like all Americans, the people of Puerto Rico went to the polls on Tuesday. But unlike their fellow citizens, Puerto Ricans cannot vote for the president, or for senators or representatives (except for one nonvoting "resident commissioner"). Instead, voters there were asked whether they wanted Puerto Rico to become the 51st state of the union: "yes" or "no." They chose "yes." With this historic vote, Puerto Ricans have staked their claim to admission as the 51st state in the Union. [...]

The painful legacy of U.S. racial bias against Puerto Rico makes the island's immediate admission into statehood a political and moral imperative. [...]

Puerto Ricans have been split down the middle between [...] two alternatives [statehood and "enhanced" commonwealth] for half a century. And even across this divide, these two groups have long agreed on two key points: All of them wish to remain U.S. citizens, and all of them wish to maintain the island's permanent union with the United States. [...]

Opponents of statehood will insist that the margin of victory was not large enough. But no other territory has ever been subjected to such a requirement — and when it comes to treating Puerto Rico differently, enough is enough. Moreover, congressional silence on statehood before the Nov. 3 referendum inevitably depressed the "yes" vote. Although 52 percent of Puerto Ricans voted for statehood, that percentage would almost certainly have been much higher if Congress had made clear *before* the vote that it stood ready and eager to welcome a state of Puerto Rico. To paraphrase a well-known maxim, for the residents of a perpetual colony, it might feel better to remain silent and only suspect that your fellow American citizens view you as inferior than to ask for equality and remove all doubt. That voting for statehood required Puerto Ricans to take a leap of faith makes the "yes" vote all the more resounding[2].

Christina D. Ponsa-Kraus,
New York Times, November 4th, 2020

1. made 2. very clear

Culture Tip

Puerto Rico is a "freely associated state" within the federal system of the US. Although Puerto Ricans have had the American citizenship since 1917, their rights are limited.

1. Read the Culture Tip and the article. Present the current status of the island.
2. Imagine why a majority of Puerto Ricans wants to keep the American citizenship and a strong link with the US.
3. **Grammar** Pick out a sentence containing an if-clause. What tense is used in the clause?
4. You meet a Puerto Rican friend. Discuss why statehood is important, why Puerto Ricans voted yes and give the American perspective.

C Australians and Inuit Canadians: moving forward?

1 Majority of Australians in favour of a republic

Audio hatier-clic.fr/21amc/149a

2 An Inuit self-government?

Audio hatier-clic.fr/21amc/149b

GROUP WORK

Student A on Australia. Student B on Canada.

1. Find the main topic of your audio. Use the following words:
   Australia: republic • lost • term • option
   Canada: Quebec • laws • self-determination • Inuit • decide
2. Identify each territory's goals and the solutions to achieve them with success.
3. You attend the Self-Determination Day conference on March 23rd. To make sure you know about the subject, swap information on what you learnt with your classmate.

I'm in!

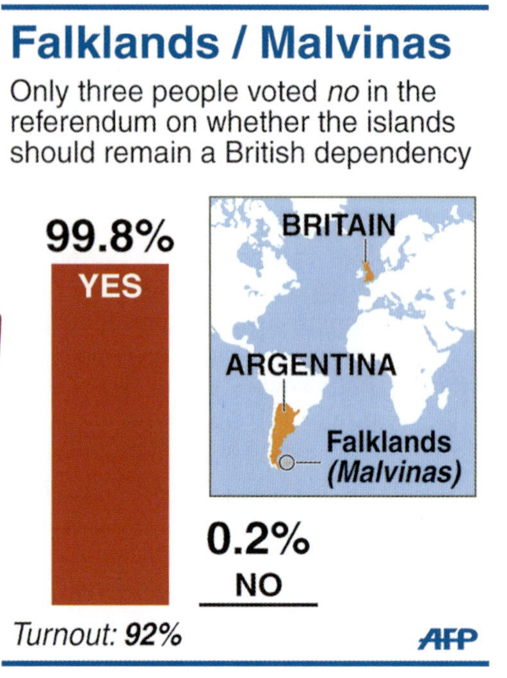

A ¿Británico or Argentinian?

1. Present the document and point out what is striking.
2. Read *Let's focus on…* n° 1, p. 152, and explain the evolution of the relationship between the Falklands and the UK.

Culture Tip

In 2013, Falklanders were asked to answer the following question in a referendum: *"Do you wish the Falkland Islands to retain their current political status as an Overseas Territory of the United Kingdom?"*

B A rock to (un)lock

EU's Gibraltar 'colony' line boosts Spain

Document issued by Brussels angers London but helps Madrid in centuries-old dispute.

MADRID — Spain was on Friday hailing what diplomats described as a historic victory in the fight over Gibraltar — thanks to a six-letter word at the bottom of a document.

"Gibraltar is a colony of the British Crown," reads a footnote in a draft regulation approved by the Council of the EU on visas for Brits after Brexit.

Spanish diplomats say it's the first time the EU has endorsed in a written text Madrid's three-centuries-old claim over the sovereignty of the Rock, as well as proof that the EU will be on Spain's side in the dispute.

"There is a controversy between Spain and the UK concerning the sovereignty over Gibraltar, a territory for which a solution has to be reached in light of the relevant resolutions and decisions of the General Assembly of the United Nations," the Council text reads.

A Spanish diplomat involved in the negotiations said his side is "satisfied" with the text and added that "Gibraltar is a colony and the EU backs that… this is the basis of our claim." [...]

A spokesperson for the UK government said "Gibraltar is not a colony and it is completely inappropriate to describe in this way," adding that the Rock is "part of the UK family and has a mature and modern constitutional relationship with the UK." [...]

Gibraltar was captured by an Anglo-Dutch force during the War of the Spanish Succession in 1704. Madrid ceded it officially in perpetuity in the Treaty of Utrecht in 1713. In 1946, the U.N. Committee on Decolonization included it in a list of non-self-governing territories, together with Hong Kong, Macao and the Falkland Islands.

An agreement for shared sovereignty of Gibraltar was discussed between former British Prime Minister Tony Blair and his Spanish counterpart José María Aznar in the early 2000s — and was overwhelmingly rejected by the people of Gibraltar in a referendum in 2002.

"The Spanish repeatedly say that they want Gibraltar to become Spanish, while here is good evidence that the Gibraltarians don't even want to countenance that possibility," Gibraltar's Chief Minister Fabian Picardo told the BBC in an interview Friday, describing Madrid's actions as "unnecessarily provocative."

The UK government has repeated its commitment to respect the wish of Gibraltar's people to remain British.

Diego Torres, www.politico.eu, February 1st, 2019

1. Say what the "historic victory" alluded to lines 2 and 3 is.
2. Explain the controversy line 16.
3. Compare and contrast the position of Spain and the one of Gibraltar concerning the independence of the peninsula.

C Falklands or Malvinas?

Home > Opinions > Politics > Should the Falklands belong to Argentina?

Should the Falklands belong to Argentina?

YES or NO

17% Say Yes — 83% Say No

Colonialism has ended! Why should Britain claim a land so far from its home country. You know, we're not in 1880, where you could just get some type of German guy to rule out that this land is British. It's not that anymore. There's Argentina, and the Falklands is an Argentine Island. The islanders can oppose this, but would it make sense that Britain claim a land so far from it. It's like America claiming Sengoku Island. The only reason Britain won the Falkland War is because Britain had support internationally.

Report Post

Like | Reply | 3 | 4

Falklands should be Argentinian, which doesn't mean necessarily to be equal to the mainland. Belonging to Argentina doesn't mean necessarily being a one more uniform part of the country... It exists something called autonomy and respect of minorities. Having a different language, culture and origin is not an excuse for not belonging to a larger neighbour territory. Look at Switzerland, with 3 or 4 official languages, or Italy, that has the German-speaking Tirol... It's a kind of British nationalist feeling that exists in this archipelago. "If we belong to Argentina, everything will go bad..." If the archipelago goes to Argentina, there won't be any kind of repression for English language and the identity of Kelppers. Argentina, maybe is not the English way of country, but it's a developed nation. Negotiation is the solution. The right of self-determination is a misleading concept of international law. It creates instability and promotes separations between territories and stagnation, rather than opportunities of unification.

Report Post

Like | Reply | 1 | 7

Absolutely NOT! The Falkland Islanders should choose their status. The Falkland Islands held a referendum on this question a few years back, and the people overwhelmingly said yes. But the Argentinians said it was void because the population "was implanted by the English!" Of course they are British, because the land WAS COLONIZED BY THEM IN THE 1800s WHEN THE SPANISH LEFT! If we give them to the Argentinians, then you might as well give all the other British colonies to Argentina! The Argentinians have gone to drastic measures just to get them, like for example saying that they should rule the Falklands because they're closer to them!! That doesn't mean anything. The Falklands have the right to say what they want...

Report Post

Like | Reply | 0 | 2

Why would Argentina of all countries own the islands? Even if the Spanish had a claim on the islands which would be passed on to Argentina, which is one of the Argentinian claims. Why would the islands be Argentinean? Peru would have the same claim to the islands as Argentina. Proximity is a bad argument since you could say Alaska belongs to Russia.

Report Post

Like | Reply | 3 | 0

1. Compare the results on page 150 and the answers of the unofficial questionnaire.
2. Sum up the arguments for and against the independence of the Falkland Islands.
3. Compare the views on independence in the Falkland Islands.

Culture Tip

Devolution:
"the transfer or delegation of power to a lower level, especially by central government to local or regional administration." (Oxford dictionary)
This means that to remain united, the UK government had to grant some powers to local assemblies in Scotland and Wales particularly. This avoided a complete break from the union.

D Caerdydd vs. Llundain

1. Identify the different interviewees and list the arguments given disapproving the current political system.
2. Focus on the street interviews and the Culture Tip on devolution. Explain the Welsh's state of mind and view on devolution.
3. Phonology Listen and repeat the following words: moment, close, vote, over. Focus on the pronunciation of the vowel *o*.
4. You are the journalist who's recorded the interviews. Write your article.

Brexit: Welsh independence 'is on the table'

Audio hatier-clic.fr/21amc/151

Let's focus on...

The Falklands war: a watershed for Mrs. Thatcher

1

In April 1982 when Argentina invaded what they called Islas Malvinas, Margaret Thatcher's political future was in serious trouble not only from the British public but from her own cabinet too. She had been Prime Minister (Conservative party) for three years and her domestic policies had led to distrust amongst the British people (cuts in public spending, a high unemployment rate…).
Prime Minister Thatcher's hasty decision to go to war to get the islands back was not supported by several Members of Parliament (MPs). Was it a master stroke or a moment of folly? But the strong-headed British Prime Minister ignored the signals. After all the Falkland Islands had been a British overseas territory since 1833.
So the UK decided to dispatch a naval task force to the archipelago 8,000 miles away in the South Atlantic Ocean to take on the Argentinian forces. The war lasted 74 days. 649 Argentinian military personnel, 255 British troops and three Falkland Islanders were killed.
This resounding victory led to a sudden increase in her popularity and subsequent reelection in 1983. The triumph also proved Margaret Thatcher's "Iron Lady" nickname was fully deserved.
The Falkland Islands were the making of her: she became renowned not only in her own country where she defended her proactive foreign policy (some say jingoism) but also on the international stage. She finally gained the stature that she had previously lacked.

Satisfaction ratings on Thatcher's policy

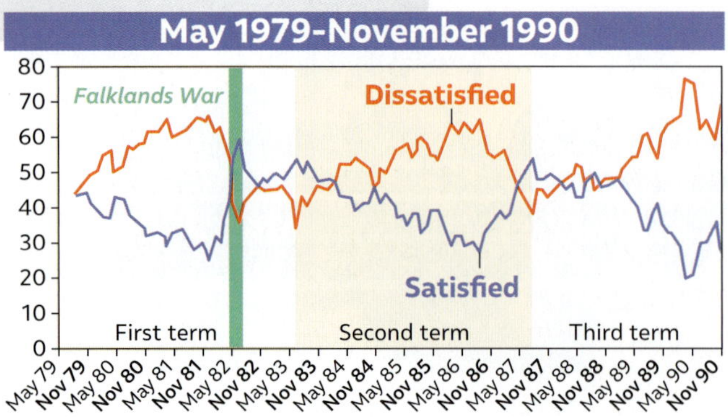

2

Referendum in Puerto Rico. The option of statehood wins with 52%.
Nov. 2020

Cameroonian separatists start a guerilla war for the independence of the anglophone region as the Federal Republic of Ambazonia.
Nov. 2016

First election of the Premier of Nunavut (Canada).
April 1st, 1999

Following devolution through the Scotland Act, 1997, a Scottish Parliament is reinstated after 292 years.
1999

First devolution referendum in Wales accepted (50.3% YES).
1997

Self-declared state of Ambazonia, abolished in 1972 by French-speaking Cameroon.
1981

First devolution referendum in Wales rejected (80% NO).
1979

Bloody Sunday: during a peaceful march against internment without trial, 14 people are killed by British troops. Bloody Sunday is often seen as the most violent event of "the Troubles". It fuels hostility, resentment and loss of trust in the British government.
Jan. 30th, 1972

A League of Nations mandate declares Cameroon to be under both British and French administrations.
1922

Easter Rising and formation of the IRA. A rebellion occurs as a group of Nationalists proclaims the establishment of the Republic of Ireland. This unrest is quashed by British troops in a bloodbath (2,000 deaths).
April 1916

The Act of Union abolishes the Irish parliament and formally united Ireland and Great Britain to become the United Kingdom of Great Britain and Ireland.
1801

Pro-independence political parties 3

Australian Labor Party (founded in 1901).The concept of an Australian Republic is officially supported by the Australian Labor Party and the Greens. A minor political party, the Republican Party of Australia, exists but remains very limited in scope.
Although all parties favoured a referendum back in the 1990s, the results of the 1999 referendum showed Australian citizens were not ready to switch to a Republic and to change their constitution, as the NO won.

Sinn Fein /ʃɪn ˈfeɪn/ is Irish for "Ourselves". The party's name affirms its ideology, i.e. national sovereignty and self-determination. Like other pro-independence parties, Sinn Fein promotes the idea of all Irish people governing themselves.
As a left-wing party, Sinn Fein's main aim is to create a united Ireland. Although it is considered Eurosceptic, in 2015, Sinn Fein supported the UK remaining in the EU. This decision was mostly based on economic issues in Northern Ireland and also on establishing a counter-power against London.
The party is active in both Northern Ireland and the Republic of Ireland. Equating the complex Irish history, the party split on numerous occasions and was even linked to the IRA (Irish Republican Army).

SNP (*Pàrtaidh Nàiseanta na h-Alba* in Scottish Gaelic) stands for Scottish National Party. This center-left party, founded in 1934, strongly supports the independence of Scotland from the UK, even more so since the Brexit referendum. It claims that Scotland would be more prosperous if it were independent.
At its creation, the SNP's ideology was based on the principle of self-determination for Scotland and was considered as a radical party that believed in redistribution of economic wealth and decentralisation of industries.
Two main schools of thought dominate the party now: the SNP gradualists (who favour a step-by-step independence) and the SNP fundamentalists (who favour independence with no negotiations).
Nicola Sturgeon has been both the leader of the party and First Minister of Scotland since 2014. On September 18th, 2014 Scotland had a referendum on national independence.
The question was: "Should Scotland be an independent country?" The result was to remain part of the UK, by 55% to 45%.
The SNP is the third biggest political party in British Parliament, just after the Conservative and Labour Parties, which just goes to show how strong their political identity is.

Palace letters or Palace papers 4

This term specifically refers to the correspondence (about 200 letters) between Queen Elizabeth II and the Australian Governor-General Sir John Kerr during the "Dismissal" crisis in November 1975 – the greatest political crisis in Australian history. Indeed, Australia witnessed a constitutional crisis when Governor-General Kerr dismissed the Australian Prime Minister (Gough Whitlam, Labour Party) and replaced him with the leader of opposition (Liberal Party).
Kerr's copies of the letters are now archived at the Australian National Archives. However, they have been classified as "personal papers" and have not been released to the public. This may change as, in 2020, the Australian High Court ruled in favour of the release of the papers.

Good Friday Agreement 5

This agreement was signed in 1998 between British PM Tony Blair, Irish Taoiseach Bertie Ahern and Northern Irish Sinn Fein leader Gerry Adams. It put an end to the violence Northern Ireland had suffered since the 1960s. This was a milestone in both the peace process and the devolution of Northern Ireland. The main provisions included:
– that the majority of Northern Irish people wanted to remain in the UK;
– a recognition of the wish to have a united Ireland.
The second provision left open the possibility for Northern Ireland to join the Republic of Ireland in the future. It came to light during Brexit negotiations that no one wanted a definitive hard border. The Irish therefore called for the British government to acknowledge the second provision and allow Northern Ireland to unite with the Republic of Ireland.

Practice your grammar

Les propositions en *if*

▶ On peut exprimer **des hypothèses** en utilisant **des propositions de condition introduites par *if***. Attention, il faut respecter la concordance des temps suivante :

	Forme du verbe dans la proposition en *if*	Forme du verbe principal
Potentiel Cela peut se réaliser un jour.	**présent simple**	***will* + V**
	*If Scotland **becomes** independent, the UK **will lose** one third of its territory.*	
Irréel On imagine une situation qui a peu de chances de se réaliser.	**prétérit simple**	***would* + V**
	*If Scotland **became** independent, the UK **would lose** one third of its territory.*	
Irréel du passé Cela ne peut plus se produire.	***pluperfect* (*had* + participe passé)**	***would have* + participe passé**
	*If Scotland **had become** independent in 2015, the UK **would have lost** one third of its territory.*	

⚠ Dans les propositions en *if*, la forme du prétérit du verbe *be* est souvent ***were*** à toutes les personnes :

*If Scotland **were** independent, the country **would be** more prosperous.*

1 **Mettez les verbes entre parenthèses à la forme qui convient.**

a. *If a referendum were held today, Britain ... (stay) in the EU.*

b. *If the opinion polls are right, the party ... (win) the election in a landslide.*

c. *If the army ... (not begin) to retaliate against the civilian population, there would have been fewer casualties.*

d. *If the turnout had been higher, the result of the referendum ... (not be) the same.*

2 **Imaginez les conséquences en complétant les amorces suivantes. Produisez deux phrases à chaque fois.**

a. *If Australia becomes a republic...*

b. *If Scotland were independent...*

c. *If Brexit hadn't happened...*

La traduction de « pendant »

▶ ***During* est une préposition qui localise un événement durant une période de temps** (*during WW2, during the class, during the film*). Les compléments de temps introduits par *during* répondent à la question ***When?***.

*Gibraltar was captured by an Anglo-Dutch force **during the War of the Spanish Succession** in 1704.*

▶ À la place de *during*, il est parfois possible d'utiliser ***throughout*** (tout au long de...) ou ***over*** (*over the holiday, over the past few years*).

▶ ***For* indique une durée** (*for two hours, for five minutes, for two weeks*). Les compléments de temps introduits par *for* répondent à la question ***How long?*** (Pendant combien de temps ?).

*__For decades__, Francophones and Anglophones **lived** in relative harmony.*

⚠ *For* peut aussi être traduit par « depuis » : dans ce cas, le verbe est au *present perfect* ou au *pluperfect* à la forme simple ou en *be* + *-ing*.

*Francophones and Anglophones **have been living** in relative harmony **for decades**.*

▶ ***While* (plus rarement *whilst*) introduit une proposition subordonnée** et est traduit par « pendant que » :

__While__ I was in Australia, I visited Canberra.

3 **Complétez par *for*, *during* ou *while*.**

a. *The UK remained in the European Union ... almost 50 years.*

b. *... the soldiers were fast asleep, they were captured by the rebels.*

c. *255 British servicemen and 3 civilians were killed ... the Falklands War.*

d. *My father campaigned for the independence of Scotland ... decades.*

e. *... the referendum campaign, former prime ministers Tony Blair and John Major teamed up to argue that Brexit could boost support for Scottish independence.*

Improve your pronunciation

Le e magique

▶ Quand une voyelle est suivie d'une consonne unique (à l'exception du *r*) puis d'un *e*, celle-ci se prononce comme dans l'alphabet.

	Prononciation de la voyelle	Exemples
a	/eɪ/ (comme dans *say*)	*state, lake, date* Exception : *have* /æ/
e	/iː/ (comme dans *see*)	*Japanese, these, Pete*
i	/aɪ/ (comme dans *my*)	*line, site, recognise* Exceptions : *give* et *live* /ɪ/
o	/əʊ/ (comme dans *no*)	*alone, hope, home, vote* Exceptions : *some, love, come, none, done* /ʌ/, *gone* /ɒ/
u	/juː/ ou /uː/ (comme dans *you*)	*tube, cube, flute*

⚠ Cette règle s'applique surtout dans **une syllabe accentuée**. Si la syllabe est inaccentuée, la voyelle est souvent réduite en *schwa* /ə/ ou en *i* bref /ɪ/ : ***Europe*** /ə/, ***image*** /ɪ/, ***active*** /ɪ/...

▶ En l'absence d'un *e* ou si la consonne qui suit est double, la voyelle est prononcée comme une voyelle brève.

site /aɪ/ ≠ *sit* /ɪ/ *later* /eɪ/ ≠ *latter* /æ/ *tube* /juː/ ≠ *tub* /ʌ/

1 Écoutez et répétez les paires de mots suivantes.

Audio hatier-clic.fr/21amc/155a

a. *not / note*
b. *cut / cute*
c. *mad / made*
d. *fat / fate*
e. *hid / hide*
f. *cop / cope*
g. *cod / code*
h. *hat / hate*

2 Les mots suivants respectent-ils tous la règle du e magique ou s'agit-il d'exceptions ? Vérifiez vos réponses et répétez les mots.

Audio hatier-clic.fr/21amc/155b

hole • cope • love • over • come • bone • none • moment • some • Anglophone • cone • gone • government • prove • milestone • oppose • rose

La syllabe nucléaire

▶ Dans une phrase ou dans un groupe de souffle (un groupe de mots entre deux pauses, voir Unité 17 p. 209), une syllabe est toujours prononcée avec plus de force que les autres. On parle parfois **de syllabe nucléaire ou de nucleus**.

*Northern Ireland is part of the United **KING**dom.*

▶ En général, il s'agit de la syllabe accentuée **du dernier mot lexical (nom, adjectif ou verbe).**

*The flag of Scotland is white and **BLUE**.*

▶ La plupart du temps, **les mots grammaticaux** (les pronoms, les prépositions ou les auxiliaires) ne portent pas l'accent nucléaire.

*I didn't **VOTE** for him.*

▶ Malgré tout, il peut arriver que l'accent nucléaire soit déplacé sur un autre mot que l'on juge particulièrement important car on considère que c'est lui qui porte **l'information vraiment nouvelle**.
C'est par exemple le cas quand on complète ou corrige une information qui a déjà été donnée.

*"The flag of Scotland is **BLUE**."*

*"Actually, it is **DARK** blue!"*

▶ De manière générale, les mots que l'on répète et qui reprennent des informations déjà connues ne portent pas l'accent nucléaire.

3 Recopiez les phrases et soulignez le mot qui contient la syllabe nucléaire. S'agit-il du dernier mot lexical ou l'accent est-il déplacé ? Justifiez votre choix. Vérifiez vos réponses en écoutant l'enregistrement. Puis répétez les phrases.

Audio hatier-clic.fr/21amc/155c

a. *She lives in Ireland.*
b. *You should tell me about your country.*
c. *You should tell me about it.*
d. *Where does her family come from?*
e. *"Did Wales vote for independence?"*
"No, but Scotland did."
f. *"Is Australia a republic?"*
"No, France is a republic."
g. *"This human rights activist was born in North Korea."*
"No, she was born in South Korea."

Let's translate

La transposition en français d'un texte

Rendez compte en français des principales idées exprimées par le document B p. 149 (*Making Puerto Rico a state*). Veillez à ne pas simplement en dresser la liste, mais à les expliciter lorsque cela vous paraît pertinent.

Organiser sa transposition

▶ La transposition doit restituer les idées du texte d'origine dans l'ordre où elles apparaissent et mettre en évidence son organisation.

▶ C'est pour cette raison que votre compte rendu doit être organisée **en paragraphes** : chaque paragraphe doit développer une idée clef dans le raisonnement de l'auteur.

▶ Dans un premier temps, il est utile de lire attentivement chaque paragraphe du texte et de déterminer quels sont **les mots importants** qui résument bien l'idée qui y est développée.

▶ Veillez également à relever **les mots de liaison** qui expriment des liens logiques : cause (*because*, *as*), conséquence (*therefore*, *that's why*), opposition (*however*, *nevertheless*, *though*), etc. Ces mots devront apparaître dans la transposition en français afin de marquer les différentes étapes du raisonnement de l'auteur.

⚠ Votre compte rendu ne doit pas comporter d'élément qui ne figure pas dans le texte d'origine. De même, il ne faut pas donner son opinion sur celui-ci.

Translation Tip

Une transposition doit également refléter le ton du texte : les faits sont-ils exposés de façon neutre et objective ou l'auteur prend-il position ?

À vous !

a. Rédigez un très court paragraphe introductif pour présenter le document : la date, la source (à souligner) et le thème de l'article. Quel est le but de ce texte ?

b. Dans chaque paragraphe du texte, relevez le mot, l'expression voire la phrase qui vous semble la plus importante et qui résume l'idée du paragraphe.

c. Relevez tous les mots de liaison qui expriment un lien logique (précisez à chaque fois quel est ce lien logique : cause, conséquence, opposition…).

Build up your vocabulary

1 Fill in your own mind map here: hatier-clic.fr/21amc/156

2 Complete the following sentences with words from your mind map.

a. The Prime Minister made a reassuring but strong speech in order to **…** people's fears and to state her will to **…** .

b. During the last referendum in Porto Rico, the **… …** was so low that it **…** the results in favour of **…** .

c. If anything **… …** in this country, the PM is to be blamed.

d. The different ministers will find a solution to **…** the crisis if they **… … … …** .

e. The majority of people in the territory of Nunavut are in favour of more **…** , but with a strong **…** with Canada.

f. Cameroon's linguistic crisis: the imminent **… … …** between the two communities.

g. It will be quite a **… … …** for the Labour Party to trust someone, as their future leader, with such conservative ideas.

3 Use any word from your mind map to create four press release headlines.

For example: Scotland's push for **independence** vote put PM in **dilemma.**

Projects

1

Forum discussion: you interact on a social media about your wish for your country to become independent or to maintain the status quo. Explain to the other users your point of view and illustrate it.

1. **Choose your role.**
   Student A: you are a Falklands Islander.
   Student B: you are Welsh.
   Student C: you are Australian.
   Student D: you are Puerto Rican.
2. **Choose a side and find arguments for or against independence in the documents of the unit or online.**
3. **Use the specific vocabulary studied in the unit (see Build up your vocabulary p. 156).**
4. **Take turns and respect your partners.**

2

Debate: you are taking part in a TV show about the different ways countries have asserted their identity and claimed their independence. Act out the televised debate.

1. **Choose your role and the country you want to represent:**
   Student A: you claim your identity and independence.
   Student B: you don't claim your identity or independence.
   Student C: you have mixed feelings.
   Student D: you are the host.
2. **Go through the unit to find the arguments you want to defend.**
3. **Review vocabulary and expressions to express your opinion, agree/disagree.**
4. **Use gap fillers in your conversation to give you time to think.**

Pour l'écrit du Bac

A Brexit: Ireland needs to press for reunification vote, says Sinn Féin

Party leader Mary Lou McDonald says Boris Johnson's attitude to EU withdrawal agreement means her country cannot trust him

Ireland cannot trust an "erratic" and "dangerous" Boris Johnson on Brexit and needs to start pressuring Downing Street for a referendum on Irish unification, according to Mary Lou McDonald, the leader of Sinn Féin.

Johnson has forfeited credibility by unpicking the withdrawal agreement and cannot be believed when he says he wants a trade deal, said McDonald. "He's the prime minister and perfidious[1] Albion just got perfidiouser, if there's such a word."

If Britain did not "honour a bargain fairly struck" it would face a backlash from Ireland's allies in the EU and US, where congressional leaders could sink Downing Street's hopes of a US trade deal, said McDonald. "If there is damage in Ireland, if there's a hardening of the border – well, then all bets are off." [...]

A government led by Sinn Féin would jolt British-Irish relations. A mouthpiece for the IRA during the Troubles, it has become a mainstream, leftwing party that appeals to voters in the south of Ireland on bread-and-butter issues, especially health and housing.

However, McDonald, 51, stressed its enduring determination to unite Ireland. "In my lifetime? Absolutely. All of the signposts, all of the markers, point in the direction of reunification," she said.

By next year, the centenary of Northern Ireland's creation, Catholics are expected to outnumber Protestants for the first time, a seismic demographic shift that comes just as Brexit has prompted some unionists[2] to question the region's position in the UK.

"The electoral majority for unionism is now gone, politics on this island has changed in ways that are profound," said McDonald, a Trinity College graduate from Dublin who succeeded Gerry Adams as party leader in 2018. [...]

McDonald said the promise of a new, progressive, inclusive Ireland, with an NHS-style health service, would win over enough voters.

Under the Good Friday agreement, the UK's Northern Ireland secretary must call a referendum when it appears likely that most people would vote in favour of a united Ireland.

However, McDonald said ministers refused to spell out the exact conditions that would trigger a vote. "I wouldn't like anybody in the British system to imagine that they hold a trump card that says 'we will forever avoid or defer a referendum in Ireland'. They don't have that right."

She said a united Ireland must offer unionists "the kinds of protections and assurances that they need" – for instance, a possible continued role for the Stormont assembly. She ruled out moving the capital from Dublin.

www.theguardian.com, Oct. 1st, 2020

1. traitorous 2. supporters for Northern Ireland remaining part of the UK

B

PARTIE 1

Prenez connaissance des documents A, B et C et traitez les sujets suivants en anglais.

a. Say what the documents reveal about the unity of the United Kingdom and how the different countries are claiming their identity within the kingdom. Pay attention to the relationship between language and cultural heritage. (300 words)

b. *"The electoral majority for unionism is now gone, politics on this island has changed in ways that are profound"* (document A, l. 36-38). Say what documents A, B and C show about the moving relationship between Northern Ireland-Wales and London; and how Brexit has changed the issue of identity and independence. (200 words)

PARTIE 2

Traduisez le passage suivant du document C en français (l. 32-41).

By 1999, this process had led to the creation of the National Assembly for Wales. For the first time in its history, Wales had a democratic institution of national self-government. Yet, in the referendum that led to its creation, only a quarter of the electorate voted in favour, while half of people chose not to vote at all. The reality was that, although a mundane sense of Welsh identity was very powerful, the political implications of this were narrow.

C A brief history of Wales: the resilient nation

In the 2016 referendum on whether to remain in the EU, there was a small majority in Wales in favour of leaving. The Brexit vote was a shock to many who cherished the idea that Welsh politics and society were more progressive than in England. Indeed, it undermined the very idea that Wales was different to England.

For many, a belief in Wales as a left-wing society has acted as compensation for the fragility of Welsh identity. Wales does not have the strong media sector, separate legal jurisdiction or national confidence that Scotland enjoys. Of course, the Welsh language is clear evidence that Wales and England have distinct cultures, but only a fifth of its people actually speak Welsh, its position as the dominant community language of the rural west is in retreat, and the legal requirements for Welsh to be taught to all children and used in all public documentation have sometimes caused controversy. Support for Welsh independence appears to be growing but it remains a minority position. Despite the patriotism evident in sport, there is often a frustration among advocates of independence that the people of Wales can appear unambitious and even regressive in their attitudes towards Welsh nationality. And yet, given the history of the nation, the fact that Welsh identity still exists at all is in many ways remarkable. [...]

By 1999, this process had led to the creation of the National Assembly for Wales. For the first time in its history, Wales had a democratic institution of national self-government. Yet, in the referendum that led to its creation, only a quarter of the electorate voted in favour, while half of people chose not to vote at all. The reality was that, although a mundane sense of Welsh identity was very powerful, the political implications of this were narrow. [...]

In the economic, political and cultural turmoil caused by a combination of Brexit, global warming and technological change, it may be that Wales will wither away. Indeed, the very concept of nations might be rejected as a quaint but divisive historical legacy. Equally, such is the level of disruption and uncertainty in British and global politics that Wales might be on a long road to becoming an independent nation.

www.historyextra.com, Nov. 22nd, 2019

13 On-screen representation in the USA

The expert's view
hatier-clic.fr/21amc/160a

In the news
hatier-clic.fr/21amc/160b

Projects

You are a journalist. Write an op-ed about a series or a movie dealing with inclusion or casting minorities.

Play an interview between a director, an actor and a TV host discussing a new series or movie dealing with minorities.

Grammar p. 168 Phonology p. 169

Someone like me?

A My identity is my superpower

1

The Maid - Hollywood loves Latinos as janitors or maids. From "Family Guy's" Consuela to Jennifer Lopez in 2002's "Maid in Manhattan," such characters have inundated pop culture. Sometimes the trope[1] comes from Latino producers. Eva Longoria's "Devious Maids" was criticized when it debuted as a "wasted opportunity," though it lasted four seasons.

www.latimes.com, April 27th, 2017

1. recurrent theme

2

America Ferrara's TED Talk

Video hatier-clic.fr/21amc/160c

GROUP WORK

e-worksheet hatier-clic.fr/21amc/160d

Group A on document 1.
Group B on document 2.

1. Pick out the stereotypes mentioned in your document.
2. Each document suggests that the stereotype is perpetrated by the community itself as well. Discuss this point of view after reading the Culture Tip below.
3. **CONNECT.** Explain how the still and the article from the *L.A. Times* illustrate America Ferrara's words.

Culture Tip

The TV drama *Devious Maids* (2013-2016) features four Latina maids working for very wealthy and influential families. The show is based on the contrast between the down to earth, ethical Latinas and the corrupt lifestyle of the affluent, powerful white people.

B Hollywood's representation of the Indian

Recently, an online petition was launched to protest against the casting of non-Native American actress Rooney Mara in the role of an Indian character in a forthcoming adaptation of *Peter Pan*. An article defending the petition states: "With so few movie heroes in the US being people of color, non-white children receive a very different message from Hollywood, one that too often relegates them to sidekicks[1], villains, or background players." Additional examples of such outcries[2] over recent miscasting[3] include Johnny Depp as Tonto in *The Lone Ranger* (2013), as well as, to a lesser extent, Benicio Del Toro as Jimmy Picard in Arnaud Desplechins's *Jimmy P.: Psychotherapy of a Plains Indian* (2013).

Neither the problem nor the outcry are new. Many studies have shown why the movie industry has often employed non-Indian actors to portray Indian characters. This trend, which Ted Jojola calls "absurd," has increasingly raised the ire[4] of Indian activists, who forced Hollywood to open its eyes on such issues in 1973, when Marlon Brando refused to accept his Oscar for his role in *The Godfather* and sent onstage in his stead Apache actress Sacheen Little Feather to make a statement against "the treatment of American Indians today by the film industry." This activism targets two issues: Indian characters are only sidekicks, villains, or background players; and Indian actors are not cast in roles of heroes. Even in Westerns, where the presence of Native Americans should be taken for granted for obvious historical reasons, Indians are only extras or fake. In a thorough study of the genre, Jane Tompkins sums up Hollywood's treatment of Natives "as props, bits of local color, textural effects. As people they had no existence. Quite often they filled the role of villains, […] a particularly dangerous form of local wildlife. But there were no Indian characters, no individuals with a personal history and a point of view."

Aaron Carr et Lionel Larré,
Hollywood Indian Sidekicks and American Identity, 2016

1. companions 2. outrage
3. giving the wrong acting role to sb 4. anger

1. Identify the two problems mentioned in the essay. Show how people have tried to raise awareness.
2. **Grammar** Translate the following sentence into French: *"Neither the problem nor the outcry are new"* (l. 16).
3. Explain the difference between "Native American" and "Indian" and conclude on the impact Hollywood has.

C The Oscar's new diversity rules

The Oscars' new diversity rules are all well and good, but will they make any difference?

The Academy has made a set of rules for best picture nominees that almost every film already meets. So will they lead to any actual change?

[...] Under the new regulations, which will come into effect for the 2025 Oscars, entries for best picture must satisfy two of four criteria to be eligible. The headline criterion is on-screen representation: at least one lead character in the movie must be from "an underrepresented racial or ethnic group"; at least 30% of the general ensemble cast must be from at least two underrepresented groups (women, racial, ethnic, LGBTQ, or people with disabilities); or the movie's subject must concern one of those groups.

[...] Still smarting from the #OscarSoWhite debacle five years ago, the Academy has been at pains to rebrand itself, at least cosmetically. The impression of the awards as being decided by a bunch of stale[1], pale, male Hollywood veterans was an increasingly bad look, and the drive to reposition the Academy as a global, 21st-century organisation has been under way for some time. Primarily this has taken the form of a membership shake-up – gently wheeling out the old white guys and welcoming in some diverse new blood. This year's intake was 45% women, 36% underrepresented ethnic/racial communities, and 49% international, from 68 countries.

A cynic might put the Academy's makeover down to concern over its own image – Hollywood is no stranger to vanity, after all. But the commitment to drive structural change is surely sincere, even if it is constrained by the twin demands of respecting "tradition" and not getting ahead of the industry's slow progress. So you could say the Academy is being seen to do something, but not too much.

www.theguardian.com, Sept. 9th, 2020

1. not fresh

1. Explain the journalist's opinion and pick out phrases typical of an op-ed article (article in which the author expresses a clear opinion).
2. List the different criticisms against the Oscars and explain the expected results of this new set of rules.
3. Write a short essay to express your point of view: will this set of rules solve the problem raised in text B?

Why representation matters

A The Asian American example

1. Explain what Constance Wu said about representation and use the poster to say the effect her movie may have.
2. List the gestures, mimics and expressions which are typical of this kind of TV show. Describe and explain the public's reaction.

PAIR WORK

3. In pairs, play the beginning of the TV show when the hosts are introducing the actress, her movie and its impact on the Asian American community.

Video hatier-clic.fr/21amc/162

B Inclusive series

1

LOGLINE[1]: A gay man with mild cerebral palsy[2] decides to rewrite his identity as an accident victim and finally go after the life he wants. Based loosely on Ryan O'Connell's upbringing and experience.

1. brief summary of a movie written to stimulate the spectator's interest
2. disorder, disease affecting muscles

"When you don't see yourself being reflected back at you, you're implicitly told that you don't matter, that your life does not matter, it's not worth being told, it's not worth being discussed."

Ryan O'Connel, author and main actor of the series

2

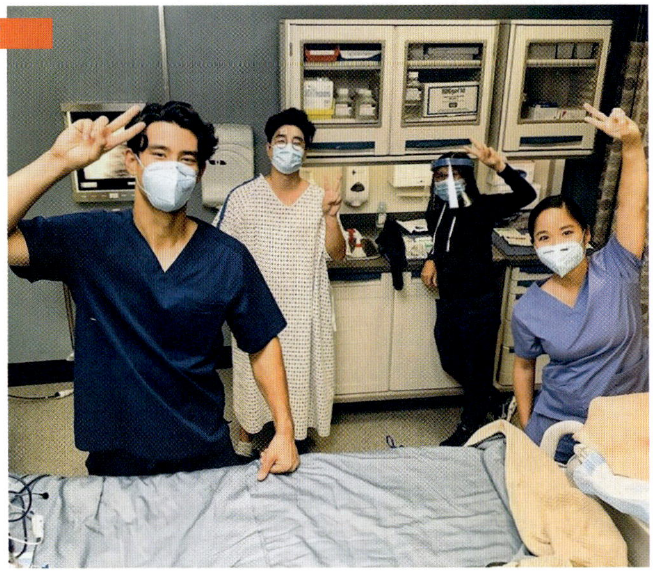

juliewong2017 When we shot this scene and I saw Nico, Mabel, and Dave on the monitor, I got teary-eyed. When you grow up virtually never seeing anyone like you on your favorite shows (or any shows), the message it sends about your place in the world is that there isn't one. What an honor to be part of a show that revolutionized how so many people are represented on TV, including the AAPI [1] community with @iamsandraohinsta's iconic Cristina Yang. Thank you, thank you, thank you @shondarhimes and @kristavernoff for changing the face of television. #greysanatomy #aapi #asianamerican #representationmatters

1. AAPI: Asian American and Pacific islander

GROUP WORK

Group A on document 1
Group B on document 2

1. Pick out information about the plot and main characters of this series. Group B: read *Let's focus on...* n° 1, p. 166.
2. Explain the message delivered in the document.
3. Present the document you have worked on to your classmate. Then, write successive messages to react to the Facebook post.

C Representation and self image

Why on-screen representation matters, according to these teens

Why does representation in pop culture matter?

For some young students, portrayals of minorities in the media not only affect how others see them, but it affects how they see themselves.

"I do think it's powerful for people of a minority race to be represented in pop culture to really show a message that everybody has a place in this world," said Alec Fields, a junior at Forest Hills High School in Pennsylvania.

Fields was one of 144 middle and high school students who were interviewed about seeing themselves reflected — or not — on the screen. PBS NewsHour turned to our Student Reporting Labs from across the country to hear what students had to say, a topic that research shows still has room for growth.

The success of recent films like "Black Panther" and "Crazy Rich Asians" have — again — sent a message about the importance of representation of minorities, not only in Hollywood but in other aspects of pop culture as well.

Only two out of every 10 lead film actors (or 19.8 percent) were people of color in 2017, this year's UCLA Hollywood Diversity Report found. Still, that's a jump from the year before, when people of color accounted for 13.9 percent of lead roles. People of color have yet to reach proportional representation within the film industry, but there have been gains in specific areas, including film leads and overall cast diversity.

According to 2018 U.S. Census Bureau estimates, the nation's population is nearly 40 percent non-white. By 2055, the country's racial makeup is expected to change dramatically, the U.S. will not have one racial or ethnic majority group by 2055, the Pew Research Center estimated.

Some students said that not seeing yourself represented in elements of pop culture can affect mental health.

"It just makes you feel like, 'Why don't I see anybody like me?' [It] kind of like brings your self-esteem down," said Kimore Willis, a junior at Etiwanda High School in California.

[…] Others, however, feel that Hollywood is overcompensating for their lack of diversity by depicting exaggerated and stereotypical characters.

Eric Wojtalewicz from Black River Falls High School in Wisconsin said that he sees a lot of gay characters that seem "over-the-top," playing on old tropes[1]. "I definitely think that not all gays are like that," he said.

Kate Casper, a junior at T.C. Williams High School in Virginia, called Hollywood's attempt at diversity "disingenuous[2]." Although there can never be enough diversity, Casper said, she feels that the entertainment industry is using diversity for economic benefit. "Diversity equals money in today's world, which is cool, I guess," she said, adding that "it's cooler to have pure motives."

The UCLA report agrees that diversity sells. It says that the median global box office has been the highest for films featuring casts that were more than 20-percent minority, making nearly $450 million in 2017.

Although public opinion may be divided about whether the entertainment industry is doing enough to represent all types of people, South Mountain High School student Dazhane Brown in Arizona said that feeling represented is "empowering."

"If you see people who look like you and act like you and speak like you and come from the same place you come from… it serves as an inspiration," Brown said.

www.pbs.org, Nov. 14th, 2019

1. stereotyped representations 2. insincere

1 Give as many details as possible about the survey that was conducted.

2 Use the figures given l. 26-45 to explain the contradiction.

3 Focus on the teenagers' answers and classify them: very positive / reserved opinion. Explain their arguments in your own words.

4 Write five questions which could have been asked to the teenagers in the survey. Then, choose one and write down what you would answer.

Minorities in the new mainstream

A Hitting the front pages

1

2

* Tipping point: important moment in a process when things are changing

1. Describe and analyse the layout of both covers. Show how it puts forward the person represented.
2. Explain what the short text on the cover suggests about the symbolic aspect of this actor / actress.
3. Write the headline and subhead of the article about this actor and this actress.

B Native American actor Wes Studi's honorary Oscar

1. Pick out information about Wes Studi (life, career).
2. Explain his reaction to the honorary Oscar (words and tone of voice).
3. Phonology Listen and repeat the following words: *nuance, Studi, lieutenant, wolves, would*. Pay particular attention to the pronunciation of the vowels in bold.
4. You are invited to hand over the Oscar to Wes Studi. Write a little speech insisting on what the actor brought to the representation of his community. Use *Let's focus on...* n° 3 and 4, p. 167 to enrich your presentation.

Audio hatier-clic.fr/21amc/164

C A genuine activist?

Why Netflix is leading the way when it comes to LGBTQ+ representation on TV
How the streaming service is besting its rivals.

[S]treaming services have led the way for a number of years now, counting more LGBTQ+ characters among their shows than all of the major US networks combined. However, GLAAD[1] recently reported that Netflix is home to more than any other, doubling the number of queer characters it streams in the past year alone.

It doesn't take more than a quick glance at the options available to confirm that's true. Just in the past six months alone, Netflix Originals like *Elite, Sex Education, The Haunting of Hill House* and *Chilling Adventures of Sabrina* have all foregrounded[2] three-dimensional queer characters who defy the stereotypes that LGBTQ+ people have long been subjected to.

[…] Bypassing the predominantly straight white cis[3] male paradigm of most networks, these new forms of distribution provide more diverse storytellers […] the opportunity to finally tell their stories and to tell them well.

But why is it that Netflix in particular has found so much success with LGBTQ+ storytelling? Well, it's been clear for a long time that the foundations of Netflix are built on its experimentation with original programming. Now that other streaming services are playing catch up, trying to match the popularity of shows like *Stranger Things*, it's easy to forget what a gamble[4] it was to pour money into programming such as *House of Cards*.

[…] Other early success stories such as *Orange Is the New Black* proved that such an approach could pay off, and including LGBTQ themes did nothing to hamper[5] their popularity. If anything, it was refreshing to hear these stories finally being told in more authentic ways than ever, and audiences responded warmly.

Unfortunately, Netflix is notorious for keeping its viewing figures close to its chest, so it's hard to determine exactly how successful these shows were. What we do know though is that Netflix certainly possesses the financial backing to fund LGBTQ+ storytelling without fear of any kind of reprise.

[…] Unfortunately, it's not all good news. Even though Netflix took an admirable stand recently against transphobic laws in North Carolina, the streaming giant still doesn't have a LGBTQ+ section on site for every region. Avoiding the inclusion of a queer category in certain countries outsides of the UK and North America suggests that Netflix still bows under local pressures, avoiding any explicit reference to LGBTQ+ representation in countries that might not welcome it.

The site's social media accounts also come under fire almost daily for cancelling some of its most popular LGBTQ+ shows too soon, including *Sense8, Everything Sucks!* and *One Day at a Time*.

www.digitalspy.com, April 18th, 2019

1. Gay & Lesbian Alliance Against Defamation 2. put in the front part 3. cisgender, not transgender 4. place bets 5. slow down progress

Culture Tip

The abbreviation LGBTQ+ was first used in the 1990s to refer to the "Lesbian, Gay, Bisexual, Transgender and Queer" community. This umbrella term intends to include all sexual orientation and identity.

1. Read the text and identify the elements that make Netflix particularly keen on including LGBTQ+ characters.
2. Read the tweets and identify the major criticisms against Netflix.

PAIR WORK

3. Let's debate: is Netflix only interested in money or is it genuinely promoting the LGBTQ+ community?

Seqi @seqilol · 7 mai 2020
necessary for your bottom line maybe

corporations don't give a sh• about your social issues please understand this

Netflix @netflix · 7 mai 2020
sorry you have yet to realize that every gay person is very necessary twitter.com/AdamSB__/stat...

5 8

"Of course we support you now that it is legal and therefore profitable to do so, why did we wait until now? No more questions! Watch our movies!" https://t.co/cfKaiA4ufQ
— Ryuuko Matoi @Kamen Rider Ex Aid (@Smug_Legend)

Let's focus on...

Grey's Anatomy 1

This medical drama TV show aired for the first time in 2005. It has broken many records and barriers for women and minorities. The show's diverse cast made Shonda Rhimes (executive producer) famous. *Grey's Anatomy* used a colour-blind casting technique: none of the characters were racially pre-determined. As a result, not only does it feature strong leading women such as Catherine Fox and Meredith Grey, but it also portrays gay and lesbian couples, many mixed-race couples, minority characters in top jobs at the hospital, intern with a hijab, etc.

Timeline 2

1915
Charlie Chaplin dresses as a woman in *A Woman.*

1920s
Anna May Wong, first Asian American to become an international star.
Sessue Hayakawa, Japanese American actor considered a sex symbol in Hollywood.

1930
The Motion Picture Production Code of 1930 (Hays Code).
- "Miscegenation (sex relationships between the white and black races) is forbidden."
- "Sex perversion or any inference to it is forbidden."

1940
Hattie Mc Daniel, first black Oscar winner for her part in *Gone With the Wind.*

1951
Pamphlet *The Dilemma of the Negro Actor* by Clarence Muse, a black pioneering Hollywood actor, about the trap African Americans are caught in.

1959
Some Like it Hot by Billy Wilder. Two male characters pretend to be women. Hint at a gay marriage at the end.

1961
West Side Story by Robert Wise, about the opposition between a white gang and a Puerto Rican gang in New York.

1970
The Boys in the Band, by William Friedkin, first Hollywood movie targetting a gay audience.

Oscars ③

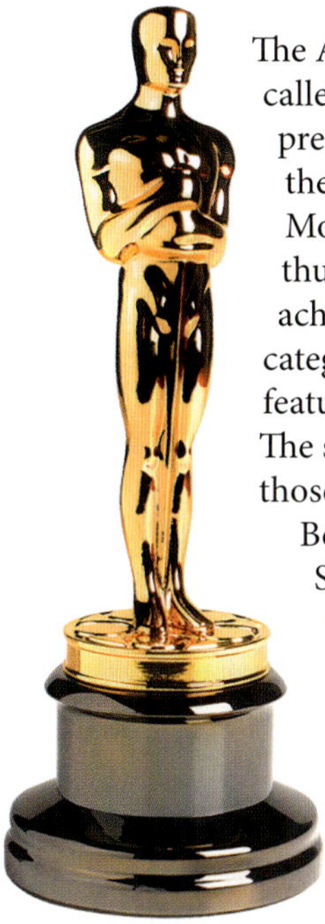

The Academy Awards, commonly called Oscars, are among the most prestigious annual awards given in the film industry. The Academy of Motion Picture Arts and Sciences thus honours the best moviemaking achievements of the year in 24 categories (acting, directing, technical features…).

The so-called "Big Five" awards are those for Best Picture, Best Director, Best Actor, Best Actress, and Best Screenplay (either Best Original Screenplay or Best Adapted Screenplay).

The first ceremony was held on May 16th, 1929 and lasted 15 minutes with only 270 guests. Nowadays, there are 6,000 voters, and 3,400 guests can attend the ceremony at the Dolby Theater.

The statuette, which was designed in 1929 by a Los Angeles sculptor called Stanley, features a knight standing on a reel of film and holding a crusader's sword.

The Academy Museum of Moving Pictures opened in September 2021.

Wesly Studi ④

Born in 1947, Wes Studi is an American Cherokee actor and director who is famous for his portrayal of Native Americans in many Hollywood movies such as *Dances with Wolves* (1990), *The Last of the Mohicans* (1992), *Geronimo: An American Legend* (1993) and *The New World* (2005). He is also known for playing Sagat in *Street Fighter* (1994). He starred in *Hostiles*, *Heat*, *Mystery Men*, *Avatar*, *A Million Ways to Die in the West*, and the television series *Penny Dreadful* too.

He received an Academy Honorary Award in 2019, becoming the first Native American and the second North American indigenous person to be honoured by the Academy (the first was Buffy Sainte-Marie in 1983).

In 2020, he was ranked #19 in the *New York Times* list of the 25 greatest actors of the 21st century.

1979
Walk Proud, movie about a Mexican gang leader played by a white actor Robby Benson.

1983
Canadian Buffy Sainte-Marie, first Native American to receive an Academy award for Best Original Song for the movie *An Officer and a Gentleman*.

1993
- *Philadelphia* by Jonathan Demme, movie about AIDS discrimination.
- *The Joy Luck Club*, first all-Asian cast movie.

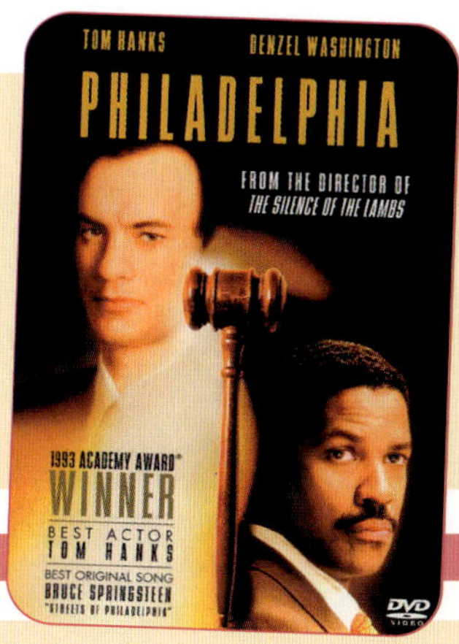

1998
Eddy Murphy's speech during the Academy Awards ceremony, accusing the organisation of racism in its selections.

2009
Tiana, first African American Disney princess.

2018
Crazy Rich Asians, by Jon M. Chu, first all-Asian cast movie since 1993.

2018
Black Panther by Ryan Coogler, first African American superhero movie.

2019
Native American actor Wes Studi gets an honorary Oscar.

Practice your grammar

As et *like*

▶ *As* a des emplois multiples. Il peut s'agir :
– d'**une conjonction** qui introduit une subordonnée. Elle peut exprimer **la simultanéité** (« lorsque »), **la cause** (« comme », « étant donné que ») ou **la comparaison** (« comme ») :

As she was born in Puerto-Rico, she was fluent in Spanish. (cause)

– d'**une préposition**. Elle signifie alors « en tant que » (elle exprime **l'identification**) et est souvent utilisée avec l'article indéfini *a / an* ou l'article Ø au pluriel :

As Ø people they had no existence.

– *As* permet de construire **des comparatifs d'égalité (*as* + adjectif + *as*)**.

*Eva Longoria isn't **as** popular **as** Jennifer Lopez.*

▶ ***Like* est une préposition** qui introduit un groupe nominal ou un pronom. Elle permet de faire **une comparaison** et se traduit par « comme ». On trouve aussi souvent *like* après des verbes d'état tels que *look*, *sound*, *smell* :

*"If you see people who **look like you** and act **like you** and speak **like you**... it serves as an inspiration," Brown said.*

⚠ Dans la langue familière, *like* est souvent utilisée pour introduire une proposition subordonnée à la place de *as*. N'utilisez pas cette structure à l'écrit.

*Nobody understands her **like I do**.* (écrivez plutôt : ***as I do***)

▶ Notez l'expression ***such as*** (« tel que ») pour introduire un exemple. ***Like*** est également courant mais moins formel.

*Other early success stories **such as** Orange Is the New Black proved that such an approach could pay off.*

1 Complétez avec *as* ou *like*.

a. *I'd love to be able to sing … Jennifer Lopez.*

b. *Today, more than 56 million Americans identify … Hispanic and Latino.*

c. *… most immigrants, my parents believed in the American dream.*

d. *… you know, LGBTQ+ is an abbreviation for "Lesbian, Gay, Bisexual, Transgender and Queer".*

e. *She was tired of always being cast … a maid because she was Latina.*

2 La conjonction *as* exprime-t-elle la cause, la simultanéité ou une comparaison dans les phrases suivantes ? Précisez son emploi, puis traduisez en français.

a. *Ten people got arrested **as** they were trying to cross the border illegally.*

b. *My husband and I are raising our children bilingual, just **as** I was raised.*

c. *Representation of women remained unchanged at 46% of series regulars, but they are still underrepresented, **as** they make up 51% of the US population.*

Les structures corrélatives

▶ Une structure corrélative permet de mettre en relation deux éléments (deux adjectifs, deux propositions, deux groupes nominaux, etc.) dans une phrase.

▶ ***Both... and...*** se traduit par « à la fois … et… » :

*Thus, **both** Indian characters **and** Native American actors remain relegated to playing sidekicks or underlings.*

▶ ***Either... or...*** (/ˈaɪðə/ ou /ˈiːðə/) se traduit par « soit… soit… » et exprime donc une alternative :

*She's the kind of actress you **either** love **or** hate.*

▶ ***Neither... nor...*** se traduit par « ni… ni… ». Le verbe est employé à la forme affirmative.

***Neither** the problem **nor** the outcry is new.*

▶ ***Whether... or...*** indique qu'aucune des deux possibilités n'a d'importance :

*Not so long ago, Asian actors - **whether** American **or** not - were asked to speak in broken English.*

3 Complétez avec *both... and...*, *either... or...*, *neither... nor...* ou *whether... or...*

a. Peter Pan *portrays Native people in a stereotypical manner that reflects … their diversity … their authentic cultural traditions.*

b. *The series has been praised by … the gay … the mainstream press.*

c. *Historically, Hispanic men have been portrayed … as villains … as Latin lovers.*

d. *Over 30% of Hispanic workers, … immigrants … US citizens, say they have experienced workplace discrimination.*

Improve your pronunciation

Les voyelles /uː/ et /ʊ/

▶ **Les voyelles /uː/ et /ʊ/** sont deux sons souvent confondus par les francophones :
- **/uː/** est **une voyelle longue**, très proche de la voyelle française de « l**ou**ve ».
- **/ʊ/** est **une voyelle brève** qui n'a pas d'équivalent en français. Il s'agit d'un son intermédiaire entre la voyelle *ou* de « n**ou**s » et le son *o* de « d**o**s ».

▶ La voyelle /uː/ peut être représentée par les graphies suivantes :

oo dans la plupart des cas	*soon, moon, too, stool*
u, ***ue***, ***ui*** ou ***ew***	*flu, truth, blue, clue, suit, fruit, crew, blew*
ou dans quelques mots	*group, soup, souvenir, you, youth, routine, route*
o dans quelques mots	*prove, lose, move, shoe, tomb, who, whose, womb, do, two*

▶ La voyelle /ʊ/ peut être représentée par les graphies suivantes :

oo* avant *k	*look, cook, book, took*
o* ou *oo dans quelques mots très courants qui sont **des exceptions**	*good, (Holly)wood, foot, (under)stood,* le suffixe *-hood (childhood), woman, wolf...*
u dans quelques mots courants à apprendre	*pull, bull, full, put, push, cushion, sugar*
ou dans **les modaux**	*could, should, would*

1 Répétez les paires de mots suivantes.

Audio hatier-clic.fr/21amc/169a

a. *fool / full*
b. *pool / pull*
c. *Luke / look*

2 Chassez l'intrus dans chacune des listes de mots suivantes. Écoutez l'enregistrement pour vérifier vos réponses, puis répétez.

Audio hatier-clic.fr/21amc/169b

a. *moon • soon • school • book*
b. *boot • root • foot • shoot*
c. *food • stood • good • Hollywood*
d. *pull • put • truth • push*

3 Pour chacun des mots suivants, trouvez un homophone (un mot qui ne s'écrit pas de la même manière mais qui se prononce de façon identique).

Audio hatier-clic.fr/21amc/169c

flu • too • through • blue • crews

L'élision

▶ Une élision est **la disparition d'un son** dans un mot.

▶ La voyelle /ə/ (appelée *schwa*) disparaît souvent en milieu de mot :

int(e)resting • happ(e)ning • p(e)rhaps

Ce phénomène est fréquent dans les terminaisons suivantes ***-ery / -ary***, ***-erence***, ***-ening***, ***-onal***, ***-erable***, ***-ically*** :

myst(e)ry • diction(a)ry • diff(e)rence • fright(e)ning • pers(o)nal • consid(e)rable • historic(a)lly

! Le son /ə/ apparaît toujours dans des syllabes inaccentuées et peut être orthographié par n'importe quelle voyelle.

▶ Les consonnes /d/ et /t/ ne sont parfois pas prononcées quand elles apparaissent entre deux consonnes.

an ol(d) car • my firs(t) professional audition

Ainsi, le *d* du mot ***and*** et le *t* des auxiliaires négatifs (*don'**t***, *isn'**t**...*) sont souvent omis quand le mot qui suit commence par une consonne :

Anyway, I didn('t) get the job.

4 Recopiez les mots suivants et soulignez les voyelles susceptibles d'être élidées. Écoutez l'enregistrement pour vérifier vos réponses, puis répétez.

Audio hatier-clic.fr/21amc/169d

professional • national • miserable • personal • national • technically • conference • history • government • police • perhaps

5 Recopiez la phrase suivante et soulignez les *t* et les *d* susceptibles d'être élidés. Écoutez l'enregistrement pour vérifier vos réponses, puis répétez.

Audio hatier-clic.fr/21amc/169e

I couldn't find my keys, so I asked my dad to take me to my first job interview.

Let's translate

Many studies have shown why the movie industry has often employed non-Indian actors to portray Indian characters. This trend, which Ted Jojola calls "absurd," has increasingly raised the ire of Indian activists, who forced Hollywood to open its eyes on such issues in 1973, when Marlon Brando refused to accept his Oscar for his role in *The Godfather* and sent onstage in his stead Apache actress Sacheen Little Feather to make a statement against "the treatment of American Indians today by the film industry." This activism targets two issues: Indian characters are only sidekicks, villains, or background players; and Indian actors are not cast in roles of heroes. Even in Westerns, where the presence of Native Americans should be taken for granted for obvious historical reasons, Indians are only extras or fake.

Aaron Carr et Lionel Larré,
Hollywood Indian Sidekicks and American Identity, 2016

L'étoffement

▶ Un étoffement consiste à traduire un mot (qui se suffit à lui-même en anglais) par un élément plus long et plus complexe en français.

▶ Les prépositions anglaises doivent par exemple souvent être étoffées pour être correctement traduites. On peut avoir recours à :

- une proposition relative :
  *He picked up the book **on** the table.*
  → Il prit le livre **qui se trouvait sur la table**.
- une proposition infinitive de but :
  *I went to the supermarket **for milk**.*
  → Je suis allé au supermarché **pour acheter du lait**.
- un participe passé ou présent :
  *According to an article **in*** The Guardian
  → D'après un article **publié dans** *The Guardian*

Translation Tip

Pour désigner les parties du corps, le français utilise souvent l'article défini « le, la, les », tandis que l'anglais a recours à un déterminant possessif (*my, your*...) :
*He washed **his** hands* → Il s'est lavé **les** mains. Attention donc à la traduction de *open **its** eyes* !

À vous !

a. Attention aux faux amis. Comment traduira-t-on : *issues, villains, extras* ?

b. Proposez des traductions pour *non-Indian, against, treatment* qui utilisent le procédé de l'étoffement.

Build up your vocabulary

1 Fill in your own mind map here: hatier-clic.fr/21amc/170

2 Fill in the blanks with words from your mind map.

a. Nowadays ... television showcases more ... in ... .

b. Teenagers ... that looks like them and debunks ... .

c. The Oscar ceremony is criticised for ... and perpetuating the white male domination on screen.

d. TV shows are pushing the limits of ... and producers are paying more attention to ... and ... characters.

e. The cast of *Grey's Anatomy* ... and ... for future generations of minorities who can ... the various characters.

3 Use the vocabulary in your mind map to create a tweet about underrepresentation in TV shows and movies.

Projects

1

You are a journalist, specialised in cinema and series.
Write an op-ed article about a TV series or movie of your choice dealing with inclusion or casting actors from minorities. Explain what you find interesting or disturbing about this fiction.

1. Select a TV show or movie you want to work on. Make sure it includes an underrepresented group.
2. Because an op-ed article expresses a subjective point of view, think of the opinion you wish to express before you start writing.
3. Make a chart with interesting and disturbing elements and compile your arguments.
4. Select specific scenes from the show or movie as illustrations of your arguments.
5. Do some research to compare this series with previous representations of the same underrepresented group in movies or series.
6. Write the article paying attention to paragraphs, expressions of opinion and the structure.

2

You are a director, an actor and a TV host for a famous American talk show. Play an interview about a new series or movie dealing with minorities.

1. Decide who is the host and who is / are the interviewee(s).
2. Imagine the main aspects of your series or movie: write the logline of the project, choose a title, make a quick ID card to make sure you know about the character.
3. Make sure your project offers a new, interesting representation of underrepresented groups.
4. The host should focus on introducing the character and the topic. The actor and director should think about their attitude towards the topic and gather arguments to convince the spectators about the originality of the project.
5. Use gap fillers and try to show emotions and reactions.
6. Act out your interview in the talk show.

Pour l'écrit du Bac

A Representation in films matter to minorities

53% of black Americans think black characters are often stereotyped

With Black Panther breaking box office records and films like Get Out and The Shape of Water bringing home Academy Awards, Hollywood seems to be moving towards more diversity in its offerings. But YouGov data shows that minority groups feel there's a long way to go before movies are representative - and fair.

When it comes to roles available in Hollywood, a new survey from YouGov Omnibus finds that most Americans believe that there are a sufficient amount of television and film roles for white people (59%), and many agree that there are enough roles for men (47%). Fewer are likely to believe that women (37%), blacks (35%), Hispanics (23%), Asians (21%), and LGBTQ people (18%) have enough roles available to them.

Looking at different aspects of representation through a lens of self-perception only amplifies these figures. For example, while 23% of Americans believe that there are a lack of characters on screen who reflect an authentic experience for blacks, black Americans are twice as likely (46%) to say the same. A similar trend emerges when a quarter of Americans (26%) cite that the same problem exists for Hispanics but over a third of Hispanics themselves (37%) believe that people like them are cast inauthentically.

Hollywood's problem with inauthenticity may stem from its use of stereotypes to portray certain groups. While 41% of Americans say that black characters are often stereotyped, 53% of black Americans feel this way.

The imbalance exists within roles too. When asked if characters who resemble them have too little dialogue, 49% of blacks and 53% of Hispanics agreed. This number soars to 61% when other minorities, comprised of Asian, Middle Eastern, Native American, and mixed people, were asked.

Those same groups were likely to call attention to power dynamics in roles where people like them were cast. Blacks (49%), Hispanics (49%), and other minorities (58%) say that they frequently see characters like them cast as sidekicks[1], but not as authority figures.

Authentic representation may be difficult to achieve with less screen time. Blacks (49%), Hispanics (40%), and other minorities (47%) were likely report that they see characters like them get killed off more and/or earlier than other characters.

Over half of black Americans (58%) say that while growing up, it was difficult for them to find role models who looked like them in movies and TV. Hispanics (55%) and other minorities (56%) also identify with the same problem. Wins for directors Jordan Peele and Guillermo Del Toro at the Oscars may move the needle on this; over half of Americans (54%) say that the industry would do a better job portraying people like them if they hired directors who've had similar life experiences.

www.today.yougov.com, March 6th, 2018

1. subordinates

PARTIE 1

Prenez connaissance des documents A, B et C et traitez le sujet suivant en anglais.

Taking into account their specificities, say how the documents illustrate the impact TV shows and films can have in empowering minorities. (500 words)

PARTIE 2

Traduisez le passage suivant du document A en français (l. 35-47).

The imbalance exists within roles too. When asked if characters who resemble them have too little dialogue, 49% of blacks and 53% of Hispanics agreed. This number soars to 61% when other minorities, comprised of Asian, Middle Eastern, Native American, and mixed people, were asked.

Those same groups were likely to call attention to power dynamics in roles where people like them were cast. Blacks (49%), Hispanics (49%), and other minorities (58%) say that they frequently see characters like them cast as sidekicks, but not as authority figures.

B

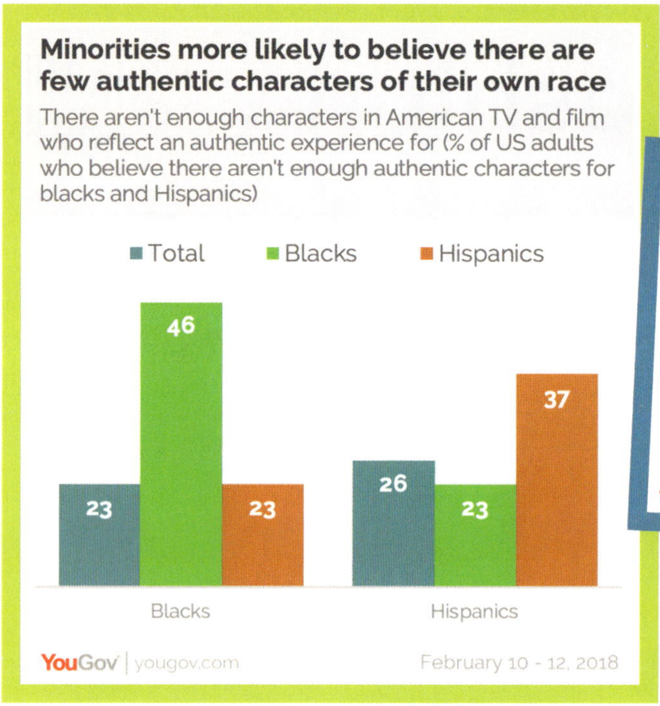

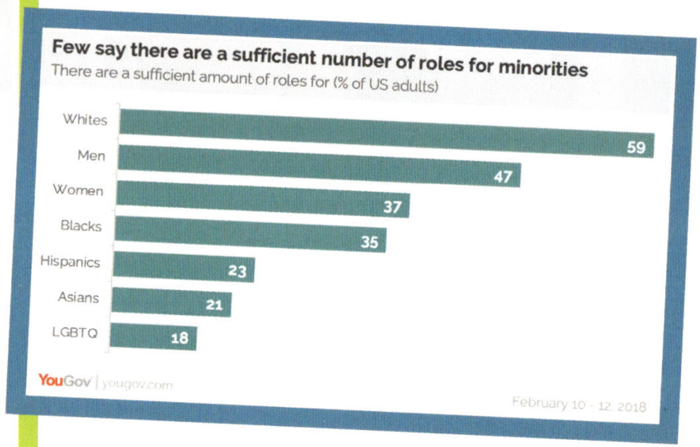

C

Kiera Allen of "Run" on Upending Disability Stereotypes

Kiera Allen makes her feature[1] debut this week, playing opposite Sarah Paulson in the Hulu suspense film "Run". It is a rare instance of a wheelchair user starring in a thriller.

In a recent Zoom interview, Allen, 22, discussed playing Chloe, a home-schooled teenager with an overprotective single mother, and how the movie upends typical narratives about disabled people.

> "This is one of the best representations of a disabled character I've ever seen," Allen said.

We don't often see an actor who uses a wheelchair in real life in this type of role — in a major thriller.

It feels like it's going to be the first time a lot of people in my generation ever see a real wheelchair user onscreen playing a wheelchair user. That's a huge honor.

There is so little media representation of people with disabilities that I feel like I'm representing an entire community because of this lack of visibility. I'm really hoping that this movie brings down some barriers and that more disabled people are cast in major movies. […]

Have you discussed the film with anyone who is disabled?

I've had some really great conversations about accessibility, about Chloe, and how she flips the narrative of abuse of disabled people. She's not a victim. She's a hero. […]

There is one scene where a broken escalator foils an escape. Did you have any input in that?

[…] Chloe gets trapped in a basement[2] and can't get out because her mother has weaponized inaccessibility against her.

It's a terrifying thing, inaccessibility, being trapped somewhere, being unable to get out, having to rely on people who may or may not have your best interests at heart, people who you may not even know, when a space is inaccessible. That stuff is really scary. And I've never, ever seen any art in any form that represents that terror. […]

What has it been like to see disabled characters portrayed by nondisabled actors?

There have been films that represent disability using able-bodied actors that have been important to me, and I felt seen and I felt like this was a representation of disability that was really true to my life. But that was also all I had. I didn't have a lot of pieces of entertainment — films, TV, plays — where I could see a genuinely disabled person in that role. I'm just so excited for young people to see that now.

The New York Times, Nov. 20th, 2020

1. film 2. underground floor

Flash

14 Fast fashion fever

In the news
hatier-clic.fr/21amc/174

Projects

- Write a blog post to raise awareness about sustainable fashion.
- Make a video on the inequalities of fast fashion for the *Fashion Channel*.

Grammar p. 178 Phonology p. 178

Not a good look

A Behind the bargain

PAIR WORK

Student A on the infographic
Student B on the cartoon

1. Describe and analyse your visual, paying attention to the designer's intentions.
2. Explain how the visuals illustrate the title of this page: "Not a good look."
3. Swap information with your partner and react.

Illustration by Alexandre Magnin - Sustainabilityillustrated.com

B What's fast fashion?

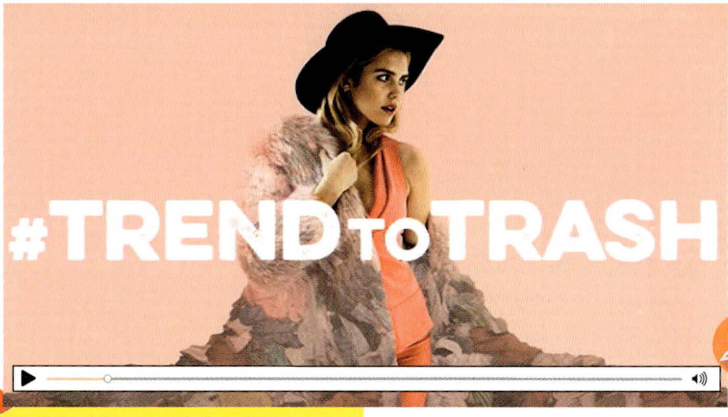

Fast fashion explained

Video hatier-clic.fr/21amc/175a

1 GROUP WORK

Group A – The brands: Pick out the strategies used by fashion retailers to make more profit.

Group B – The employees: Explain how workers' rights are ignored.

Group C – The environmentalists: Find elements showing the impact of fast fashion on the environment.

2 Report to the other groups.

3 Define fast fashion and write a short paragraph entitled "The dark side of fast fashion."

C The downside of fast fashion

Exploitation and sweatshops are at the core of fast fashion: it's time to dismantle the system.

This week, an investigation into sweatshops in Leicester shed an unwelcome light onto the UK's dark relationship with fast fashion.

Companies like Boohoo, who are one of the most successful brands on the market, have been using factories in Leicester to produce their cheap clothing for years. But for the most part, British consumers seem to imagine their clothes are made (albeit in sweatshops[1]) in countries like India and Bangladesh where the exploitation of workers is widely reported.

Earlier this month all eyes were focused on H&M and Topshop as reports came flooding in[2] that due to cancelled and unpaid orders, thousands of garment[3] workers in Bangalore had been fired on the spot to cut costs at struggling factories.

For many, the realisation that such abuses are taking place so much closer to home has been seemingly harder to swallow. Fast fashion relies on globalisation and like all exploitative industries, it is powered by cheap labour used to generate huge profits with low production costs. From Bangalore to Leicester, the fashion industry is built upon the mass exploitation of those who work within its supply chains[4]. […]

The Clean Clothes Campaign said about exploitation in the industry: "The garment industry, not only the fast fashion industry, is built on poverty wages[5] and sweatshop conditions. These working conditions are no mere flaws[6] of individual factories, but they are driven by an industry practice of pushing for the lowest price and shortest lead times in an eternal race to the bottom."

"The awkward truth is, that as long as this dynamic is not addressed, scandals about working conditions in factories in the UK, Bangladesh or Ethiopia will continue to resurface from time to time."

"As long as brands respond by cutting and running or just addressing conditions in a single factory, the overall level of exploitation will not change. Only if brands change their purchasing practices for the better, can the workers stitching their clothes start to receive decent wages and better conditions."

"The sweatshop conditions in factories in Leicester are no new discovery. It is paramount that this time the issues are addressed properly by moving beyond a factory level approach to holding the brands at the top of the supply chain responsible for the conditions under which their clothes are produced." […]

Much like the consumer's aim to find the cheapest, most readily available clothing, brands use the same logic to find suppliers across the world. The only way we can begin to tackle exploitation in the fashion industry is to look at dismantling the systems that make it all possible in the first place.

www.euronews.com

1. small factories where workers are exploited 2. arrived in great quantity 3. piece of clothing 4. supply chain: network between a company and its suppliers to produce and distribute a product 5. salary 6. defects

1 Complete the e-worksheet, then pick out elements to demonstrate that fashion brands are responsible for certain inequalities in the fashion industry.

2 Explain how such unjustness is not limited to developing countries.

3 Present the unfairness of fast fashion on the programme *The Fashion Spot*.

e-worksheet hatier-clic.fr/21amc/175b

Breaking up with fast fashion

Not a good look

Audio hatier-clic.fr/21amc/176

A Destroying the world

1. Pick out the negative effects of fast fashion.
2. List the tips that are given.
3. Record a podcast to encourage your peers to break up with fast fashion.

B Fast fashion and sustainability

As people start to become more conscious of their ecological footprint in the world, people are looking to find ways of making their lives more sustainable. Avoiding fast fashion is one of the ways that people can try to limit their impact on the ecosystem.

What is fast fashion?

Fast fashion was born after the Industrial Revolution. With the introduction of sewing machines, dressmaking could now be outsourced to stores instead of the home. This transition quickly created life-altering challenges for workers.

One of the first-ever major garment factory fires happened in 1911 at New York's Triangle Shirtwaist building. Close to 150 workers lost their lives and the majority of those workers were immigrant women.

Fast fashion today has been described as cheap clothes inspired by high fashion – trendy items offered at 'affordable' prices for the everyday consumer. However, unsafe labour practices that plagued[1] fashion factory workers in the early 20th century, including a lack of training, defective equipment or unreasonable work schedules and pay, still largely persist today.

The 'fast' part of fast fashion comes from the speed at which these clothes are produced, which can only be done through the use of sweatshops in developing countries providing cheap and poorly regulated labour.

What is sustainable fashion?

"More sustainable fashion can be defined as clothing, shoes and accessories that are manufactured, marketed and used in the most sustainable manner possible, taking into account both environmental and socio-economic aspects," according to Green Strategy – an organization that has been helping fashion companies pivot to sustainable fashion since 2012.

Sustainability can be achieved through repurposing fabric and looking for improvements throughout the overall manufacturing process. There is no way to be 100 per cent sustainable, but trying to find better ways to produce clothes should be the goal.

https://charlatan.ca

1. Explain the success of fast fashion.
2. Outline the differences between fast fashion and sustainable fashion.
3. Read the Culture Tip and write the synopsis of the documentary called *The Price of Fast Fashion*.

Culture Tip

A *sweater* in the 1850s was an employer who demanded monotonous work for very low wages. So the term ***sweatshop*** was born, meaning a workplace where unskilled employees, sometimes children, work many hours in unhealthy or oppressive conditions, for poverty-level pay.

C Sustainable clothing: a good look

The 21 most ethical and sustainable clothing brands from the UK

Share for change

There's no denying it: sustainability is becoming increasingly important. More and more people are trying to reduce their impact on the planet and, as a result, a growing number of ethical and sustainable fashion brands are arising to both meet the demand and help change the fashion industry for the better. But which clothing brands are ethical? First, let's learn about what makes a brand ethical in the first place.

What makes an ethical brand?

Long story short, an ethical brand makes sure it positively impacts on people, the planet, and animals.

An ethical brand ensures its workers are treated fairly across the supply chain[1]. This includes policies and practices on child labour[2], forced labour, worker safety, the right to join a union[3], and payment of a living wage[4].

An ethical brand also cares about its use of resources and energy, reducing its carbon emissions, impact on our waterways, as well as using and disposing of chemicals safely.

Finally, an ethical brand uses no or very few animal products, like wool, leather, fur, angora, down feather, shearling[5], karakul[6], and exotic animal skin and hair. Ideally, the brand is 100% vegan!

Now that you know what to look for to determine whether a brand is ethical or not, you might decide to shop from companies located in your country or region. Whether it is to support your local communities or reduce your carbon footprint when shopping online, shopping locally has many great benefits.

So if you live in the UK, you might be wondering which clothing brands are ethical. We know how you feel, which is why we compiled this list of eco-friendly and conscious fashion brands from UK.

https://goodonyou.eco

1. network between a company and its suppliers to produce and distribute a product 2. jobs exploiting children 3. organisation of workers 4. salary 5. wool from a sheep less than two years old 6. sheep from Central Asia

1 Determine the subjects of the two documents.

2 Compare and contrast both documents. Then explain the latest fashion trends.

3 CONNECT. Explain how the inequalities of fast fashion are being countered.

Total Secondhand Apparel Market to Double in 5 Years With Resale Sector Driving the Growth[1]

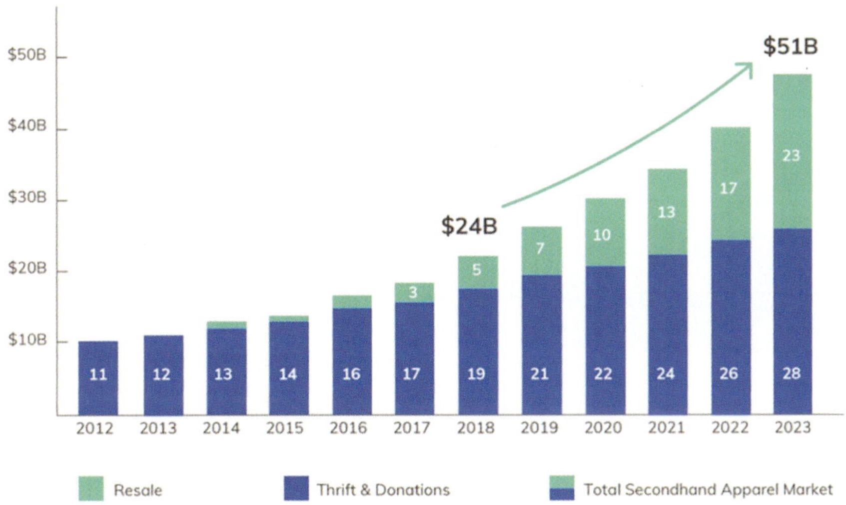

Resale has grown

21X

faster than the retail apparel market over the past three years.[1]

Leading Resale Sector Players

THREDUP
Managed marketplace for all brands—from GAP to Gucci.

The RealReal
Managed marketplace for luxury and designer brands.

POSHMARK
Peer-to-peer marketplace focused on social commerce.

Practice your grammar

Le *present perfect* avec *for* et *since*

▶ Pour traduire « depuis », on a recours :
– à ***for*** pour introduire **une durée** : *for three hours, for 10 years, for long.*
- à ***since*** pour introduire **une date** ou **un moment ponctuel** : *since 2012, since September, since then.*

Since peut également introduire **une proposition subordonnée**. On le traduit alors par « depuis que ». Notez l'emploi du prétérit dans la proposition subordonnée ci-dessous :

I've been working** as a fashion designer **since I was 23.

▶ Dans une phrase contenant *for* ou *since*, si l'on veut indiquer qu'une action ou un état a commencé dans le passé et est encore en cours au moment où l'on parle, on met le verbe principal au ***present perfect* en *be + ing* (*have / has been* + V-*ing*)**. On le traduit en français par un présent :

*Companies like Boohoo **have been using** factories in Leicester to produce their cheap clothing **for years**.*

▶ La forme simple peut être utilisée surtout avec les verbes d'état qui ne s'emploient normalement pas avec *be* + V-*ing* :

***I've known** this fashion brand **for a long time**.*

⚠ Il est possible d'utiliser le prétérit avec *for*. Dans ce cas, on le traduit par « pendant » et non par « depuis » :

***I worked** for this company **for 10 years**.* → J'ai travaillé pour cette entreprise **pendant 10 ans**.

1 Complétez les phrases avec *for* ou *since* et mettez le verbe entre parenthèses à la forme qui convient.

a. *This clothes shop ... (be) open ... two months.*

b. *... 1990, more than 400 sweatshop workers ... (die) in factory fires.*

c. *I ... (sew) my own clothes ... years.*

d. *... February, online clothing sales ... (grow) by 17% in Britain, while in-store sales ... (slump) by 22%.*

e. *The textile industry ... (thrive) ... the 1960s.*

2 Traduisez.

a. Depuis plusieurs mois, la production augmente plus rapidement que la demande.

b. Cette usine fabrique des vêtements de sport depuis 10 ans.

c. Cette usine a fabriqué des vêtements de sport pendant 10 ans.

Build up your vocabulary

Fast fashion

The dark side

- **sweat**shop
- **fac**tory
- exploi**ta**tion
- cheap/child **la**bour
- **haz**ardous work
- **pov**erty **wa**ges
- **wor**king con**di**tions
- ine**qual**ities
- **plas**tic pol**lu**tion

The players

- brand
- **la**bel
- sup**ply** chain
- re**tail**er
- **bar**gain
- good deal
- high street store
- the **fash**ion **in**dustry
- **cus**tomer de**mands**
- **fash**ion trends

Looking to the future

- **sec**ond-hand ap**pa**rel
- **vin**tage **clo**thing
- sustaina**bil**ity
- eco**lo**gical **foot**print
- ethical **gar**ments
- treat sb **fair**ly
- dis**man**tle
- **tack**le an **is**sue
- swap
- rent

Projects

1 Write a blog post to raise awareness about sustainable fashion.

1. Gather information from this unit and do some research yourself.
2. Mindmap your ideas: the positive aspects of sustainable fashion versus the downside of fast fashion.
3. You can raise awareness by using figures, maps, infographics.
4. Think up an attractive, appealing layout for your blog post: add images, maps...
5. Show what is being done to change things.

2 Make a short video for *Fashion Channel* to illustrate the inequalities of fast fashion.

1. Make a snappy and interesting introduction to your video to encourage your audience to keep on watching: a quote, some statistics, a definition...
2. Plan out the main part of your video, using knowledge from this unit or information from the media.
3. Illustrate your arguments with pictures, graphs etc.
4. Only use key words to give structure to your work and to avoid reading.
5. Check the pronunciation of unfamiliar words.

Flash

15 Black Lives Matter in the UK

In the news
hatier-clic.fr/21amc/180

Projects

- Let's debate: Is removing statues erasing history?
- Write a poem or a slam focusing on racial progress in the UK.

Grammar p. 180 Phonology p. 180

How the past shaped UK cities

A Historical landmarks

1. Study the map and explain how Bristol is linked to slavery.
2. Show why it's important artists like Banksy join the debate.
3. CONNECT. Explain how both documents symbolise a kind of racial frontier in the UK.

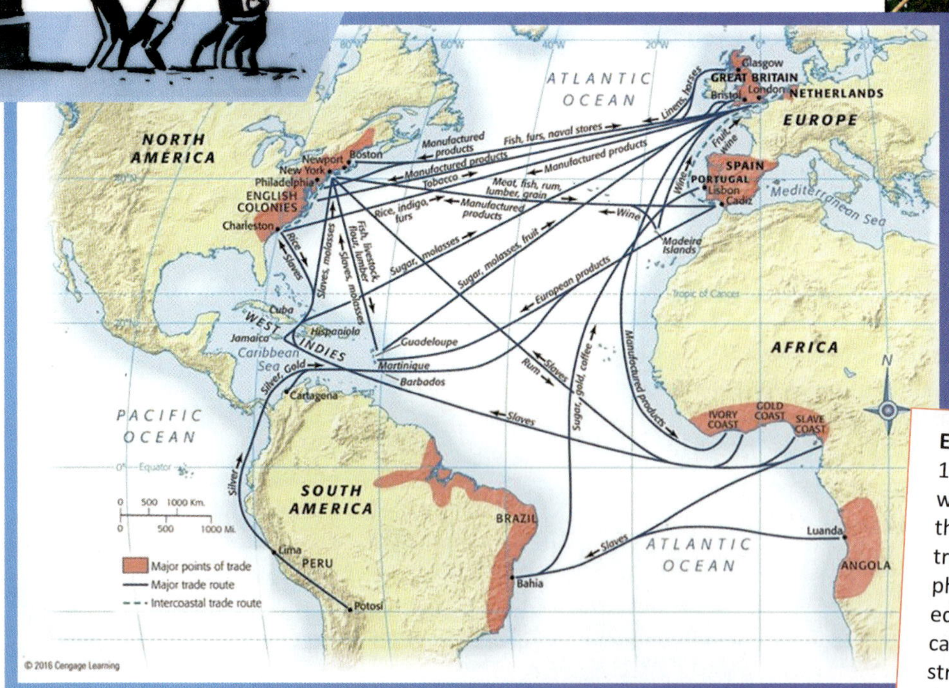

Culture Tip

Edward Colston (1636-1721) was a politician who made a fortune with the transatlantic slave trade. He later became a philanthropist and donated to several charitable causes in Bristol. Many streets and buildings in the city bear his name.

B Glasgow's darker past

1. Show why Graham Campbell is an excellent symbol for this fight and comment on the tone of his message.
2. Explain Glasgow's involvement in slave trade.
3. Demonstrate how black people contributed to Glasgow's wealth.
4. Describe Glasgow's part in slave trade for your school's gazette's Black History Month special.

How slavery shaped some of the UK's biggest cities

Video hatier-clic.fr/21amc/181

C Facing the past

British cities face a long overdue reckoning with racist monuments

With Liverpool, it was cotton. For Bristol, it was sugar; Glasgow, it was tobacco. Then there's London which, aside from being a hub for shipping, also developed many of the financial instruments that allowed the industry to operate. It's a grim[1] fact that many of Britain's most progressive cities were built on the profits of the Atlantic slave trade.

The evidence of all this has been fully visible – in statues and plaques, and in the names of streets and buildings – without ever being truly accounted for. As with so much of Britain's imperial history, this issue has rarely troubled mainstream[2] politics, even as it defines the country in the eyes of the world.

The closest the idea of decolonisation has come to bothering that mainstream was in 2015, when the Rhodes Must Fall movement, which protested the commemoration of Cecil Rhodes and his record in southern Africa, spread from the University of Cape Town to Oxford. But that was reported largely as a matter of campus politics, of wokeness[3] gone mad, rather than one of Britain's history of racism. What's more, five years later, the statue at Oriel College that the Oxford students were protesting still stands.

This week, though, something seems to have shifted. On Sunday night, attendees at a Black Lives Matter protest in Bristol pulled down a statue of slaver Edward Colston that had stood in the city centre since 1895. Colston, who lived from 1636 to 1721, was a major local philanthropist who did much to shape the city, endowing almshouses[4] and churches, hospitals and schools. But he made his money through the Royal African Company, which is estimated to have transported over 84,000 African men, women and children to the Americas. The BLM protestors threw his statue into the harbour.

The incident has been criticised by some, mostly on the political right, as a symptom of mob rule[5]: Remove the statue, they say, but not like this. Such critiques ignore the fact that, as Labour's shadow foreign secretary Lisa Nandy said Wednesday night, "For 20 years, protesters and campaigners had used every democratic lever at their disposal, petitions, meetings, protests, trying to get elected politicians to act. And they couldn't reach a consensus and they couldn't get anything done." The mob got it done. […]

The right's other critique of this movement is that it amounts to rewriting history. But it's very far from clear that a monument without context teaches history. (Surely a museum would be better?) It's also not clear why, when everything else about the fabric and identity of our cities is continuously in flux, they are required to leave any statue, let alone one of a racist who treated other human beings as property, in its place forever. As historian David Olusoga argued in the Guardian this week, "The toppling of Edward Colston's statue is not an attack on history. It is history."

Oxford's Rhodes Must Fall protest has restarted, incidentally. Perhaps, this time, he will.

Jonn Elledge, June 11th, 2020
http://citymonitor.ai

1. ugly 2. conventional 3. state of being aware 4. shelters for the poor and homeless 5. large groups acting without the consent of the authorities

1. List the references to slave trade (dates, places, people) and create a timeline.
2. Show that peaceful protests have not been successful to remove a statue in the past.
3. Prepare a speech defending the toppling of the statue that you will give at Bristol speaker's corner.

Erasing frontiers

A Black voices matter

1. Watch the video and note down the keywords. Write the message of the song in your own words.
2. Listen to the beginning of the first verse. Rephrase his idea concerning "work".
3. Focus on the second verse. Show Dave's goal when citing names of African countries.
4. You have just watched the video on YouTube: leave a comment.

Dave delivers political rap at the Brits Awards 2020

Video hatier-clic.fr/21amc/182a

e-worksheet hatier-clic.fr/21amc/182b

B Creating new symbols

BLAM app lets users erect augmented reality statues of historical black figures

London non-profit BLAM has developed an augmented reality (AR) app called History Bites, which gives users the chance to see black history memorialised through virtual plaques and sculptures.

Developed as part of Black History Month, the mobile application is aimed at kids and profiles five different figures, including Mae Jemison, the first black woman to travel to space.

Completing a quiz about each of them allows users to place a corresponding monument in the world around them using AR, so they can see their heritage and history represented wherever they want – whether in prominent public spaces or their own neighbourhood.

"At BLAM we are constantly seeking new ways to counterbalance the effects of Eurocentricity and racism on Black lives and the creation of this app can help Black children reaffirm positive ideas and notions about their black identity," BLAM founder Ife Thompson told Dezeen.

"Through racism and the media, Black children are disproportionately exposed to negative narratives and concepts about their blackness. This often leads to them internalising negative stereotypes about themselves and others that look like them." [...]

The only event to be included is the four-month-long Bristol Bus Boycott, which took place in the UK in 1963 and forced the Bristol Omnibus Company to back down from its discriminatory ban on black and Asian drivers.

This is immortalised in the app through a sculpture of a raised black fist, serving as a symbol of solidarity and resistance.

"We do not have enough statues of Black people in the UK," Thompson said.

"The UK education system remains a white space. And since we do not learn truthful narratives about our past, it is almost impossible to honour something you have never even been taught about."

Out of thousands of statues in the UK, only 15 are of named, black individuals, according to estimates by the BBC – the same number as the approximately 15 statues of people directly involved in the transatlantic slave trade which still stand in places across the UK today.

Jennifer Hann, Nov. 6th, 2020
www.dezeen.com

C Teaching a new narrative

1

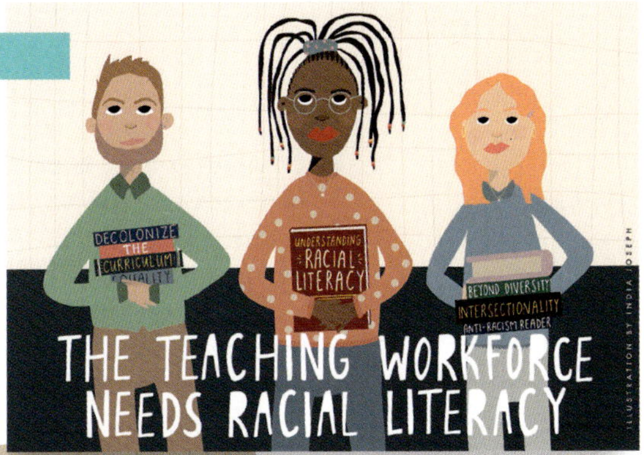

2

3

GROUP WORK

Student A: poster 1
Student B: poster 2
Student C: poster 3

1. Describe your poster (layout and what it shows).
2. Rephrase the caption or the titles in your own words, and show the aim of your poster. Present it to the two other students.
3. Read the caption and/or the titles of the books and guess the meaning of the words "literacy", "overwhelming", "decolonizing", or use a monolingual dictionary.
4. Explain to a friend why these posters have been created.

Sculptor unveils "black everywoman" as UK row over statues and race grows

What kind of statue can represent black British women today? It is a question the sculptor Thomas J Price believes he has answered.

After the controversial appearance of the statue of a Black Lives Matter protester on the plinth formerly occupied by an effigy of Edward Colston in Bristol last Wednesday, Price has unveiled a new work destined for east London.

Reaching Out shows a woman looking down at her mobile phone and is intended as a black "everywoman", shown in a relaxed, modern pose.

"It was important to me not to have to fulfil a certain expectation, like the idea you would have to be a top athlete, or a Black Panther or a politician to be up there," Price told the Observer. "It is a fictional character based on various references. I did have someone model for part of it but she remains anonymous.

"All the characters in my work are anonymous. I want to show something about their inner world, rather than their public roles. I want to show people at a natural moment. That can look vulnerable, but it is strong really, because there is no facade." […]

Price, who studied at Chelsea College of Art and the Royal College of Art, and who has had major shows at the National Portrait Gallery and the Yorkshire Sculpture Park, says the title of the work has a double meaning. The figure is using her phone, but she is also allowing the artist to reach out. "Is she calling someone or being called? There is a bit of push and pull, a feedback loop there," he said.

Vanessa Thorpe, *The Guardian*, July 19th, 2020

Activities for texts 1 and 2

1. Pick out adjectives from the articles and use them to show what both men want to fight and convey with their creations.
2. Explain why they think artistic creation can help build a new narrative regarding black lives in the UK.
3. **CONNECT.** Show that the use of public spaces can be positive for the cause of Black British cultural and creativity.

Practice your grammar

Prépositions et gérondif

▶ Le gérondif (en anglais *gerund*) est une forme nominalisée du verbe. On le construit **en ajoutant *-ing* au verbe**. On le trouve souvent après **des prépositions** telles que *of, for, about* ou bien encore *without* :

*The protesters left the square **without** be**ing** arrested.*

▶ Le gérondif est fréquent après **des verbes qui se construisent avec des prépositions**. En voici quelques exemples :

- *apologise **for** V-ing*
- *criticise sb **for** V-ing*
- *succeed **in** V-ing*
- *prevent sb **from** V-ing*
- *accuse sb **of** V-ing*
- *blame sb **for** V-ing*
- *discourage sb **from** V-ing*
- *insist **on** V-ing*

*Some rioters were accused **of** loot**ing** stores.*

⚠ On traduit souvent ces gérondifs en français par des **infinitifs.** Pour marquer une antériorité, on a également recours à **un infinitif passé** (*avoir* ou *être* + participe passé) :
*Certains émeutiers ont été accusés d'**avoir pillé** des magasins.*

▶ Quelques verbes et expressions qui se construisent avec **la préposition *to*** sont susceptibles d'être suivies d'un gérondif :

- *be used / get used **to** V-ing*
- *look forward **to** V-ing*
- *contribute **to** V-ing*
- *amount **to** V-ing*
- *object **to** V-ing*
- *when it comes **to** V-ing*

*Removing statues from public places **amounts to** rewrit**ing** history.*

1 Complétez avec la préposition qui convient : *for, of, on, from* ou *in*.

a. *She insisted ... visiting the International Slavery Museum in Liverpool.*

b. *A lot of activists and celebrities blamed the government ... not supporting the Black Lives Matter movement.*

c. *The police prevented the protesters ... entering the city hall.*

d. *The crowd ultimately succeeded ... toppling the statue.*

e. *The mayor was criticised ... taking part in the demonstration.*

2 Traduisez en utilisant le verbe entre parenthèses. Veillez à utiliser la bonne préposition.

a. Mes parents m'**ont dissuadé** de manifester contre les violences policières. *(discourage)*

b. J'**ai hâte** de visiter le vieux port. *(look forward)*

c. Ils **ont été arrêtés** pour avoir pillé des magasins. *(be arrested)*

d. Je **n'ai pas l'habitude** de me plaindre. *(be used)*

Build up your vocabulary

BLACK LIVES MATTER

Denouncing

- make a clean break with the past
- **re**proach sb with **do**ing sth
- pull down
- put sth up: e**rect**
- ropes
- **heart**-wrenching: **caus**ing great **sad**ness or **sym**pathy
- trans**at**lantic slave trade
- **hope**lessness

Being equal

- be on an **e**qual **foot**ing with
- turn the clock back
- **lev**el the **play**ing field: make oppor**tu**nities **e**qual for all
- bridge the **diff**erences: over**come**
- **per**sonal i**den**tity /aɪˈden.tə.ti/
- strong-**willed**: de**ter**mined
- **sym**pathy: com**pass**ion
- **hall**mark: dis**tinc**tive characte**ris**tic

Narrating

- ac**count**: **sto**ry
- **try**ing: an**noy**ing and **dif**ficult
- im**ply**
- break new grounds: **in**novate
- teach sb sth
- depersonali**sa**tion
- em**brace** one's **sto**ry: ac**cept** enthusi**as**tically

(Re)shaping space

- be **sep**arated from
- be dragged a**way**: be **phys**ically moved
- cross the **thresh**old: cross a **fron**tier
- im**port** ≠ ex**port** goods
- turn sth **in**to: trans**form**
- **topp**le **stat**ues

Projects

1 Let's debate: Is removing statues erasing history?

1 Create groups of five and choose your part.
- a historian for the removals and one against
- a town mayor in Bristol, Liverpool or Glasgow
- an expert in art and symbols

2 Think about your character.
- name
- personality
- views...

3 Prepare your arguments.
- Find examples to supports your views.
- Collect information in the unit and on the web.

4 Prepare a list of link words and 10 to 15 key words to be more natural when you speak.

5 Be convincing with your tone and the words you use (*should*, *must*...).

2 Write a poem or a slam questioning racial progress in the UK.

1 Think of the messages you want to convey.
- Refer to a special event or place to start your slam or your poem.
- Write a mind map with two or three keywords/key events.
- Use ideas from the unit and do some research on the web.

2 Write your slam or poem.
- Decide the numbers of stanzas or verses you want to write.
- Make the lines rhyme or not (patterns: AABB, ABAB, ABBA...).
- Use metaphors or alliterations to spice up your creation.
- Use verbs of your five senses to describe your emotions.

3 Memorise your slam or your poem.
- Use an online dictionary to make sure you know the pronunciation of the words.
- Read it aloud in front a mirror.
- Record yourself to check what can be improved.

4 Perform your slam or poem.
- Use your body language to match your words.
- Play with your voice (whispers/shouts...).
- Accentuate the words that are important to you.

16 Megacities: a threat to sustainability?

The expert's view
hatier-clic.fr/21amc/186a

In the news
hatier-clic.fr/21amc/186b

Projects

- You are a journalist working for National Geographic. Write a report on how megacities tackle sustainability.
- You are an American architect. Deliver a speech to help shape a sustainable future for Mumbai.

Grammar p. 194 **Phonology** p. 195

The emergence of megacities

A A new distribution of megacities

1

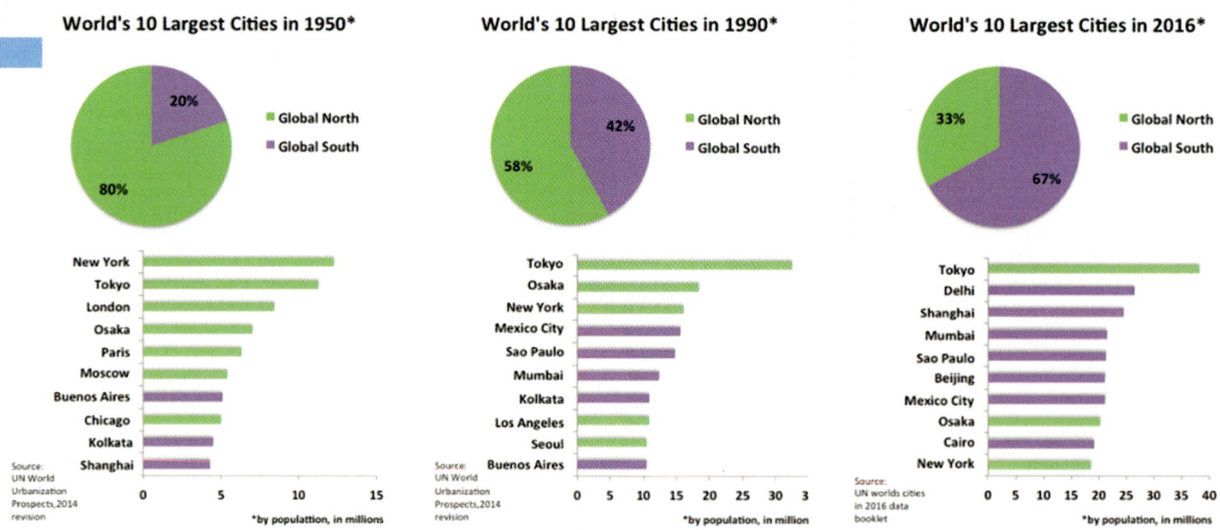

1. Focus on the title, the quote and the pie charts. Explain what the pie charts represent.
2. Concentrate on the bar charts. Comment on the evolution of the situation of New York, London and Delhi.
3. Read *Let's focus on...* n° 4, p. 193 and explain what could be an obstacle to the power of megacities of the Global South.
4. **CONNECT.** Find elements in the charts justifying Michael Bloomberg's vision of cities.

2

> *"Cities have played a more important role in shaping the world than empires."*
>
> Michael Bloomberg, former Mayor of New York (in office 2002-2013)

B "Cities on a different scale"

1. Pick out three figures and explain what is new on Planet Earth.
2. Find adjectives and sentences characterising megacities. Classify them into two groups: positive or negative aspects.
3. Send a message to your Indian pen pal to share what you have learnt in this documentary.

Living in the city

Video hatier-clic.fr/21amc/187

C Managing megacities

These are the cities that will dominate the global economy in the next 15 years

Despite the west's experience of managing the process of urbanisation, it doesn't have all the answers

New York will continue to be the world's largest urban economy in 2035, but Jakarta will have passed Tokyo to become the most populous city. However, cities in the Indian subcontinent, led by Bengaluru (Bangalore) and Dhaka, will be the fastest-growing. Those are three of the conclusions from a study by Oxford Economics of the way the economies of global cities will develop over the next couple of decades. […]

What should we make of all this? These are projections for nearly 20 years ahead, and will inevitably be off the mark[1] in terms of detail, but the broad thrust[2] of the study is likely to be correct. So we have to accept, massive urbanisation will continue for a generation at least, probably longer. That leads to several conclusions.

One is that this will change the planet in social as well as economic terms. We know from our experience in the west, moving from the countryside to a large city is socially liberating. No one knows who you are. People are free from their social backgrounds, or at least more free* than they would have been, had they remained on the land.

Another observation is that people are not just richer – though measured living standards are generally higher in great cities than the surrounding countryside – but they benefit in other ways. For example they have, in general, better access to healthcare and education. Probably – though this is a huge generalisation – they are better fed – I recall being told, when visiting Dharavi, the huge informal city near Mumbai airport, that for all its mess and apparent disorder, no one went to bed hungry.

A third conclusion is that urbanisation is a huge investment opportunity. We know a lot about what to do and what not to do when developing attractive cities. There are the basics of water, sewage[3] and transport. We know land should be set aside for parks and recreation. We know informal settlements spring up[4], and converting these into more organised housing has to be handled with sensitivity.

All this costs money, so part of the wealth generated by a fast-growing city has to be channelled[5] back into its infrastructure.

But alongside the developed world's knowledge of how to manage cities lies one big lesson: the model a rich city follows is not necessarily best for a city in an emerging market. […]

I think the challenge of megacities is more about the growing gap between the most successful ones and less successful middle-rankers[6], rather than the movement to cities as such.

Hamish McRae, *The Independent*, Dec. 5th, 2018

1. inaccurate 2. the whole idea 3. facilities for the disposal of waste matter 4. appear suddenly 5. used for 6. quite successful megacities

*"freer" should be the correct form but language is evolving and "more free" is now frequent

1. Read from the beginning to line 8. Pick out adjectives that define megacities in the future. Draw your own conclusion.
2. Read from line 9 to line 21. Show to what extent this phenomenon will have an impact on people and the planet.
3. Explain the challenge urban planners have to face when organising future megacities.
4. Record a one-minute podcast about the advantages of moving to a megacity and the issues it raises.

Enhancing liveability

A What is urban sprawl?

1. Read *Let's focus on…* n° 1, p. 192 and define urban sprawl in your own words.
2. Watch the video and list the causes of urban sprawl in a city.
3. **Phonology** Listen to the video and repeat the following words: *land lots*, *lifestyle*, *day-care*. Which element carries the main stress? What do you notice?
4. As the mayor of a developing city, you have attended a conference on urban planning. Share your knowledge with one of your local councillors.

B Addressing challenges

1 Johannesburg: a megacity-to-be choosing densification

Johannesburg, the largest city in South Africa, provides a very different – but also promising – case study. Under apartheid, the urban poor were forcibly relocated into outer-city settlements[1] – often located between five and 40km from the urban periphery. Many of these turned into slums[2] as population numbers far exceeded what these settlements were designed to accommodate.

After democratisation in 1994, there was a major inward flow of people into the urban core that could not be accommodated, despite a massive housing construction programme. Land invasions took place in all South African cities, including on inner-city land.

Johannesburg's metropolitan government realised it could not build an integrated city by moving millions of people around, because so many already lived in formal townships[3]. Instead, it identified a set of strategically located urban development hotspots, and then invested in mass transit services to link them together.

The aim is to rapidly intensify job and residential densities in these development hotspots, thus increasing the number of people who can access publicly funded mass-transit services.

This will increase average densities over time, and integrate the city via transit rather than expensive residential relocations. This, coupled with strategies to upgrade informal settlements rather than building new houses on the peripheries, has contributed significantly to enhancing densification, rather than encouraging the sprawl promoted by Johannesburg's property developers and banks since 1994.

There is no doubt that sprawling[4], de-densifying cities are a major threat to the future sustainability of the planet. Neither the UN's sustainable development goals nor the Paris agreement's climate targets will be achieved if this challenge is not addressed – but it means going up against property developers who tend to prefer greenfield developments on the peripheries to the complexities of brownfield regeneration.

The Guardian, July 12th, 2016

1. neighbourhoods 2. very poor and overcrowded districts 3. towns or suburbs where only black people lived under apartheid 4. extending

Student A: text 1

1. Compare urbanisation before apartheid and after apartheid.
2. Concentrate on the choice made by Johannesburg's metropolitan government. Explain it.
3. Read *Let's focus on…* n° 1, p. 192 and show what is at stake in this decision.

C Eating away into the countryside

1 Contrast the right and left-hand sides of the picture. Explain what is to be lost or won.

2 Read *Let's focus on...* n° 1, p. 192 and define urban sprawl with your own words.

3 You are involved in the Australian Conservation Foundation. As such, email your Member of Parliament to oppose urban sprawl.

2 Common issues associated with urbanisation

Understanding the common issues associated with urbanization will be critical to develop a better food supply model that is customized to large and smaller urban regions. First, urbanization is strongly correlated[1] with economic growth and better standards of living. Countries that are the least urbanized tend to be among the poorest. Urbanization provides considerable advantages, including economic growth, centralized infrastructures, and government, political, education, social, and health services. […]. However, urbanization has also resulted in many issues, such as urban poverty, food and nutrition insecurity, and health disparities.

Second, food demands and dietary patterns in urbanized regions have shifted to more convenient[2] and prepared foods, attributable in part to long working hours and better economic income among consumers. Many of the convenient foods available in cities are also higher in salt, fats, and sugar than home-prepared foods. […] These factors have contributed to increased risks of deaths from chronic diseases such as obesity, cardiovascular disease, diabetes, and renal failure.

Third, not all urban environments evolved similarly, and there is vast diversity in the characteristics of cities depending on their size (e.g., a small settlement with under half a million inhabitants or a large metropolis with over 10 million). Close to half of the world's urban dwellers[3] reside in relatively small settlements of fewer than 500,000 inhabitants, whereas only around one in eight live in the 28 megacities with more than 10 million inhabitants. By 2030, 41 megacities will surface in the Global South, and medium-size cities will be located in Asia and Africa.

Fourth, urbanization makes cities more susceptible to natural and human-made disasters (floods, droughts[4], and pollution). Climate change will affect food security and water access in areas that are already currently vulnerable (e.g., megacities).

Fifth, societal trends and consumer preferences have driven the rise in peri-urban agriculture, as the urban population demands food from agricultural systems in close proximity to where they live. However, peri-urban land for agriculture has to compete with non-farming uses such as housing and regional industry, driving up the prices for land for agriculture in the city fringes[5]. […] The search for alternative methods to access fresh produce in cities has resulted in the growth of urban agriculture, as seen in urban orchards[6] in streets tended to by neighborhood communities, vertical farming on buildings, and rooftop gardens.

Dietrich Knorr, Chor San Heng Khoo, Mary Ann Augustin, "Food for an Urban Planet: Challenges and Research Opportunities", *Frontiers in Nutrition*, Jan. 19th, 2018

1. connected to 2. requiring little effort 3. inhabitants 4. dry periods 5. periphery 6. gardens planted with fruit trees

Student B: text 2

1 Pick out the advantages and drawbacks of living in a megacity.

2 List the different challenges raised by megacities.

3 Find three innovations linked to those challenges.

PAIR WORK

4 **CONNECT.** Use both texts to debate what is to be done to make fast-growing megacities sustainable liveable places.

Becoming sustainable

A Aiming for zero emission

1. Focus on the document and explain what the yellow, black and white texts represent.
2. Sum up what is advocated.
3. Show to what extent London could rank among the most sustainable megacities.

What is needed to put London on track to zero carbon by 2050

2016 Zero carbon new homes

2017 Central London transport emissions surcharge (T-Charge)

2018 Minimum energy efficiency performance standards for all rented properties

2019 All new buildings zero carbon | Central London Ultra Low Emission Zone (ULESZ)

2020

2020 Smart meter in every home and SME

2018-2022 40% CO_2 reduction

2021 ULEZ expanded to inner London for light vehicles

yellow text = London lead, black text = UK government lead

2020s Insulation of remaining lofts and cavity walls and replacement of remaining low efficiency gas boilers

By 2030 15% of demand met by renewable and district energy

2028-2032 60% CO_2 reduction

2030

By 2030 UK government decision on long term decarbonisation of heat

From 2030 All GLA group heavy vehicles are fossil fuel-free

By 2030 100 MW solar PV installations

By 2030 1 GW of solar PV installations

2030s City wide deployment of low carbon heating systems eg. heat pumps

2037 All bus fleet zero emission

2040

2040s Gasand electricity networks reach zero carbon

2050 2 GW of solar PV installations

2050 Any remaining residual emissions offset

2050 Zero emissions from all transport and buildings

C Taking the pressure off megacities

Smart cities
Video hatier-clic.fr/21amc/190

1. Watch the video. Find figures to explain what is now at stake for engineering services.
2. List the different missions civil engineers will have to accomplish. Read *Let's focus on...* n° 1, p. 192. Say what could help civil engineers face all the engineering challenges.
3. You'd like to study in this institution. Explain how civil engineering will help address tomorrow's major global challenges.

B Damage control

1 The question of how to achieve a Sustainable City is one which is frequently tackled[1] by think tanks and research institutes. However, the term 'sustainability' does not have a clearly defined meaning when used by these organisations, and the sub-themes and agendas encompassed[2] can be quite different. For example, Sustainable Cities International focuses on the traditional 'resource based' interpretation of sustainability –it looks primarily at energy use, urban air and water. For the Future Cities Collaborative, however, the stated aim of 'building sustainable cities' is an umbrella for a broader remit[3]. The Collaborative: works with mayors to encourage urban revitalisation and improved liveability; looks at alternative transport possibilities; place making, disaster management and urban design; and researches more adaptive solutions to energy and water demands. Meanwhile, the Intel Collaborative Research Institute on Sustainable Connected Cities adopts a 'human centred' interpretation of sustainable cities and is concerned with enhancing and changing how people live, interact and engage with cities (Schöning et al., 2012).

Emily Moir, Tim Moonen, Greg Clark, *What are future cities?*, 2014, p. 49

1. dealt with 2. included 3. responsibility

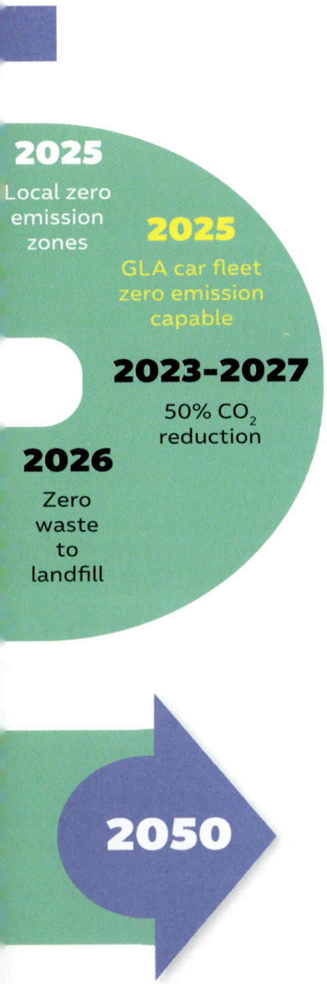

2 Here in New York we are seeing the birth of our own sustainable city. It started with Mike Bloomberg's path-breaking[1] and continued with Mayor de Blasio's OneNYC development plan. It included the multi-billion-dollar resiliency plan developed and funded in the wake of Hurricane Sandy to reinforce our shoreline[2] and build a more climate adapted city. Mass transit is slowly attracting reinvestment. We have built new urban parks like the High Line, the newly opened Domino Sugar Factory Park, and the Freshkills Park at the site of Staten Island's infamous landfill[3]. We see the development of a more sustainable city with the growth of bike lanes and Citibike bike-sharing stations. We see it with on-going and institutionalized efforts to protect the ecosystems around our upstate reservoirs and the construction of a multi-billion-dollar third water tunnel. We see it in the slow and steady investment in energy efficiency and renewable energy sponsored by New York state and its electric utilities (and paid for by consumers).

A more sustainable New York City will need to invest in new forms of solid waste management, including recycling, waste-to-energy, and fertilizer technologies such as anaerobic digestion[4]. The city already recycles food waste from 400,000 residents. Renewable energy, smart grids, energy efficiency, electric vehicle charging infrastructure, enhanced mass transit and improved public spaces will also need to be built. We've done this before in New York: the street grid, park system, electrical grid[5], subway and water system did not appear by magic. They were built by forward-looking government and business leaders seeking to build a more prosperous city. It worked. The next step is to adapt and, where necessary, rebuild that infrastructure for a sustainable future.

Steve Cohen, "The Transition to the Sustainable City, here in New York", *State of the Planet*, April 9th, 2018

1. different and new approach 2. coastline 3. dump 4. a biological process 5. network supplying people with electricity

1. Read text 1. Pick out the different definitions given to "sustainable cities". Sum them up in your own words.
2. Read text 2. List all the actions taken. Say to what end.
3. Find out what is left to be done.
4. Concentrate on the passage from line 1 to line 20 (text 2). Say what the people behind New York's plan mean by "sustainable city."
5. **Grammar** Pick out two compound adjectives. How are they formed?
6. **CONNECT.** Use both documents to show how defining sustainability is a prerequisite for the development of liveable megacities.

Let's focus on...

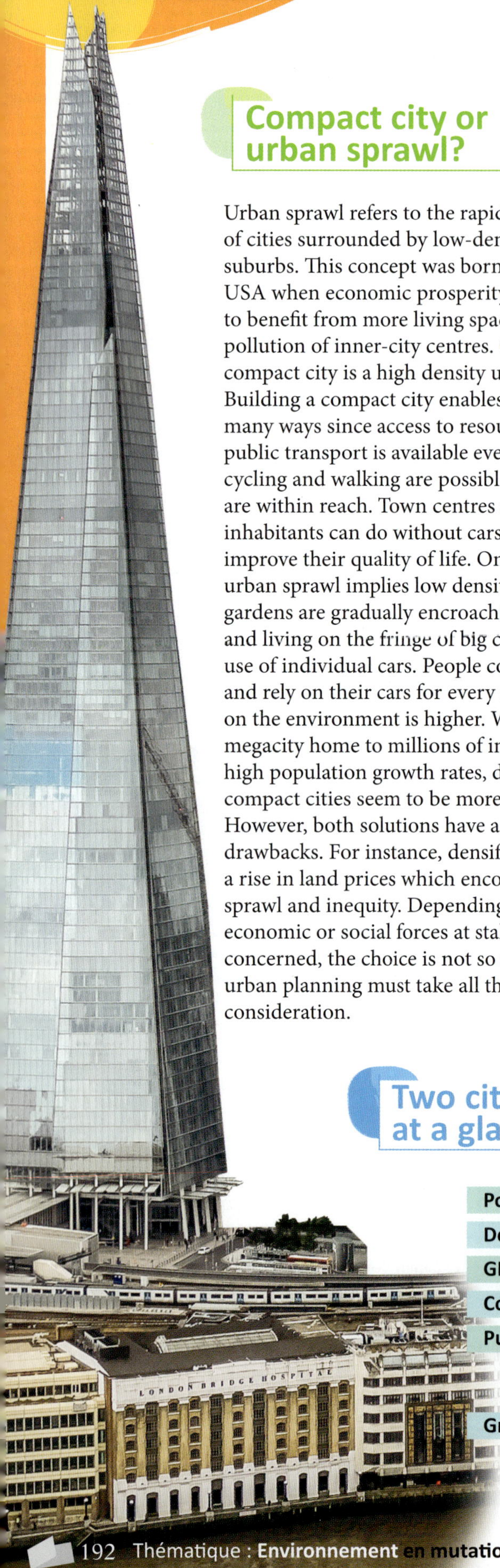

Compact city or urban sprawl? ❶

Urban sprawl refers to the rapid development of cities surrounded by low-density residential suburbs. This concept was born after WWII in the USA when economic prosperity allowed families to benefit from more living space away from the pollution of inner-city centres. On the contrary, a compact city is a high density urban settlement. Building a compact city enables to save energy in many ways since access to resources is easier and public transport is available everywhere. Even cycling and walking are possible as all the facilities are within reach. Town centres are revitalised. The inhabitants can do without cars, and low emissions improve their quality of life. On the other hand urban sprawl implies low density areas, private gardens are gradually encroaching on farmland and living on the fringe of big cities requires the use of individual cars. People commute to work and rely on their cars for every move. The impact on the environment is higher. When planning a megacity home to millions of inhabitants, with high population growth rates, densification or compact cities seem to be more sustainable. However, both solutions have advantages and drawbacks. For instance, densification can lead to a rise in land prices which encourages informal sprawl and inequity. Depending on the different economic or social forces at stake in the country concerned, the choice is not so simple. Careful urban planning must take all the criteria into consideration.

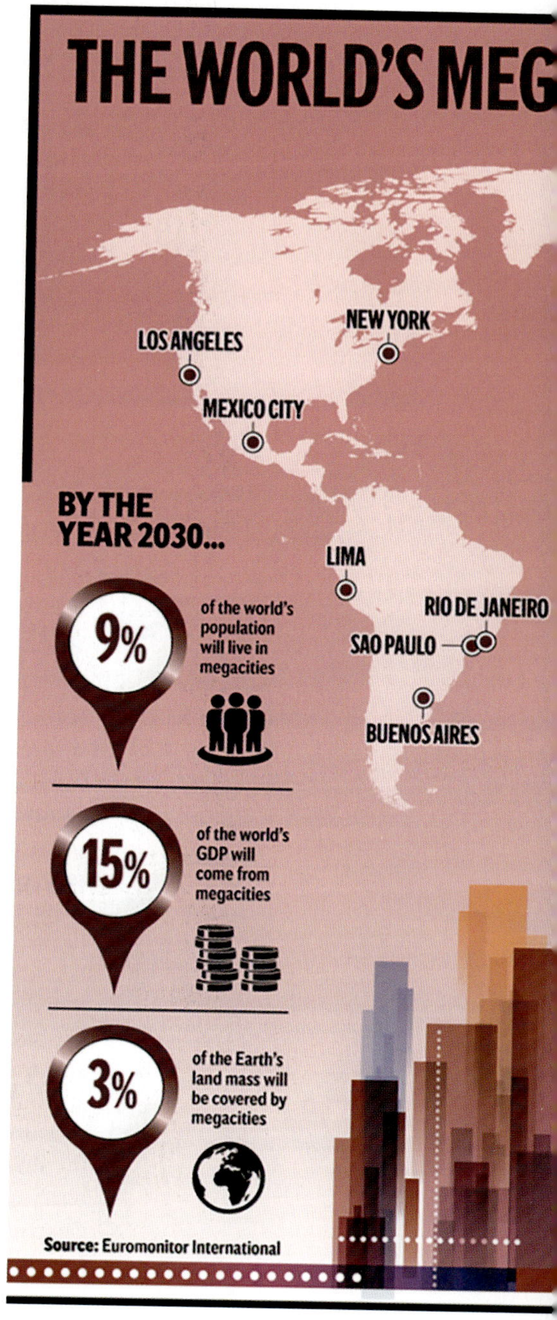

Two cities at a glance ❷

	London
Population (2019)	8,961,989
Density	5,701 people/km^2
GDP (billions)	approximately $649 (2018)
Cost of living index	81.63
Public transport	Great transportation system, ex.: the tube (11 lines, 270 stations, and 249 miles of track, 24/7)
Green space	47% 8 million trees

Megacities in the world

3

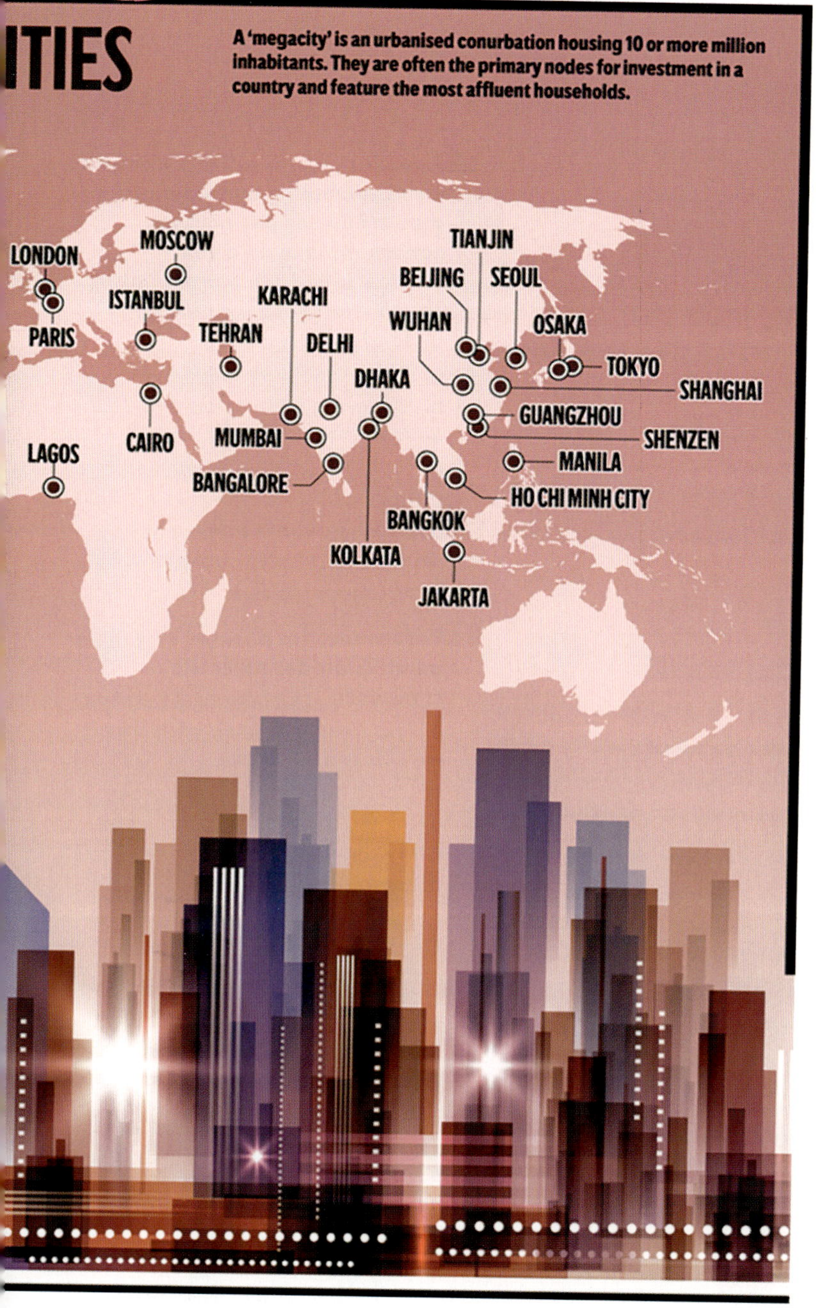

New York City

8,336,817

10,716/km²

$1,065 (2019)

100

Great transportation system,
ex.: the subway (27 lines, 472 stations, and 665 mainline track miles)

14%
over 1,700 parks, playgrounds, and recreational facilities

Megacities vs Global cities

4

Defining the boundaries of a city is complex. A megacity could mean the city itself or the urban agglomeration. For example, when London is mentioned, what is meant is Greater London. Still, what defines a megacity is its urban area which accommodates a population of several million inhabitants (more than 10 million according to the United Nations). These megacities are not necessarily global cities. The concept of Global cities implies political, financial and economic power. This concept was defined in 1991 by a sociologist called Saskia Sassen in *The Global City – New York, London, Tokyo*. Global cities are home to prominent companies which are networked across the world. They are technologically advanced and have enormous influence on the world economy. While megacities located in the Global North are innovative urban centers and global hubs, most megacities of the Global South deal with massive urban expansion leading to informal planning, economic, social and environmental problems, and shortages of resources.

Practice your grammar

Les adjectifs composés

▶ Il est possible de former des adjectifs composés à partir de divers éléments :

nom + adjectif	*world-famous, environment-friendly*
adjectif + nom	*high-quality, long-term, last-minute*
adjectif + adjectif	*dark-blue, light-green, red-hot*
nombre + nom	*five-page, 30-storey*

⚠ Lorsqu'un mot composé est formé d'un nombre suivi d'un nom, ce dernier n'est jamais mis au pluriel : *a **five-minute** speech, a **100-page** book, a **two-room** flat, a **100-storey** building*.

▶ Le second élément peut être également formé à partir d'un verbe à la forme en *-ing* (participe présent) ou au participe passé. Le premier élément peut alors être :

un nom	*home-prepared, time-saving, record-breaking*
un adjectif	*good-looking, easy-going* (facile à vivre)
un adverbe	*fast-growing, hard-working, well-behaved*

▶ Le second élément est parfois **un nom auquel on a ajouté le suffixe *-ed*** : *dark-haired*, *absent-minded* (distrait), *old-fashioned*, *left-handed* (gaucher)...

1 Associez chaque adjectif composé à son synonyme ou sa définition, puis produisez des phrases contenant chacun d'eux.

old-fashioned • forward-thinking • thought-provoking • narrow-minded • far-reaching

a. *intolerant, prejudiced*

b. *favouring innovation and development; progressive*

c. *having a great influence or effect*

d. *making people think seriously about a particular subject*

e. *no longer modern*

2 Reformulez les phrases suivantes en utilisant des adjectifs composés.

a. *This avenue is lined with trees.* → *This is a ... avenue.*

b. *David has red hair and green eyes.* → *David is a ... and ... boy.*

c. *My son is 11 years old.* → *I have a ... son.*

Les propositions de temps

▶ En anglais, on peut introduire les propositions de temps par :

- *when*	- *before*	- *until / till*
- *while* (pendant que)	- *after*	- *as soon as* (dès que)
- *since* (depuis que)	- *as*	- *once* (une fois que)
- *by the time*	- *every time*	- *whenever*

▶ Les propositions de temps sont parfois **réduites** : le sujet est alors supprimé et le verbe est à la forme en ***-ing***

*We know a lot about what to do and what not to do when **developing** attractive cities.* (= *when we develop attractive cities*).

Si le verbe est *be*, le sujet et le verbe peuvent être tous les deux omis :

However, the term 'sustainability' does not have a clearly defined meaning when (it is) used by these organisations.

⚠ Ces transformations ne sont possibles que si le sujet du verbe principal est le même que celui de la subordonnée.

▶ On ne peut pas utiliser **un futur en *will* dans une proposition de temps**. Il faut employer à la place un présent simple :

*When I **live** in Brooklyn, I'll commute to Manhattan every day.*
(et non : *When I ~~will~~ live in Brooklyn...*)

3 Réduisez les propositions de temps quand cela est possible

a. *Before I leave my house, I turn off all the lights.*

b. *After the mayor was elected, he took action to reduce traffic congestion.*

c. *Since I moved to Tokyo, I've mainly had contact with locals.*

d. *When she was a child, my grandmother lived in a slum in New Orleans.*

e. *After the crisis was over, the council made a great effort to provide cheap housing and more public facilities.*

4 Traduisez.

a. *Quand je serai riche et célèbre, je vivrai à New-York.*

b. *Dès que tu seras à Londres, appelle-moi.*

Improve your pronunciation

Les voyelles /ɜː/ et /ʌ/

▶ Il s'agit de deux sons souvent confondus par les francophones :
- le son /ɜː/ est une **voyelle longue** qui ressemble à la voyelle du français *d**eu**x*.
- le son /ʌ/ est une **voyelle brève**. La bouche est légèrement plus ouverte.

▶ La voyelle /ɜː/ est représentée par des graphies qui contiennent toutes un *r*, en position accentuée :

ir	***girl, third, first***
er	***service, version, eternity***
ur	***burn, urban, Johannesburg***
***ear* + consonne**	***heard, pearl, early, learn*** Exception : ***heart*** /ɑː/
or* après un *w	***world, word, worse***

⚠ Les terminaisons inaccentuées *-er* et *-or* se prononcent /ə/ : ***father***, ***bigger***, ***inspector***…

▶ La voyelle /ʌ/ est représentée par les graphies suivantes, en général en position accentuée :

u	dans un mot d'une syllabe, avant une consonne simple ou double : ***slum***, ***bus***, ***duck***, ***up*** Exceptions : ***pull***, ***bull***, ***put***, ***push***, ***full***, ***butch*** /ʊ/
u	en milieu de mot, avant une consonne double : ***summary***, ***funny***, ***subject***
o	dans des mots très courants qui sont des exceptions, surtout avant un *n*, un *m*, *th* ou un *v* : ***son***, ***some***, ***come***, ***done***, ***none***, ***money***, ***love***, ***other***, ***mother***, ***brother***, ***London***, ***front***, ***nothing***
ou	dans quelques mots : ***young***, ***country***, ***couple***, ***touch***
oo	uniquement dans ***flood*** et ***blood***

1 Dans les paires de mots suivantes, dites quel mot contient /ɜː/ et lequel contient /ʌ/. Écoutez l'enregistrement pour vérifier vos réponses et répétez.

Audio hatier-clic.fr/21amc/195a

a. *girl / gull* **b.** *bud / bird*
c. *hurt / hut* **d.** *shirt / shut*

2 Chassez l'intrus : quel mot ne se prononce pas comme les autres ? Écoutez l'enregistrement pour vérifier vos réponses et répétez.

Audio hatier-clic.fr/21amc/195b

a. *cut • nut • put • shut*
b. *push • rush • brush • flush*
c. *love • glove • oven • flush*
d. *early • heart • earn • earth*
e. *enough • rough • tough • though*

3 Pour chacun de ces mots, trouvez un homophone (un mot qui ne s'écrit pas de la même manière mais qui se prononce de façon identique).
nun • son • some • won • fir

L'accentuation des mots composés

Pour bien accentuer un mot composé, il faut examiner sa nature :

Adjectifs composés	Noms composés
L'accent principal est sur le **second** élément : ***old-fashioned*** ***hard-working***	L'accent principal est sur le **premier** élément : ***lifestyle*** ***post office*** **Exceptions :** C'est le second élément qui porte l'accent principal lorsque le premier élément désigne : - un lieu : ***a London pub***, ***a city hall*** - ce dont est constitué le second élément : ***an apple pie***

4 Recopiez ces mots et dites si ces mots composés sont des noms ou des adjectifs. Puis, soulignez la syllabe qui porte l'accent principal. Écoutez l'enregistrement pour vérifier vos réponses et répétez.

Audio hatier-clic.fr/21amc/195c

police station • climate change • world-famous • postcard • Park Avenue • city centre • world-famous • Greenwich Village • pickpocket • credit card • good-looking

Let's translate

We know from our experience in the west, moving from the countryside to a large city is socially liberating. No one knows who you are. People are free from their social backgrounds, or at least more free* than they would have been, had they remained on the land.

Another observation is that people are not just richer – though measured living standards are generally higher in great cities than the surrounding countryside – but they benefit in other ways. For example they have, in general, better access to healthcare and education. Probably – though this is a huge generalisation – they are better fed – I recall being told, when visiting Dharavi, the huge informal city near Mumbai airport, that for all its mess and apparent disorder, no one went to bed hungry.

*freer should be the correct form.

The Independent, May 30th, 2018

La ponctuation : quelques pièges

▶ **Le tiret long (–)** est un signe de ponctuation assez fréquent en anglais. On le remplace en français le plus souvent par **des points de suspension, deux points ou des parenthèses.**

▶ **Les guillemets à chevrons** « … » ne sont utilisés qu'en français. En anglais, il faut utiliser les guillemets qui ont la forme "…" ou bien '…' .

▶ Les virgules servent de séparateurs de milliers. En français, on les remplace par des espaces :
3,000 inhabitants → 3 000 habitants

▶ **Les adjectifs de nationalité et les noms de langue** prennent une majuscule en anglais mais une minuscule en français :
a French village → un village français

▶ Il en va de même des noms de mois dans les dates (*in January 2020* → en janvier 2020).

Translation Tip

À vous !

a. Qu'exprime l'inversion sujet – auxiliaire dans *had they remained on the land* ? Reformulez cette proposition afin d'en faire apparaître clairement le sens.

b. Quel lien logique exprime *for all* dans ***for all** its mess and apparent disorder* ? Par quelle préposition française pourra-t-on le traduire ?

c. Par quels signes de ponctuation français replacera-t-on les tirets longs anglais dans ce texte ?

Build up your vocabulary

1 Fill in your own mind map here: hatier-clic.fr/21amc/196

2 Draw this grid on your copy book and complete the missing words.

Nouns	Adjectives	Verbs
regulation		
		commute
challenge		
	sustainable	
	urban	

3 Complete these sentences with words from your mind map.

a. … are in charge of the development of liveable and … megacities.

b. Due to … , megacities have to build … to … a huge number of people.

c. Because of urban sprawl, some megacities … over a large area.

d. In LEDCs, the arrival of millions of … has … the development of … and … .

e. Contrary to most megacities situated in … , New York and London are global hubs with a … and all sorts of … they … .

4 Use ten words / expressions of the mind map to write a paragraph about the rapid growth of a megacity in developing countries.

Projects

1
You are a journalist working for National Geographic. Write a report on how megacities tackle sustainability.

1. Think about the structure of your report. You need to have:
   - a title - an introduction - recommendations - a conclusion
2. Speak about the past, the present and the future of megacities.
3. Choose the information you want to give about sustainability and support it with facts and figures.
4. Use link words and appropriate grammatical structures.

2
You are an American architect. Deliver a speech to help shape a sustainable future for Mumbai.

1. Look at the unit and pick out the most relevant arguments concerning:
   - overpopulation
   - the environment
   - strategies, initiatives, and solutions
   - sustainable standards
2. Find examples to illustrate each argument.
3. Use link words: for instance, namely, as, given that, therefore, consequently, besides...
4. Check the pronunciation of difficult or new words with an online dictionary.
5. Do not read: have a list of 10 to 15 keywords.
6. Remember to greet your audience and introduce yourself. Thank your audience for listening at the end.
7. Rehearse! Practice makes perfect!

Pour l'écrit du Bac

A Green Square: from a rich industrial past to a vibrant, sustainable and connected community

Through the innovative financing tool of land value capture, Sydney is creating a new, sustainable urban neighbourhood for over 80,000 people to live and work on an old industrial parcel.

Australia's leading global city is facing a space crunch. With rising demand, especially from overseas residents who now represent over half the city's population, Sydney must think creatively about where and how to create new urban neighbourhoods to meet this demand. Green Square, Australia's largest urban redevelopment project, will transform a 278-hectare brownfield site that is 4 km equidistant from both the CBD[1] and the airport into a mixed-use neighbourhood that will accomodate 61,000 residents and 21,000 workers by 2030.

The ambitious project launched in 1994 but stalled over land ownership issues, industrial cleanup needs, and a lack of funding. However, Green Square received a major boost in 2000 when Sydney built a rail line from the airport to the CBD for the Olympics and included a stop in the neighborhood. That accessibility to the rest of the city has led planners to brand the Green Square Town Centre as "Sydney's global village" that is "10 minutes from anywhere." […]

City leaders envision Green Square as a showpiece for the Sustainable Sydney 2030 plan. They believe the project demonstrates how the city can increase its population and job base, grow via high-density urban infill rather than suburban sprawl, and still maintain a low environmental footprint through energy efficient building design and high rates of public transport, cycling, and walking." An industrial area doesn't have much of a public domain, much permeability, but what we are trying to solve is to bring forth a new way of living in Australia," Contziu* said. Green Square contributes to SDG3 with its focus on a healthy living environment, SDG11 as a sustainable urban neighbourhood, and SDG13 by helping Sydney reduce per capita[2] carbon emissions.

*Lila Contziu, Green Square Placemaking Manager

Metropolis, World Association of the Major Metropolises, *Solutions for and by Cities*, 2019, p. 70

1. Central Business District 2. per habitant

PARTIE 1

Prenez connaissance du dossier proposé, composé des documents A, B et C non hiérarchisés, et traitez en anglais le sujet suivant (500 mots maximum) :

Taking into account their specificities and viewpoints, show how the documents illustrate some of the challenges awaiting Sydney and Toronto, and future megacities. You will pay particular attention to the relationship between densification and sustainability, the sustainable development goals that have to be achieved, and the concept of liveability.

PARTIE 2

Traduisez le passage suivant du document 2 en français.

As urbanist Richard Florida has repeatedly forewarned, Toronto, in the absence of major civil ambition, is at risk of failing to realize its full potential as a modern global metropolis. What is needed, he argues, is a new, regionwide model for growth: no more outward sprawl, much more densification, making the most of the space it has, replete with ambitious transit investments akin to what New York City undertook decades ago.

B The population of the Toronto area will hit 8 million in the next 10 years. It's make or break time – are we ready?

Transit crunches. Housing shortages. Climate change. Will the Toronto of 2030 be a prosperous, livable city – or a gridlocked[1] urban nightmare? As we enter a new decade, the Star is embarking on an ambitious yearlong project to find practical solutions for the most pressing problems facing Toronto as it takes its place among the world's megacities.

Urbanization is, of course, a global trend. The most recent data from the United Nations puts the number of the world's megacities – cities with more than 10 million inhabitants – at 33 in 2018, projected to rise to 43 in 2030. But well before Greater Toronto enters into the 10-million club, we will hit a demographic turning point – in 2033 – with fully half of all Ontarians living in the region for the first time.

That growth will come with increased political clout[2], federally and provincially, as Toronto increases its share of seats at Queen's Park and in the House of Commons, giving the city even greater influence in shaping election outcomes to its urbanized will.

As more and more Boomers downsize, demand for smaller living spaces is expected to rise, favouring units with maximum livability, walkability, accessibility and transit options. But the generational shift could also help solve a challenge that has vexed planners for years – how to win zoning changes to add multi-unit density in the city's "yellowbelt," that vast expanse of semi-detached and detached housing that comprises an estimated 70 per cent of Toronto's residential neighbourhoods.

As urbanist Richard Florida has repeatedly forewarned, Toronto, in the absence of major civil ambition, is at risk of failing to realize its full potential as a modern global metropolis. What is needed, he argues, is a new, regionwide model for growth: no more outward sprawl, much more densification, making the most of the space it has, replete with ambitious transit investments akin to what New York City undertook decades ago. […]

One thing business and politicos alike know for certain: more and more, our climate crisis is going to drive planning, including redevelopment and retrofitting aimed at net-zero emissions, replete[3] with heat pumps, rainwater collection, solar panels and electric-vehicle charging stations. That's partly because by 2030 a much more demanding demographic cohort – Generation Z – will ascend to adulthood.

Mitch Potter, www.thestar.com, Jan. 31st, 2020

1. blocked by traffic 2. power 3. supplied

C

17 Travelling without footprints

The expert's view
hatier-clic.fr/21amc/200a

In the news
hatier-clic.fr/21amc/200b

Projects

- Organise and host a radio show about a national park of your choice.
- You are an experienced traveller. Write an article on the consequences of ecotourism.

Grammar p. 208 Phonology p. 209

Last-chance tourism

A Enjoy while you can

1

Timeless change at the Columbia Icefield: two generations of photographers mark the passing of time.

2

Australia's iconic coral reefs are in trouble. Man-induced pollution affects this biodiversity hotspot.

PAIR WORK

Student A on visual 1
Student B on visual 2

1. Read *Let's focus on...* n° 2, p. 206 and explain the differences between now and then.
2. Swap information and guess the motivations of modern-day tourists.
3. You are a travel agent. Create a marketing slogan about visiting either of these places before it's too late.

B Intrepid travallers?

Is this trend just causing more damage?

One of the greatest ironies of our time is that humans are simultaneously intrepid travellers, and one of the main causes of the irreversible damage happening to our planet. Rising sea levels, erosion, deforestation and urban development are just some of the man-made reasons our most treasured corners of the earth are changing beyond recognition.

But this irony is big business; visiting parts of the world before they disappear is becoming increasingly common. Last chance tourism, which Forbes named as one of this year's top travel trends, is attracting visitors to the Amazon rainforest, the retreating mangroves in the Everglades in Florida, Australia's bleaching[1] Great Barrier Reef, the melting ice in Montana's Glacier National Park and the sinking city of Venice. […]

One defense of last chance tourism is that it helps raise awareness of climate change, which offsets[2] the damage caused. But the researchers have found that while tourists to Churchill perceive climate change to have a negative impact on polar bears, they don't necessarily understand how they themselves contribute to greenhouse gas emissions.

Similarly, a survey of Antarctic cruise passengers found that 59 per cent felt that their travel did not impact on climate change, and fewer than 7 per cent said they had or might offset their emissions as a result of their experience.

Another argued benefit of last chance tourism is that it raises money and publicity for conservation efforts. The president of the Maldives, Abdulla Yameen, said last year that mass tourism will create the funds it needs to adapt to climate change, and has backed[3] plans to increase tourism from 1.3 million people a year to more than 7 million in 10 years.

Money from tourism to the Great Barrier Reef contributes to the marine park that is tasked with protecting the reef. But the downside to this is that human activity also pollutes the individual reefs, which can be damaged by tourists getting sun lotion into the sea, research has found.

In 2012, scientists estimated that the Great Barrier Reef had already lost more than half of its coral cover since 1985, but the way research is reported, and the threats that drive tourists to visit such endangered places, are misplaced, according to ecologist Peter Mumby.

"The reef has experienced a very serious impact over the last few years in particular, but remember that it's the size of Italy," he says. "There remain many wonderful areas, and I've little doubt that tourists will always find something valuable to enjoy."

"Yes, the reef is likely to deteriorate, and we need to accelerate action to protect it, but the notion that it will die is wrong."

The Independent, May 30th, 2018

1. coral bleaching happens when corals lose their vibrant colors and turn white 2. compensates 3. supported

1. Read *Let's focus on…* n° 2, p. 206 and explain the dark side of last-chance tourism. Comment on the irony of the situation.
2. List the positive consequences of last-chance tourism on environmental protection and explain the ambivalent situation in The Maldives.
3. Focusing on the last four paragraphs, explain why there is no rush to visit the reef before it is gone.
4. You work for an NGO. Write the three golden rules of sustainable tourism.

C Antarctica: room for concern

John Oliver, Last week tonight - Antarctica

Video hatier-clic.fr/21amc/201

1. Watch the video, pick out the stressed words and use them to present it.
2. List the reasons tourists give to justify their trip. Choose the best words to describe them: naïve, ridiculous, adventurous, glamorous, arrogant, smart?
3. Identify all the different arguments given by John Oliver not to go to Antarctica.
4. You are John Oliver's script writer. Imagine what jokes he could make about visiting the Great Barrier Reef.

Ecotourism: a win-win for everyone?

A Dry ice humour

A

B

C

D

GROUP WORK

Student 1 on A – Student 2 on B
Student 3 on C – Student 4 on D

1. Match your row with one of these issues: noise pollution – carbon emissions and global warming – loss of food source for animals - the failure of carbon offsetting

2. Match your row with one of these behaviour traits and explain how the comic strip makes fun of ecotourists: narcissism – carelessness (lack of attention) – self-righteousness (moral superiority) – misguided search for authenticity

3. Swap information and create a comic strip illustrating the irony of ecotourism.

B The latest frontier

1 Read *Let's focus on...* n° 1, p. 206 and listen to the recording. Explain where polar bears are now making theirs dens and how they have been affected by climate change.

2 Show how and why Kaktovik suddenly became a tourist destination.

3 Report on how the locals feel about the sudden popularity of Kaktovik.

4 **Phonology** Listen to and write down the following passage: "Suddenly the whole world [...] before they went extinct". Now listen to it again and group words into speech units. Use the symbol | to mark the boundaries between these units.

5 You are part of a wildlife protection group. Give a one-minute talk to the press in which you sound the alarm about the situation in Kaktovik.

Polar bears in Kaktovic

Audio hatier-clic.fr/21amc/203

C The human cost of ecotourism

Ecotourism and neocolonialism: the human cost of wildlife conservation

Around the world, people, often indigenous, are becoming "conservation refugees" forced to leave their ancestral homelands for the creation of protected areas and wildlife reserves.

Indigenous people and conservationists[1] share a vital and mutual goal: to protect and preserve biological diversity. Their collaboration would produce great results for both people and the environment, yet for decades the imaginary of "pristine[2]" nature has prevented that these two key actors reconcile their forces, resulting in the creation of high numbers of unmanageable protected areas and the degradation of native peoples as nothing more than trespassers on their ancestral lands.

The idea of "virgin and pristine" nature that is in need of protection and thus enclosure[3] has been at the core of the conservation movement for decades. This concept of 'untouched land', spread and reinforced through the media and Western environmental NGOs[4], has dangerous consequences, because places can only be considered "wilderness", if they are (supposedly) devoid of human inhabitants. The creation of national parks and wildlife reserves, purposefully enclosed areas of "pristine nature" – places saved in a seemingly unaltered state for future generations – has led to the systematic eviction of natives from their lands.

In the United States, national parks like Yosemite or Yellowstone were once home to thriving indigenous communities that had treasured the environment around them before their displacement for the enclosure of their lands by national park authorities. This phenomenon is not unique to the United States, it is happening almost everywhere, and is particularly widespread on the African continent: Groups such as the nomadic Massai and the forest-dwelling Batwa have lost much of their traditional land to large animal conservation projects in Kenya and central Africa.

It is even more of a paradox really, how the displacement of native people from their lands for the formation of wildlife parks, goes hand in hand with the arrival Western conservationists for the management of these lands. Lands, tribal peoples have not only lived off sustainably but also whose biodiversity they have preserved for millennia – yet conservation experts and specialists from Europe and the Americas are flown in to help assess the progress and assist in developing teaching programs for locals and anti-poaching[5] unit.

blogs.lse.ac.uk

1. people who work for the preservation of the environment 2. untouched 3. protected areas 4. Non-Governmental Organisations (NGO) 5. against illegal hunting of wild animals

1 Read *Let's focus on...* n° 4, p. 207 the headline and the first paragraph. Explain the downside of the protection of the environment.

2 Identify why conservationists and indigenous populations do not work well together.

3 You are a spokesperson for one of the local populations. Explain to a Westerner why a radical interpretation of conservation can hurt your community.

Doing the right thing

A Soaring CO_2 emissions

Global carbon dioxide emissions from aviation

Our World in Data

Aviation emissions includes passenger air travel, freight and military operations. It does not include non-CO_2 climate forcings, or a multiplier for warming effects at altitude.

1

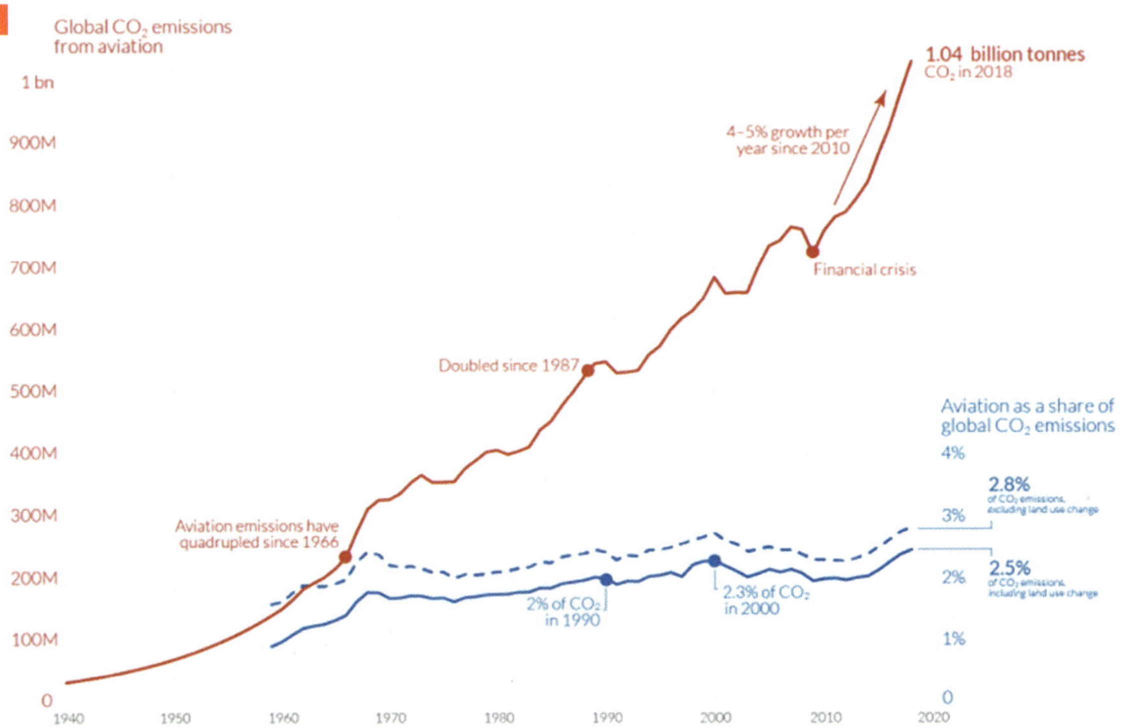

OurWorldinData.org - Research and data to make progress against the world's largest problems.
Source: Lee et al. (2020). The contribution of global aviation to anthropogenic climate forcing for 2000 to 2018; based on Sausen and Schumann (2000) & IEA.
Share of global emissions calculated based on total CO_2 data from the Global Carbon Project.

2 Emissions from different modes of transport

Emissions per passenger per km travelled

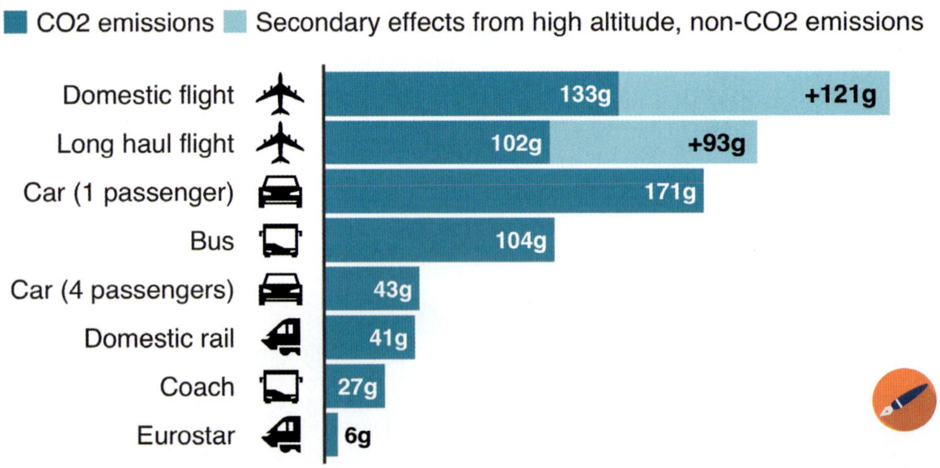

Note: Car refers to average diesel car

Source: BEIS/Defra Greenhouse Gas Conversion Factors 2019 BBC

1. Look at graph 1 and describe the recent trend in CO_2 emissions from aviation.
2. Look at document 2. Compare the emissions from different modes of transport. Determine the most reasonable mode of transport.
3. **CONNECT.** Look at both graphs and explain why flying is criticised.

B Flight shame

Despite flying being the single fastest way to grow our individual carbon footprint, people still want to fly. Passenger numbers even grew by 3.3% globally last year alone. The hype[1] around "Flygskam" – a global movement championed by climate activist Greta Thunberg that encourages people to stop travelling by plane – seems to have attracted more media attention than actual followers.

The industry has reacted quickly. Websites like Skyscanner, used to compare flight options between destinations, now show customers a "greener choice" – displaying how much less C02 a certain flight emits, compared to the average for that route. These green choices are determined to be flights that use more direct routes, airlines that have newer aircraft, or can carry more passengers.

Meanwhile, popular budget airline Ryanair – whose CEO only recently admitted climate change isn't a hoax[2] – now claims to have the greenest fleet of air planes in Europe. The company's modern, fuel efficient planes – alongside its ability to fill them with passengers – does make it the "greenest" air travel option out there. However, Ryanair had a total of 450 planes in operation in 2019 (compared to only 250 in 2010) – meaning that despite its fuel-efficient planes, the sheer quantity of fuel they burn is why they were named one of Europe's top ten polluting companies in 2019.

Last year also saw carbon offset schemes[3] become popular. These schemes allow passengers to pay extra so their airline can invest in environmental projects on their behalf – thereby making a flight theoretically "carbon-neutral". British Airways now offsets all of its customers' domestic UK flights, while Ryanair also has a scheme allowing passengers to buy offsets for their flights, with proceeds going to projects including a whale protection scheme – which appears completely unconnected to reducing carbon at all.

Passengers might feel satisfied, but whether their offsets actually reduce carbon is less clear. Critics question the time-lag associated with offsets, especially tree-planting schemes. A plane that flies today pollutes today – but a tree planted today won't remove carbon for years. As for "avoided deforestation" projects, which aim to protect existing trees, proving these trees wouldn't have survived without offset funding is almost impossible.

The other danger of these cheap offsets is that travellers might believe they solve the problems caused by flying – so they won't change their travel behaviour. Indeed, one government minister even argues that there's no need for people to fly less, because low-carbon and electric flights are around the corner. Despite reports that solar or battery-powered planes are coming to the rescue, current plane technology is going nowhere fast.

This is partly because jet fuel on international flights isn't taxed, which leaves little financial incentive for the industry to invest in big technological shifts. Aircraft manufacturers Boeing even predicts it will produce 44,000 planes by 2038 to accommodate the 8 billion passengers flying each year by then. Those planes will look, sound and pollute much like today's ones.

Roger Tyers, theconversation.com, Feb. 4th, 2020

1. publicity 2. a fabrication 3. compensation initiatives

1. Read the first paragraph and explain in your own words what Greta Thunberg champions.
2. Pick out the elements showing the reaction of the air travel industry and the changes that eco-friendly travellers can make.
3. List the reasons why this recent evolution is not enough. Focus on the final paragraph and explain which unexplored option holds a lot of promise.
4. **Grammar** Observe the following sentence: "Websites ... destinations" (l. 9-11) and complete this statement: "We use *used to* + V to insist that repeated actions or a state in the ... are no longer true. The negative of *used to* is ...".

PAIR WORK

5. Act out a conversation between Greta Thunberg and the CEO of an airline company: can you agree on a compromise between flying and not flying at all?

C Fly clean

1. Watch the BBC video. Give the most ecologically responsible option for the planet.
2. List the recommendations if you must fly.

PAIR WORK

3. Make a proposal for a green project to offset the carbon footprint of flying. Give a one-minute presentation.

How to reduce your carbon footprint when you fly

Video hatier-clic.fr/21amc/205

Let's focus on...

Climate change and wildlife tourism 1

Whales, tigers and polar bears: these iconic species have become the poster animals warning us about climate change. Insects and frogs are disappearing fast too, but they do not capture the public's imagination the way big mammals do. Consequently, wildlife watching tours have been developing fast, and they raise both admiration and criticism depending on where you're standing. Advocates will praise them because they often go hand in hand with conservation projects, while critics insist that travellers need to be kept away from these animals.

Conservation includes a variety of actions: it's about saving the animals as well as their habitats, so it involves campaigns to raise awareness among the local populations. For instance, the hunting of whales or *whaling* has been part of native cultures for centuries: the animals are killed for their usable products, and they are the cornerstone of the economy of many communities. Smart tourism initiatives may help these communities understand that they have a vested interest in the *survival* of whales, and that living whales are as profitable, or even more profitable than dead whales! Wildlife tourism is about finding the right balance, and making sure that travellers leave no footprints behind them – other than the cash that will help local communities thrive.

Last-chance tourism 2

Some of the world's breath-taking natural wonders may be gone in a matter of years. Last-chance tourism gives you the opportunity to experience them up close while that window is still open. No one should pass up the chance to view near-extinct wild animals or gaze at movingly beautiful landscapes that will be tragically spoiled as a result of climate change. Last chance tourism has thrived in parallel with mass tourism. Cheap air travel and tailor-made adventure package tours mean that more middle-class visitors are able to tick off items on their "bucket list" of places they want to see before it is too late. On the downside, the increasing popularity of last chance destinations and higher visitor traffic have contributed to further erosion of natural habitats, increased environmental pollution and disruption of local populations. Without sensible eco-friendly options to mitigate its negative impact, last chance tourism may just take another toll on nature's priceless wonders.

Tours and tourism: a social phenomenon 3

Have you ever wondered where the word "tourism" comes from? Long before "tourism" became the mass phenomenon we are familiar with, it was the preserve of a "happy few". As early as the 17th century, the daughters and (mostly) the sons of the British nobility would visit Europe upon reaching adulthood. It was considered as a "rite of passage" that would make a permanent impression on the young soul, and though the itinerary could vary, it generally included Greek and Italian cultural hotspots, places boasting a lot of art, and where the contemplation of ruins was thought to shape one's sense of aesthetics. This is known as the Grand Tour. Over time, the phenomenon expanded, and it was emulated by all social classes. Tour-ism was coined at the turn of the 19th century and, soon enough, it stopped being an individual adventure and sightseeing was undertaken in groups, in the wake of pioneer Thomas Cook.
Tours for a happy few are back in fashion! The rich have found new frontiers for their holidays, always looking for unchartered territory, in a never-ending quest for exoticism that has taken them to wild areas, mountaintops, the poles. The richest people want the most exceptional landscapes, so disappearing vistas are at the top of their list.

4

VACATION WITH A POSITIVE IMPACT:

ECOTOURISM

Since travellers have been seeking natural respites for ages, it seems that ecotourism may not be a new practice, but rather just a new term.

HISTORY OF ECOTOURISM

MID-17TH CENTURY: The Beginning of the Grand Tour

An artistic/cultural pilgrimage popularized by travel writers, like Roman Catholic Priest Richard Lassels

The Italian Peninsula's warmer climates and alluring landscapes make it a primary destination

1797 Alexander von Humboldt

Travels to Central and South America with botanist Aime Bonpland

Travels 6,000 miles over 5 years crossing the countries by foot, horse, and canoe

1835 Charles Darwin

Darwin explores the lush Galapagos Islands in the HMS Beagle, collecting specimens

1848 Alfred Russel Wallace

Wallace, along with Henry Walter Bates, explores the Amazon River basin to collect insect and animal specimens and seek evidence of evolution

1968 Owen Lee

After working with Jacques Cousteau, he moves to Zihuatanejo, Mexico

Founds a Nature Study Center at Las Gatas Beach, intending to help bring people closer back into our ecosystem

1983 "Ecotourism" Coined as a Term

Environmentally conscious Mexican architect Héctor Ceballos-Lascuráin first coins the term, defined as traveling to fairly undisturbed areas to enjoy the scenery and culture

1996 Ecotourism Explodes

For example, South Africa's Conservation Corporation spent $60M on 60-100 luxury lodges for ecotourism destinations

2003 Center for Responsible Travel

Martha D. Honey, PhD, co-founds the center in order to support efficient ecotourism

Practice your grammar

Le relatif *whose* et la traduction de « dont »

▶ Le relatif *whose* /huːz/ est toujours suivi d'un nom. Il s'agit d'un équivalent du relatif français *dont*.

*Ryanair, **whose CEO** only recently admitted climate change isn't a hoax, now claims to have the greenest fleet of airplanes in Europe.*

⚠ Le nom suit directement *whose*. Il n'est jamais précédé d'un article comme c'est le cas de *dont* en français.

▶ *Whose* fonctionne comme **un génitif** : il permet d'établir une relation d'appartenance (ou de parenté, etc.) entre le nom antécédent et celui qui le suit. On peut ainsi relier ces deux noms par ***of*** ou par la marque du génitif ***'s*** :

*China, **whose greenhouse gas emissions** have significantly increased since 1990, is currently the world's biggest polluter.* (= *China**'s** greenhouse gas emissions*)

*Tourists visit these national parks to view and photograph **the wildlife**, **whose habitat** is increasingly threatened by climate change.* (= *the habitat **of** the wildlife*)

⚠ *Dont* ne se traduit pas toujours en anglais par *whose*, en particulier quand l'antécédent est complément du verbe :

Le livre **dont** tu as besoin est sur la table. → *The book **that / which / Ø** you need is on the table.* (= *you need this book*)

1 **Réunissez les deux phrases en une seule en utilisant le relatif *whose*.**

a. *The airline had to accommodate 100 passengers in a hotel. These passengers' flight had been canceled.*

b. *The travel industry won't recover until 2023. The revenues of the travel industry nosedived during the COVID-19 pandemic.*

b. *The government should protect polar bears. Their ecosystem is at risk due to the negative effects of global warming.*

d. *Brazil contains about 60% of the Amazon rainforest. The degradation of the Amazon rainforest could have severe consequences for global climate and rainfall.*

Used to

▶ ***Used to*** est employé pour mettre en valeur **un contraste entre une situation passée (en général un état ou une habitude) et une situation présente**. On le traduit souvent par ***avant* ou *jadis* + imparfait**.

*There have always been polar bears around Kaktovik. But they **used to be out** on the sea ice, hunting their prey of choice: seals.*

▶ *Used to* est souvent suivi de ***(but) now...*** pour souligner ce contraste :

*Websites like Skyscanner **used to compare** flight options between destinations, **now** they show customers a "greener choice" – displaying how much less C02 a certain flight emits.*

▶ Voici comment il se forme :

Forme affirmative	Forme négative	Forme interrogative
I used to + V	*I didn't use to* + V	*Did you use to* + V ?

Notons qu'à la forme négative, on trouve aussi parfois ***didn't used to*** ou ***used not to***.

▶ Il n'est pas rare que le verbe qui suit *to* soit sous-entendu, surtout après un comparatif :

*In the Arctic Ocean, sea ice melts **earlier than it used to**.*

⚠ Il ne faut pas confondre ***used to* + V** et ***be used to* + V-*ing***, qui exprime l'habitude et qui peut se mettre à tous les temps :

*I'**m** not **used to** travel**ing** so far away.*

2 **Comparez la situation écologique actuelle avec celle d'avant le changement climatique.** Produisez quatre phrases qui utilisent la structure *used to* + V.

Ex. : *Heatwaves **used to be** rare, but now, they occur almost every year.*

3 **Traduisez en utilisant *used to* + V ou *be used to* + V-*ing*.**

a. Avant, j'allais au travail en voiture. Maintenant, j'y vais à vélo.

b. Je voyage moins qu'avant.

c. Je n'ai pas l'habitude d'aller au travail en voiture.

Improve your pronunciation

Le *l* sombre et le *l* clair

▶ La consonne *l* peut se prononcer de deux manières différentes en anglais britannique standard, en fonction du contexte dans lequel elle apparaît.

• Le premier son, appelé ***l* clair**, pose peu de problèmes : il ressemble beaucoup au *l* français que l'on trouve dans *livre*, par exemple. En anglais, on le trouve en début de syllabe, avant une voyelle : ***look***, ***black***, ***let***, ***ugly*** …

• La seconde prononciation, appelée ***l* sombre (parfois représentée par le symbole ɫ)**, n'a pas d'équivalent en français. Pour prononcer correctement ce *l*, la langue doit être dirigée vers les incisives du haut, puis être redirigée vers le fond de la bouche, vers la zone du palais. On trouve le *l* sombre en fin de syllabe après une voyelle : ***well***, ***tell***, ***help***, ***full***, ***real***…

1 Écoutez et répétez les mots suivants. Tous ces mots existent en français : soyez attentif.ve à la différence de prononciation entre le *l* français et le *l* sombre anglais.

Audio hatier-clic.fr/21amc/209a

Churchill • cool • cocktail • fuel • football • milkshake

2 Recopiez les mots suivants et soulignez en rouge les *l* clairs et en vert les *l* sombres. Écoutez l'enregistrement pour confirmer vos réponses et répétez.

Audio hatier-clic.fr/21amc/209b

climate • holiday • melt • travel • pollute • help • tell • last • almost • seal • wild

Les groupes de souffle

▶ Un groupe de souffle est un groupe de mots prononcé sans pause dans le débit de parole. Par convention, on sépare les groupes de souffle par le symbole | qui représente une très courte pause.

▶ Il peut y avoir plusieurs groupes de souffle dans une même phrase. C'est **la structure grammaticale de la phrase** qui permet de rythmer sa prononciation. Par ailleurs, la ponctuation, et en particulier **les virgules**, nous aident souvent à délimiter les groupes de souffle :

| ***Welcome to Antarctica,*** | ***the majestic seventh continent,*** | ***an unspoiled land of incredible ice formations that you simply have to see.*** |

⚠ Attention toutefois, tous les groupes de souffle ne sont pas isolés par des virgules.

▶ **Les compléments circonstanciels** constituent en général des groupes de souffle, surtout quand ils sont placés en début ou en fin de phrase :

| ***Every year,*** | ***more than 40,000 people visit Antarctica.*** |

⚠ Les adverbes de manière ne sont en général pas séparés du reste de la phrase par une pause :

| ***He answered my question very honestly.*** |

▶ Les groupes nominaux longs constituent généralement des groupes de souffle à part, surtout s'ils sont sujet de la phrase :

| ***The most beautiful landscapes in the world*** | ***are in Alaska.*** |

▶ Quand on fait une énumération, chaque élément est souvent séparé des autres par une pause :

| ***Polar bears,*** | ***elephants*** | ***and whales*** | ***are endangered species.*** |

3 Découpez les phrases en groupes de souffle (utilisez le symbole | pour les séparer) et prononcez-les. Plusieurs découpages sont parfois possibles. Écoutez l'enregistrement pour vérifier vos réponses.

Audio hatier-clic.fr/21amc/209c

a. *I think he's wrong.*

b. *Andrew, could I have a word?*

c. *New research from Australian scientists says tourists are threatening the park's biodiversity.*

d. *Yesterday we visited Yosemite National Park.*

e. *Many of the people I know don't believe in climate change.*

f. *If you have to travel by air, offset your carbon emissions by donating money to sustainable projects.*

Let's translate

In 2012, scientists estimated that the Great Barrier Reef had already lost more than half of its coral cover since 1985, but the way research is reported, and the threats that drive tourists to visit such endangered places, are misplaced, according to ecologist Peter Mumby.

"The reef has experienced a very serious impact over the last few years in particular, but remember that it's the size of Italy," he says. "There remain many wonderful areas, and I've little doubt that tourists will always find something valuable to enjoy."

"Yes, the reef is likely to deteriorate, and we need to accelerate action to protect it, but the notion that it will die is wrong."

The Independent, May 30th, 2018

La modulation

▶ **Une modulation** est un procédé de traduction qui consiste **à changer de point de vue**. Elle permet souvent d'éviter le mot-à-mot et d'obtenir une traduction naturelle et idiomatique.

▶ La modulation **peut être grammaticale**. Il peut s'agir :

– d'un passage de **la forme négative à la forme affirmative** (ou inversement) :

She may be right. → Elle n'a peut-être pas tort.

– d'un passage de **la voix passive à la voix active** :

I'm obsessed by him. → Il m'obsède.

– traduire **un singulier par un pluriel** : *my luggage* → **mes** bagages.

On parle aussi de **modulation** quand on est amené à désigner la partie par le tout (*She shut the door in **my face*** → Elle me ferma la porte **au nez**.) ou quand on effectue un changement de point de vue spatio-temporel (***up** the street* → **au bout de** la rue), etc.

Translation Tip

À vous !

a. Traduisez les segments suivants au moyen d'une modulation grammaticale : *I've little doubt that..., the way research is reported*. Décrivez les changements apportés.

b. Attention aux faux amis. Comment traduira-t-on : *misplaced, serious, notion* ?

c. Proposez des traductions pour *its coral cover, is likely to deteriorate* qui utilisent le procédé de la transposition (voir Unit 22, p. 266). Décrivez les changements apportés.

Build up your vocabulary

1 Fill in your own mind map here: hatier-clic.fr/21am/210

2 Fill the gaps with words from your mind map.
With unprecedented growth, tourism has reached a ... , putting severe pressure on the Amazon ... or Australia's ... to name but two common destinations on top of many tourists' ... (the things they plan on doing before they die) . They all want to see the endangered places before it's too late! There are so many ... flocking to the same places that they cause ... damage. As a consequence, locally, ... people have started to raise ... about their changing life conditions. Meanwhile environment activists would like to see Westerners adopt a different ... and pay more attention to their individual carbon footprint. It looks as though ... is what it takes to cut down the number of people flying around the world, and consequently reduce carbon ... .

3 Write an email to your American friend to influence his/her choice for his/her next trip.

Projects

1 Organise and host your NPR show about a national park of your choice.

1. **Choose the part you want to play**
   - Student A: the radio host
   - Student B: a local that is critical of tourism
   - Student C: a local hotel manager
2. **Prepare your contribution to the show.**
   - Choose the park (for ex. Yosemite National Park in the US, Kakadu National Park in Australia, Abel Tasman National Park in New Zealand or Banff National Park in Canada).
   - Note down some arguments, figures and keywords found in the unit or on the web.
   - Use expressions to defend your point of view: I strongly believe, I have mixed feelings about,I've witnessed such and such…
3. **No reading please! Get ready to speak with a dozen key words or bullet points.**
   - As the host, prepare an introduction, a summary of facts and questions.
   - As the locals, anticipate the questions and prepare answers.
4. **Get ready for the recording. Check the voice recorder on your smartphone. Review your notes one last time While on air, stay calm and confident. You can always do another take.**

2 You are an experienced traveller. Write a travel blog explaining the potential damage caused by eco-tourism.

1. **Review the unit, your personal knowledge and the web to collect information.**
2. **Find examples, facts and figures in the headlines of https://www.sciencedaily.com/terms/ecotourism.htm to find examples in the headlines.**
3. **Write a first draft laying out your arguments and match each of your ideas with supporting evidence.**
4. **Find an attention-grabbing headline and draft your article.**
5. **Follow the standard layout of an online article (headline, date, by-line…) and type the final version.**

Pour l'écrit du Bac

A

Last chance tourism is the tourism industry that is built around the last chance to see something. It could be the last chance to see wild rhinoceros in Africa, the last chance to see the Great Barrier Reef or the last chance to see Argentina's glacier fields. If you knew that before long something would be gone forever, you would likely make an effort to experience it before it is too late.

Last chance tourism is something that has been increasing in popularity since travel fairs began to fall in price with budget airlines. Flights from the UK to Australia can be had for under £500, a historically low price and as the destinations tourism industry continues to increase, prices will only decrease.

However, what people don't seem to be considering is the effect that the last chance tourism industry has on the very elements that people are so eager[1] to see 'for the last time'.

The increase in traffic flocking to see endangered species in their natural habitat disturbs their environment and potential highlights their position to poachers and hunters. Increased local boat traffic boosts water pollution in the area around The Great Barrier Reef, increasing ocean acidity and a decline in the death of coral population. Increased air travel to see natural places of beauty, Argentina's glacier fields for example, very obviously increases pollution, green houses gases and speeds up climate change.

Our selfish need to tick off items on our 'holiday bucket list', ironically only furthers the decline of our planet's natural beauty. It's a downward spiral that only gets worse the more and more people realise that this is their last chance to visit these amazing places.

How do we stop this downward spiral of self-perpetuating destruction?

People need to be educated to the fact that their (albeit small) contribution to global warming, habitat destruction and pollution is still a contribution. A contribution, no matter how small, is huge. However, this notion and mind set doesn't stop at the negative, it applies to the positive also. A small contribution to sustainability, recycling and conservation isn't as small as it may seem.

thisiseco.co.uk

1. excited

PARTIE 1

Prenez connaissance du dossier proposé, composé des documents A, B et C non hiérarchisés, et traitez en anglais le sujet suivant (500 mots maximum) :

Taking into account their specificities and viewpoints, show how the documents illustrate some of the challenges of sustainable travel. You will pay particular attention to the impact of climate change on holiday habits and the factors that actually contribute to a sustainable and responsible approach to tourism.

PARTIE 2

Traduisez en français le passage suivant du document C.

But guilt rarely leads to constructive change. The answer isn't to never travel again, then, but to travel more thoughtfully, more creatively, more intentionally.

Clearly, the closer to home you stay, the smaller your carbon footprint is likely to be. It's not to say you should never go abroad again; more than a good place to start is by embracing previously overlooked domestic destinations before you go rushing off to Fiji.

B

C A green guide to going on holiday

"Guilt" is a word we increasingly associate with our lifestyle choices as we hunker down[1] into the 2020s. Many people are reassessing their holiday habits. In light of previous frequent headlines about overtourism, Greta Thunberg's famous shunning[2] of flights and the uncomfortable disconnect between many rich Westerners and the reality of life in whatever "exotic" destination they've just touched down in, it can be difficult to see how travel can ever be truly sustainable.

But guilt rarely leads to constructive change. The answer isn't to never travel again, then, but to travel more thoughtfully, more creatively, more intentionally.

Clearly, the closer to home you stay, the smaller your carbon footprint is likely to be. It's not to say you should never go abroad again; more than a good place to start is by embracing previously overlooked domestic destinations before you go rushing off to Fiji. [...]

Picking the right business to book with can be instrumental in having a positive impact when you travel. Luckily, there's an ever-growing market of companies committed to offering sustainable trips – ones that put the concepts of bolstering local communities and adding value back into destinations at the very heart of their products.

Much Better Adventures, for example, gives 5 per cent of revenues to help support conservation projects and the families of local guides who have been badly affected by the pandemic; this year, the brand became the first international travel company to add carbon footprint labels to all its trips, enabling customers to compare when choosing their holiday.

Helen Coffey, *The Independent*, Feb. 3rd, 2021

1. (here) settle 2. avoidance

18 The challenge of policing UK & US cities

The expert's view
hatier-clic.fr/21amc/214a

In the news
hatier-clic.fr/21amc/214b

Projects

- You are a journalist. Write an article dealing with the mayor's new decision about law enforcement in the city.
- One of you is a journalist, the other a film director. Record a podcast about a series on big cities policing issues.

Grammar p. 222 Phonology p. 223

Policing the city

A Police, crime and the city

2

1

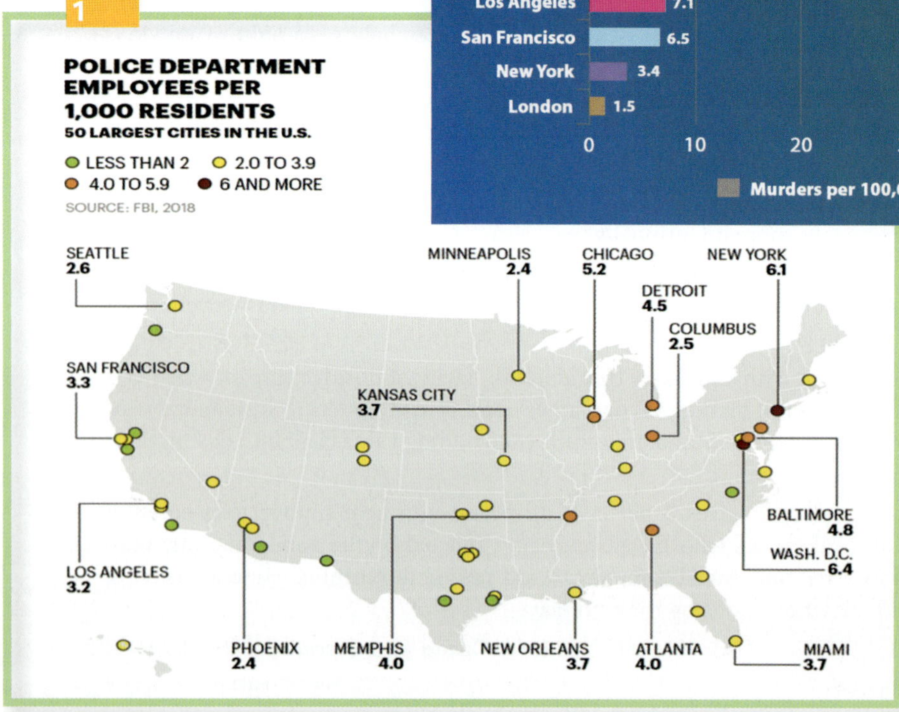

1. Present the two documents and explain what the figures reveal for each of them.
2. Make suppositions about the gap between the murder rates in London and in US cities.
3. **CONNECT.** Focus on a few US cities. Compare the figures given in the two documents and deduce the link.

B Join the Met

1 **Becoming an officer in The Met**
Video hatier-clic.fr/21amc/215a

2 **Join the LAPD**
Audio hatier-clic.fr/21amc/215b

PAIR WORK

Student A on document 1
Student B on document 2

1. Explain the nature of the document and its purpose.
2. Pick out information about the job and list the challenges of urban policing.
3. Exchange on your videos and compare the slogans.
4. Give a short speech to present the job of police officer to new recruits.

C Police in the modern city

1 The history of modern policing

Before the Industrial Revolution, policing in America and England was typically carried out voluntarily by individual citizens concerned with maintaining law and order in their communities. […]

The beginning of modern policing

Sir Robert Peel, […] known as the "father of modern policing," established the Metropolitan Police Services in London in 1829. Then as now, British police officers were called "Bobbies" in honor of his first name.

Sir Peel is credited with establishing the three core principles of policing, which remain as essential today as they were two centuries ago:

- The goal of policing is preventing crime, not catching criminals. Effective police departments have low arrest rates because their communities have low crime rates.

- To prevent crime, police must earn public support. If the community trusts and supports the police, all citizens will share the responsibility of preventing crime as if they were a volunteer police force.

- To earn public support, the police must respect community principles. Police earn a good reputation by enforcing the laws impartially, hiring officers who reflect and represent the community, and using force only as a last resort.

History of police in America

[…] The first dedicated, centralized, city police department was established in Boston in 1838. Similar police forces in New York City, Chicago, New Orleans, and Philadelphia soon followed. By the turn of the century, most large American cities had formal police forces.

The era of city political machines during the late 19th century brought the first obvious cases of police corruption. Local political party ward leaders, many of whom owned bars or ran street gangs, often appointed and paid off high ranking police officials to allow illegal drinking, gambling, and prostitution in their precincts. […]

Law enforcement today

Beginning in the early 2000s, however, many Americans came to criticize local police agencies as operating more like occupying soldiers than community protectors. After the 2014 Ferguson Riots in Ferguson, Missouri, the Black Lives Matter movement came to illustrate the public's concern over the use of unnecessary, often excessive force by police.

Robert Longley, www.thoughtco.com, July 13th, 2020

2

The making of copper
Video hatier-clic.fr/21amc/215c

e-worksheet hatier-clic.fr/21amc/215d

1. Watch the video. Show how Sir Peele's principles echo the recent evolution of the police.
2. Read the text. Sum up the police values and show how they have been betrayed by different scandals. Explain how the video illustrates it with a precise example.
3. **CONNECT.** Using both the text and the video, explain the link between the development of cities and the need for a professional police force in the UK and in the USA.

Urban policing: topical issues

A Patrolling the city

1 **Bosch**
Video hatier-clic.fr/21amc/216a

1. Watch the two videos. List their common points and differences.
2. Show how fighting crime in the city is presented as a heroic mission (rhythm, shots, soundtrack).
3. Use examples from the videos to comment on this sentence from video 1: "Every murder is the tale of the city."
4. You are the director of the documentary series *The Met: Policing London*. Explain how movies and series about the police have influenced your style.

2 **The Met: Policing London**
Video hatier-clic.fr/21amc/216b

B Debate over police methods

1

NEW YORK (CBS NewYork) – There's demand for wholesale[1] change at the NYPD after a damming report by the Department of Investigation finds the NYPD was unprepared to deal with protests over the murder of George Floyd, and that excessive force exacerbated tensions.

As CBS2's political reporter Marcia Kramer reports, New Yorkers were appalled by the video of the police response to the George Floyd protests: Bystanders sprayed with pepper spray, a squad car driving into a crowd of protesters, a woman pushed to the ground by police.

A new report by the Department of Investigation tears the Band-Aid off that wound.

"Our investigation found that the NYPD, as an institution, made a number of key errors or commissions that likely escalated tensions and a potential for violence," said DOI Commissioner Margaret Garnett.

Among the findings:

- The NYPD lacks a clearly defined strategy to respond to large scale protests
- Police used excessive force that heightened tensions
- Cops lacked sufficient training

"The NYPD's tactics often failed to discriminate between lawful, peaceful protesters and unlawful actors," Garnett said. […]

"These tactics, which included encirclement, also known as kettling[2], mass arrests, baton and pepper spray use, and other tactics, reflect a failure to calibrate an appropriate balance between valid public safety, or officer safety, interest and the rights of protesters to assemble and express their views," Garnett said.

PROTESTS AND POLICE REFORMS

Mayor Bill de Blasio and Police Commissioner Dermot Shea vowed to make changes.

"I am saying to everyone in the NYPD – everyone needs to accept the results of this report. Everyone needs to implement them," de Blasio said. "If there's anyone in leadership in the NYPD who reads that report and disagrees… they should leave now."

Marcia Kramer, newyork.cbslocal.com, Dec. 8th, 2020

1. large-scale 2. containing protesters

Text 1:

1. Point out the events commented on in this article and show how the police reacted. Explain what makes these reactions questionable.
2. Identify whose opinion is voiced in the report and why it differs from common thinking.

C Denouncing police violence in the city

1

George Floyd and Black Lives Matter

PAIR WORK

Student A on visual 1
Student B on visual 2

1 Describe your piece of street art (characters, layout, colors) and explain which country is concerned.

2 Comment on the issue tackled and explain the message of the artist. Swap information with your partner.

3 You have just walked past one of these artworks and decide to post the photograph on Instagram. Write the short text which would go with it.

2

Banksy

2

Met police to begin using live facial recognition cameras in London

The Metropolitan police is to start using live facial recognition (LFR) cameras linked to powerful computers on London's streets despite scepticism from experts over how efficient the system is and widespread concerns over civil liberties. […]

The Met said it would deploy the technology overtly and only after consulting communities in which it is to be used.

It said the cameras would be linked to a database of suspects uploaded using the latest intelligence. If the system detects someone who is not on the database, their information will be deleted in seconds. But if it generates an alert because the person is wanted, an officer will speak to them.

Using facial recognition linked to databases of suspects is potentially the next big leap[1] for law enforcement, as big as the introduction of fingerprints. […] Nick Ephgrave, an assistant commissioner at the Met, said: "As a modern police force, I believe that we have a duty to use new technologies to keep people safe in London. Independent research has shown that the public support us in this regard." […]

The Met has made promises to the mayor of London, Sadiq Khan, after an independent ethics review raised concerns over its earlier trials of facial recognition software. The system will not be linked to other official databases. It is not designed to allow the authorities to scan every corner of London or allow them to be confidently capable of tracking anyone down.

Vikram Dodd, *The Guardian*, Jan. 24th, 2020

1. important step

Text 2:

3 Explain how the system works and why it is "modern".

4 Identify opposing views and comment on the opinion expressed.

Both texts 1 and 2:

5 **CONNECT.** Show that both the NYPD and the Met in London are aware of the controversial issues regarding their methods and trying to address them. Use *Let's focus on…* nos 2 and 5, p. 220-221 to enrich your paragraph.

Time for a change

A "Defunding the police"?

1

What does "Defund the police" mean and does it have merit?

George Floyd's death has galvanized much of America to move the needle toward police reform ideas – such as defunding police – that were previously viewed as radical.

"Defund the police" means reallocating or redirecting funding away from the police department to other government agencies funded by the local municipality. That's it. It's that simple. Defund does not mean abolish policing. And, even some who say abolish, do not necessarily mean to do away with law enforcement altogether. Rather, they want to see the rotten trees of policing chopped down and fresh roots replanted anew. [...]

One consistent finding in the social science literature is that if we really want to reduce crime, education equity and the establishment of a work infrastructure is the best approach. A study using 60 years of data found that an increase in funding for police did not significantly relate to a decrease in crime. Throwing more police on the street to solve a structural problem is one of the reasons why people are protesting in the streets. Defunding police – reallocating funding away from police departments to other sectors of government – may be more beneficial for reducing crime and police violence.

Rashaw Ray, www.brookings.edu, June 9th, 2020

2

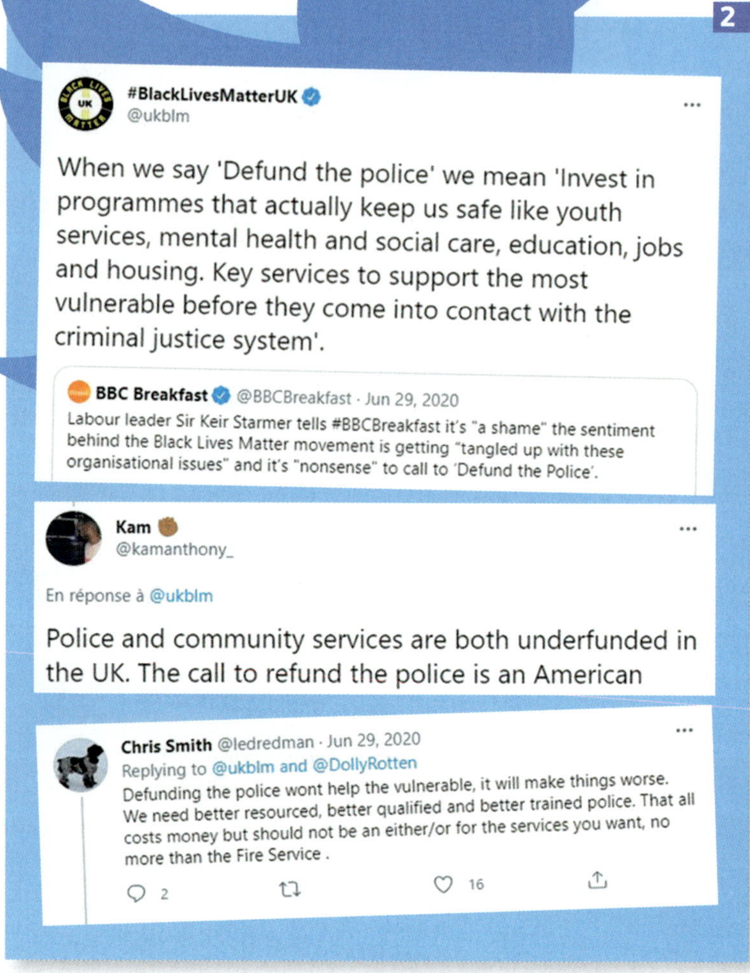

#BlackLivesMatterUK
@ukblm

When we say 'Defund the police' we mean 'Invest in programmes that actually keep us safe like youth services, mental health and social care, education, jobs and housing. Key services to support the most vulnerable before they come into contact with the criminal justice system'.

BBC Breakfast @BBCBreakfast · Jun 29, 2020
Labour leader Sir Keir Starmer tells #BBCBreakfast it's "a shame" the sentiment behind the Black Lives Matter movement is getting "tangled up with these organisational issues" and it's "nonsense" to call to 'Defund the Police'.

Kam
@kamanthony_

En réponse à @ukblm

Police and community services are both underfunded in the UK. The call to refund the police is an American

Chris Smith @ledredman · Jun 29, 2020
Replying to @ukblm and @DollyRotten
Defunding the police wont help the vulnerable, it will make things worse. We need better resourced, better qualified and better trained police. That all costs money but should not be an either/or for the services you want, no more than the Fire Service .

2 16

3

Kamala Harris on Defunding the police

Video hatier-clic.fr/21amc/218

GROUP WORK

Group 1 on the article – Group 2 on the tweets – Group 3 on the video

1. Explain the definition of the concept "defunding the police" and pick out the references to recent history. Compare it to the definition given in *Let's focus on ...* n° 6, p. 221.
2. Give the arguments for and against such a decision.
3. Present your document to two classmates from the other groups and discuss the concept.
4. **Grammar** "**Throwing** more police on the street [...] is one of the reasons why people are protesting in the streets." Analyse the word in bold. Focus on the role of the *ing* ending. What do you call this verb form?
5. Reply to one of the tweets.

B Community-Oriented Policing

1

Detroit Police Dept. @detroitpolice · 21 oct. 2020

@detroitpolice @ChiefJECraigDPD **announced the establishment of the Office of Internal and External Relations**, a new office designed to strengthen the relationship between the police & community through procedural justice, police legitimacy & community engagement.

2

PAIR WORK

Student A on document 1
Student B on document 2

1. Analyse your document and explain how the initiative illustrates the concept of Community-Oriented Policing (COP).
2. Present your document to your classmate. Together, find the common points and discuss the relevance of this COP (communication technique, visual elements).
3. Play a coffee meeting between a Boston police officer and a citizen. Choose one topic among the ones discussed previously in class.

C Addressing problems

1. Use words from the audio to define "institutional racism" and "individual racism" and explain Cressida Dick's position about these issues.
2. Pick out expressions used by the two speakers that reveal the tension in the interview.
3. Phonology Listen to the following words: *for*ce, *Geor*ge Floyd, *cau*se. Focus on the British pronunciation of the letters in bold. How would an American speaker pronounce these words? What are the main differences?
4. Continue the interview with questions about recent issues such as facial recognition or police violence.

Met Police Commissioner Cressida Dick

Audio hatier-clic.fr/21amc/219

Let's focus on...

FBI vs NYPD

1

Law enforcement in US cities is handled by police departments while the FBI (Federal Bureau of Investigation) is the national investigative agency, in charge of major cases, like murder, inter-state crimes and kidnappings. Any activity which compromises the security of the United States is also investigated by the FBI.

The Met

2

In 1829, British statesman Sir Robert Peel, then Home Secretary in Lord Liverpool's cabinet, passed The Metropolitan Police Act which led to the creation of The Metropolitan Police Force. Constables were then appointed permanently and paid to enforce the law in London streets. These "Peelers", also called "Bobbies", had to fulfill several conditions, like be aged between 20 and 27, at least 5 foot 7 inches tall and also be fit and literate. The "Bobbies" have been wearing the same iconic helmet since 1863. The headquarters had an entrance on a street called Great Scotland Yard, that is why the Met is often referred to as Scotland Yard (or New Scotland Yard now).
In 2019, there were 8,911 officers at the Met to enforce the law in 32 London boroughs. It is the City of London Police which polices the very center of London.

Bosch and other famous fictional police officers

3

You probably know fictional private detectives, like Agatha Christie's Hercule Poirot, Sir Arthur Conna Doyle's Sherlock Holmes or Raymond Chandler's Philip Marlowe, but police officers also feature in fiction and some of them have become famous characters, especially when they become recurring characters in movies or series. These officers are often hard working, successful in their enquiries, and yet their troubled personalities make them stand apart from their colleagues.
Michal Connelly, a former journalist, spent most of his career reporting on the crime beat before becoming a bestselling author. LAPD detective **Harry Bosch**, his most popular character, has seduced millions of readers since he appeared in print in 1992. His admirers have followed him onto the screen thanks to Amazon Prime's adaptation. In getting justice for people who have been wronged, Bosch often oversteps procedures.
Harry Callahan, nicknamed "Dirty Harry" is a movie character who appeared in 5 movies by Don Spiegel and was played by Clint Eastwood. This police officer from San Francisco Police Department is famous for his violent and pitiless methods, hence the use of the adjective "dirty" to qualify him.
Luther is the main character of a British psychological crime drama series. This DCI (Detective Chief Inspector) of the "Serious and Serial Unit" in London city is quite an obsessive, possessed, and sometimes violent officer who feels consumed by the darkness of the crimes which he has to investigate.

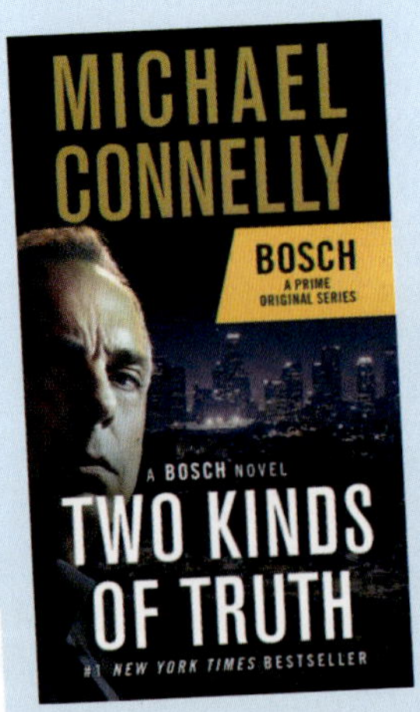

Timeline 4

UK

Cressida Dick, first female commissioner of the Met.
2017

G20 protests in London. One demonstrator killed by the police.
2009

Macpherson report stating that institutional racism existed at the Met.
1999

New headquarters: The New Scotland Yard.
1960s

First women to become full police officers at the Met.
1919

Jack the Ripper investigation by the Met.
1888

Henry Owen first police officer to fire a revolver while on duty.
1887

Creation of the Metropolitan Police in London by Robert Peel.
1829

USA

George Floyd killed by the police during his arrestation.
25th May 2020

35783 officers in the NYPD.
2020

Arrest of NYPD officer Adrian Schoolcraft accused by his fellow officers of manipulating crime statistics and carrying out intentional wrongful arrests (to meet arrest quotas).
2009

NYPD develops the CompStat computer system to track crime geographically.
1984

Creation of a Gang Intelligence Unit by a Sergeant Robert Michael (LAPD).
1977

First black officer (NYPD).
1911

Alice Stebbins Wells (LAPD), first female police officer in the USA to be sworn in with full powers.
1910

Birth of the LAPD.
1869

Creation of the NYPD to replace an old night watch system.
1845

First city police department in Boston.
1838

First federal law enforcement agency, the US marshalls service.
1789

NYPD 5

The New York City Police Department (NYPD) appeared when the Government of NYC intended to control rising crimes in the 1820s. In 1845, the idea of a full-time professional police force was copied from London's Metropolitan Police service. This replaced the night watch system which had originally been implemented in the 17th century. The NYPD has now about 55,000 employees, including 36,000 uniformed officers. It includes services such as the Emergency Service Unit, harbor patrol, air support, bomb squad, counter-terrorism, criminal intelligence, narcotics, anti-organised crime, public transportation or public housing. In 2019, the NYPD dealt with 500,00 reports of crimes and arrested over 200,000 people. In 2020 its budget was 6 billion US dollars.

Defund the police 6

Following the protests of May 2020 after George Floyd's death, many activists of Black Live Matters and other organisations came up with the need for "defunding the police". Behind this term lies the idea of reimagining the role of the police forces in American society, redistributing some of the money allocated to law enforcement to budgets like education, health or housing. Some more extremist organisations, gathered around the hashtags #8Can'tWait and #8toAbolition, go further, claiming the police should be abolished.

Practice your grammar

Les propositions gérondives

▶ Une proposition gérondive est **une proposition dont le verbe est à la forme en *-ing*** et qui occupe la place d'un pronom ou d'un groupe nominal dans la phrase.

▶ Une proposition gérondive peut être **sujet de la phrase** :

Using facial recognition linked to databases of suspects is potentially the next big leap.

▶ Elle peut être également **complément du verbe** :

The suspect denied murdering his boss.

⚠ Tous les verbes ne sont pas susceptibles d'être suivis d'un verbe au gérondif. **La plupart des verbes sont suivis de l'infinitif en *to*.**

▶ Voici une liste de verbes suivis du gérondif :

- *avoid*
- *can't help*
- *deny*
- *finish*
- *stop / give up*
- *admit*
- *mind*
- *enjoy*
- *risk*
- *contemplate*
- *consider*
- *imagine*

Par ailleurs, quelques verbes acceptent les deux constructions : *start, begin, continue, try, remember,* certains verbes de goût (*like, hate, love*...), etc.

▶ On trouve des propositions gérondives après **des prépositions** telles que *with, of, for* ou *without* (voir Unit 15, page 184) :

*Sir Peel is credited **with** establishing the three core principles of policing.*

1 Mettez le verbe entre parenthèses à l'infinitif en *to* ou au gérondif.

a. *I usually avoid ... (go) out late at night.*

b. *The suspect denied ... (break) into the house and refused ... (answer) the police's questions.*

c. *She advised him ... (call) the police.*

d. *The convict hopes ... (be released) on parole.*

e. *My son wants ... (become) a detective. That's why he's contemplating ... (join) the police force.*

f. *He was charged with ... (kill) two people.*

2 Traduisez. Utilisez le mot entre parenthèses le cas échéant.

a. Réformer la police pourrait prendre des années.

b. Je ne pouvais pas m'empêcher de crier. *(can't help)*

c. Il envisage de porter plainte contre son agresseur. *(consider)*

Les noms collectifs

▶ Certains noms qui désignent **des groupes ou des collectivités** peuvent être tantôt suivis d'un verbe au singulier, tantôt suivis d'un verbe au pluriel.

*The government **are / is planning** to defund the police.*

De même, ces noms sont parfois repris par un pronom pluriel *they / them* ou employés avec le possessif *their*.

▶ L'accord au singulier est employé si l'on veut insister sur l'unité et la cohésion du groupe :

*The government **has decided** to increase taxes.*

▶ Le pluriel est employé si l'on désire insister sur la diversité des individus qui constituent le groupe, par exemple quand ils agissent différemment.

*The jury **were** allowed to go to **their** homes every night.*

▶ Voici quelques exemples de noms collectifs :

- *family*
- *government*
- *class*
- *team*
- *staff*
- *jury*
- *committee*
- *audience*

À ces noms, il faut ajouter ceux qui désignent **des équipes sportives, des entreprises ou des organisations** (*the FBI, Interpol*...).

▶ **Le mot *police*** est, quant à lui, toujours suivi d'un verbe au pluriel.

***The police are investigating** the circumstances that led to the killing of three people.*

3 Choisissez la forme qui convient. Les deux réponses sont parfois possibles.

a. *The jury **has / have** reached a decision.*

b. *The family **are / is taking** separate holidays this year.*

c. *The police **have / has charged** her husband with murder.*

d. *The crew **is / are wearing** new uniforms.*

e. *An average family **consists / consist** of four people.*

f. *The orchestra **was / were** tuning **their / its** instruments.*

Improve your pronunciation

La voyelle longue /ɔː/

▶ **La voyelle** /ɔː/ est **une voyelle longue**. Ce son ressemble à la voyelle du français d*o*s, mais est légèrement plus longue.

▶ Elle est souvent représentée par **les graphies suivantes contenant un *o* et un *r*** :

or	*force, before, store*	***our***	*your, fourth, source*
oor	*door, poor, floor*	***oar***	*board, roar*

Dans ces graphies, le *r* ne se prononce pas en anglais GB standard. Il est, en revanche, prononcé en anglais US standard.

! En fin de mot ou en position inaccentuée, le suffixe *-o(u)r* se prononce /ə/ : *error, spectator, colour...*

▶ Cette voyelle apparaît aussi en anglais britannique dans les contextes suivants :

au / aw	*law, draw, saw, cause*
al(l), alk	*all, tall, walk, talk*
augh / ough	surtout dans des verbes irréguliers : *thought, taught, ought*

! En anglais américain, les graphies du tableau ci-dessus sont prononcées avec la voyelle longue /ɑː/, un son plus ouvert qui ressemble à la voyelle de *calm* ou de *car*.

1 **Prononcez les mots suivants.** Écoutez l'enregistrement pour vérifier vos réponses.

Audio hatier-clic.fr/21amc/223a

uniform • order • your • enforcement • important • support • New York • George Floyd • informer

2 **Vous allez entendre des mots prononcés par un locuteur britannique, puis par un locuteur américain.** Répétez-les en fonction de l'accent que vous aurez choisi.

Audio hatier-clic.fr/21amc/223b

law and order • support • store • thought • bought • walk • talk • cause

Les suffixes neutres

▶ Certaines terminaisons dites « contraignantes » influencent la place de l'accent principal dans le mot (voir Unit 20, p. 243). C'est par exemple le cas de la terminaison *-ian* : ***mu**sic* Oo → *mu**si**cian* oOo

▶ À l'inverse, **les suffixes dits « neutres » n'influencent pas la place de l'accent tonique**. Les mots contenant ces suffixes sont donc accentués de la même manière que les mots racines dont ils sont issus :

-age /ɪdʒ/	*orphan → orphanage*
-ful /fəl/	*meaning → meaningful*
-hood /hʊd/	*neighbour → neighbourhood*
-ing	*police → policing*
-ism /ɪzəm/	*sceptic → scepticism*
-less /ləs/	*meaning → meaningless*
-ly	*confident → confidently*
-ment /mənt/	*enforce → enforcement*
-ness /nəs/	*conscious → consciousness*
-or / er /ə/	*office → officer*
-ship	*citizen → citizenship*

! Ces suffixes sont **inaccentués**. Leur voyelle est par conséquent souvent **réduite**, c'est-à-dire prononcée avec la voyelle /ə/ ou /ɪ/.

3 **Prononcez les mots suivants. Attention à l'accentuation et à la prononciation du suffixe.** Écoutez l'enregistrement pour vérifier vos réponses.

Audio hatier-clic.fr/21amc/223c

damage • advantage • unlawful • terrorism • racism • demonstrator • useless • development • enforcement

4 **Recopiez les mots et soulignez la syllabe qui porte l'accent principal.** Écoutez l'enregistrement pour vérifier vos réponses et répétez.

Audio hatier-clic.fr/21amc/223d

a. *impartial → impartially*
b. *overt → overtly*
c. *success → successful*
d. *leader → leadership*
e. *begin → beginning*
f. *punish → punishment*

Let's translate

Before the Industrial Revolution, policing in America and England was typically carried out voluntarily by individual citizens concerned with maintaining law and order in their communities. This part-time citizen volunteer model of policing worked well until the late 1700s and early 1800s, when exploding population growth resulted in more frequent incidents of crime and violent civil unrest in cities throughout England and the United States. It soon became clear that full-time, professional policing – sanctioned and endorsed by the government – had become a necessity.

Robert Longley,
www.thoughtco.com,
July 13th, 2020

La traduction des mots composés

▶ Les noms composés sont très fréquents en anglais, surtout dans la presse écrite. Leur traduction peut donc poser problème.

▶ Dans un nom composé, le nom principal est celui qui est placé le plus droite. Il peut comporter deux termes, voire bien plus.

▶ Le plus souvent, pour traduire un nom composé anglais, le français a recours à **une préposition** (surtout *de* ou *à*) :
the police force → les forces **de** police.

▶ Il est, dans certains cas, possible de traduire le premier nom par **un adjectif** :
a New York lawyer → un avocat **new-yorkais**.

▶ Il est parfois nécessaire **d'étoffer** le nom composé, en ajoutant un ou plusieurs mots (un adjectif, un participe passé, etc.) :
this tabloid scandal → ce scandale **digne** d'un tabloïde.

Translation Tip

À vous !

a. Traduisez les noms composés suivants : *part-time citizen volunteer model, population growth.*

b. Quelle est la nature grammaticale d'*exploding* et de *of crime* ? Ne faudra-t-il pas avoir recours à des transpositions (voir Unit 22, p. 266) pour traduire ces expressions ?

Build up your vocabulary

1 Fill in your own mind map here:
hatier-clic.fr/21am/224

2 Use your mind map to find the word corresponding to the definition.
a. someone who gives information to the police
b. the district of a police station
c. make people respect the law
d. a crime consisting in breaking into a house to steal something
e. someone who has aggressed someone else

3 Complete the sentences with words from the unit.
a. When police officers are informed about a bank ... they rush to the place in their ... with the ... on to warn all the cars around. Then, they get out of the car, and have to put on a ... and a ... in case the suspects are armed.
b. During a violent demonstration, ... may be used to scatter the crowd and the demonstrators who are arrested are ... to prevent them from defending themselves.
c. There have been many scandals about ... who took advantage of their power to ... criminals or to accept ... .

4 Describe a usual policeman's day in the city for a leaflet on the NYPD.

Projects

1

You are a journalist in 2040. The mayor of a British or American metropolis has made an important decision about the police in his or her city. Write an article about the announcement.

1. Choose the main elements: mayor's name, city, decision, motivation.
2. Do some research about this city and its police system now to be able to refer to this period when you write in 2040.
3. Choose a point of view you want to defend (praising or criticising the police force) and express it in the last paragraph, after presenting the facts.
4. Write a catchy headline. Choose a photograph to illustrate it and write a caption.
5. Proofread your writing, present it as a press article.

2

One of you is a journalist, the other a film director. Record a podcast interview of the director of a series illustrating today's issues of big cities policing.

1. In pairs, imagine a series involving the London Met or an American big city police (LAPD, NYPD...). List the main elements: title, characters (names, personalities, complicated history), places, plots (repetitive patterns), music for the credits, general visual style and genre (action, comedy, drama).
2. Think of the issues you want to tackle (urban criminality, police violence, use of new technologies, community-oriented policing) and the message you wish to convey.
3. Choose a particular context for the podcast interview: release of a new season, award, controversy about the series (among the public or the police). The journalist may be admirative or critical.
4. Without writing down any script, prepare the main steps of the interview.
5. Record the podcast using an appropriate tone.

Pour l'écrit du Bac

A Transcript: Mayor de Blasio delivers 2021 state of the city address

Mayor Bill de Blasio: Let me tell you a story, a story about a city that bore the brunt[1] of the COVID crisis, a city that was the epicenter, a city that was laid low, but refused to be held down. Let me tell you a story about how things change, about the way we come back, about the way we build something better. Let me tell you a tale of a new city. […]

The new city we need to build has to be a city where everyone belongs. That new city we build has to be one where everyone feels fairness and the decency they deserve. To do that, we have to transform the relationship between our police and our communities. We have to change the culture of policing, fundamentally […] by bringing community closer, by deepening neighborhood policing, by ensuring there is trust. To overcome the challenge of violence […], we're creating a new joint force to end gun violence and fight back against shootings. This will not just be the NYPD, it'll be leaders of communities all over New York City. It means getting the community involved. […]

We know it is only a very few who commit the violence in New York City. But with this new approach, we will identify, individual by individual, who's creating the violence that afflicts everyone else, and will bring to bear[2] all the energies of community and law enforcement to end that violence. […]

The way forward in this city depends on trust. The forward depends on accountability. Where there is accountability there is also trust. Trust between neighborhoods and police. And that's why we are announcing the David Dinkins Plan to expand and strengthen the Civilian Complaint Review Board. We named it after Mayor David Dinkins because he made the CCRB a reality. And this new plan takes historic steps forward. We will grant the CCRB new review powers, we'll make sure the NYPD patrol guide is reviewed, and expand the power of the CCRB to do the kind of proactive work necessary to improve the relationship between police and community, to give people more confidence. That trust and confidence ultimately means more cooperation between community and police, and that is the way to reduce crime and violence. That is the ultimate expression of neighborhood policing.

And we'll also change the value we put on community engagement, by changing the training of our police officers to focus more on a real dialogue with the community. We'll expand the People's Police Academy, ensuring that officers are trained by neighborhood residents before they ever walk the streets of our neighborhoods.

[…] If you want to know if New York City is going to come back, and come back strong, and come back better, just listen to the voices of your fellow New Yorkers. They will tell the story.

www1.nyc.gov, Jan. 28th, 2021

1. be badly impacted by 2. use

B

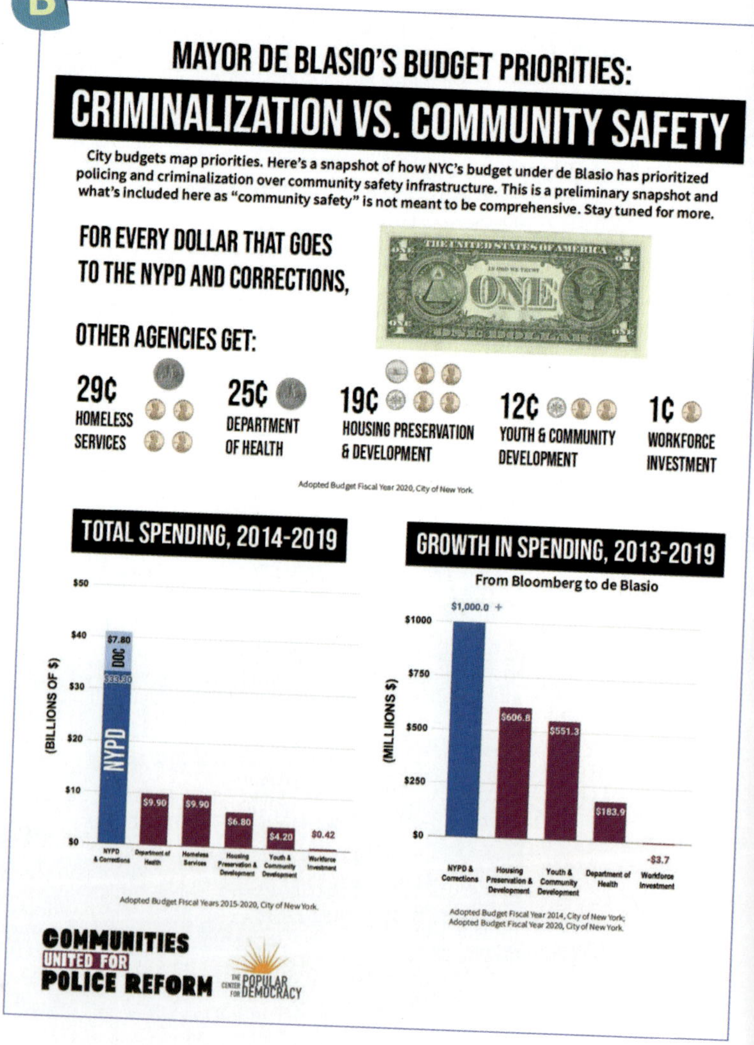

C New York Police arrest dozens as M.L.K. Day marchers gather near City Hall

The confrontation came days after the state's attorney general sued the New York Police Department for its handling of protests following the death of George Floyd.

Dozens of people were arrested on Monday night in Lower Manhattan as hundreds participated in a march on Martin Luther King's Birthday organized by Black activist groups, according to the police and witnesses.

Videos posted online by witnesses and participants show New York Police Department officers with helmets, batons and zip ties[1] trying to clear protesters who had gathered on the streets and sidewalks near City Hall. Some of the marchers went to the area after walking across the Brooklyn Bridge.

A spokesman for the department said dozens of arrests were made between 8 p.m. and 10 p.m. in the vicinity of Chambers and Centre Streets. According to some videos posted online, the police began arresting people after urging the crowd to disperse.

The episode came in the late hours of Martin Luther King's Birthday, and just days after the New York State attorney general, Letitia James, sued the New York Police Department over its handling of protests this summer after the death of George Floyd.

[…] One witness to Monday night's events, Jordan Plaza of the Bronx, said a relatively small number of protesters had spilled off the sidewalks and into the street when the police announced that they were obstructing the road and would soon be arrested.

"They weren't approaching the police in a violent manner," Ms. Plaza, 20, said. "Police randomly surged[2]."

Ms. Plaza said she had stumbled upon the protest earlier in the night on the way to see friends and joined on a whim[3]. She said she was startled by what she saw and contrasted the treatment of protesters in New York City with the treatment of those loyal to President Trump who rioted[4] inside the U.S. Capitol two weeks ago. […]

On Monday night, images of officers yanking individuals out of a crowd of protesters began circulating widely on social media, and echoed scenes from last summer, when Black Lives Matter demonstrators flooded the streets in New York and other cities. A number of those videos helped fuel the lawsuit[5] by Ms. James, the state's attorney general.

The lawsuit she filed in federal court in Manhattan is the first time that the state attorney general has sued a police department, according to Ms. James's office.

"There was ample ability and opportunity for the city and N.Y.P.D. leadership to make important changes to the way that officers interact with peaceful protesters, but time and time again, they did not," Ms. James said.

Bazi Paybarah and Alex Traub,
The New York Times, Jan. 18th, 2021

1. easily fastened links 2. moved forcefully 3. sudden desire 4. protested violently 5. legal action

PARTIE 1

Prenez connaissance du dossier proposé, composé des documents A, B et C non hiérarchisés, et traitez en anglais le sujet suivant (500 mots maximum).

Taking into account their specificities and viewpoints, say what the documents show about the difficulties, risks, and issues of city-policing. You will pay particular attention to:

- the challenges of city-policing
- the relationship between city-dwellers and their police
- the recent evolutions

PARTIE 2

Traduisez en français le passage suivant du document 1.

The new city we need to build has to be a city where everyone belongs. That new city we build has to be one where everyone feels fairness and the decency they deserve. To do that, we have to transform the relationship between our police and our communities. We have to change the culture of policing, fundamentally […] by bringing community closer, by deepening neighborhood policing, by ensuring there is trust. To overcome the challenge of violence […], we're creating a new joint force to end gun violence and fight back against shootings. This will not just be the NYPD, it'll be leaders of communities all over New York City. It means getting the community involved.

Flash

19 Policing the seas

In the news
hatier-clic.fr/21amc/228

Projects

You join a TV news panel. Debate the need for armed guards onboard merchant ships.

Your are a Communications Officer on board a USN ship. Write a news article for a webzine.

Grammar p. 232

Combatting crime

A Piracy data

1

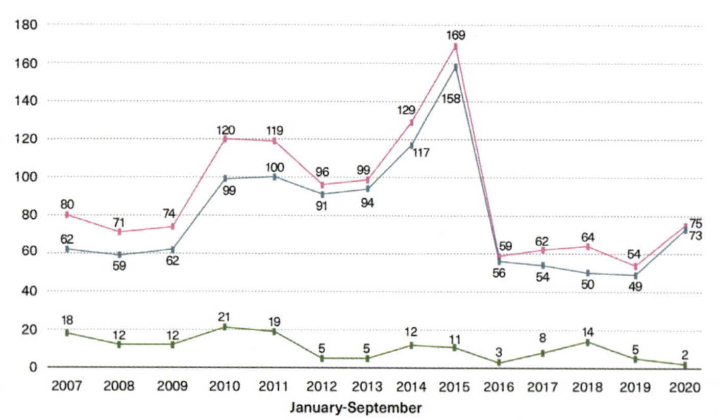

Graph 1 – Number of incidents (January-September of 2007-2020)
Total | Actual | Attempted

2

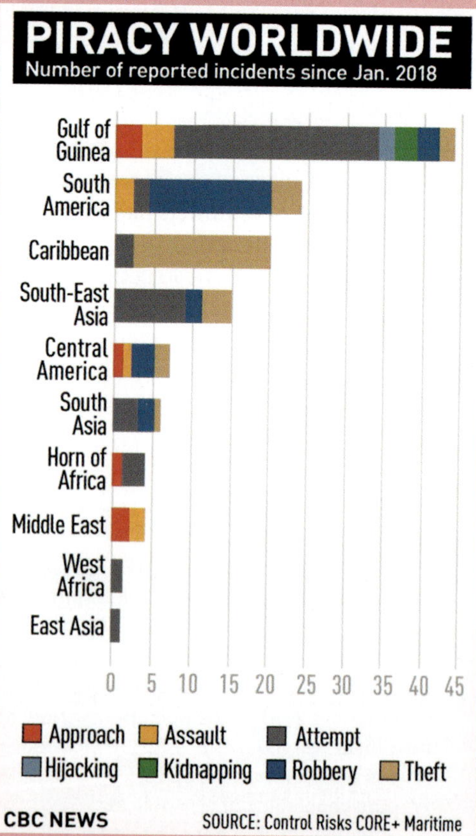

1 Analyse the two graphs: type of graph, title, subject of comparison.

2 CONNECT. Use the two documents to draw some conclusions about piracy.

B Crime on the high seas

PAIR WORK

Student A on video 1
Student B on video 2

1

Captain Phillips

Video hatier-clic.fr/21amc/229a

2

Coast guard busts submarine

Video hatier-clic.fr/21amc229b

1. Identify the maritime crime being committed.
2. Gather precise information on the criminals.
3. Explain the navy or coast guard's role in the situation.
4. You're a reporter. Swap information to write your article: "Combatting crime on the high seas."

C Fighting crime at sea

U.S. Navy stops pirate attack

The U.S. navy ship Pinckney succeeds in rescuing a merchant vessel following a boarding by pirates.

At approximately 11:00 a.m., the M/V Heather, operating 30 nautical miles from Nordic Apollo, reported suspicious activity by a skiff[1]. Pakistan Navy Rear Adm[2]. Kaleem Shaukat, CTF 151's commander, authorized Pinckney to investigate. Nordic Apollo confirmed the pirate attack, but stated they no longer had sight of the skiff. In response to the distress call, Pinckney made best speed to the area, issued a radio warning to other vessels in the vicinity[3] and launched its MH-60R helicopter. The helicopter crew successfully tracked and located the skiff, observing nine suspected pirates and pirate paraphernalia on board, including several ladders, weapons and fuel containers. The suspected pirates were seen attempting to cover their weapons with blankets and throwing the ladders overboard as Pinckney closed their position. Intercepted by the helicopter and Pinckney, the skiff stopped and the suspected pirates threw their weapons, identified as five AK-47 rifles, one rocket propelled grenade (RPG) launcher and three RPG rounds, overboard. Pinckney was given authorization to conduct a boarding using their visit, board, search and seizure (VBSS) team and once aboard, the VBSS team confirmed there were nine suspected pirates, one grappling hook[4], 36 barrels of fuel, and 75 and 45 horsepower outboard engines. The VBSS team scuttled[5] one outboard motor and left the skiff with enough fuel and water to return back to shore. Cmdr[6]. Matthew M. McGonigle, Pinckney's commanding officer, praised the crew for their efforts. "My crew responded in an exceptional reaction time and with complete professionalism. With the helicopter in the air, acting in conjunction with the ship, we were able to have full coverage of the situation and stop them carrying out any further illegal activities. The operation was carried out in accordance with our pre-rehearsed responses to such an event, and I am very proud of the Pinckney's crew and all those involved."

Piracy is a threat to the security of all nations and requires an international solution. The presence of coalition navy vessels in the region demonstrates a commitment to regional security and stability. To continue to counter and deter[7] piracy successfully, coalition efforts must be complimented by proactive measures by commercial shippers, regional governments, and the international community.

https://www.oceanuslive.org

1. small boat used for leisure 2. admiral 3. area 4. instrument on the end of a rope thrown by pirates to board a ship 5. threw in the water to sink 6. Commander 7. discourage

1. Analyse the role of naval forces in the fight against maritime crime.
2. Report on the pirates' *modus operandi*: how they operate.
3. Report to the class: outline the risks and importance of policing the seas.

Defending freedom of navigation

A Protecting the seas

The U.S. Will "Keep Up the Pace"[1] of South China Sea Freedom of Navigation Operations (FONOps)

Freedom of navigation operations are operations conducted to demonstrate American or international rights to navigate air or sea routes.

Last year marked "the greatest number of freedom of navigations operations in the South China Sea in the 40-year history of the FONOps program, and we will keep up the pace this year." Said Secretary for Defense Esper.

The Navy conducted nine FONOps operations in the South China Sea in 2019. Six FONOps have been conducted in the South China Sea this year.

Esper reiterated the United States government's rejection of China's maritime claims[2] (in the area) and that the new U.S. policy on the South China Sea "plainly states that our recognition of maritime claims is consistent with international law, favors the sovereign rights of Southeast Asian partners and rejects the PRC's (People's Republic of China) excessive and unlawful maritime claims that have been used to bully smaller countries from accessing offshore resources in their own Exclusive Economic Zones."

Recent dual-carrier strike force[3] exercises in the South China Sea have been a "clear and powerful signal" that the U.S. will operate wherever international law allows. Later on in the session, he challenged Chinese claims that the U.S. carriers were only allowed to operate in the South China Sea because the People's Liberation Army allowed it to.

"I don't know what the Chinese meant by that hollow[4] statement about American carriers being there by the pleasure of the PLA. Look, American aircraft carriers have been in the South China Sea and the Indo Pacific since World War II, and we will continue to be there, and we're not going to be stopped by anybody. We're going to sail, fly and operate where international law allows," he said, adding that the United States does so to assert international laws and rights and to support the sovereignty of its friends and partners and reassure them that the United States will be there in support of such.

Esper added that the United States was committed to Taiwan and will continue to conduct arms sales to it and continue to conduct FONOps in the Taiwan Straits. He also stated, though, in the case of Taiwan and also the rest of the Indo-Pacific region, it was China that was aggravating the situation

Esper stated that the U.S. was not in search of a conflict but was committed to a constructive and result-orientated relationship with China in regard to the defense relationship, to open lines of communication and to reduce risk. But at the same time, the United States "firmly believe no single nation can or should dominate the public commons, and we will continue to work alongside our allies and partners to support a prosperous and secure Indo-Pacific for all."

https://news.usni.org

1. maintain the rhythm 2. right to get sth from sb 3. group of ships, armed and ready for attack 4. no real value

"It follows then as certain as that night succeeds the day, that without a decisive naval force we can do nothing definitive, and with it, everything honorable and glorious."

George Washington, 1781

1. Pick out information to demonstrate what China and the US disagree about.
2. Compare and contrast the US navy's determination to maintain FONOps and the George Washington quote.
3. Find evidence that the US is not looking to escalate the tensions with China in the area.
4. Prepare a short update for the Foreign Office on the situation in the South China Sea.

B South China Sea tensions

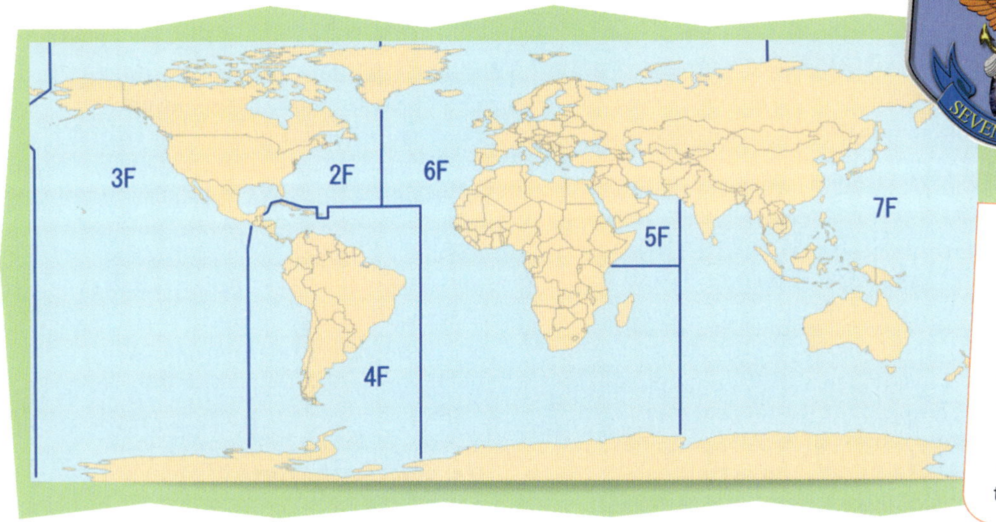

Culture Tip

The Seventh Fleet is the largest US Navy deployed fleet (50-70 ships and submarines, 150 aircraft). It operates in an area which encompasses 36 maritime countries including China, Russia, India, North Korea, and the Republic of Korea.

PAIR WORK

Student A on the cartoon
Student B on the map

1. Student A: Read the Culture Tip and describe the cartoon. Then analyse the speech bubbles to define the atmosphere between the two countries.
   Student B: Describe the Seventh Fleet's badge. Study the map and read the Culture Tip. Determine this fleet's area of responsibility.
2. Swap information with your partner.
3. Discuss how the documents are related to the title of the page "Defending freedom of navigation."

C The Royal Navy

What the Royal Navy does

Video hatier-clic.fr/21amc/231

1. Pick out places and numbers to show that the "Royal Navy is fully engaged around the world."
2. Identify the Royal Navy's different missions.
3. Find elements which characterise Royal Navy personnel, then say what the Navy's ultimate goal is.
4. Brief an American Admiral on how the Royal Navy is tackling challenges on the high seas.

Practice your grammar

Relatives et quantifieurs

▶ On peut associer **un pronom relatif à un quantifieur** (*some, all, many...*) pour extraire une partie d'un ensemble :

some	
many / a lot	
one / two / three...	***of which / whom...***
a few	
all	
none	

On a recours à ***of which*** si l'antécédent est non humain, et à ***of whom*** si l'antécédent est humain :

*The ship was attacked by pirates, **some of whom** were arrested by the US Coast Guard.*

*Six people were suffering from gunshot injuries, **none of which** were life-threatening.*

▶ On traduit cette structure en français par ***dont* + quantifieur** (*dont certains, dont beaucoup, dont un / deux / trois, etc.*) :

*Le bateau a été attaqué par des pirates, **dont certains** ont été arrêtés par la police maritime américaine.*

1 À partir des deux phrases, produisez une phrase unique contenant une relative. Utilisez le quantifieur en gras.

Ex. : *Five Chinese vessels docked at Honolulu Harbor. Two of them were carrying stolen luxury goods.* → *Five Chinese vessels, two of which were carrying stolen luxury goods, docked at Honolulu Harbor*

a. *The attackers killed eight passengers. **All** these passengers were American citizens.*

b. *Next year, the company will buy five new vessels. **Three** of them will transport oil and hydrocarbon.*

c. *Last year, the Coast Guard apprehended more than 500 suspected drug smugglers. **Most** of them were transferred to the U.S. for prosecution.*

d. *A scuba diver has discovered the wrecks of two Japanese battleships. **Both** were sunk by an American submarine during WW2.*

Build up your vocabulary

POLICING THE SEAS

Crimes
- drug **traffi**cking
- **pi**racy
- **hi**jacking
- **kid**napping
- un**law**ful **mar**itime claims
- **ran**som
- cause **ten**sions
- **trigg**er **con**flict

Piracy
- board (v.)
- **wea**pons
- **assault** (n.)
- **rob**bery
- steal
- skiff
- **threat**en
- **pi**rates
- AK-47 **ri**fles
- **rock**et **pro**pelled gre**nade laun**cher
- **ill**egal acti**vi**ties

Fighting crime
- **coun**ter
- de**ter**
- **car**ry out
- con**duct**
- sup**port**
- com**mit** to
- de**ploy**
- se**cure**
- **com**bat

Defending freedom
- **na**val en**gage**ment
- strike force pro**tec**tion
- **for**eign **po**licy
- inter**na**tional law
- **so**vereign rights
- **al**lies and **part**ners
- **Free**dom Of Navi**ga**tion Oper**a**tions
- Ex**clu**sive Eco**no**mic Zone
- se**cu**rity
- sta**bil**ity
- coa**li**tion **for**ces

Projects

1 In light of the numerous piracy incidents on the high seas, join a TV news panel and debate the need for armed guards onboard merchant ships.

1. Ensure you fully understand the role assigned to you.
2. Search through the unit to find information about incidents at sea that you can use in an introductory statement.
3. Organise your ideas into a mind map. Then, try to anticipate some counter arguments.
4. Think how to speak in a convincing way, to give extra substance to your arguments.
5. During the discussion, listen carefully to the opposition, to deliver made-to-measure rebuttals and win the debate!

2 As Communications Officer on board a USN ship, you have been tasked to write a news article for a webzine about a recent piracy or drug trafficking incident involving your ship.

1. Research recent piracy and drug-trafficking incidents on the Net and make a note of the information.
2. As Communications Officer, your job is to convey a positive image of your ship. The article should reflect this.
3. Your writing should be clear and structured. Don't forget to include link words.
4. Re-read you work, checking for misspellings and grammar inaccuracies.

20 Secret agents, symbols of power?

The expert's view
hatier-clic.fr/21amc/234a

In the news
hatier-clic.fr/21amc/234b

Projects

- You are a film critic. Write a review of a spy movie explaining the evolution of espionage.
- You are a recruiting agent at the CIA or MI6. Record a recruiting video for a cyber threat analyst.

Grammar p. 242 Phonology p. 243

When fiction combats the enemy

A The spy swap

1

The Bridge of Spies (Steven Spielberg, 2015)

Video hatier-clic.fr/21amc/234c

e-worksheet hatier-clic.fr/21amc/234d

1. Pick out elements in the trailer (sounds/soundtrack/images/words) that illustrate the adjective "tense" used several times in the text.
2. Use elements from the text showing this film stages Cold War spy craft.
3. Phonology Listen and repeat the following words: *information, Constitution, negotiation, civilization, position*. Focus on the syllable that carries the main stress. What do you notice?
4. **CONNECT.** Using elements from the review and the trailer, explain the stakes of the Cold War and the role of spies.

2 *Tom Hanks and Mark Rylance red hot in Steven Spielberg's magnificent cold war thriller*

With terrific craftsmanship, pure storytelling gusto and that Midas-touch ability to find grounds for optimism everywhere, Steven Spielberg has dramatised a true-life cold war spy-swap[1] drama, starring Tom Hanks and Mark Rylance. [...]

In 1962, America prepared to recover Gary Powers, the U2 spy-plane pilot captured by the Soviets. The plan was hand over their own incarcerated Russian spy Rudolf Abel, in a classic Cold War prisoner exchange at dawn on the Glienecke bridge spanning East and West Berlin – the so-called "Bridge of Spies" – with snipers waiting on both sides ready to take their man out in case of last-second betrayal.

Spielberg's movie shows that the build-up involved agonisingly tense, deniable negotiations in bad faith, with each side calculating and re-calculating, with every day that went past, how likely it was that their man had cracked under interrogation, given up secrets, and therefore become valueless as an asset[2]. To their opponents' rage the US was actually insisting on a two-for-one: they also wanted an American student named Frederic Pryor wrongfully imprisoned in East Berlin, a deal which would make them look they'd had the best of the bargain.

The Guardian, Oct. 5th, 2015

1. swap: exchange 2. advantage

C Sisterhood of spies

1

Number of women holding top jobs at the CIA

1 Read *Let's focus on...* n° 1, p. 240. List the places, the dates, the people and terrorist organisations that you find in the article and create a timeline or drawing.

2 Sum up what the infographic shows.

3 Read the text. Quote four assets women analysts have in the world of espionage. Show women bring something more to the fieldwork.

4 Indicate why female spies are asked to carry out interrogations of terrorists. Say why it is ambiguous.

5 **CONNECT.** Explain how the infographic and the article illustrate a shift from cliché to modernism in espionage.

2

This is a women's world

Navy SEALs may have killed Osama Bin Laden, but women led them to their prey.

Women made up the majority of analysts – at one point all the analysts – in "Alec Station," the unit charged with finding Bin Laden, managed the ramp-up[1] at the CIA's Counter Terrorism Center after 9-11, and participated in the interrogation, and the waterboarding[2], of all Qaeda suspects.

They were critical to the first capture of a major all Qaeda target, Abu Zubaydah; helped find and kill Abu Musab al Zarqawi, the leader of al Qaeda in Iraq; ran "black sites," the secret CIA prisons used to interrogate terror suspects; and in the case of two senior analysts, died in an attack by al Qaeda on a CIA compound in Afghanistan.

Fran Moore, then and now the CIA's director of intelligence, its fourth-ranking official, said she doesn't know if there was "something explicit" about their gender that sparked the female al Qaeda hunters. "But I can say," said Moore, "that if those individuals hadn't been working the issue, I am not confident we would've been successful." [...]

So why are the women of the war on terror so driven, and so valuable as analysts?

Nada Bakos, the head of the targeting team that killed Zarqawi, said her team was "three quarters women," and their relentless focus on taking down. Zarqawi and other al Qaeda leaders may have been influenced by a distinctly female view of security.

After 9-11, she said, the women working for her seemed to have vowed, "You're not going to do that to me again." "We're aggressive in the protection of our children," said Bakos. "We see risks differently, longer term."

Carol Rollie-Flynn, former executive director of the agency's Counter Terrorism Center, said she thinks "the real strengths of these women were their intense dedication[3] and incredible attention to detail."

Detail and more detail, said Bakos, was a big part of the Zarqawi team's day. The women sifted through communications intercepts, interrogation reports, snippets[4] from human spies, and satellite images, trying to make their analysis "operational" – meaning good enough to find their target and strike him. [...]

A former CIA official told NBC News that he thought women might have been especially effective at interrogating terror suspects because of the combination of surprise and shame. Jihadis were stunned that women, whom they saw as inferior, had been chosen to question them. [...]

John Brennan, the director of the agency [2013-2017], told NBC News women have a unique perspective.

"We all are products of our experiences," said Brennan.

"In addition to the innate intelligence and capability and creativity that women bring to the workforce, I think they have the opportunity to see the world through – and I think this is very important-- the eyes of a woman."

Robert Windrem, *NBC News*, Nov. 14th, 2013

1. intensification 2. a form of torture that simulates drowning 3. commitment 4. information

Modern warfare

A The donought

Secrets and spies: Behind the doors of the UK's most enigmatic government agency

Over a century GCHQ has evolved from a codebreaker into a critical defence against the most advanced technological threats to national security. And while changes are afoot, some old habits die hard.

THEY CALL IT "THE DOUGHNUT:" 180 metres in diameter, this massive circular building in Cheltenham houses GCHQ, the government's intelligence, cyber and security agency. It's here that some of the country's greatest hackers, technophiles and spooks[1] ply[2] their trade in espionage. [...]

GCHQ (Government Communications Headquarters) is the agency charged with keeping our nation safe. Employing around 10,000 people, it also includes the National Cyber Security Centre, based in London. [...]

The mission

On the agency website, director Jeremy Fleming explains the key functions: "We focus on communications: how to access, analyse and – occasionally – disrupt the communications of the UK's adversaries; and on the nation's cyber security."

He pinpoints[3] what he calls the "mission areas". These are: preventing terrorist attacks, cyber security, thwarting[4] serious and organised crime, supporting the armed forces, and something called strategic advantage - which includes "managing threats from hostile states, promoting the UK's prosperity and shaping the international environment".

Out of the shadows

Times have changed since then, though. During the last decade GCHQ has emerged from the shadows and is now actively recruiting a more diverse workforce. Having its base in the very bourgeois environs of Cheltenham probably doesn't help. One of the reasons the agency recently opened a new station in Manchester was to attract employees from varied backgrounds, perhaps realising that a diversity of social class, race, language and neurodiversity can only help in the business of spying. It now has social media feeds, and publishes GCHQ-branded puzzles for the public.

Dominic Bliss, www.nationalgeographic.co.uk, Nov. 5th, 2020

1. slang for spies 2. carry out your business 3. shows the exact cause of 4. stop from happening

1. Read *Let's focus on...* n° 4, p. 241 and rephrase the mission statement of the GCHQ.
2. Explain the advantages of diversifying the recruitment.
3. As a journalist, you interview a new recruit for GCHQ: talk about their motivations and aspirations.

B Becoming an MI6 agent

GROUP WORK

Group A: on the video "Intelligence officer job"

1. List the tasks done by an intelligence officer and imagine the skills needed for the job.
2. Read the paragraph which is part of the video and explain what skills are crucial for the job and why.
3. Imagine why languages are a key component to the job.

Careers at SIS

Videos hatier-clic.fr/21amc/238

Group B: Connor – Group C: Amelia – Group D: Raj

1. Watch your video and pick out information about the background of the person speaking.
2. Find information about their early career and explain their decision to change paths.
3. Explain how SIS has managed to fulfil the professional and personal life of the person.
4. **CONNECT.** Act out a job interview between a recruiter and an applicant. Talk about their motivations and aspirations.

C The whistle blower

1 **Edward Snowden says "the most powerful institutions in society have become the least accountable"**

LISBON, Portugal — "What do you do when the most powerful institutions in society have become the least accountable to society?" […]

In 2013, Snowden's name hit the headlines after the whistleblower leaked[1] classified documents with journalists that detailed surveillance programs run by the NSA that tapped[2] people's cell phone and internet communications.

Washington subsequently charged Snowden with espionage and theft of government property, while his passport was also revoked. He was then granted asylum in Russia, and has lived there ever since.

Snowden recently released a memoir, "Permanent Record," detailing the events that led up to his leaking of classified documents with journalists. The U.S. has sued him over the book, alleging he violated non-disclosure agreements he signed with the NSA and CIA.

"They don't like books like this being written," Snowden said Monday, in response to pressure from U.S. authorities on his autobiography.

"We have legalized the abuse of the person through the personal," he said, adding that the widespread collection of data by governments and corporations entrenches[4] "a system that makes the population vulnerable for the benefit of the privileged."

EU privacy overhaul[5] "misplaces the problem"

Snowden also directed some criticism at data privacy authorities that have tried to step up regulation on companies over how they handle user data. He said the EU's General Data Protection Regulation, which is aimed at giving people control of the information collected on them by businesses, "misplaces the problem."

"The problem isn't data protection, the problem is data collection," Snowden said. "Regulation and protection of data presumes that the collection of data in the first place was proper, that it is appropriate, that it doesn't represent a threat or a danger."

www.cnbc.com, Nov. 5th, 2019

1. blow the whistle = inform on, denounce 2. revealed secrets 3. bugged 4. establishes 5. revision

2

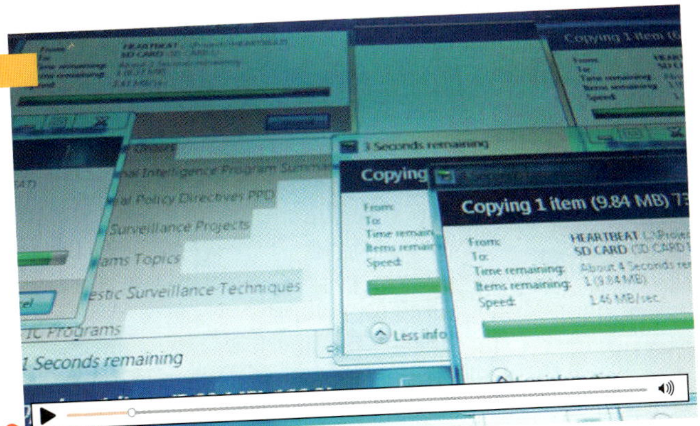

Enemy of the state?

Video hatier-clic.fr/21amc/239

GROUP WORK

Group A: on the text

1. Gather information about Snowden from the text and *Let's focus on…* n° 5, p. 141. Then explain the difference Snowden makes between "data protection" and "data collection".

Group B: on the video

2. Gather information about Snowden from the trailer and *Let's focus on…* n° 5, p. 141. Then pinpoint the turning point in his vision of the CIA and explain his reaction and decision.

3. **Grammar** Pick out two superlative adjectives. How are they formed?

4. **CONNECT.** Debate whether Edward Snowden is a symbol of power or counter-power and whether he is a traitor.

D Rambo vs. Snowden

1. Look at the cartoon and list the stereotypes of the "warrior" and "the geek". Explain why it is a caricature.

2. Show why it is humorous/ironic. Explain the message of the cartoonist and react.

Let's focus on...

CIA 1

The CIA (**Central Intelligence Agency**) is the main civilian foreign intelligence service in the United States of America. It was founded after WWII in 1947 and is located in Langley, Virginia. The agents' mission is "straight-forward but critical: protect America's national security." They "collect valuable foreign intelligence, conduct timely analyses and execute effective covert actions" (source CIA website). The agency does not directly answer to the US federal government and laws. Its motto is: "The Work of a Nation. The Center of Intelligence," its unofficial motto: "And ye shall know the truth and the truth shall make you free." (John 8:32). Gina Haspel is the 7th director of the CIA; she is the first woman to hold this post. The CIA has been the subject of many controversies such as waterboarding or attempted assassinations of foreign leaders.

Ronald Reagan 2

Ronald Reagan served as the 40th President of the United States (1981-1989). He is said to have escalated the Cold War in the 1980s, reversing the "Détente" period. His speech in front of the British Parliament in 1982 clearly denounced the USSR's ideology. In 1983, continuing in the same vein, he even called them "an evil empire".

The Cold War 3

Right after World War Two, the world got divided into two parts: the Eastern Bloc (with a communist ideology) and the Western Bloc (with a capitalist ideology). This binary opposition resulted in many local conflicts and great political tensions. This war of ideology was based on the competition between the two blocs on many different levels (economic, political, colonial, spatial), which led to the increased importance of intelligence services and spies. The doctrine of MAD (Mutually Assured Destruction) kept both sides on edge and nuclear threats paralysed the world on a regular basis.

Major phases of the war:

1947-1953 Implementation of the Truman Doctrine of containment (local conflicts such as Korean War, Panama Canal)

1953-1962 Crisis and escalation (Cuban missile crisis)

1962-1979 Détente

1979-1985 New Cold War

1985-1991 Final years with Gorbachev's reforms, the end of the Berlin Wall and the reunification of Germany

Espionage in the English-speaking world 8

A joint declaration issued by the US and UK against Nazi Germany.
1941 (August)

1943
UKUSA Agreement is signed between the USA and the UK on signals intelligence.

The 1943 secrets treaty between NASA and GCHQ (British intel and security organisation) is formalised.
1946 (March)

1946
Canada's Communications Security Establishment Canada (CSEC) + CSIS (Canadian Secret Service, 1984).

The CIA (Central Intelligence Agency) is created (USA).
1947

1948
The secrets treaty is extended to Canada, Norway (1952), Denmark (1954), West Germany (1955), Australia (1956), and New Zealand (1956). But only the Commonwealth countries are regarded as collaborating members. Known as FVEY (Five Eyes).

NSA (National Security Agency, USA) and ASIS (Australia) are created.
1952

NZSIS is created (New Zealand).
1956

MI6 4

SECRET INTELLIGENCE SERVICE MI6

The **Secret Intelligence Service** (SIS) is known as MI6. This agency is the foreign intelligence service of the United Kingdom. Its tasks are mainly focused on the collecting of overseas intelligence and on the analysis of human data. For now, its priority is to thwart terrorism and cyberterrorism. Author Graham Greene was a former SIS officer. Ian Fleming, the famous author of James Bond novels, was also a former Naval Intelligence Division officer and John Le Carré, the renowned novelist, worked for the MI5 (National Security) and MI6.

Edward Snowden 5

Edward Snowdon is a former CIA agent who leaked secret information and details about the government's system of surveillance back in 2013. Contrary to hackers who illegally hack into the government's computers, Snowden was an inside agent who decided to unveil classified information he thought American citizens should be aware of.
His revelations have triggered much debate about mass surveillance, national security and information privacy. He now resides in Russia that granted him a right of asylum. Recently, he published his memoirs entitled *Permanent Record*.
On Sept. 2nd 2020 a US federal court ruled that the surveillance program unveiled by Snowden was illegal, and potentially unconstitutional.

J. Robert Oppenheimer 6

Oppenheimer is "the father of the Atomic bomb". He was an American scientist who, during the Cold War, advocated against nuclear proliferation and against the nuclear arms race with the USSR.

Nikita Khrushchev 7

Leader of the USSR at the time of the Cold War, Khrushchev is known for supporting the country's space race program and is also associated with the Cuban Missile Crisis. He led the USSR at the height of the Cold War tensions.

1960s ECHELON programme is launched (monitoring diplomatic and military communications from the Eastern Bloc). It becomes effective in 1971.

1985-1991 Perestroika, referring to the restructuring of the Soviet political and economic system.

1990-1991 Gulf War. The Five Eyes + France + Argentina.

2001 (September 11) Terrorist attacks on the Twin Towers in New York. More than 3,000 deaths. Global war on terror begins.

2010 The full text of the UKUSA Agreement is released.

2010s New alliance: 5 Eyes + four countries (France, Denmark, Norway, the Netherlands): Nine Eyes.

2011 Military NATO-led intervention to overthrow Gaddafi. Nine Eyes involved.

March 2014 The International Court of Justice (ICJ) orders Australia to stop spying on East Timor. This marks the first such restriction imposed on a member of the FVEY.

Practice your grammar

Les verbes prépositionnels

▶ Certains verbes ne sont pas directement suivis de leur complément : ce dernier doit être introduit par **une préposition** (*of*, *with*, *for*, *about*...). Par exemple, le complément du verbe *wait* est toujours introduit par la préposition *for* :

*"He's waiting **for** the dark," Leamas muttered.*

⚠ Il n'est en général pas possible de prévoir si un verbe se construit avec une préposition ou non. Il faut donc **vérifier sa construction dans le dictionnaire** et l'apprendre.

▶ Voici quelques exemples de verbes prépositionnels :

on	***spy on sb***	espionner qn
	comment on sth	commenter qc
	rely / count on sb	compter sur qn
	depend on sth	dépendre de qc
for	***look / search for sth***	chercher qc
	ask for sth	demander qc (mais *ask a question*)
	pay for sth	payer qc (mais *pay taxes / $10*)
at	***look / stare at sth***	regarder qc (fixement)
	smile at sb	sourire à qn
	laugh at sb	se moquer de qn
to	***listen to sth***	écouter qc
of	***(dis)approve of sth***	(dés)approuver qc

▶ Certains verbes peuvent se construire avec différentes prépositions et changer de sens :

hear
- **Ø** *sth* : entendre qc
- ***from*** *sb* : avoir des nouvelles de qn
- ***of*** *sth* : entendre parler de qc
- ***about*** *sth* : être au courant de qc

1 Complétez avec la préposition qui convient : *on*, *of*, *for* ou *at*.

a. *James Bond smiled ... the driver and paid ... the taxi ride.*

b. *During the Cold War, the CIA spied ... Russian technology.*

c. *I don't approve ... hackers' methods.*

d. *In 2013, Snowden asked ... political asylum in Russia.*

e. *The Senator said he was not in a position to comment ... the FBI's investigation.*

f. *The police searched the crime scene ... clues.*

2 Traduisez.

a. Tu ne peux pas compter sur lui : c'est un espion russe.

b. Je n'ai jamais entendu parler de Ian Fleming.

c. As-tu eu récemment des nouvelles de ton oncle ?

d. Je cherche des informations sur les services secrets américains.

Les superlatifs

▶ On forme les superlatifs des adjectifs de la manière suivante :

Supériorité (le plus...)	*the* adj. court + *-est* ***the greatest** hacker*	*the most* adj. long ***the most famous** spy*
Infériorité (le moins...)	*the least* adjectif ***the least dangerous** hacker*	

▶ Les adjectifs courts sont les adjectifs d'**une syllabe**. Ceux de deux syllabes qui se terminent par ***-y*** (*happy* → *happiest*), ***-le*** (*simple* → *simplest*) ou ***-ow*** (*narrow* → *narrowest*) peuvent aussi former leur superlatif au moyen de la terminaison *-est*.

▶ Notez ces formes irrégulières :

good → ***the best*** *bad* → ***the worst*** *far* → ***the farthest / the furthest***

▶ **Le complément du superlatif** est soit introduit par *in* (s'il s'agit d'un lieu), soit par *of* (s'il s'agit d'une période).

*James bond is **the most famous** spy **of** all time.*

***The most powerful** institutions **in** society have become the least accountable to society.*

3 Mettez l'adjectif entre parenthèses au superlatif de supériorité.

a. *What is the ... (easy) way to hack a Facebook account?*

b. *The Pentagon has reportedly been targeted by hackers in what may be one of the ... (large) cyberattacks to date.*

c. *In my opinion, Octopussy is the ... (bad) James Bond movie ever.*

d. *The CIA is the ... (well-known) US spying agency.*

e. *What is the ... (safe) place to store your data?*

Improve your pronunciation

La consonne /ŋ/

▶ **La consonne /ŋ/** n'existe pas en français. Il s'agit d'**une consonne nasale** : quand on la prononce, l'air passe par le nez et la langue est dirigée vers le palais. Cette consonne a la particularité de ne jamais apparaître en début de mot ou de syllabe.

▶ Elle est le plus souvent représentée par la graphie *ng* : ***working***, ***English***, ***strong***, ***ring***, ***lung***...

⚠ Lorsque /ŋ/ apparaît en fin de mot et est représentée par la graphie *ng*, **on ne prononce pas le *g*** (***spring***, ***sing***, ***young***), y compris quand on ajoute un suffixe (***singer***, ***singing***). Le *g* est en revanche prononcé en milieu de mot : ***English***, ***single***.

▶ Lorsque la graphie *n* est suivie de la consonne /k/, elle est également prononcée /ŋ/ : ***Tom Hanks***, ***thank***, ***think***, ***uncle***...

1 Écoutez ces paires de mots et répétez. Attention à bien distinguer la consonne /n/ (de *bin*) et la consonne /ŋ/ (*bing*).

Audio hatier-clic.fr/21amc/243a

a. *thin / thing* **b.** *sin / sing*
c. *singer / sinner* **d.** *win / wing*
e. *kin / king*

2 Dans les mots suivants, la graphie *n* est toujours prononcée /ŋ/. Pour autant, la consonne *g* se prononce-t-elle ? Justifiez votre réponse. Lisez les mots à haute voix et écoutez l'enregistrement pour vérifier vos réponses.

Audio hatier-clic.fr/21amc/243b

gang • Washington • longer • single • Sting • Fleming • wrongfully • strength • mingle • younger • language • United Kingdom

Les terminaisons contraignantes

▶ Parfois la terminaison d'un mot permet de prédire **quelle syllabe porte l'accent principal**. On parle de « terminaisons contraignantes » (en anglais : *stress-imposing suffixes*).

▶ Par exemple, les mots se terminant par les suffixes suivants sont accentués sur **la syllabe qui précède immédiatement ce suffixe**.

-ible	*incredible*
-ify	*classify, qualify*
-ity / -ety	*security, diversity, society*
-logy / -logist	*sociology, ideology*
-ic(s) / -ical	*technological, strategic, political* Exceptions : *rhetoric, Catholic, politics, lunatic*
-ia / -ial / -iar / -ian	*familiar, civilian, Virginia*
-ion	*institution, addition* Exception : *television*

▶ Il peut arriver que l'accent d'un mot soit **déplacé** si on lui ajoute l'une de ces terminaisons. Les mots de la même famille n'ont donc pas toujours la même accentuation.

Canada /'kænədə/ → *Canadian* /kə'neɪdiən/

3 Recopiez les mots suivants et soulignez la syllabe qui porte l'accent principal. Écoutez l'enregistrement pour vérifier vos réponses, puis répétez les mots.

Audio hatier-clic.fr/21amc/243c

protection • interrogation • communication • population • television • opportunity • creativity • priority • activities • prosperity • political • terrific • specific

4 Recopiez ces mots appartenant à la même famille et soulignez la syllabe qui porte l'accent principal. Écoutez l'enregistrement pour vérifier vos réponses, puis répétez les mots.

Audio hatier-clic.fr/21amc/243d

a. *history* → *historical / historian*
b. *social* → *sociologist*
c. *technology* → *technological*
d. *politics* → *politician / political*
e. *irony* → *ironical*
f. *specific* → *specificity*
g. *office* → *official*
h. *economy* → *economic*

Let's translate

In 2013, Snowden's name hit the headlines after the whistleblower leaked classified documents with journalists that detailed surveillance programs run by the NSA that tapped people's cell phone and internet communications.

Washington subsequently charged Snowden with espionage and theft of government property, while his passport was also revoked. He was then granted asylum in Russia, and has lived there ever since.

www.cnbc.com

L'équivalence

▶ L'équivalence est un procédé de traduction utilisé lorsque le texte d'origine nécessite **une réécriture complète**. On l'utilise pour traduire :
- les expressions idiomatiques ou les proverbes :
It's none of your business. → *Ce ne sont pas tes oignons.*

- des expressions de la vie quotidienne qui ne peuvent être traduites littéralement :
Enjoy your meal! → *Bon appétit !*

▶ Il peut aussi s'agir **de faits ou d'allusions culturels** que le lecteur francophone ne peut comprendre et qu'il faut donc expliciter :
I owe money to ***the IRS****.* → *Je dois de l'argent* ***au fisc****.*

Translation Tip

Quand une phrase est trop longue, il est parfois nécessaire de la scinder en deux parties ou plus. Cela sera sans doute indispensable dans la première phrase.

À vous !

a. Traduisez les segments suivants en ayant recours à des équivalences : *hit the headlines, the whistleblower*. Utilisez le dictionnaire unilingue si nécessaire.

b. Les mots *while*, *charged* et *run* sont polysémiques (= ont plusieurs significations). Cherchez leurs acceptions possibles dans le dictionnaire unilingue. Quel sens avez-vous retenu à chaque fois ?

c. Identifiez dans le texte un verbe conjugué à la voix passive. Pourra-t-on le traduire par un passif français ?

Build up your vocabulary

1 Fill in your own mind map here:
hatier-clic.fr/21amc/244

2 Complete the sentences with words from your mind map. One blank = one word.

a. Despite long hours of interrogation, the agent and the suspect remained locked in a **...** .
b. If you want to start a new **...** in MI6, you need to **... ... ...** such as speaking foreign languages and offer a comprehensive **...** .
c. Stephan, a famous **...** has revealed that the company CEO's has been involved in some **...** .
d. A **... ...** is someone who **... ... ...** to **... ...** .
e. The CIA was reluctant to get its **...** forces **...** in an unnecessary conflict.

3 Use the words from the mind map to create four top secret messages back to your government.
Example: The **undercover agent** 009 **wiretapped** the spy in an attempt to secure **intelligence** and avoid **warmongering.**

Projects

1

You are a film critic for a teen magazine. Write a review of a spy movie explaining the evolution of espionage and the power displayed in such movies.

1. Choose a spy movie that you know well: make sure you know the director, actors, date of release, when it happens...
2. Select one or two stills from the movie that you can include in your article and write down the gist of the story.
3. List the important elements in the evolution of the spy and see how your movie refers to them.
4. Use adjectives and adverbs to nuance your presentation. Think of ways to praise or criticise aspects of the movie, acting, directing, special effects, soundtrack.
5. Make sure your article is clear and well-structured with short and clear paragraphs. Create suspense, no spoilers!

2

You are a recruiting agent at the CIA or MI6. Make a 3-minute recruiting video for a cyber threat analyst in the secret services, including the assets and skills required.

1. Choose the agency you work for.
2. Think of the skills necessary to be a cyber threat analyst: language, sports, computer-knowledge...
3. List the tasks a cyber analyst would do in your service. You may also think about the dos and the don'ts.
4. You should list your aspirations and the career opportunities you may offer the applicant.
5. Prepare and rehearse your presentation. Put extra care on the accentuation of the words. Record your video.

Pour l'écrit du Bac

A Inside the C.I.A., she became a spy for planet Earth

Linda Zall is disclosing how she toiled[1] anonymously within the intelligence agency to help scientists intensify their studies of a changing planet.

Linda Zall played a starring role in American science that led to decades of major advances. But she never described her breakthroughs on television, or had books written about her, or received high scientific honors. One database of scientific publications lists her contributions as consisting of just three papers, with a conspicuous gap running from 1980 to 2020.

The reason is that Dr. Zall's decades of service to science were done in the secretive warrens of the Central Intelligence Agency.

Now, at 70, she's telling her story – at least the parts she's allowed to talk about – and admirers are praising her highly classified struggle to put the nation's spy satellites onto a radical new job: environmental sleuthing[2]. […]

The top-secret images that Dr. Zall succeeded in repurposing[3] for environmental inquiries came from satellites that were some of Washington's crown jewels. The spy satellites would zero in on such targets as deadly weapons and render images that in some cases were said to be good enough to show a car's license plate. The first reconnaissance satellite, known as Corona, was launched in 1960. Federal experts have put the overall cost of its hundreds of successors at more than $50 billion.

An accident of fate let the fleet assess a top environmental concern – the extent to which vast expanses of Arctic and Antarctic ice were retreating.[…]

In early 1995, Medea[4] was the driving force when President Bill Clinton ordered the declassification of more than 800,000 spy-satellite images, including ones for mapping and area surveillance. Taken from 1960 through 1972, the images showed not only airfields and missile bases but also giant swaths of land marked by deforestation and environmental ills. […]

President George W. Bush's administration and conservatives in Congress, questioning the scientific consensus on global warming, let Medea languish for many years. But in late 2008 it was revived in cooperation with a Democratic Congress, and continued by the Obama administration. […]

She retired from the C.I.A. in 2013. Medea was never the same. The agency shut it down in 2015, and the Trump administration made sure there was no revival of the program.

In interviews, former Medea members said the incoming Biden administration might want to establish a similar panel for helping the world push ahead on knotty issues of environmental change.

The New Yorker, Jan. 7th, 2021

1. worked 2. investigating 3. putting to new use
4. name of the task force of scientists Dr. Zall recruited

B

C Cyber-attack is brutal reminder of the Russia problem facing Joe Biden

Analysis: new president must find a way to contain such hyper-aggressive behaviour from Moscow

It is Joe Biden's biggest foreign policy headache. As well as confronting the Covid pandemic, the president-elect has to deal with a more familiar problem: Russia. Moscow's meddling in the 2016 US presidential election cast a shadow over US politics for four long years.

And now the Kremlin appears to have struck again. This week details emerged of an unprecedented cyber-attack against US government departments. Beginning in March, suspected Russian hackers penetrated Washington's signature institutions.

They include the commerce and treasury departments, homeland security, nuclear laboratories and the Pentagon, as well as leading Fortune companies. For months the Russian spies roamed[1] at will, apparently undetected. Only now are aghast[2] officials scoping the damage.

The hacking is a brutal reminder of how Vladimir Putin and the KGB agents around him view the world. They regard the US as the *glavniy protivnik* or main enemy. This adversarial cold war mindset endures, regardless of whether a Trump or a Biden sits in the White House.

This latest cyber-attack can be explained as part of Moscow's continuous almost-but-not-quite war against the west. It is an asymmetric conflict, fought on Moscow's side by shadow state operatives. Some are assassins, deployed in Salisbury and Siberia. Others are backroom computer or chemical experts.

In recent years the Kremlin used hacking extensively. It is cheap, deniable, and psychologically effective – inducing panic. Despite billions spent by the US on cyber defence, the hackers were able to discover a vulnerability in a software update, and to infiltrate dozens of US federal computer systems.

A central conundrum[3] for Biden's presidency is how to contain such hyper-aggressive Russian behaviour. The answer eluded Barack Obama, who tried unsuccessfully to reset relations with Putin. The person who led this doomed mission was the then secretary of state, Hillary Clinton, herself a Russian hacking victim in 2016.

On Thursday Biden pledged to "disrupt and deter our adversaries from undertaking significant cyber-attacks in the first place". But what this means concretely is unclear. In the meantime billions will be spent on trying to shore up American cyber-defences against the next inevitable Moscow attack. [...]

The FSB is the domestic spy agency which Putin headed before he became prime minister and president. Its hackers – known as Cozy Bear or APT29 – broke into Democratic party servers in summer 2015. They got there a few months earlier than a rival Russian hacking group, Fancy Bear, working for GRU military intelligence.

Cozy Bear's activities are impressively global. They have previously infiltrated unclassified systems belonging to the White House, state department and the US chiefs of staff, as well as other organisations, universities and thinktanks. Victims are in western Europe as well as in Brazil, China, Japan, South Korea and New Zealand. [...]

Establishing exactly who is behind the raids will be tortuous. "I never never heard anything about SVR hackers. Which says something in Moscow where everything leaks," Soldatov said. Somewhere in Moscow, Russia's hacking operatives will be toasting another successful mission.

The Guardian, Dec. 18th, 2020

1. wandered 2. horrified 3. puzzling question

PARTIE 1

Prenez connaissance du dossier proposé, composé des documents A, B et C non hiérarchisés, et traitez en anglais le sujet suivant (300 mots maximum).

Taking into account their specificities, say how the documents illustrate the complexities and new challenges that intelligence agencies are facing, focusing on the use of power.

PARTIE 2

Traduisez en français le passage suivant du document C (l. 1-12).

It is Joe Biden's biggest foreign policy headache. As well as confronting the Covid pandemic, the president-elect has to deal with a more familiar problem: Russia. Moscow's meddling in the 2016 US presidential election cast a shadow over US politics for four long years.

And now the Kremlin appears to have struck again. This week details emerged of an unprecedented cyber-attack against US government departments. Beginning in March, suspected Russian hackers penetrated Washington's signature institutions.

21 Battle for the Arctic, a new cold war?

The expert's view
hatier-clic.fr/21amc/248a

In the news
hatier-clic.fr/21amc/248b

Projects

You are an intern at the UN. Take part in a panel discussion on geopolitical affairs.

As a junior researcher you have been asked to write an article about what is at stake for the US in the Arctic.

Grammar p. 256 Phonology p. 257

Arctic assets

A What's going on in the Far North?

1

2

1. Read *Let's focus on…* n° 1 p. 254 and determine which countries/peoples have territorial claims and why.
2. Use the four icons at the bottom of document 2 as prompts to answer this question: why is there a race to the Arctic?
3. **CONNECT.** Make a link between the two visuals.

B Who owns the Arctic?

Who owns the Arctic Ocean?

Video hatier-clic.fr/21amc/249a

e-worksheet hatier-clic.fr/21amc/249b

GROUP WORK

Group 1: 0:00-1:52
Group 2: 1:53-4:28
Group 3: 4:29-the end

1. Read *Let's Focus on …* n° 1, p. 254 and complete the e-worksheet.
2. Present your findings to the other groups.
3. **Phonology** Listen and repeat the following words: *resource*, *Russia*, *increase*, *exclusive*. Focus on the pronunciation of the letter *s*.
4. Create your own infographic on "Arctic assets."

C The importance of Lomonosov Ridge

The rush to claim an undersea mountain range

One of the most mysterious mountain ranges in the world is not visible on any ordinary map. You can't see it on the most popularly used flat map of the world, the Mercator projection, or on the Peters projection that is a popular (and more accurate) alternative. On a spinning globe, the plastic axle at the North Pole often covers it up, as if there's nothing to see.

But this is where you can find the Lomonosov Ridge, a vast mountain range running from the continental shelf of Siberia towards Greenland and Canada. The mountain range stretches for more than 1,700km (1,060 miles), its highest peak is 3.4km (2.1 miles) above the ocean floor.

This little-known mountain range is at the centre of three nations seeking sovereignty over the seabed around the North Pole. According to Denmark, the mountain range is an extension of its autonomous territory of Greenland. According to Russia, it is an extension of the Siberian archipelago Franz Josef Land. And according to Canada, it is an extension of Ellesmere Island in the Canadian territory of Nunavut.

So who is right?

As coastal nations, Russia, Denmark and Canada of course already have sovereign rights over the seafloor close to their own shores. Coastal countries can establish an Exclusive Economic Zone that stretches up to 200 nautical miles (370km) from shore, which gives them rights to activities like fishing, building infrastructure and extracting natural resources, under the UN Convention on the Law of the Sea. That law also permits a country to extend its rights over the seabed further – if there are seafloor features that they can prove are an extension of their continental shelves.

For such a seafloor feature to count in a country's favour, there has to be evidence that it is a piece of submerged land – and not an oceanic ridge that has always been underwater and has little to do with the country's land mass.

www.bbc.com, July 27th, 2020

1. Pick out the geographical features of Lomonosov Ridge and identify which countries are fighting over it.
2. Explain why it is important to map the area and define the benefits of an Exclusive Economic Zone.
3. Post an entry on the blog *Arctic Today* explaining the importance of Lomonosov Ridge.

Cold Rush

A

1. Suggest a title for this visual.
2. Comment on the map explaining what it reveals about the Arctic countries.
3. You work for Nordregio International Research centre. Present your map.

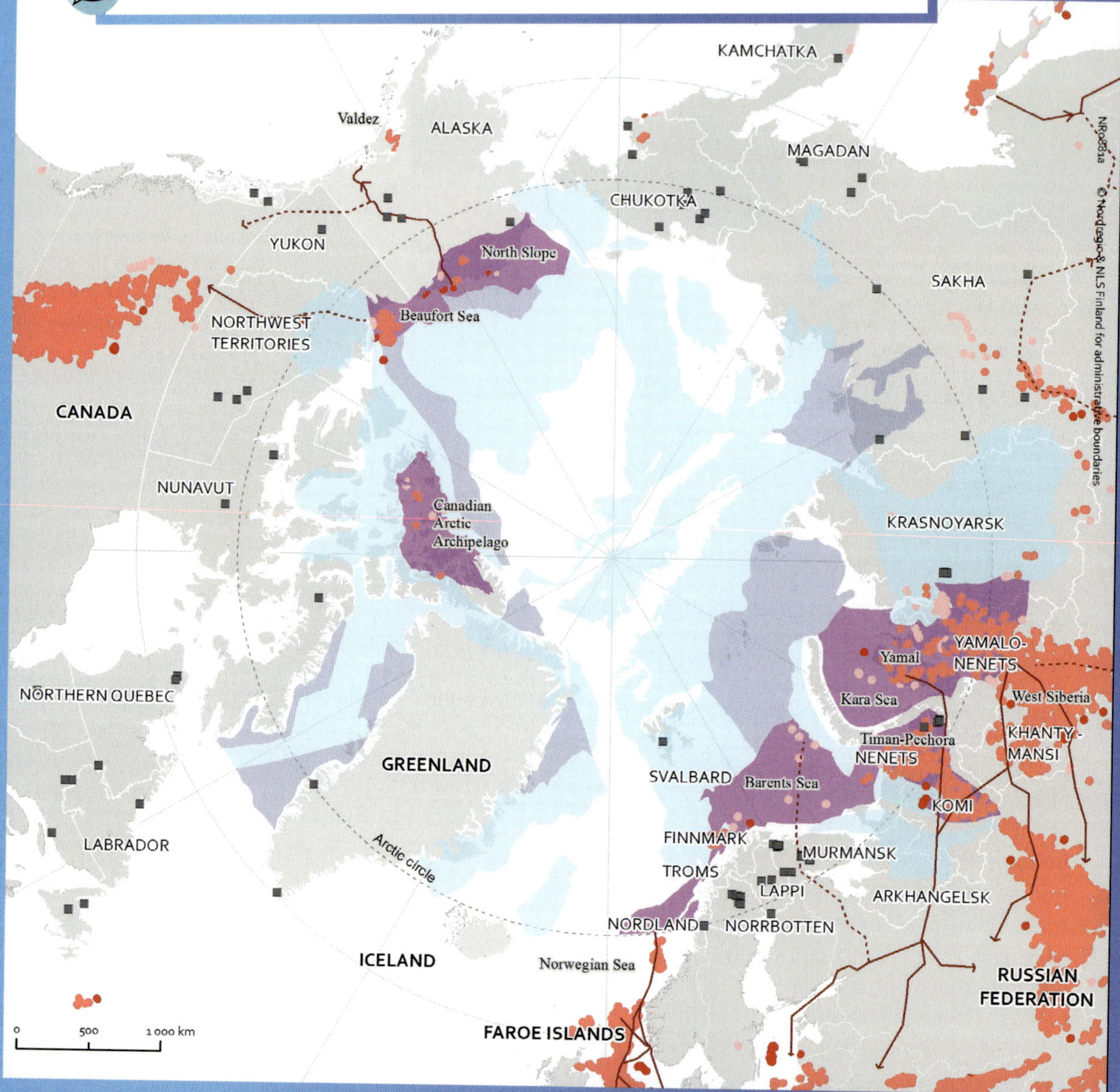

Main oil and gas resources & Mining activities in the Arctic

Oil/gas: exploration and production
- Gas
- Oil
- Oil and gas

Oil/gas: prospective areas and reserves
- < 50 %
- 50-99 %
- 100 %

Probability that at least one accumulation over 50 million barrels of oil or oil-equivalent gas exist after USGS (areas North of Arctic Circle included)

- ■ Main mining site

- Main existing oil/gas pipeline (indicative direction)
- Main proposed oil/gas pipeline (indicative direction)

Regions included:

US - Alaska; CA - Yukon, Northwest Territories, Nunavut, Newfoundland & Labrador, Northern Quebec; GL; IS; FO; NO - Nordland, Troms, Finnmark, Svalbard; SE - Norrbotten; FI - Lappi; RU - Komi, Arkhangelsk, Nenets, Khanty-Mansi, Yamalo-Nenets, Krasnoyarsk, Sakha, Kamchatka, Magadan, Chukotka.

Data source: Nordregio, NSIDC, PRIO, United Sates Geological Survey USGS and several homepages for oil, gas and mining companies.

B Understanding the source of tensions

Potential for conflict in the Arctic: The New Cold War?

Examining the potential for conflict as major states look towards the newly accessible Arctic region with its abundant resources

For the majority of human history, this region has been largely inaccessible due to harsh conditions, freezing temperatures, and a wall of Arctic sea ice. But in recent years, that wall of sea ice is melting away and the Arctic is now warming faster than any place on earth (National Geographic, 2020). Because of this newfound accessibility, large and powerful nations are beginning to take interest in the region, with military and economic ambitions. […]

Why are Nations interested in the Arctic?

The following are some reasons why:

Resources

The melting away of Arctic sea ice is exposing more land, ripe for potential exploitation of resources. It is also making it easier to access offshore resources. Some of the newly available resources in the Arctic include fish, natural gas, oil, and valuable mineral resources. According to the U.S. Secretary of State Mike Pompeo, these resources include "13 percent of the world's undiscovered oil, 30 percent of its undiscovered gas and an abundance of uranium, rare earth minerals, gold and diamonds; fisheries galore." (Politico, 2020). The interactive map from Esri shows the melting of Arctic sea ice over time.

Trading routes

The melting of sea ice is also making way for new trading routes via seaways. This could be a major opportunity for exporters that ship goods in bulk from Asia to the West. Two new major shipping routes are being developed in the Arctic as a result of this: the Northern Sea Route, which runs along Russia's north coast, and the Northwest Passage, which threads through Canada's northern islands (Politico, 2020). With forecasts suggesting that the Arctic Ocean could be ice-free as early as 2040 (SWIPA Assessment, 2005), this could lead to conflict over control of the new trading routes. […]

Tourism

Another reason why nations are interested in the Arctic is the positive economic impact of tourism. The cruise industry is looking to expand operations in the Arctic, offering customers views of the Northern Lights and authentic interactions with local communities. There are some potential issues with expanding the industry there though, as it can be dangerous and unpredictable traveling through Arctic waters, cruise operators have concerns about passenger safety. Furthermore, increased operations would further contribute to climate change and the warming of the Arctic.

https://storymaps.arcgis.com

1 Pick out information explaining why nations are starting to show an interest in the Arctic and what had happened previously.

2 GROUP WORK

Group 1 on *Resources*
Group 2 on *Trading routes*
Group 3 on *Tourism*

Find out why nations are interested in the Arctic. Read your paragraph, then report back to the other groups.

3 **Grammar** Pick out all the words and phrases expressing a cause-and-effect relationship.

4 Use information from the article to explain the title of these two pages "Cold Rush."

C Resources of the Cold War

1 Ships in the (polar) night
Video hatier-clic.fr/21amc/251a

GROUP WORK

Group 1 on video 1
Group 2 on video 2
Group 3 on video 3

2 The New Cold War
Video hatier-clic.fr/21amc/251b

3 Natural resource race
Video hatier-clic.fr/21amc/251c

1 Identify what aspect of the Arctic features in your video and explain the title.

2 Pick out precise details on the issue in question and then swap information with the other groups.

3 You have an idea for a new mini documentary on the Arctic. Pitch your ideas to a TV producer.

A geopolitical issue

A Who is winning the battle for the Arctic?

Battle for the Arctic: U.S. warns Russia "Is way ahead of us" in race to control new frontier

The U.S. Coast Guard has warned that America is falling behind Russia in the race to dominate the Arctic, as warming global temperatures open up areas previously inaccessible due to ice.

Speaking at the Aspen Security Conference, U.S. Coast Guard Commandant Admiral Karl Schultz said American leaders had serious concerns that they were lagging behind Russia in the world's newest military frontier.

"Russia has a huge Arctic coastline, they have clear Arctic interest, they derive their GDP[1] from there," Schultz explained, according to Russian state news agency Tass. "From the security standpoint and the militarizing of the Arctic, that is probably the future place for a contentious situation."

The Pentagon recently released a new Arctic strategy document that indicated it considers the far north increasingly important in a new era of great power competition with Russia and China.

Moscow is deploying more resources northwards and investing in Arctic-capable forces, while Beijing has declared itself a "near-Arctic" power. The U.S. is moving to meet this challenge and give the region more prominence[2] in its strategic planning.

Schultz said the U.S. "should be concerned about Russia, who is way ahead of us in this game, and the emerging aggressive China, who is pushing into the game." He noted that while Americans may "think about the Arctic as a very faraway place," the "Russian world view is very much based on the Arctic."

Its importance to Russia is reflected in Moscow's investment in Arctic resources. Though its economy and military budget are dwarfed[3] by those of the U.S., Russia maintains a fleet of dozens of icebreakers while the U.S. only has two. Schultz also warned that while China is still behind both nations, it will "outbuild" the U.S. by 2025.

A "polar security cutter" is currently under construction for the Coast Guard, effectively a militarized ice breaker. Its order demonstrates the U.S military pivot towards the Arctic and an effort to close the gap with its rivals, particularly Russia.

In May, Schultz told *Defense News*, "We talk about the Arctic through a different lense now. We talk about the Arctic as a competitive space." He noted that both Russia and China are bolstering[4] their Arctic capability[5] and stressed the U.S. must do the same.

"We're championing increased capabilities in the Arctic, we're championing better communications, better domain awareness, we're talking about innovation, we're talking about resiliency, we're talking about rule-based order," he continued.

"I want to see the Arctic remain a peaceful domain. China's a self-declared Arctic state. They're not one of the eight Arctic nations, so for me, for the service, its presence equals influence."

Schultz told the Aspen Security Conference that the U.S. above all desires a "peaceful, environmentally safe" Arctic region. He noted that American forces currently cooperate with Russia on search and rescue missions and a satellite system used by mariners worldwide. "I think we absolutely need to find the common ground[6]," he said.

www.newsweek.com

1. Gross Domestic Product 2. importance 3. made to seem small 4. reinforcing 5. military capacity 6. shared interests

1. Compare and contrast Russia and China's strategy in the Arctic.
2. Pick out elements to show how the US might be lagging behind. Then explain how it intends to catch up.
3. Give a one-minute introduction to the panel discussion programme entitled: "Power struggle in the Arctic."

Arctic race heats up for U.S., Russia and China

Video hatier-clic.fr/21amc/252

B The battle for the Arctic heats up

1

2

PAIR WORK

Student A on visual 1
Student B on visual 2

1. Define the nature of your visual, identify the characters and what they represent.
2. Analyse the cartoonists' intentions.
3. Swap information with a partner.
4. Write speech bubbles for the characters in your visual. Then give it a title.

C High stakes

GROUP WORK

Group 1: Russia (1:17-2:42)
Group 2: China (2:43-3:54)
Group 3: USA (3:55-6.03)

1. Complete the e-worksheet. Then pick out elements that show your country's economic, political or geopolitical strategy in the Arctic.
2. Compare and contrast your findings with those of the other groups.
3. Find arguments to justify the title of this unit: "Battle for the Arctic, a new cold war?"

e-worksheet
hatier-clic.fr/21amc/253

Let's focus on...

Indigenous peoples and the Arctic Council 1

Arctic Athabaskan Council
AAC

Saami Council

The Arctic was once referred to as *terra nullius* on maps, meaning "nobody's land". However, communities and cultures set up in the Arctic thousands of years ago and continue to survive in the *Frozen North*. Living and thriving in the Arctic with the specific challenges posed by the region's extreme climate, is no mean feat.

In total, only about 4 million people live in the Arctic and a minority of 500,000 are indigenous people. The Inuit in Canada and Greenland, the Yu'pik, Inupiat and Athabascan in Alaska are among the Indigenous peoples, as are the Saami in circumpolar areas of Finland, Sweden, Norway and Northwest Russia. Other indigenous groups in Russia include Nenets, Khanty, Evenk and Chukchi.

The governance of such a region, with such a wide range of peoples and stakeholders might seem a difficult task. Hence the creation of the high-level forum called the Arctic Council. The Council includes the Arctic states, the Arctic Eight (Canada, Denmark, Finland, Iceland, Norway, Russia, Sweden and the USA) and the region's indigenous peoples.

Lately, these communities have been facing other challenges. With the scramble for natural resources, military tensions and the quest for new shipping routes, rights to land and natural resources might be overlooked. To protect them, the Indigenous peoples' organisations have been granted Permanent Participants status in the Arctic Council which gives rights and enables the organisations to affect the policy making in the Council and fully participate in negotiations and decisions.

INUIT
Inuit Circumpolar Council
IC

Aleut International Association
AIA

Russian Association of Indigenous Peoples of the North
RAIPON

Gwich'in Council International
GCI

802799AI (R02112) 4-01

Defining the Arctic 2

The Arctic is the northernmost region on Earth. It is dominated by the Arctic Ocean and countries such as Scandinavia, Russia, the US, Canada and Greenland. It is nearly all covered by water and most of that is frozen.

Did you know that there are three definitions of the Arctic?

First and foremost, **the Arctic Circle**, as defined by certain scientists, is an imaginary line that circles the globe at roughly 66°34'N, north of the Equator, and is about 16,000 kms long. Above this latitude, the sun does not set on summer solstice (June 21st) and does not rise on winter solstice (December 21st). North of the Arctic Circle, though, at lower latitudes, the length of the continuous day and night is shorter. At the North Pole, the sun only rises and sets once each year.

Then some researchers determine the Arctic region based on **temperature**. They maintain that the Arctic includes any places in high latitudes where the mean day-time temperature in summer does not rise above 10 degrees Celsius.

The third definition is characterised by **vegetation**. Scientists assert that the Arctic is the area north of the arctic tree line. This is the northernmost latitude in the Northern hemisphere where trees can grow. Farther north, prolonged and extremely cold temperatures freeze the sap and make it impossible for trees to survive. Furthermore, permafrost in the soil stops trees from putting down roots deep enough to support them.

Practice your grammar

L'expression de la cause et de la conséquence

▶ On peut exprimer **la cause** au moyen **des locutions prépositionnelles suivantes :**

owing to..., because of..., due to...	à cause de...
thanks to...	grâce à...

Elles introduisent des groupes nominaux ou des pronoms :

*For the majority of human history, this region has been largely inaccessible **due to / because of / owing to harsh conditions and freezing temperatures**.*

▶ La cause peut être exprimée par **des propositions subordonnées** introduites par **des conjonctions** telles que ***because*** (parce que), ***as*** (comme), ***since*** (puisque).

***As it can be dangerous and unpredictable traveling through Arctic waters**, cruise operators have concerns about passenger safety.*

▶ La conséquence peut être exprimée par **des adverbes de liaison** :

that's (the reason) why	c'est pourquoi
therefore / consequently / as a result / accordingly	par conséquent
thus	ainsi
so	donc

Ils permettent de relier deux phrases ou propositions indépendantes.

*The greenhouse effect is making the Earth warmer. **That's why / Therefore** the polar ice caps are melting.*

1 Complétez les phrases avec les mots ou expressions ci-dessous. Donnez toutes les possibilités.

therefore • due to • as • because • owing to • that's why • because of

a. *The Arctic holds 13% of the world's undiscovered oil. ... offshore drilling activities are increasing in the Arctic Ocean.*

b. *Polar bears may face extinction by the end of the century, ... their sea ice habitat is under threat ... climate change.*

c. *The Arctic is becoming a geopolitical hotspot ... vast reserves of oil and gas.*

2 Reliez les phrases en mettant en évidence le lien de cause à effet. Produisez six phrases en utilisant ces mots et expressions.

because • consequently • as a result • therefore • as • that's why

a. *The Greenland ice sheet is receding at a record pace.*

b. *Global sea levels are rising.*

c. *Some countries might face flooding in the future.*

d. *New trade routes and sea lanes are opening in the Arctic.*

Les relatives réduites

▶ En anglais, il est fréquent de trouver à la place d'une relative **une proposition participiale** dont le verbe est à la forme en *-ing*. On parle parfois de **relatives réduites** :

*The Arctic refers to the geographical areas **which surround the North Pole**. → The Arctic refers to the geographical areas **surrounding the North Pole**.*

▶ Si le verbe de la relative correspondante est au passif, le verbe de la participiale sera **un participe passé (V-*en*)** :

*According to a scientific report **which was published last year**, the Arctic might be free of ice in the summer by 2100. → According to a scientific report **published last year**...*

▶ Ces structures sont très fréquentes et sont même préférées aux relatives, jugées stylistiquement plus lourdes. Utilisez-les autant que possible à l'écrit !

3 Réduisez les relatives en gras en propositions participiales.

a. *An oil tanker **which was carrying about 30 million gallons of crude oil** ran aground on the shores of Alaska.*

b. *The oil spill poses a serious threat to the people **who live in the area**.*

c. *The territory **which is claimed by Russia** includes the Lomonosov Ridge, an underwater mountain ridge passing near the North Pole.*

d. *Environmental organisations and lobby groups **who represent the oil industry** will meet at the Arctic Ocean Conference tomorrow.*

Improve your pronunciation

La prononciation des graphies *s* et *ss*

▶ La graphie s entre deux voyelles se prononce normalement /z/ : *rose, these, rise*

▶ ⚠ Ne confondez pas **le verbe *close*** /kləʊz/ et **la préposition *close to sth*** /kləʊs/.

▶ Notez les exceptions suivantes où le *s* entre deux voyelles se prononce /s/ (comme dans ***s**ame*) :
- dans la terminaison ***s**ive* : *intrusive, explosive*
- dans la terminaison *a**s**e* : *base, case, chase*
- dans la terminaison *ea**s**e* : *increase, decrease*
- dans **les noms** *house, mouse, use, excuse* et leur dérivés (*useful*, *useless*).

⚠ Quand ces quatre mots sont des **verbes** ou dans les dérivés de ces verbes, *s* est prononcé /z/ : *user, housing*.

▶ **La graphie *ss*** se prononce normalement /s/ : *accessible, impressive*.
- elle se prononce /ʃ/ (comme dans ***sh**oot*) dans **les terminaisons *-ssion*, *-ssure*, *-ssue*** : *pressure, discussion, tissue*.
- elle se prononce /z/ dans les mots suivants, qui sont des exceptions : *dissolve, possess, dessert* /di'zɜːt/, *scissors, Missouri*.

Verbe ou nom ? L'accentuation des homonymes

▶ En anglais, il est fréquent qu'un même mot fonctionne à la fois comme un nom et comme un verbe (par exemple : *an increase / to increase*).

▶ Certains mots de deux syllabes n'ont pas la même accentuation s'ils fonctionnent comme nom ou comme verbe. La règle est la suivante :

Nom (accentué sur la 1ère syllabe)	Verbe (accentué sur la 2nde syllabe)
present	*present*
increase	*increase*
export	*export*

⚠ Ce changement accentuel peut modifier la prononciation des voyelles. Les syllabes inaccentuées sont en effet souvent réduites et prononcées avec **un *schwa* /ə/** ou **un *i* bref**.
present (verbe) /prɪ'zent/ ≠ *present* (nom) /'prezənt/

▶ Voici d'autres mots qui ont ce fonctionnement : *conflict, contrast, suspect, rebel, insult, extract, progress, protest...*

▶ Si on ajoute certains suffixes à un verbe (*-er, -or, -ing, -ed*...), l'accent reste sur la deuxième syllabe :
export (verbe) → *exporter*

1 **Classez les mots suivants en fonction de la prononciation de la graphie *s* ou *ss* : /s/, /z/ ou /ʃ/.** Vérifiez vos réponses en écoutant l'enregistrement, puis répétez les mots.

Audio hatier-clic.fr/21amc/257a

issue • accessible • lose • cause basic • exclusive • close to the house • mission • cruise • increased • useful • episode • basin • sensitive

2 **Classez les mots en gras en fonction de la prononciation de la graphie *s* ou *ss* : /s/, /z/ ou /ʃ/.** Vérifiez vos réponses en écoutant l'enregistrement, puis répétez les mots.

Audio hatier-clic.fr/21amc/257b

a. ***Russia possesses*** *more than half of all the Arctic's estimated oil* ***resources****.*

b. ***Release*** *of methane and carbon dioxide stored in permafrost could* ***cause*** *severe global warming,* ***as*** *they are potent* ***greenhouse gases****.*

3 **Les mots en gras sont-ils des noms ou des verbes ? Recopiez-les et soulignez la syllabe accentuée, puis vérifiez vos réponses en écoutant l'enregistrement. Répétez les phrases.**

Audio hatier-clic.fr/21amc/257c

a. *Recent studies have shown a significant* ***decrease*** *in the snow-covered area over the Arctic during winter.*

b. *Oil* ***exports*** *from Canada* ***decreased*** *last year.*

c. *The country needs to* ***export*** *more gas.*

d. *I've only read short* ***extracts*** *from the book.*

e. *The company* ***extracts*** *oil in Alaska.*

Let's translate

Transposition en français d'un texte

Rendez compte en français des principales idées exprimées par le document B p. 252. Veillez à ne pas simplement en dresser la liste, mais à les expliciter lorsque cela vous paraît pertinent.

Contourner les difficultés lexicales d'un texte

Afin de bien synthétiser un texte, il faut impérativement dissiper tout problème de compréhension en décryptant les mots inconnus. Deux stratégies sont possibles :

▶ On peut **inférer** le sens du mot inconnu (c'est-à-dire en déduire le sens en se basant sur des indices). Pour cela, il est possible :
- de **s'aider du contexte** : la proximité du mot inconnu avec d'autres mots familiers, situation, type de texte, ton du passage, registre de langue...
- d'examiner **la formation du mot** : contient-il un suffixe ou un préfixe connu ? S'agit-il d'un mot composé dont un élément vous est familier ?

▶ Il est possible d'utiliser **un dictionnaire unilingue** : dans ce type de dictionnaire, on ne trouve pas de traductions de mots (comme dans les dictionnaires bilingues) mais des définitions en anglais.

⚠ Tous les mots inconnus d'un texte n'ont pas la même importance. Seuls les mots clefs figureront dans votre synthèse. C'est le sens de ces mots qu'il faut élucider en priorité.

Translation Tip

- Attention aux **acronymes** qui diffèrent d'une langue à l'autre et qu'il faut le cas échéant expliciter. Comment devra-t-on restituer GDP ?
- Attention **aux faux amis** qui peuvent entraver la compréhension du texte : quel est le sens de *concerns* ici ?

À vous !

a. Inférez le sens des mots suivants. Formulez des hypothèses que vous justifierez : *lag behind, coastline, ice-breakers, outbuild*. Proposez pour chaque mot une traduction que vous pourrez utiliser dans votre synthèse.

b. Utilisez le dictionnaire unilingue pour accéder au sens puis proposez une traduction en français : *prominence, gap, lense*.

c. Parmi les mots ci-dessus, dont le sens a été élucidé, certains sont des mots clefs qui devront impérativement figurer dans la synthèse, d'autres non. Lesquels sont indispensables ?

Build up your vocabulary

1 Fill in your own mind map here: hatier-clic.fr/21amc/258

2 Know your zones! Find a word from your mind map that corresponds to the definitions below.

a. a line running currently at around 66°33 north of the Equator
b. a zone potentially containing natural resources
c. an area stretching from the coast to 200 nautical miles out to sea
d. an area covering up to 12 miles from the coast
e. a portion of a continent that is submerged in shallow water

3 Choose from the terms below to complete the summary.

seabed – heats up – shipping routes – oil – military buildup – ice melt – race – rivalry – asset

Deposits of natural resources including ... and gas have been discovered in the Arctic. A ... between several countries is on to see who can be the first to exploit these ... , thus boosting their economy. There is intense ... with some countries competing for territory underwater on the ... . Due to increased temperatures, there has been significant ... . This has lead to the opening of new ice-free ... which will enable goods to be transported quicker, allowing companies to save both fuel and time. However, the downside of the discoveries has been a ... : the presence of troops and military icebreakers in the area. This has caused additional tension in the area as the quest for territory ... .

Projects

1

You are an intern at the UN. Take part in a panel discussion on geopolitical affairs.

1. Look through the unit for information and do your own research.
2. Define which aspects of the Arctic you are going to speak about and mind map a plan.
3. Make your introduction a hook to grab the audience's attention: use statistics, anecdotes or unusual facts.
4. Write down just key words to avoid reading. Check the pronunciation of the words you are not sure about.

2

As a junior researcher you have been asked to write an article about what is at stake for the USA in the Arctic.

1. As you are a junior researcher, your style is going to be direct, straight to the point.
2. Prepare your arguments, remembering to back them up with facts and data. Each argument should, in part, answer the question: "What is at stake for the US in the Arctic?"
3. Think about what to include in the introduction. The information in *Let's Focus on ...* n° 2, p. 255 might help.
4. Find relevant examples from the unit or from your own research.
5. In the conclusion you should briefly summarise the main points.

Pour l'écrit du Bac

1

A

AFTER THE ICE:

MINERAL RICHES OF THE ARCTIC

Receding Arctic ice is unlocking fathomless mineral resources – if you don't mind frost and cost.

90 Billion Barrels

IS THE ESTIMATED SIZE OF UNDISCOVERED OIL DEPOSITS BEYOND THE ARCTIC CIRCLE.

1,525 BILLION BARRELS WORLD TOTAL KNOWN OIL RESERVES

5.9% OF WORLD'S KNOWN OIL RESERVES

That's equivalent to:

110% OF RUSSIA'S RESERVES	**1,677%** OF NORWAY'S KNOWN RESERVES	**339%** OF U.S. RESERVES	**52%** OF CANADA'S KNOWN RESERVES

B

84% of hydrocarbon resources lie offshore

MINERALS BEYOND THE ARCTIC CIRCLE

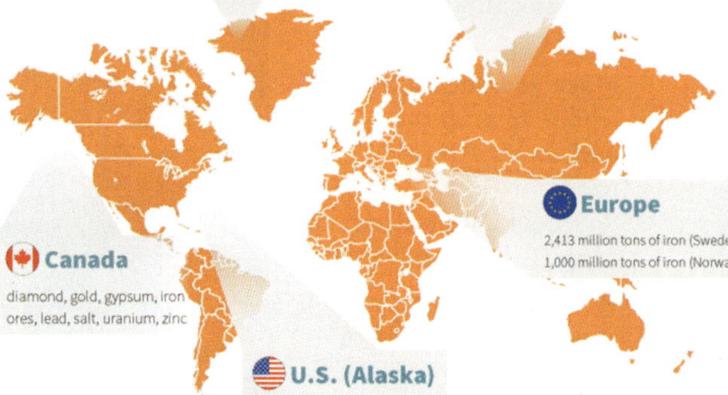

Greenland
gold, molybdenum, nickel, platinum group elements, rare earth elements (tantalum, niobium).

Russia (Arctic Siberia)
Apatite, ceramic raw materials, coal, cobalt, copper, diamonds, gold, gypsum, iron ores, mica, molybdenum, nickel, palladium, platinum, silver, precious stones, rare metals, tin, titanium, zinc
+ fossil ivory (mammoth tusks from melting permafrost)
$1.5-2 trillion – the estimated value of Russian mineral reserves

Europe
2,413 million tons of iron (Sweden)
1,000 million tons of iron (Norway)

Canada
diamond, gold, gypsum, iron ores, lead, salt, uranium, zinc

U.S. (Alaska)
67 million tons of zinc
67.6 million tons of lead

But before you start crowd-funding your first Arctic mine, consider these icy realities...

MAIN DIFFICULTIES OF ARCTIC MINING

- **An iceberg of costs**: starting up mine operation may cost $ billions
- **Short shipping season**: difficult to transport goods and supplies
- **Melting permafrost**: built infrastructure crumbles as deep-ground ice melts
- **Summer swamps**: drilling and road transport nearly impossible in summer
- **Icebergs**: Calving ice sheets a menace sea transport
- **Polar bears**: permanent threat to mine staff
- **-50°C in winter**: frostbite, mechanical failure, blocked shipping channels

C

1,669 trillion cubic feet

THE ESTIMATED SIZE OF ARCTIC NATURAL GAS RESOURCES

11,671 TRILLION CUBIC FEET WORLD TOTAL KNOWN GAS RESERVES

24.3% OF THE WORLD'S KNOWN GAS RESERVES

That's equivalent to:

99% OF RUSSIA'S KNOWN RESERVES	**2,354%** OF NORWAY'S RESERVES	**500%** OF U.S. RESERVES	**2,736%** OF CANADA'S RESERVES

2 World powers increasingly see icy Arctic as a hot property

From a helicopter, Greenland's brilliant white ice and dark mountains make the desolation seem to go on forever. And the few people who live here — its whole population wouldn't fill a football stadium — are poor, with a high rate of substance abuse and suicide.

One scientist called it the "end of the planet."

When U.S. President Donald Trump floated the idea of buying Greenland, it was met with derision, seen as an awkward and inappropriate approach of an erstwhile[1] ally.

But it might also be an Aladdin's Cave of oil, natural gas and rare earth minerals just waiting to be tapped as the ice recedes[2].

The northern island and the rest of the Arctic aren't just hotter due to global warming. As melting ice opens shipping lanes and reveals incredible riches, the region is seen as a new geopolitical and economic asset, with the U.S., Russia, China and others wanting in.

In April, Russian President Vladimir Putin put forward an ambitious program to reaffirm his country's presence in the Arctic, including efforts to build ports and other infrastructure and expand its icebreaker fleet. Russia wants to stake its claim in the region that is believed to hold up to one-fourth of the Earth's undiscovered oil and gas.

China sees Greenland as a possible source of rare earths and other minerals and a port for shipping through the Arctic to the eastern U.S. It called last year for joint development of a "Polar Silk Road" as part of Beijing's Belt and Road Initiative to build railways, ports and other facilities in dozens of countries.

But while global warming pushes the cold and ice farther north each year, experts caution that the race to the Arctic is an incredibly challenging marathon, not a sprint.

On the other hand, while mining in Greenland has been expensive due to the environment, development costs have fallen as the ice has melted, making it more attractive to potential buyers, she said.

Strategically, Greenland forms part of what the U.S. views as a key corridor for naval operations between the Arctic and the North Atlantic. It is also part of the broader Arctic region, considered strategically important because of its proximity to the U.S. and economically vital for its natural resources.

Bangkok Post, Aug. 23rd, 2019

1. former 2. retreats

PARTIE 1

Prenez connaissance des documents 1 A, B, C et 2 et traitez le sujet suivant en anglais :

Write a short commentary on the four documents (minimum 300 words) taking into account their specificities. Analyse how the documents deal with these themes: rivalry - interdependence - global relations.

PARTIE 2

Traduisez le passage suivant du document 2 en français.

When U.S. President Donald Trump floated the idea of buying Greenland, it was met with derision, seen as an awkward and inappropriate approach of an erstwhile ally.

But it might also be an Aladdin's Cave of oil, natural gas and rare earth minerals just waiting to be tapped as the ice recedes.

The northern island and the rest of the Arctic aren't just hotter due to global warming. As melting ice opens shipping lanes and reveals incredible riches, the region is seen as a new geopolitical and economic asset, with the U.S., Russia, China and others wanting in.

22 The royals: ambassadors for Britain?

The expert's view
hatier-clic.fr/21amc/262a

In the news
hatier-clic.fr/21amc/262b

Projects

- You have a youtube channel about the royal family. Try to convince your subscribers that today's royals represent a modern image of Britain.
- Imagine an interview with a member of the royal family to question whether the members have evolved over time on the question of diversity.

Grammar p. 270 Phonology p. 271

Queens of the Anglo-Saxon world

A A united Empire

1. List the symbols which suggest the Empire is showing a united front.
2. Imagine this poster was sent as a postcard by the Queen to a general in a country of the Commonwealth. Write down what could be the message to the troops.

Poster celebrating cooperation across the Empire, 1942

B The future Queen's speech

A Commonwealth speech

Audio hatier-clic.fr/21amc/263a

1. Explain Princess Elizabeth's message when she says she is at home in Cape Town.
2. Pick out the words referring to the Commonwealth as a family/community. Use them in a paragraph to give a definition of the Commonwealth as described by Elizabeth. Then check your definition with *Let's focus on...* n° 3, p. 269.
3. **Phonology** Focus on Princess Elizabeth's pronunciation of the word "year". How do you pronounce this word? Is Elizabeth's pronunciation still common nowadays?
4. You are a Canadian journalist writing a piece about the speech. Indicate why this is a remarkable message sent from the monarchy.

C The Empress of India

It is rare that I leave the cinema *deeply* offended with what I've just seen. Yesterday, after watching the just released *Victoria & Abdul*, was one such day. [...]

Based on true events – "mostly," as the opening credits confess – Stephen Frears' latest work tells the story of an unlikely friendship between Queen Victoria and an Indian servant (who is shipped from India, without a say in the matter, to gift the queen with a coin).

Queen Victoria, played by Judi Dench, is portrayed as what seems to be the most woke[1] monarch in British history; when met with antagonism about her new friendship, she is furious with her court for being "racialists" (she, conveniently, absolves herself of the accusation).

Abdul, her servant, is written with offensive two-dimensionality. In *every single scene*, he is unwittingly wonderstruck[2] with the Queen. In fact, he worships the ground she walks on (literally, he kisses her feet). For she is the "Empress of India" – a fact we are reminded of *over* and over again.

While Queen Victoria, by treating Abdul like an exotic pet, is offered a new lease[3] of life, what does Abdul gain? Well, as he gleefully expresses, "the great privilege" of being among the "glorious people" of the British Empire (what else?!). [...]

Period dramas such as this are dangerous. They are pitched as light entertainment: tonally soft with a peppering of low stakes conflict – but they are rooted in the merciless grip of British imperialism. Films like *Victoria & Abdul* seek to absolve our barbaric behaviour in colonised countries.

The Victorian era was responsible for unimaginable atrocities in India. Indian MP Shashi Tharoor, author of *Inglorious Empire: What the British did to India*, demonstrates how Britain economised its industrial revolution through plundering[4] India, reducing the country's share of the world economy from 23 percent to 4 percent.

British exploitations of India – like that of local produce, such as grain – led to unprecedented poverty under the British Raj; both the Great Famine of 1876-1878 and the Indian famine of 1899-1900 are thought to have killed up to 10 million people each. [...]

We have a cultural and social responsibility to honourably interrogate our colonial past, even if it makes us uncomfortable. But we don't teach our past racism and enslavement in British schools. Rather than respecting the lives torn apart at our imperialism, we mute and erase them.

Amrou Al-Kadhi, *The Independent*, Sept. 16th, 2017

1. aware of political and social issues, especially racism 2. amazed 3. an opportunity to be more active 4. pillaging

Victoria & Abdul (Stephen Frears, 2017)

Video hatier-clic.fr/21amc/263b

GROUP WORK

Student A on the text, student B on the trailer.

e-worksheet hatier-clic.fr/21amc/263c

1. List the symbols of British monarchy and indicate if they represent common heritage, diversity or colonialism.
2. Explain the point of view expressed in your document.
3. Exchange your answers and discuss whether this film depicts the royals as good ambassadors in the Commonwealth.

A diversity of voices

A Coming together

1. Imagine the context of this visit and list the western symbols.
2. Explain the difference between the royals and the locals (attitude, outfits...).
3. You are a student attending the event. Report your thoughts in the school gazette. Indicate why this visit is special.

B Leading the change

Prince William's speech at the BAFTA

Audio hatier-clic.fr/21amc/264

1. Show that the BAFTA (British Academy of Film and Television Arts) is a good place for the royal family to get its voice heard.
2. Indicate how Prince William uses humour to pass on his message.
3. List the words he uses about diversity and use them in a sentence to show what he means.
4. You're a humourist handing out the next prize after Prince William. Show the limits of his speech.

C The people's Princess

9 reasons Princess Diana was so much more than a style icon

Princess Diana captured the world's attention as a royal trendsetter, but during her time in the public eye, she also became a prominent philanthropic force. Diana worked tirelessly on behalf of charities around the world, using her fame to raise awareness of a number of important humanitarian issues. Twenty years after her death, here's why Diana will always be remembered as the "People's Princess."

1) She changed the face of the British monarchy.

Through her charity work, Diana highlighted how royalty, which had previously been known for its stuffiness[1], could be in touch with the public. In her interview with BBC's Panorama in 1995, she said, "I would like a monarchy that has more contact with its people." This statement became something of a personal mission for the Princess. Diana was at some point patron[2] of over 100 charities. […]

2) She led a campaign for a worldwide ban on landmines.

After a visit to Angola in 1997, Diana became anti-landmine activists' most prominent advocate. During that trip, which was captured by the BBC for a Heart of the Matter documentary, the Princess was photographed putting her own safety at risk as she walked through a recently cleared minefield. […] Her son Prince Harry, who is now patron of leading landmine charity, The HALO Trust, recently called for the world to become free of the weapons by 2025.

3) She changed the world's perception of HIV and AIDS.

In April 1987, when speculation around the virus was rife[3], Diana was invited to open Britain's first AIDS ward at Middlesex hospital. A photograph, which made front-page news around the world, showed her shaking hands with HIV-positive patients without wearing gloves. This publicly challenged the notion that HIV/AIDS was passed from person to person by touch and highlighted Diana's affection and compassion for people living with the disease. […] At the time of her death, Gavin Hart, of the National AIDS Trust, told the BBC: "In our opinion, Diana was the foremost ambassador for AIDS awareness on the planet and no one can fill her shoes in terms of the work she did."

4) She raised awareness of leprosy.

Like her AIDS efforts, Diana traveled to countries with a high leprosy rate in order to remove the stigma surrounding the disease. As patron of The Leprosy Mission, she visited hospitals in India, Nepal and Zimbabwe and by spending time with patients, she dispelled one of the myths surrounding the illness – that it can be passed on by touch. […]

5) She made regular personal visits to London's homeless centers.

Despite relinquishing most of her charitable causes after her divorce from Prince Charles in 1996, Diana became patron of Centrepoint in 1992 and remained in the role until her death in 1997. Both William and Harry were taken by the Princess to see the help offered at the charity's shelters and, at the age of 23, William followed in his mother's footsteps when he became patron. Speaking at the time, he told The Telegraph: "My mother introduced that sort of area to me a long time ago. It was a real eye-opener and I am very glad she did. It has been something I have held close to me for a long time." […]

Katie Frost, *Harper's Bazar*, Aug. 31st, 2018
This article is from May 2017, and has been republished in remembrance of Princess Diana on the anniversary of her death.

1. formality 2. supporter 3. common

1. List the reasons why Diana was a good ambassador for Britain and show she trained her children to follow her path.
2. Comment on how she used the media to communicate about the causes she defended.
3. Explain why she will be remembered as "the people's Princess."
4. Imagine a list of actions Diana and her children could have been involved in to show the evolution of the British monarchy. Explain your choices in a paragraph.

The royals facing modernity

A Star ambassador

Prince Charles named Katy Perry ambassador of his British Asian Trust philanthropic project, drawing backlash[1] from those who pointed out Perry's lack of ties to the community and history of cultural appropriation.

Perry's new role was announced by the heir[2] apparent on Tuesday night at the charity's annual Royal Dinner, with the singer posting a tweet announcing it on Wednesday. The 35-year-old singer will be working under the trust's Children's Protection Fund and its efforts to combat child trafficking in South Asia.

Prince Charles founded the British Asian Trust in 2007 in an effort to tackle poverty in South Asia.

Perry, who served as an UNICEF Goodwill Ambassador since 2013, said Wednesday that she was excited to work with the British Trust Fund and that she has a "magnetic connection" with India.

Some of the singer's fans quickly congratulated her on the announcement, but other Twitter users expressed confusion at the choice to name a non-Asian from the U.S. to the role.

"I can't believe the fact that Katy Perry, a white American, has been chosen to be the British Asian trust ambassador???? I just- what?," one user wrote.

> **Zarik | Stream** *folklore*
> @zyusaf13
>
> I love Katy but seriously? She's not British or is she Asian. There are SO MANY BRITISH ASIAN celebrities who should be in her place: Dev Patel, Jameela Jamil, Anjali Mohindra, Parminder Nagra and Riz Ahmed to name a few.
>
> > **Yahoo News UK** @YahooNewsUK
> > Prince Charles announces Katy Perry as British Asian Trust ambassador
> > https://trib.al/bsrJyQ9
>
> 9:12 AM · Feb 5, 2020
>
> 2.9K — 543 people are Tweeting about this

People named several celebrities who may have been better fits for the role, such as Zayn Malik, Dev Patel or Jameela Jamil.

Another wrote that while they meant no offense, "could we not find a British Asian to fill this role? there's plenty of us."

Others referred back to instances where Perry has drawn criticism for culturally appropriating minorities in her past performances and appearances.

A notable instance that resurfaced Wednesday was a 2013 American Music Awards geisha-inspired performance. Perry, who donned a kimono to sing her song "Unconditionally," was called culturally insensitive for perpetuating harmful stereotypes of Asian women.

Perry apologized for the incident, as well as several other times she was criticized for cultural appropriation, in 2017 during a livestream to promote her album, "Witness."

"I've made several mistakes," Perry said in the stream, according to Billboard. "I won't ever understand some of those things because of who I am. I will never understand, but I can educate myself and that's what I'm trying to do along the way."

Doha Mahani, nbcnews.com, Feb. 5th, 2020

1. criticism 2. successor

1 Find out why this choice is criticised and imagine what the objective could be with this new ambassador.

2 Read *Let's focus on...* n° 4, p. 269. Explain the sentence "Perry has drawn criticism for culturally appropriating minorities" l. 25-27.

3 **Grammar** Observe the following compound words: *the 35-year-old singer, child trafficking* and complete the following sentence:
A compound noun consists of ... or more words (usually two ... or an adjective and a noun - but other combinations are also possible) functioning as a single unit.

4 The journalist exchanges tweets with readers who do not understand The Prince's choice. Student A is the journalist and Student B a reader.

Omid Scobie @scobie · Mar 7
I rarely add my own opinion to reporting but if there was ever a photo that illustrates what the Royal Family is about to lose — it's this. Diversity, modernity, inclusivity and representation.

B Royal diversity

1. Describe the image and comment on the attitude of the people.
2. Explain the tweet in your own words.
3. You are in charge of Megan Markle's communication. Record a short podcast explaining the situation and why she is a good symbol of Britain.

C Modernising the Establishment

Meghan Markle bringing diversity to the royal family
Video hatier-clic.fr/21amc/267

1. Analyse the presenters' and the reporter's angle on the story. Show what is key for them with this wedding.
2. Show why Megan will help change the image of the monarchy in Britain for the public.
3. Enact an interview between the journalist and a member of the public who believes this wedding will not help the royal family modernise its image.

Let's focus on...

A royal family tree

1

A floating royal residence

2

The Royal Yacht Britannia served the British Royal Family for over 44 years. She was a successful ambassador and played a key role in major historic events. Britannia travelled over one million nautical miles on 968 state visits, the equivalent of once round the world for each year, calling at over 600 ports in 135 countries, most of them part of the Commonwealth including, Australia, Canada and New Zealand.

Britannia was famously used by the Royal family to host glorious state receptions and banquets during its numerous journeys across the world. It allowed the Queen to display Britain's grandeur to heads of State as well as to the world's leading business leaders as if they had been invited to one of Her Majesty's Royal palaces.

Britannia was thus also seen as an ambassador for British business, as the Queen and her aides promoted trade and industry around the globe onboard the yacht. It had become indispensable for captains of industry and business magnates to attend what was then called 'Sea Days' which were merely overseas trade missions. It was estimated that over £3 billion were made for the Exchequer (ministry of finance) on Britannia between 1991 and 1995 alone.

The yacht was even involved in the evacuation of British nationals during civil war in South Yemen in 1986, another event underlining her special status.

Timeline

5

1837-1901 Reign of Queen Victoria.

1930-1950 British Empire Games.

20/01/1936 King George V dies, succeeded by Edward VIII.

11/12/1936 Edward VIII's abdication and succession by George VI.

1947 Princess Elizabeth's Commonwealth speech.

1949 Commonwealth.

The Commonwealth

3

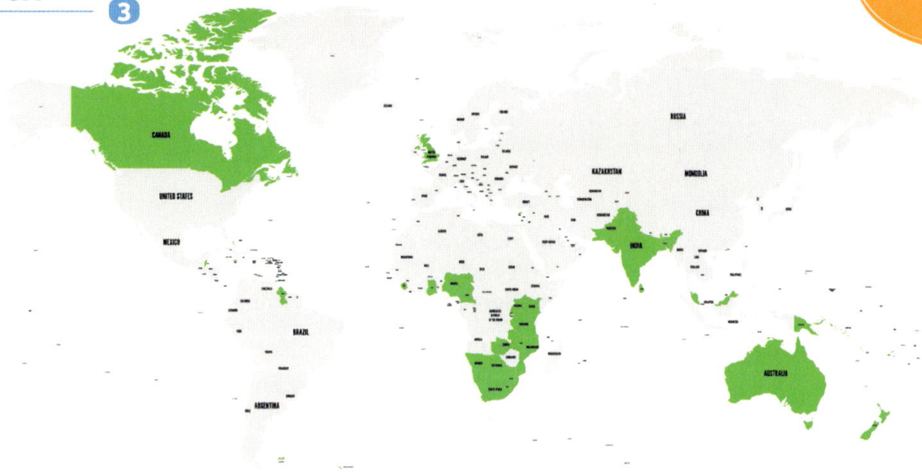

The Commonwealth is also known as the Commonwealth of Nations. It was called the British Commonwealth of Nations and was founded in 1926 when the Empire started to break-up. Today, there are 53 member countries. It is a free association of sovereign states including the United Kingdom and a number of its former dependent territories, which it governed like Australia or New Zealand as well as independent members. Most of the older dependencies are colonies like Anguilla, Bermuda, the Cayman Islands, the Falkland Islands, Gibraltar… These territories have decided to continue to be linked to the UK and therefore cooperate at different levels. They also acknowledge Queen Elisabeth as the symbolic head of this association. The Commonwealth doesn't have a constitution and its members are connected through shared traditions, institutions but also through economic interest.

Fun facts

The Commonwealth has a combined population of 2.4 billion, almost a third of the population of the whole world. More than 60 per cent of its population is aged 29 or under.

Culture appropriation

4

The unacknowledged or inappropriate act of taking or using things from a culture that is not your own such as customs, practices, ideas, hairstyles, clothing…
The problem is usually when someone from a dominant culture takes something from a less dominant culture for aesthetic reasons or personal enrichment. For example, when Pharrel wore a Native American headdress as a costume.

- **1952** Reign Queen Elisabeth.
- **6/2/52** George VI dies, succeeded by Elizabeth II.
- **1954-1966** British Empire and Commonwealth Games.
- **1970-1974** British Commonwealth Games.
- **1978** Commonwealth Games.
- **2018** Prince Harry appointed Commonwealth youth ambassador by the Queen.

Practice your grammar

Les noms composés

- Un nom composé est un nom complexe formé de plusieurs éléments juxtaposés. Ce procédé est fréquent **pour créer des mots nouveaux. Les anglophones en créent constamment.**
- On trouve, entre autres, les formations suivantes :
  - nom + nom : ***a Twitter user, a period drama***
  - V-ing + nom : ***a washing machine, a living room***
  - adjectif + nom : ***a high school***
  - nom + préposition : ***a passer-by*** (un passant)
- L'élément le plus important est en général celui **situé en dernière position** :

  *a newspaper **article** → un **article** de presse*

  ⚠ Le premier élément est généralement au singulier, même s'il renvoie à une réalité plurielle ou s'il contient un nombre : ***child trafficking, the 35-year-old singer, an eleven-day trip***
- **Il n'existe pas de règle orthographique.** Ainsi, les éléments peuvent être séparés (***a newspaper article***), reliés par un trait d'union (***a brother-in-law***) ou bien accolés (***a birthday, the Commonwealth***).

1 À partir des définitions suivantes, construisez des noms composés, puis complétez les phrases en utilisant les noms ainsi formés.

the father of your husband or wife • a person who pays tax • an event organised to collect money for a charity • a trip that lasted 10 days

a. *Meghan Markle and Prince Harry's … to Africa cost … £250,000, making it the most expensive royal tour last year.*

b. *Kate Middletown and her …, Prince Charles, attended a … in London yesterday.*

2 Traduisez les expressions suivantes par un nom composé.

a. les dirigeants du Commonwealth
b. une interview de vingt minutes
c. un livre de deux cents pages
d. un fan de Ketty Perry
e. une star hollywoodienne

Le passif des verbes d'opinion et de parole

- Il est possible d'utiliser certains verbes d'opinion ou de parole (*think, believe, report, say, know, consider, expect…*) à la voix passive dans une phrase impersonnelle dont le sujet est *it* :

  It is believed that Prince Harry is currently in India.
- Une autre structure consiste à placer le sujet de la proposition en *that* en tête. Son verbe est alors à l'infinitif en *to*.

  Prince Harry is believed to be currently in India.
- S'il est question d'un fait passé, on utilise un infinitif parfait (***to have* + participe passé**) pour marquer cette antériorité : ***The Indian famine of 1899-1900 is thought to have killed up to 10 million people.***
- Ces tournures sont souvent utilisées dans la presse pour indiquer qu'une nouvelle n'est pas vérifiée ou que sa source est inconnue.
- Pour les traduire, la meilleure solution consiste à utiliser **le pronom *on*** (***on pense que…***) ou la tournure impersonnelle ***il paraît que***, ou bien à mettre le verbe au **conditionnel** : ***Le Prince Harry serait actuellement en Inde.***

3 Mettez les phrases à la voix passive en suivant le modèle ci-dessous.

Some people say that Meghan Markle is a symbol of diversity and modernity. → Meghan Markle is said to be a symbol of diversity and modernity.

a. *Some historians consider that Queen Elizabeth is one of the greatest monarchs of all time.*

b. *Everyone knows that Britain is a multicultural country.*

c. *A lot of people think that Meghan Markle followed in Princess Diana's footsteps.*

d. *Some journalists expect William and Kate to make an official visit to South Africa next year.*

e. *Some people believe that Princess Diana was assassinated.*

Improve your pronunciation

La prononciation de la graphie *ea(r)*

▶ **La graphie *ea*** peut se prononcer :

/iː/ (comme dans *keep*)	***read, speak, mean***
/e/ (comme dans *bed*)	***Commonwealth, head, dead***
/eɪ/ (comme dans *say*)	***great, steak, break*** (mais ***breakfast*** /e/)

⚠ Les verbes irréguliers *read, mean, dream, deal, leap* changent de prononciation au prétérit et au participe passé.

Infinitif	Prétérit	Participe passé
mean /iː/	***meant*** /e/	***meant*** /e/

▶ **La graphie *ear*** se prononce :

/ɪə/ (comme dans *here*) en fin de mot, y compris quand on ajoute un suffixe	***dear(ly), fear, appear(ance)*** Exceptions : ***wear, tear*** (déchirer), ***swear, bear, pear*** se prononcent /eə/
/ɜː/ (comme dans *girl*) avant une consonne	***learn, pearl, early*** Exception : ***heart*** (prononcé /ɑː/ comme dans *car*)

1 Classez les mots suivants dans un tableau en fonction de la prononciation de la graphie *ea* : /iː/ (comme dans *see*), /e/ (comme dans *bed*) ou /eɪ/ (comme dans *say*). Écoutez l'enregistrement pour vérifier vos réponses et répétez.

Audio hatier-clic.fr/21amc/271a

stream • feather • steak • ready • release • disease • break • breakfast • team • weapon • instead • deal • I dealt • health • New Zealand

2 Dans les suites de mots suivantes, chassez l'intrus. Puis écoutez l'enregistrement pour vérifier vos réponses et répétez.

Audio hatier-clic.fr/21amc/271b

a. *dear – fear – near – pear*
b. *wear – swear – clear – bear*
c. *dearly – early – nearly*
d. *earth – heart – heard – earl*

La prononciation des prépositions

▶ Certaines prépositions ont deux prononciations en fonction du contexte. Il s'agit des prépositions ***at, for, of, from*** et ***to.***

▶ Dans la plupart des contextes, elles sont prononcées **avec la voyelle /ə/** souvent appelée *schwa*. Il s'agit d'un son très bref qui ressemble à un e muet. On dit parfois que la voyelle est « réduite ».

Princess Diana is famous for /ə/ ***her fairy-tale wedding and her tragic death.***

Il s'agit-là de la prononciation la plus courante et la plus naturelle de ces prépositions.

▶ Plus rarement, en particulier quand elles apparaissent seules en fin de phrase ou de proposition (par exemple, dans les questions), on prononce la voyelle telle qu'elle est écrite. On dit alors que la voyelle est « pleine ».

What is Princess Diana famous for? /ɔː/

▶ Les autres prépositions (*on, with, in, by...*) n'ont normalement pas de forme réduite.

3 Dans les phrases suivantes, les prépositions en gras sont-elles susceptibles d'être prononcées avec la voyelle *schwa* /ə/ ? Écoutez l'enregistrement pour vérifier vos réponses et répétez.

Audio hatier-clic.fr/21amc/271c

a. *Diana Spencer became a member **of** the British royal family when she married Charles, Prince **of** Wales, **in** 1981.*

b. *What did Diana campaign **for**?*

c. ***In** the late 1990s Diana campaigned **for** a ban **on** the manufacture and use **of** landmines.*

d. *What did Princess Diana die **of**?*

e. ***On** August 31, 1997, she was involved **in** a terrible car accident in Paris. She died **from** her injuries a few hours later.*

Let's translate

The Victorian era was responsible for unimaginable atrocities in India. Indian MP Shashi Tharoor, author of *Inglorious Empire: What the British did to India,* demonstrates how Britain economised its industrial revolution through plundering India, reducing the country's share of the world economy from 23 percent to 4 percent. British exploitations of India – like that of local produce, such as grain – led to unprecedented poverty under the British Raj[1]; both the Great Famine of 1876-1878 and the Indian famine of 1899-1900 are thought to have killed up to 10 million people each.

Amrou Al-Kadhi, www.independent.co.uk

1. the rule of the British government in India before India became independent in 1947

La transposition

▶ Une transposition est un procédé de traduction qui consiste à **changer la catégorie grammaticale d'un mot** ou d'un groupe de mots (groupe nominal, verbe, adjectif, adverbe, etc.) par une autre, sans pour autant changer sa signification.

▶ On peut, entre autres, transformer :

- un adverbe en verbe : *He **finally** stepped down.* → *Il **a fini** par démissionner.*
- un verbe en adverbe : *She **may** be wrong.* → ***Peut-être** a-t-elle tort.*
- un nom en adjectif : *a **period** drama* → *un drame / film **historique***

Translation Tip

▶ Les abréviations et acronymes diffèrent d'une langue à l'autre et doivent souvent être explicités. Comment devra-t-on traduire *MP* ?

▶ Le tiret long (–) est un signe de ponctuation fréquent en anglais et très peu utilisé en français. On le remplace le plus souvent par des points de suspension, deux points ou des parenthèses.

À vous !

a. Doit-on traduire le titre *Inglorious Empire: What the British did to India* ?

b. Traduisez à l'aide d'une transposition : *unprecedented, are thought to have killed, inglorious.*

c. Qu'exprime la préposition *through* dans *through plundering India* ? N'existe-t-il pas une structure en français qui exprime la même idée ?

Build up your vocabulary

1 Fill in your own mind map here:

hatier-clic.fr/21amc/272

2 Complete the following paragraph with words from your mind map.

a. The ... ... has evolved and has tried to be more ... .

b. The countries which belong to the ... have often been ... of the UK.

c. Most British citizens believe it is high time Royals ... .

d. Commonwealth countries and their traditions should be ... by the Royal family.

e. People across the world of proud of their British ... but more ... is needed nowadays.

3 Translate these 5 words and use them in a paragraph to explain why the Royal Family should champion diversity: rassembler – modernité – partager – évoluer – soutenir

Projects

1

You have a youtube channel about the royal family and you believe today's royals represent a modern image of Britain. Try to convince your subscribers in a 2-minute speech.

1. Select some arguments in the documents you have studied in class.
2. Look at the past to show how the royal family has evolved over time.
3. Choose not only royal family members but also causes they defend.
4. Don't learn your speech by heart: only use a list of ten words.
5. Practice in front of family/ friends/ a camera. Use their feedback and the images to improve.
6. Film yourself in a neutral environment and play the part!

2

You work for the think tank Diversity UK, which tries to improve diversity and inclusion in Britain. Imagine an interview with a member of the royal family to question whether the members have evolved over time on the topic of diversity.

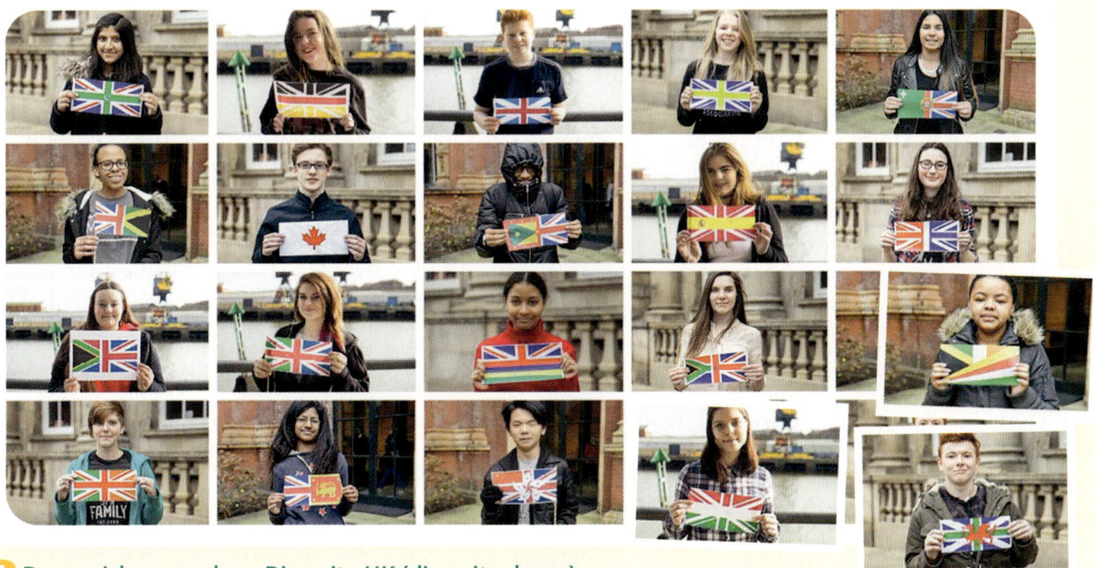

1. Do a quick research on Diversity UK (diversityuk.org).
2. Prepare a list of arguments to convince the public.
3. Give some examples to illustrate your arguments.
4. Carefully choose the member of the royal family who will best represent this shift.
5. Make sure your questions are respectful and not too insistent.
6. Write a short paragraph to introduce your interviewee and set up the setting.
7. Conclude your interview with a hopeful view on the future.

Pour l'écrit du Bac

A

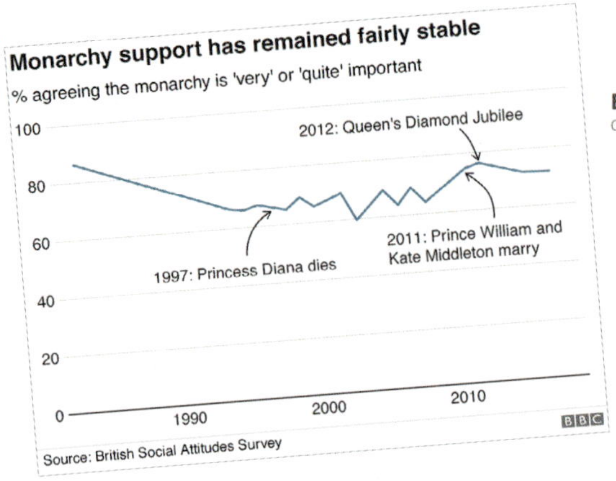

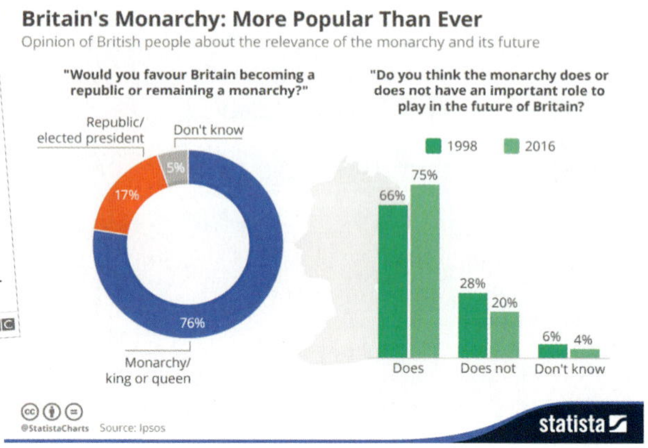

B Charles praises Commonwealth: Diversity can help counter globalisation

Prince Charles praised the Commonwealth's diversity of people, cultures and religions

Charles spoke passionately about the potential of the family of nations to make a difference on the major challenges facing the world, in his final speech as his tour of south-east Asia and India with the Duchess of Cornwall came to a close.

The heir[1] to the throne sat down for talks with India's prime minister Narendra Modi in New Delhi on Wednesday night and he described in his address how the pair discussed the "crucial" role India can play.

In a lighter moment the Prince affectionately referred to Camilla as "mehabooba" – the Urdu word for darling – and got a laugh from invited guests at the residence of Britain's High Commissioner to India, Sir Dominic Asquith.

Charles highlighted how London is due to host the next gathering of Commonwealth leaders in April and said the "sheer diversity" of the body is one its greatest strengths.

Charles spoke passionately about the potential of the family of nations to make a difference

With the UK leaving the European Union, Britain's relationship with its Commonwealth partners - in terms of trade, security and investment – will take on greater importance.

The Prince said: "This diversity is to be celebrated and cherished, not only because it is so central to our identities and our sense of belonging, but also, if I may say so, because it offers us the best hope of addressing the most pressing challenges of our time.

"A one-size-fits-all approach to globalisation simply cannot be the answer and will, I am convinced, lead us into a sterile, monocultural homogeneity that creates ever greater problems whilst simultaneously robbing us of the solutions to address them."

Charles's 11-day trip had been billed as a major Commonwealth tour, with stops in Singapore, Brunei and Malaysia, and with the heir to the throne speaking a number of times about his passion for the family of nations.

Prince Charles releases a rehabilitated turtle into the sea on Golden Bay

He also stressed the importance of India's position in the institution, as it is home to 60 per cent of the Commonwealth's population of 2.3 billion.

He said the Commonwealth offered "an unparalleled means to build bridges between our countries and fairer societies within them so that understanding and aspiration might be the inheritance of the generations that follow us".

He added: "The world can learn so much from India today, as indeed it has done through history, and, ladies and gentlemen, as I have done throughout my own life."

Charles highlighted how London is due to host the next gathering of Commonwealth leaders in April.

Charles concluded by saying "All these bonds between our people are of course emblematic of the Commonwealth itself.

"The challenges we face together and the aspirations we share make it as relevant[2] and as necessary as it has ever been.

"It offers us all the hope that by working together and drawing strength from our diversity we might secure a safer, more prosperous and fairer future for our children and our grandchildren."

www.express.co.uk, Nov. 9th, 2017

1. successor 2. appropriate

C The Queen's 2020 Commonwealth Day message

9/3/2020

On Commonwealth occasions, it is always inspiring to be reminded of the diversity of the people and countries that make up our worldwide family. We are made aware of the many associations and influences that combine through Commonwealth connection, helping us to imagine and deliver a common future.

This is particularly striking when we see people from nations, large and small, gathering for the Commonwealth Games, for meetings of Commonwealth governments, and on Commonwealth Day. Such a blend[1] of traditions serves to make us stronger, individually and collectively, by providing the ingredients needed for social, political and economic resilience[2].

Throughout my life, I have had the opportunity to see and hear how membership of the Commonwealth family means so much to those living in all parts of the world, often in places that are quite remote. Advances in technology and modern media have now enabled many more people to witness and enjoy - with remarkable immediacy - this experience of Commonwealth connection, in areas such as education, medicine and conservation.

Looking to the future, this connectivity means we are also aware, perhaps as never before, that wherever we live, our choices and actions affect the well-being of people and communities living far away, and in very different circumstances. For many, this awareness awakens a desire to employ our planet's natural resources with greater care, and it is encouraging to see how the countries of the Commonwealth continue to devise new ways of working together to achieve prosperity, whilst protecting our planet.

As members of this very special community, on this Commonwealth Day, I hope that the people and countries of the Commonwealth will be inspired by all that we share, and move forward with fresh resolve to enhance the Commonwealth's influence for good in our world.

ELIZABETH R

1. mix 2. strength

PARTIE 1

a) Prenez connaissance du dossier proposé, composé des documents A, B et C non hiérarchisés, et traitez en anglais le sujet suivant (300 mots maximum).

Say what the documents reveal about how the royal family is trying to extend its influence abroad.

b) Vous rédigerez, au choix, l'un des deux écrits complémentaires demandés ci-dessous :

- "The world can learn so much from India today, as indeed it has done through history, and, ladies and gentlemen, as I have done throughout my own life." (document B, l. 51-53). Expliquez en anglais et en 200 mots maximum en quoi les documents A et C illustrent ce propos de Prince Charles cité ici.

Ou

- "On Commonwealth occasions, it is always inspiring to be reminded of the diversity of the people and countries that make up our worldwide family." (document C, l. 1-2). À la lumière des documents A et B, expliquez, en anglais et en 200 mots maximum, en quoi cette diversité est fragile.

PARTIE 2

Rendez compte en français des principales idées exprimées par le document B. Veillez à ne pas simplement en dresser la liste, mais à les expliciter lorsque cela vous paraît pertinent.

Analyser un article de presse

Identification du document

- Nature : article d'opinion ? d'information ? article de fond ?
- Éléments visuels dans le texte qui peuvent vous aider : cartes, graphiques, format, illustrations.
- Dates et sources.
- Article d'opinion : qui est l'auteur·e ?

Lecture de l'article

- Repérer qui parle.
- Faire attention au titre et aux sous-titres.
- Identifier le sujet principal (*key ideas*).
- Entourer les mots de liaison pour comprendre la logique de l'article.
- Prendre en compte le style d'écriture.
- Surligner les mots clés (chiffres, dates, lieux, personnes…).

Comprendre les arguments

- Faire attention à la 1ère phrase de chaque paragraphe.
- Relever les exemples donnés → quelle est la conclusion du/de la journaliste ?
- Dans un article de presse, les éléments sont présentés de façon pyramidale : du plus factuel au plus important.
- Dans un article d'opinion : trouver le point de vue de l'auteur·e.

Repérer l'implicite

- Être capable de repérer les adjectifs / adverbes / expressions qui montrent un point de vue spécifique.
- Déterminer le ton de l'article.
- Relever les incohérences et les contradictions dans l'argumentation du journaliste. Cela révèle-t-il quelque chose ?

Tip
→ Aidez-vous du lexique sur les rabats.

Ma checklist
hatier-clic.fr/21amc/276a

Exemple d'analyse
hatier-clic.fr/21amc/276b

Analyser un reportage

L'analyse d'un reportage (= *news report*) suit la même méthodologie que celle d'un article de presse. Il faut cependant ajouter une analyse du ton et des images qui jouent un rôle important, s'il s'agit d'une vidéo.

Dans les studios

Anchorman/woman, presenter : c'est lui/elle qui donne l'information.

➔ Examiner la posture et la gestuelle.

- Prêter attention à la voix : quel est le ton utilisé ?
- Utilisation d'images ? de graphiques ? d'aide visuelle ?

Sur le terrain

➔ L'envoyé spécial (= *field reporter*), est un·e autre journaliste qui apporte des précisions sur un sujet : quel type d'informations ? Quel est le ton du/de la journaliste ?

➔ Est-il/elle essentiel·le ? Sert-il/elle un but ?

➔ Le/la présentateur·trice pose-t-il/elle des questions ? Dans quel but ?

Angles et mouvement de la caméra

Le choix du cadrage influence fortement la façon dont on donne et perçoit l'information. Les reportages utilisent souvent un cadrage neutre, mais ils peuvent être amenés à en utiliser d'autres. En voici quelques exemples :

Wide shot : permet à l'audience de voir tout l'environnement. C'est un bon moyen pour établir une scène, montrer la situation dans laquelle se trouve le/la journaliste.

Mid shot : permet de se concentrer sur la personne tout en gardant un arrière-plan.

Close-up : permet de montrer un détail du reportage. Cela est souvent utilisé pour montrer les visages des personnes présentes dans le reportage, ou bien un détail significatif.

Interviews

➔ Sujet et but de l'interview ?

➔ Qui interviewe ? Qui est interviewé·e ?

Two-shot : un cadrage qui met deux personnes sur le même plan et ont la même importance.

Reverse over the shoulder : un plan qui permet de voir l'interviewé·e par-dessus l'épaule du/de la journaliste.

Over the shoulder : la caméra se trouve derrière la personne pour montrer une activité.

Décrire et analyser un dessin de presse

Présenter le document

- **Quel type de document ?** ➔ *a **com**ic strip, an edi**to**rial car**toon**, a **draw**ing, a **mag**azine **cov**er*
- **La source et la date** ➔ *It was published in… / It dates from…*

⚠ N'oubliez pas le format des dates : *in* + (mois) année : *in June 2020*, ou bien *on* + date complète (mois + jour, année) : *on September 7, 2020.*

Décrire le document

Pour décrire une image, il faut utiliser le présent en *be + ing* : *The main character **is wearing** sunglasses.*

a caption **(= une légende)**

Analyser puis interpréter

N'oubliez pas qu'un dessin de presse vise non seulement à faire rire, mais aussi à faire réfléchir et bien souvent à révéler l'absurde d'une situation. Analyser un dessin de presse revient donc à…

- **le contextualiser :** à quelle actualité fait-il référence ou allusion ? Y reconnaît-on des personnages publics connus liés à cette actualité ?
- **analyser les procédés comiques :** qu'est-ce qui rend le dessin drôle, critique ou provocateur ? Des procédés graphiques ou rhétoriques y contribuent-ils ? Dans la presse, on a souvent recours aux procédés suivants :
  - **l'allégorie** (***al**legory*) : l'utilisation d'éléments concrets pour illustrer un contenu abstrait.
  - **la caricature** (***car**icature* /ˈkærɪkətʃʊə/) : une représentation qui, par la déformation et l'exagération, tend à ridiculiser le modèle.
  - **la métaphore** (***met**aphor*), **l'analogie** (*a**nal**ogy*) **ou la comparaison** (*com**par**ison* /kəmˈpærɪsən/).
  - **des stéréotypes** (***ster**eotypes*).

Adjectives:
- ab**surd**
- **fun**ny = hi**lar**ious
- **hu**morous /ˈhjuːmərəs/
- **mor**dant /ˈmɔːdənt/ = **bi**ting
- ri**dic**ulous = **lu**dicrous

Nouns:
- **al**legory
- **cri**ticism
- pun
- **sat**ire /ˈsætaɪə/
- **ster**eotype

Verbs:
- poke fun **at** sb
- make fun **of** sb = mock sb
- spoof sb = **par**ody sb
- **rid**icule sb = de**ride** sb
- **cri**ticise sth = lam**poon** sth = pan sth
- re**fer** to sth
- al**lude** to sth = hint at sth
- draw a **par**allel be**tween** X and Y

Les courants politiques

L'échiquier politique dans six pays anglophones

Pour vous aider à bien analyser un article de presse, il vous sera utile de connaître les principaux partis politiques de ces six pays anglophones : l'Australie, le Canada, l'Irlande, l'Afrique du Sud, le Royaume-Uni et les États-Unis.

Chaque drapeau représente le pays dans lequel le parti est actif.

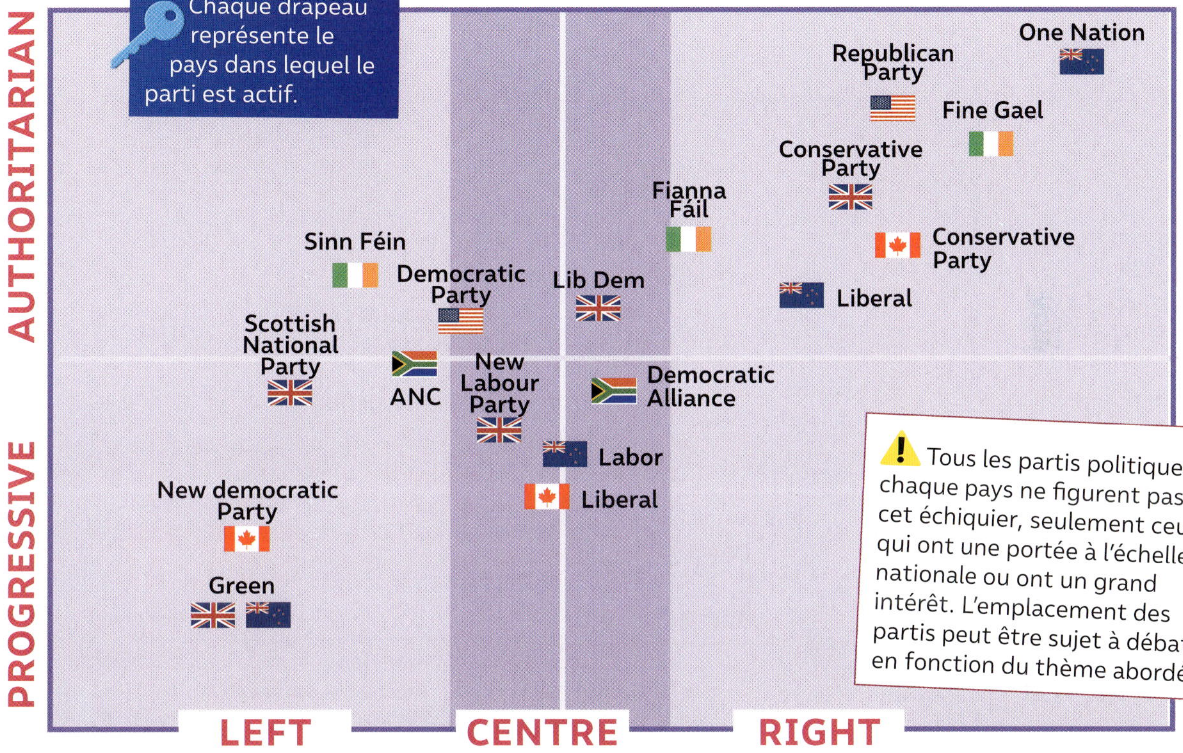

⚠ Tous les partis politiques de chaque pays ne figurent pas sur cet échiquier, seulement ceux qui ont une portée à l'échelle nationale ou ont un grand intérêt. L'emplacement des partis peut être sujet à débat, en fonction du thème abordé.

Lexique politique

Noms

- grass roots: the ordinary people in a society
- **hin**drance: obstacle
- **mouth**piece: a person who represents others
- **pol**itics: actions of a government, the study of it
- **pol**icy: a set of ideas agreed by a political party
- un**rest**: social agitation
- **watch**dog: a guardian, a defender

Adjectives

- bold /'bəʊld/: audacious
- counter-in**tui**tive: not logical
- de**fi**ant: proudly rebellious
- **du**bious: suspicious en**thra**lling /ɪn'θrɔː.lɪŋ/: captivating
- ill-ad**vised**: unwise, not relevant
- re**li**able /rɪ'laɪ.ə.bəl/: trustworthy
- un**yiel**ding: firm, not giving way, determined

Verbes

- **appoint**: choose so officially for a job
- de**ceive** sb /dɪ'siːv/: fool sb, not be honest
- de**fy** sb or sthg: go against, resist
- en**thral** sb: fascinate
- **plumm**et: fall quickly and suddenly
- soar: go up very rapidly and at a high level
- yield (to): surrender, bend, give up

Expressions

- be power-**hun**gry: *être assoiffé de pouvoir*
- catch off-guard: *prendre par surprise*
- em**brace** o**pin**ions: *adhérer à des opinions*
- it stems from…: *cela provient de…*
- pioneer a **pol**icy: *inventer une nouvelle politique*
- spin **doc**tor: *conseiller·ère en communication*
- think out**side** the box: *penser en dehors des sentiers battus*

Les principaux titres de presse
hatier-clic.fr/21amc/279

Passer la presse en revue

Vous trouverez ici quelques pistes pour vous aider dans l'étude d'un document issu des médias anglo-saxons (articles / reportages de presse écrite, radio et télévision, Internet).

Quels acteurs ?

Pour bien comprendre les enjeux d'un article ou d'un reportage, il est important de prendre en compte sa source : de quel pays vient le journal ou l'émission audiovisuelle ? Ces médias sont-ils politiquement ancrés ?

Voici un schéma regroupant les principaux organes de presse anglo-saxons selon leur orientation.

Printed press

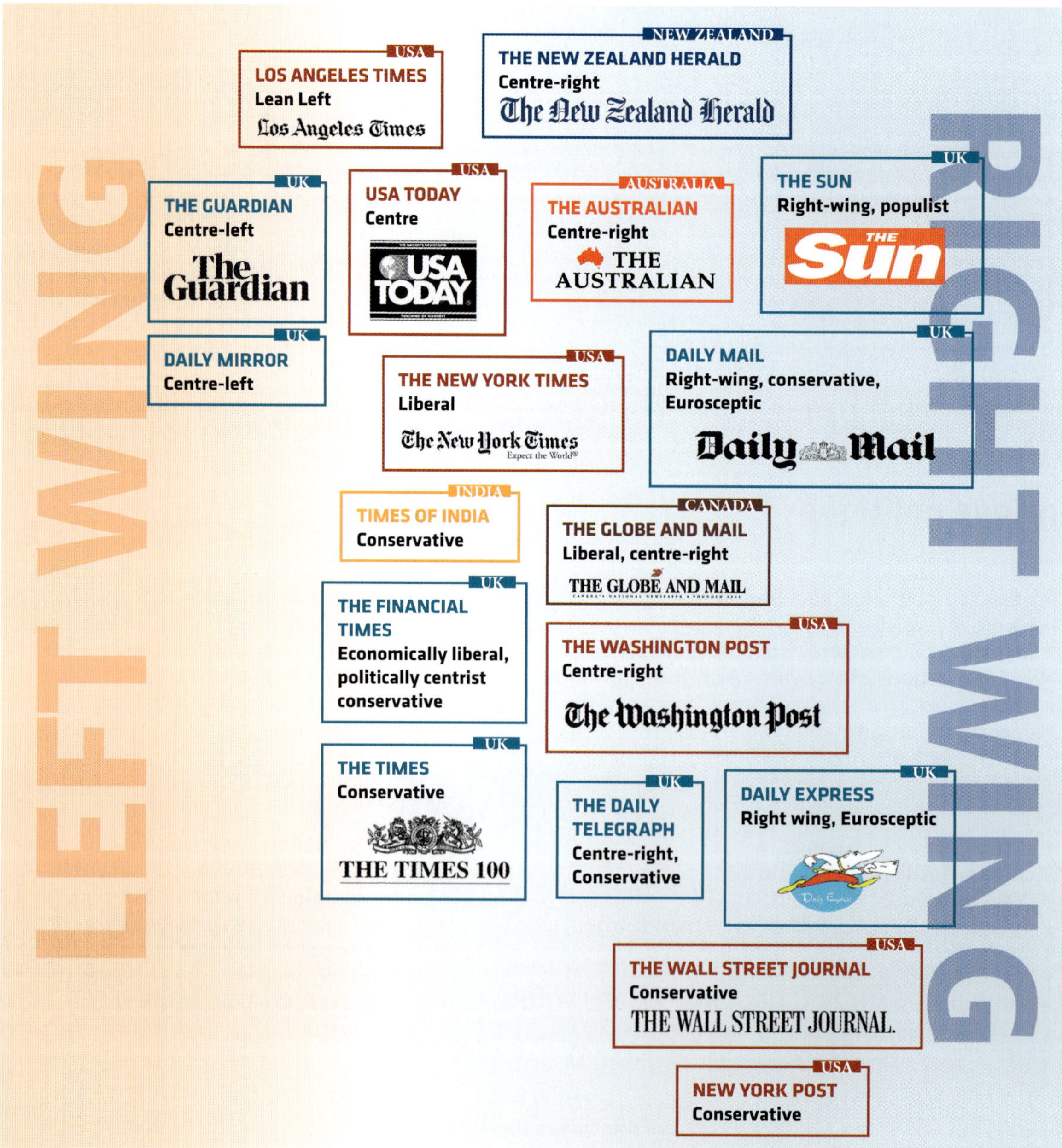

Identifier les sources : repérer une fake news

Le titre & le message

En majuscules ? Avec des points d'exclamation ? C'est louche, analysez-le bien ! Vous incite-t-on à partager le message, à le diffuser au plus grand nombre ? Méfiance ! Le but est sûrement d'obtenir un grand nombre de clics et de diffuser de la publicité ou une infox.

La source !

Vérifiez le site et les liens proposés afin de vous assurer que ces liens sont bien en relation avec l'article que vous lisez. Il faut vérifier la crédibilité du site. Regardez l'adresse URL du site : des extensions par .infonet ou .offer ont de grandes chances d'être des infox.

L'auteur·e

Qui a publié l'article ? Est-ce une personne fiable ? Quelle est sa fonction ? Journaliste ? Blogueur ? Si vous ne la connaissez pas, faites une recherche et vous serez vite fixé·e.

Les images

Il est important de décrypter l'image : la photo est-elle originale ? Est-elle sortie de son contexte ou semble-t-elle retouchée ? Quelle est sa source ? Vous pouvez utiliser des outils en ligne qui vous aident à vérifier, comme Décodex du journal *Le Monde*, par exemple.

La date !

Il n'est pas rare de publier de nouveau un vieil article ou une photo ancienne afin de faire croire qu'il s'agit d'une nouvelle histoire.

D'autres articles ?

Si l'information est vraie, d'autres articles auront été écrits à ce sujet et vous pourrez ainsi aisément recouper les informations. Faites des recherches !

Analyser un graphique

En **LLCER Anglais Monde Contemporain**, vous aurez des graphiques à commenter. Pour cela, mieux vaut maîtriser le lexique adéquat, la méthodologie et savoir lire les données chiffrées.

Numbers and figures

0 nought / zero

3.5: three point five **0.35**: point three five

200 two hundred **3,000** three thousand

8,605 eight thousand six hundred (and) five **6,000,000 = 6 m / 6M**: six million

2bn: two billion / 2 thousand million

Percentages **40%** forty per cent

Fractions **½** one half **1/3** one third **¼** one quarter

Dates **1904** nineteen o four **2015** twenty fifteen / two thousand (and) fifteen

Le point marque les décimales

la virgule marque les milliers

Pas de s

In depth

	Verbs	Nouns
UP ↑	in**crease**, /ɪn'kriːs/ rise	an in**crease**, /'ɪn.kriːs/ a rise
	➡ it has in**creased by** 10%	➡ an **in**crease in the **num**ber of...
	+soar ++ **sky**rocket +++ peak	a peak

	Verbs	Nouns
DOWN ↓	de**crease** /dɪ'kriːs/, fall, de**cline**	a **de**crease /'diː.kriːs/, a fall, a de**cline**
	➡ it has de**creased by** 10 %...	➡ a **de**crease in the **num**ber of...
	+ drop ++ **plum**met +++ col**lapse**	a col**lapse** a drop

	Verbs	Nouns
→	**stag**nate, re**main** **sta**ble/ **stead**y, **sta**bilise, stay **con**stant, **lev**el off	sta**bi**lity
↝	**fluc**tuate, go up and down	fluctu**a**tion

An example

Presentation

This document **published by** Smartairfilters.com is **a line graph** showing air quality in five of India's major cities from 2015 to 2018. **It indicates** the levels of PM2.5 pollution.

Analysis

According to this chart, pollution is still acute in Delhi, in spite of efforts. It has indeed the worst air quality **peaking at** around 122 microgrammes (µg) of PM2.5 per cubic metres in 2016, while Chennai is the least polluted city. The year 2016 **saw a rise in** the pollution rate in three cities out of 5. Air quality in Hyderabad **has remained quite steady** since 2015, whereas pollution levels **have risen slightly** in two cities (Kolkata and Mumbai); however, they **still remain below** those in Delhi.

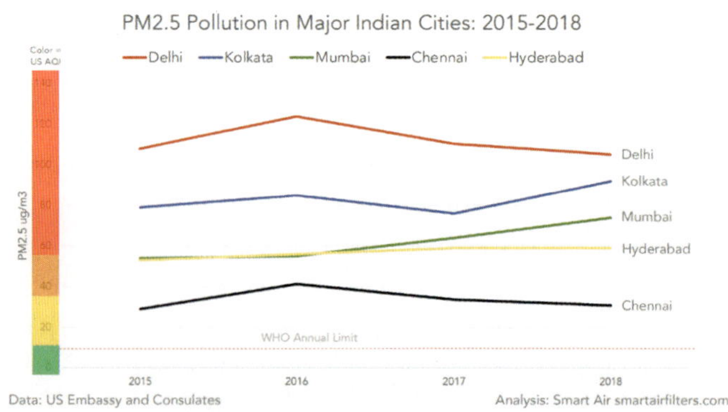

Conclusion

The graph reflects the Indian government's lack of action to fight pollution, which is critical in 4 out of 5 cities mentionned.

Analyser une carte

Pour décrire et analyser une carte, vous devrez répondre à quatre questions (voir p. 60).

1 ? **A trustworthy source:** 270towin. With the title "2020 Presidential Election Live", we learn that Joe Biden, who is a Democrat, won the US election. The second useful title is "BIDEN 306 - 232 TRUMP" (which is also the map key) shows the numbers of electoral votes Biden won. The two little blue arrows show the line that a candidate needs to reach to win (270 electoral votes). The map shows how the American voted in their 50 states (information given in the map). The boundaries in the map show the different states and the two letters in the state are their abbreviations. The column made of rectangles on the right-hand side represents the eastern states that are too small to be represented on the map.

2 ? We can contrast the **colours** (= political parties) shown on the map thanks to the key. The Democrats in blue and the Republicans in red which is the exact opposite in most European countries. We can notice that there is no other colour, so no other significant political parties. There are roughly as many blue states as red states. However, the Democrats won, because they added up more populous states that have more electoral colleges.

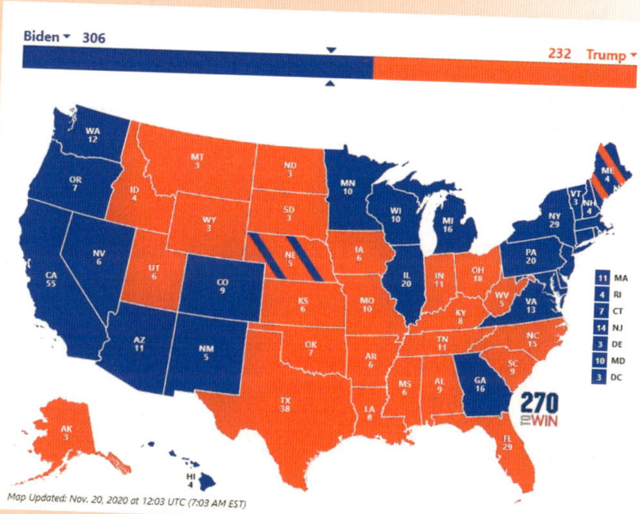

3 ? The map shows the **location** of the states that voted Democrat or Republican. We can also deduce the population distribution thanks to the number of electoral votes. The higher it is, the more populous the state is.

4 ? Looking at the map we can conclude that:

First, the democratic states are situated on the east and west coasts, as well as in the north at the Canadian border and around the Big Lake area (northeastern states). Some of them represent the "blue wall", it means that these states continue to vote Democrat no matter what (California, Illinois, New York, Washington DC, Rhode Island, Massachusetts...). There is also a "red wall" which is located in the centre and in the southern part of the country with states like Texas, Kansas, Mississippi and in the northern part of the USA with Alaska, Idaho, Nebraska...

Secondly, all the democratic states have large metropolitan areas that are populated by diverse groups of people. These groups (ethnic minorities, intellectuals, the young...) are more likely to vote for the Democrats and showcase more liberal views in urban areas.

Thirdly, the strongest red states in the country are mostly situated in rural areas (Midwest), they are often less populated than the blue states. People that vote Republican are likely to be older and live in small or average-sized cities. Finally, we can deduce that the place of urban and rural areas has politically shaped the USA.

Utiliser le dictionnaire unilingue

Que trouve-t-on dans un dictionnaire unilingue ?

➡ Dans un **dictionnaire unilingue**, on ne trouve pas de traductions de mots (comme dans les dictionnaires bilingues) mais **des définitions en anglais**. Le dictionnaire unilingue vous aidera donc surtout **à comprendre le sens des mots inconnus**.

➡ Certains d'entre eux proposent **des synonymes** ou bien **des antonymes** (des mots de sens contraire), qui peuvent aussi aider à la compréhension. Les définitions sont souvent accompagnées de citations qui illustrent les différents emplois du mot en contexte.

➡ Le dictionnaire unilingue donne d'autres informations utiles :

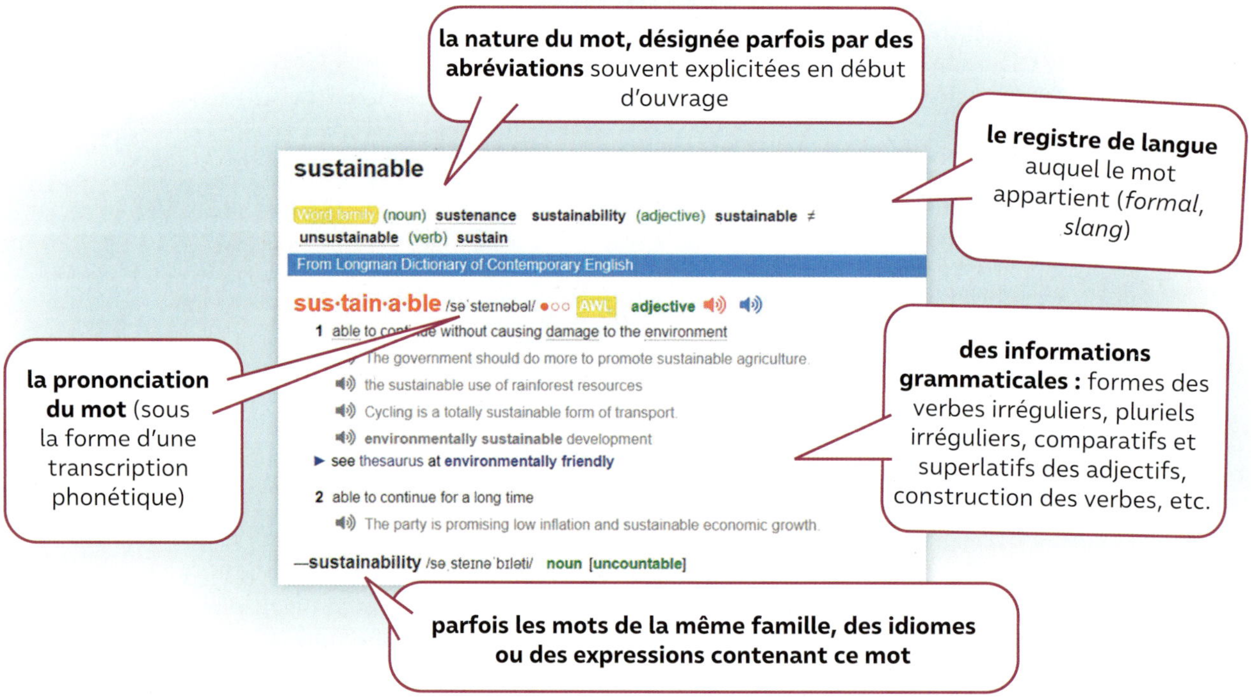

Comment utiliser le dictionnaire unilingue ?

➡ Le jour de l'épreuve écrite du baccalauréat, vous aurez droit au dictionnaire unilingue. Il vous sera utile pour dissiper des incompréhensions dans les documents mais aussi pour vous aider à traduire un court passage.

➡ Il faut bien veiller à déjouer certains pièges :
- certains mots peuvent avoir plusieurs **natures grammaticales** (verbe et nom par exemple) ;
- certains mots peuvent avoir **plusieurs sens** et donc être associés à plusieurs définitions. Il convient donc de choisir la définition adéquate qui correspond au contexte du texte à traduire ;
- il faut bien veiller à connaître **les abréviations** utilisées (*v.*, *adj.*, *n.*, etc.).

Tip

Le jour de l'épreuve, utilisez le dictionnaire unilingue en dernier recours. En effet, passer trop de temps à le consulter vous fera perdre un temps précieux. En cas de problème de compréhension, essayez dans un premier temps d'inférer le sens du mot inconnu à partir du contexte ou de sa formation (suffixes, préfixes, etc.).

Le Grand oral

Cette épreuve n'est pas une épreuve de spécialité mais elle s'adosse à des connaissances liées à votre ou vos spécialités. Vous devez présenter au jury deux questions qui peuvent porter sur une ou deux spécialités : par exemple, vous pouvez choisir un sujet qui concerne seulement la spécialité LLCER Monde Contemporain ou un sujet transversal (LLCER Monde Contemporain et votre deuxième spécialité).

Le Grand oral : pour quoi faire ?

- Mettre en œuvre des techniques de prise de parole en public
- Synthétiser des connaissances acquises au cycle terminal
- Faire des recherches
- Mettre en pratique les compétences d'argumentation et d'interaction
- Exposer son projet d'orientation

SE PRÉPARER AUX ÉTUDES SUPÉRIEURES

ÊTRE PERFORMANT DANS LE MONDE PROFESSIONNEL

Le déroulement de l'épreuve

Durée : 20 minutes

Préparation : 20 minutes (pour organiser vos idées et éventuellement créer un support, non évalué, à donner au jury).

Coefficient : 10 [voie générale]

Vous serez debout pendant la première partie de l'épreuve, au moins.
Vous n'aurez pas droit à vos notes pendant toute la durée de passage.

5 minutes – Présentation d'une problématique
Expliquez votre choix de sujet, développez en 2 ou 3 parties, concluez en répondant à votre problématique.

10 minutes – Interaction avec le jury
Approfondissez votre pensée, donnez des exemples, argumentez, montrez vos connaissances.

5 minutes – Échange sur le projet d'orientation
Liez votre problématique à votre projet d'études.
➔ **En français**

« Le candidat peut recourir en partie, **mais pas en totalité** [à l'anglais]. » « Le candidat peut faire le choix de s'exprimer totalement en français tout en recourant à quelques citations dans la langue de spécialité. »
https://eduscol.education.fr

Le Grand oral

Préparation · Interaction · Connaissances · Problématisation · Réflexion personnelle · Esprit critique · Clarté · Structure · Conviction · Argumentation

Exemples de problématiques avec les croisements de spécialités possibles

- *To what extent are megacities of the English-speaking world a model?* ➨ AMC + HGCGSP.
- *Is there still a gap between social classes in the UK?* ➨ AMC + SES ou AMC + HGGSP
- *Transhumanism: a threat or an opportunity?* ➨ AMC + SVT ou AMC + HLP ou AMC + Numérique et Sciences Informatiques ou AMC + Sciences de l'Ingénieur.
- *Does Anglo-Saxon journalism still have ethics?* ➨ AMC + HLP ou AMC + HGGSP

Exemple de sketchnote

Does Anglo-Saxon journalism still have ethics?

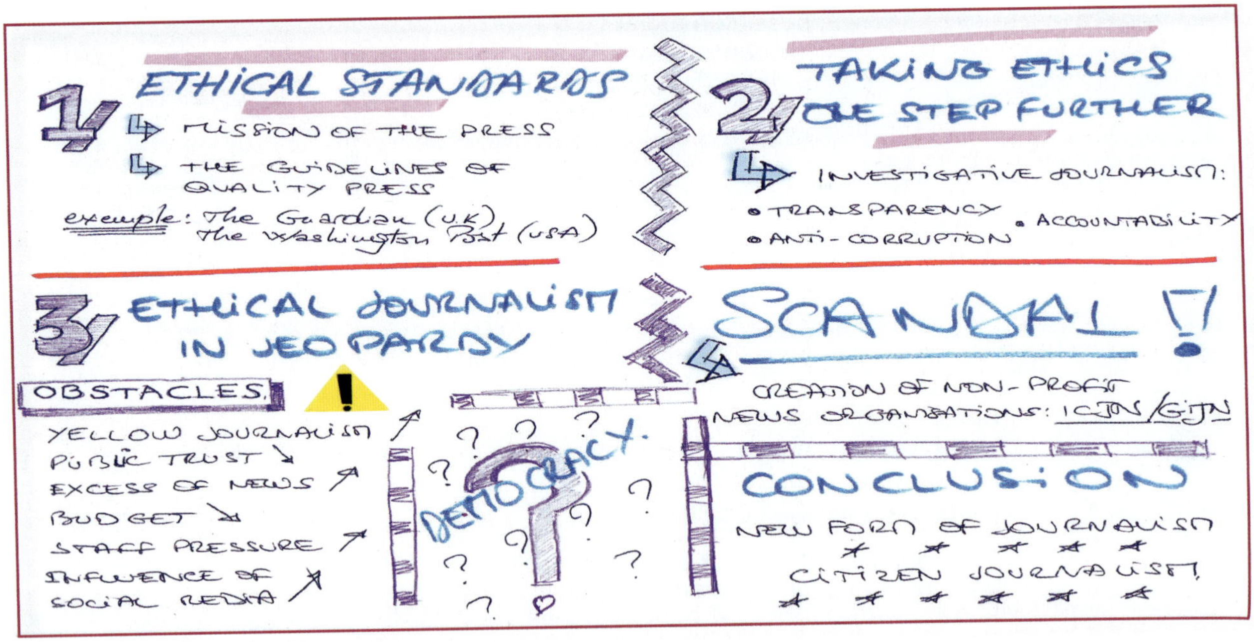

Voici un exemple de phrase d'accroche pour débuter votre présentation:
With the increasing use of fake news in American politics and also around the world, the notion of ethics in journalism seems to be very much at stake today.

Memo
#clarté #intelligibilité
Tous les membres du jury ne sont pas spécialistes.

Memo
#Annonce ton plan !
Le jury se repérera mieux si l'annonce du plan et les transitions sont claires.

Memo
#oublieleparcœur
La récitation ruine la restitution !
Mais apprendre votre introduction vous donnera confiance.